DIAGNOSING AND CORRECTING READING DISABILITIES

DIAGNOSING AND CORRECTING READING DISABILITIES

GEORGE D. SPACHE

Professor Emeritus
University of Florida

Allyn and Bacon, Inc.
Boston · London · Sydney · Toronto

Library of Congress Cataloging in Publication Data

Spache, George Daniel, 1909–
Diagnosing and correcting reading disabilities.

Bibliography: p.
Includes index.
1. Reading—Remedial teaching. 2. Reading disability. I. Title.
LB1050.5.S59 428'.4'2 75-31826

ISBN 0-205-04916-8

Fifth printing . . . May, 1978

contents

preface

This text was planned as part of a three-book correlated series on reading disabilities. It was our belief that the ideal materials for training reading specialists in diagnosis and remediation demanded a more thorough treatment of the whole field than any textbook available has ever offered. Certainly there have been many "how-to-do-it" texts based almost entirely on the author's experiences and opinions. But, in our opinion, those instructional aides have failed to provide an adequate background in the research literature of the area. They have usually presented the tests, teaching practices, and the principles of diagnosis and remediation without the critical evaluation that could have been derived from the pertinent research. In a word, to us these texts have never touched upon the "why" of these tools and procedures.

For these reasons, we undertook to prepare the kind of textbooks that we felt were essential. One of these, *Investigating the Issues of Reading Disabilities,* reviews the research in depth and provides an informational background for those entering the field. Another, the present text, implements the implications and conclusions that can be drawn from the research and deals with the practices of diagnosis and remediation. The third book, which is still to be written, will offer case studies in a format intended to help sharpen the diagnostic insights of the practitioner in this field.

We realize, of course, that not all graduate students in reading, or even some instructors, will want to explore the field in such depth as this series tries to offer. Others will welcome the manner in which the related book summarizes our knowledge of the significance of etiological factors, points out the strengths and weaknesses of common diagnostic instruments and remedial approaches, and attempts to provide the information needed for a critical evaluation of our practices. Some will perhaps use it as preparation to discussing the practical steps suggested in this text.

To facilitate student comprehension and learnings in this field, each book features chapter previews. If used by the student and discussed by the instructor, as the research indicates, these provocative questions will aid in better student understanding and retention. At the close of each chapter, in both books, we offer a learning activity that will enable the reader to apply immediately some of the major concepts of each portion. Some of these will be especially feasible for in-service teachers or reading specialists, while others will be practical for almost any graduate student to try after having read the relevant chapter. We hope that these learning activities will support the instructor's efforts to provide meaningful, firsthand experiences in this field.

For the sake of simplicity and consistency, we have used the pronoun *she* to refer to the teacher or clinician and *he* to refer to the pupil throughout the text. This avoids ambiguity when both teacher and pupil are referred to in the same sentence.

Sarasota, Florida

George D. Spache

acknowledgments

We are indebted to a number of sources for permission to use some of the matter and illustrations of this text. We are grateful to the following:

Keystone View Division of Mast Development Co. (Keystone Visual Survey Tests).

Titmus Optical Co. (The Titmus Vision Tester).

Bausch and Lomb Co. (The Ortho-Rater—Industrial Model).

The Psychological Corporation (Farnsworth Dichotomous Test for Color Blindness and illustrations of subtests of the 1974 WISC-R).

Eckstein Bros. Inc.; Beltone Electronics Corp.; and Maico Hearing Instruments (photos of their audiometers).

American Guidance Service, Inc. (Peabody Picture Vocabulary Test).

Harcourt Brace Jovanovich (Durrell Analysis of Reading Difficulty and Gilmore Oral Reading Test).

Follett Publishing Co. (Botel Reading Inventory and Individual Reading Placement Inventory).

California Test Bureau (Diagnostic Reading Scales).

Educational Developmental Laboratories (photo of the Reading Eye Camera).

Several examples of perceptual-motor training activities by courtesy of the Phillippi Shores School of Sarasota, Florida, Frank Rivers, principal.

We are also appreciative of the permission of the National Reading Conference for us to adapt an article that appeared in the Seventh Annual Yearbook of the Southwest Reading Conference.

acknowledgments

DIAGNOSING AND CORRECTING READING DISABILITIES

part one

DEFINING THE BASIC PREMISES

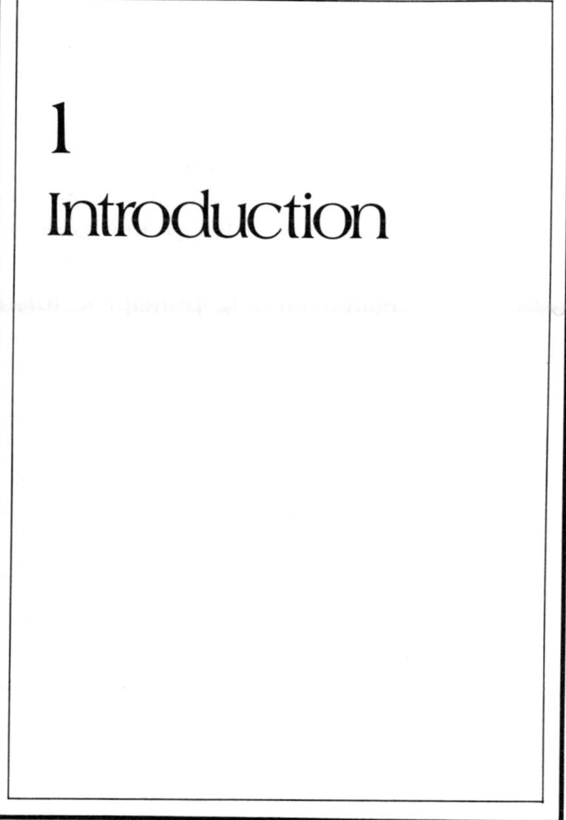

1 Introduction

The definition of reading disability is a very crucial element in the field of diagnosis and remedial work. It enters into such important decisions as the selection of cases and their discharge from treatment. It affects the meaningfulness of most experiments with methods and materials because the lack of a realistic definition of what retardation in reading is limits the generalization of the results. The definition of retardation also influences the planning for treatment, the duration and intensity of the therapy, and even the nature of the treatment in many cases. And finally, our definition of what constitutes a severe retardation modifies our estimates of the student's potential for improvement and hence our evaluation of the success of our treatment programs. For these many reasons, we offer a broad but realistic definition of retardation in reading that requires the consideration of a number of significant facets of each case.

Since diagnosis and remediation are actually elements of the same process of treatment of a reading disability, the principles offered to guide such efforts are not discrete; they are presented jointly. In considering the definition of a disability and the principles that may guide our treatment, use these questions to organize your reactions.

1. Do you agree with the author's criteria of a reading disability? If not, can you support your disagreements by factual data?
2. Would you add any additional criteria that are widely applicable to those offered by the author?
3. Do you accept the concept that diagnosis and remediation are a continuous, single process? Would you suggest any additional very significant guiding principles that might be acceptable?

PARTS TWO THROUGH FIVE of this book and its accompanying collection of readings, *Investigating the Issues of Reading Disabilities,* will discuss the disabled reader and the diagnosis and correction of his difficulties. It is only fitting that we should now define these terms and the related guiding principles, for, despite the existence of this profession for some forty years, there is no commonly accepted description of these terms.

THE DISABLED READER

We could quote a dozen descriptions of the average pupil who is experiencing failure in reading from as many sources. They would be sprinkled with such terms as: *dyslexic, minimal brain damage, specific reading disability, perceptual deficit, maturational lag, associative learning disability,* and so on. We could quote other authorities who would tell us that the disabled reader is any child who falls below expectancy (usually meaning his mental age) by as little as three to six months at primary grade levels, or slightly larger amounts at higher grades. Still another group consider any pupil reading any material aloud at sight who makes more than five oral errors of any kind per 100 running words, regardless of their effect upon comprehension, as a poor reader.

Our personal reaction to these definitions is that they are "armchair" descriptions without reference to the realities of the classroom or to the educational data that would refute them. We shall offer and defend a more pragmatic definition of the retarded reader.

The retarded reader is one who:

Is retarded in a number of major reading skills. Weakness in one area of reading such as rate or vocabulary, or comprehension or word analysis is relatively readily overcome by direct training of the missing skills in many cases. In fact, in some cases, a few interviews with the classroom teacher or the school remedial teacher will suffice to outline the corrective steps that can often be employed in the course of classroom reading lessons. Simple developmental training parallel to that usually offered in reading instruction can readily overcome a problem of inflexible, slow rate, sight or meaning vocabulary lack, or a weakness in phonic, structural, contextual, or visual word analysis. There are ample, well-organized training materials in each of these areas that can be used under ordinary teacher supervision with good results. Only when there are manifest deficiencies in several or almost all of these major skills will the expensive process of diagnosis and remedial therapy seem justified, in our opinion. This portion of the definition would, of course, include the child who has never really learned to read despite one or several years of instruction. But it would exclude from clinical diagnosis the 25–30 percent of cases who are referred to reading services but who are found to have only one or even no area of skill weakness.

Is retarded by one year or more, if in the primary grades, or by two years or more if older. We are here defining the disabled reader in terms of a degree of retardation that cannot readily be treated by the average classroom teacher. Any teacher who is flexible in her instruction and use of materials can certainly handle pupils who vary by only six months or so from exact grade placement in the primary grades. In fact, most effective primary teachers recognize and overcome this degree of retardation in some of their pupils every year that they teach. For example, second-grade teachers readily adapt to the fact that some of their pupils need instruction at a primer level at the beginning of the year. Since primers are usually introduced sometime between the third and the fifth month of the first grade for average-ability pupils, these beginning second graders are exhibiting at least a six-month retardation. Yet the teacher adapts her group instruction to these facts and, while she may not be entirely successful in accelerating their growth, offers appropriate instruction with reasonable results. This degree of retardation of three–seven months that is supposed to characterize candidates for remedial attention is equally insignificant in the third grade at the hands of competent teachers.

In contrast, the child entering a second grade who is still functioning on a prereading level, or the third grader entrant who is struggling with a high first reader (that is, one year or more retarded below grade placement) may present a demand for specialized or individualized instruction that the average teacher does not recognize or meet readily. This child is a candidate for diagnosis of his difficulties and, perhaps, for remedial therapy.

Above the primary grades, as in fourth and fifth, school surveys indicate that about 60 percent of pupils fall outside of their grade placement in group tests. That is, only about 40 percent are within a year of grade placement. Using the standard of one-year retardation as a criterion of reading disability would automatically classify about 30 percent of all school children as disabled readers. This seems unrealistic, for there is ample evidence that this 30 percent progresses reasonably satisfactorily in school in terms of grades, promotions, graduations and the like, including the poorer readers. In fact, as is pointed out later in considering the ultimate outcomes of remedial services, there is little difference in the school success of the poorer readers from that of their peers. Again, our criterion of two years or more, and three or more years at secondary level, is the dividing line between poor readers who need diagnosis and remediation and those who can be dealt with in the classroom.

Charles A. Ullmann* has shown that use of a constant criterion of retardation of one year would result in classifying an increasing number of pupils as retarded in each higher grade. For example, using the norms from the Stanford Achievement Test, a one-year criterion in grades three to six gradually increases the suspected proportion of retardees from 16 to 30 percent. In grades seven to nine, a criterion of two years below grade placement produces the artificial increase from 19 to 31 percent. Above the ninth grade, either the one- or two-year standard would again gradually increase the proportion of pupils supposed to be retarded. This artificial increase is due to the decelerating nature of the reading curve and to the decreasing differences between successive grades. Hence a single, fixed cut-off point for determining which pupils are really retarded in reading would produce an ever-increasing number as the grade level increases. Like many reading authorities, Ullmann considers that approximately 15 percent of each group may be considered severely retarded in reading. Our criteria of one year at primary, two years from grades four–eight, and three years at secondary does produce about this type of estimate of the retarded population.

Is retarded below that level necessary for full participation in the reading tasks of his age or grade or socioeconomic group. An individual's needs for reading are related to his occupational goals and to his cultural status. To apply "national" norms from some reading test indiscriminately to all segments of the population is both unrealistic and unfair. We cannot expect the same degree of reading achievement of all pupils, regardless of their backgrounds, their goals, and their educational opportunities. This is not to say that every effort should not be made to help each pupil read adequately for his capacities and his needs. But, in the subskills as well as in the major areas of reading, as in all human traits, variability not similarity is the normal expectation. Not until the millennium is reached when no children are handicapped by language differences, socioeconomic status, educational opportunities, or the middle-class orientation of the public school can we begin to consider a common standard. Even then, there will continue to be many children who cannot meet that standard because their progress has been hindered by some of the other factors that tend to determine reading success, as sensory defects.

When a pupil is unable to compete on favorable terms with his sociocultural peers, he may be considered for diagnosis and remediation, if that retardation is of the degrees suggested above. This, of course, is a subjective judgment based on his school record, teachers' judgments, intelligence record, and related information. But the alternative of declaring as disabled readers most of the pupils who differ from the middle-class majority in a reading test is even more subjective.

Is an individual who has had normal opportunities for schooling. The

*Charles A. Ullmann, "Prevalence of Reading Disability as a Function of the Measure Used," *Journal of Learning Disabilities,* 2 (November 1969), 556–58.

child or adult who has not had adequate schooling and hence has not learned to read sufficiently for his life needs is more properly described as an illiterate than a disabled reader. He is not a candidate for expensive diagnosis and remediation, but rather for good introductory instruction in the appropriate centers for such work. The gradual equalization of the quality of schooling available to minority groups has reduced, but not entirely eliminated, the need to recognize that this proviso of adequate schooling may still be relevant when the pupils of some school systems are to be evaluated.

Has continued to show this degree of retardation below his sociocultural peers despite corrective efforts. A reading disability does not usually suddenly appear, as in the results of a single reading test, or a teacher's judgment. It develops gradually over time and is manifest by continued poor performances or decreasing scores consistently below those of his peers. Referral to a diagnostic center should be based on this pattern of gradually increasing retardation, not upon a sudden drop in status or a simple plateau in growth. Pupils who lag behind their peers for a short period of time may be reflecting the effects of family problems, health, attendance, changes in instructional procedures, school transfers, and the like. Only when definite attempts to overcome the slowed developmental rate as tried in the classroom have failed over a period of months should the possibility of reading disability be considered. Reading disability is not a slowing down of progress for temporary causes, but a persistent failure to perform at expectancy levels.

There are many other ways of identifying the disabled reader by comparison with some criterion of what he might be expected to accomplish in terms of his capacities. For example, the student's mental age is widely used as a criterion of his expectancy. Or mental and chronological ages are combined in a weighted formula that is supposed to indicate his expectancy level. Another approach is by the comparison of his auditory comprehension level with his present silent comprehension level. When the first of these is markedly higher, this is supposed to indicate that the student is functioning below capacity. There are serious flaws in all three of these systems for identifying the disabled reader, flaws too numerous to repeat at this time. The arguments against their use are offered in detail in chapter 4, "Diagnosis in the Intellectual Area," in this book and in our related book, *Investigating the Issues of Reading Disabilities.*

The greatest problem that most remedial teachers and reading clinics face is the tremendous number of potential applicants who need their services. Hence it is imperative to establish a realistic definition of a disabled reader and to declare the bases for the selection of remedial cases. The apparently simple comparison of mental age and reading level or the deceptively easy formulas for predicting the existence of a reading disability would result in categorizing more than half the school population as disabled readers. Aside from their lack of foundation in representing actual pupil performances, they are manifestly unrealistic in the proportions of the population that they characterize as retarded in reading.

The selection and definition of disabled readers, as in our definition, must consider such mitigating factors as the student's sociocultural status, the nature of his reading difficulties, the degree of retardation below a level common to his peers, the duration of his problem, and the need for special professional assistance beyond what has or can be done in the classroom. Although they may not be part of the operational definition of a reading disability, there are a number of other facts that must be considered before selecting pupils for intensive diagnosis and remedial therapy. These include tentative estimates of the duration of the treatment program that may be necessary in view of his degree of retardation, his age and grade level, his I.Q., and similar facts. Lengthy illustrations of how these facts influence selection and treatment procedures will be found in chapters 12 and 13. These chapters will help convey to the reader a more complete picture of the planning that enters into the apparently simple matter of deciding whether a student needs, and will profit from, professional services.

We may have succeeded here only in conveying to the reader that we believe identification of the disabled reader is a very complex decision. But it is. A few simple mathematical steps, we are certain, will convince the reader that the other simplistic methods of formulas, and the like, actually are correct in only perhaps 20–30 percent of the population. Only in that small portion—and it decreases with age as at secondary and college levels—do these formulas, tables, and indexes of expectancy really work. What proportion, then, will be incorrectly evaluated and falsely labeled? Even Bond and Tinker, who have proposed one of these quick ways of estimating retardation, have, at the same time, quoted these statistics that refute their formula and the others.

PRINCIPLES OF DIAGNOSIS AND REMEDIATION

We are not certain of the values of enunciating a group of principles of diagnosis, for many of them sound like clichés. But, on the other hand, if the reader is engaged in, or about to begin, work in this field, even these trite statements may influence his thinking and future procedures. These principles have been collated from this writer's unpublished materials, other sources, and a group enunciated by Peter D. Pumfrey of the Department of Education, the University of Manchester, at the 8th Annual Study Conference of the United Kingdom Reading Association in 1971.* Since diagnosis and remediation are really part of the same process and occur simultaneously during the treatment program, we shall not dichotomize these principles.

1. Diagnosis is a continuous process of proposing hypotheses, testing them by teaching strategies and referring or discarding them (3). All the information and understanding of any disabled reader that is needed to help him, cannot be obtained in the initial testing at the beginning of the program. As we test and as we begin instruction that seems relevant in terms of our first impressions, we must constantly observe the pupil's behavior, responses to the approach we are using, and its apparent impact upon his development. Just as there is seldom a single cause for his difficulties, there is also very infrequently an answer in one type or kind of treatment. Flexibility is the heart of the test and observation-hypothesis-strategy trial-conclusion process of diagnosis and remediation.

2. Diagnosis is pragmatic and directly related to remedial practice. As Pumfrey phrases it, "the heart of diagnosis is the interpretation of a series of observations coupled with the ability to relate the interpretation to a plan for remedial teaching." The purpose of testing is analytic not descriptive; the end result is not a label placed on the child, as *minimal brain-damaged, dyslexic, perceptually handicapped,* or the like, but a direct suggestion for the trial of a specific treatment strategy. The mere listing of the results of a whole group of tests is not a diagnosis, despite its prevalence at the hands of many psychologists and reading centers. The diagnosis would be the interpretation of the probable meaning, educationally speaking, of the patterns of test scores. We want to know, as in intelligence testing, not only how bright this child is, but also what clues to cognitive strengths and weaknesses, what hypotheses about the child's language background can be formed from the test results?

This principle implies also that the reading teacher refrains from using esoteric tests, such as eyedness, handedness, memory for designs, figure-ground perception, and the like, unless these relate the results directly to a treatment strategy. Wide use of tests like the Frostig, the Bender, and the Illinois Test of Psycholinguistic Abilities (ITPA) does not guarantee their validity or their values in yielding information that can be directly translated into treatments. The diagnostician must gradually evolve a group of familiar testing instruments (the use of which is supported by the relevant literature) that help in the understanding of, and attempt to treat, subjects. The gradual selection of a testing battery grows out of the testing and proving of the hypotheses generated by these instruments.

3. Diagnosis is eclectic and thorough. All basic etiological areas must be covered to obtain the total picture of the development of the disability. The process requires much more than an assessment of reading skills

*Personal correspondence with Peter D. Pumfrey.

because difficulties with these may be symptomatic of a wide range of causative factors (Pumfrey). This principle implies the collating of information from schools, parents, agencies working with the family, the pupil's health history, and developmental history, as well as analytic testing in the areas of vision, hearing, personality, and intelligence. With older pupils, measures and observations of study habits and practices, and handling of materials with flexibility would be added. Most of this data gathering and testing can be done relatively adequately by the trained remedial teacher, but she should be flexible in seeking help from other professionals and parents on many occasions to aid in interpreting the observed behaviors.

A diagnosis is not a failure when obvious causes cannot be pinpointed during this exploratory process. There are no nice, neat ways of proving that this or that area is the precise reason for the student's problem, in most cases. All we can derive from the facts that we have accumulated are clues as to probable causes, clues to be tested by related treatment when this is conceivable. When a contributing factor cannot be eradicated by treatment, then we must try to diminish its influence by developing counterbalancing strengths of the pupil.

4. Beware of the tendency to fractionate behavior into minute subskills, which are then assumed to be major causes if the pupil's performance is weak (2). Unfortunately for the reader's ability to integrate diagnostic areas, it is necessary for us to present each area of exploration separately and to review it thoroughly, as though it were independent of the total picture. To provide the essential professional background for the reading teacher, we must review each specific visual skill, each auditory ability, each perceptual performance, as though they were unrelated within each sensory area or across sensory channels. Similarly, for instructional purposes, we isolate and explore the intellectual, the sociocultural, the personality and self-concept factors even when we know that this atomizing gives a false view of the integration of these as manifest in each individual pupil.

This overemphasis leads to all sorts of malpractices in our field as exemplified in those that find panaceas for all their cases in one type of treatment, or those that have only one or two tests that suffice for diagnosis of all causes. We know one clinic where all cases apparently need correction of the convergence-divergence visual ratio, for which, of course, this clinic has a corrective gadget. We know another group of clinics where about 96 percent of the cases of disability are found to be due to lack of phonic skills, for which, of course, the clinics have their own training materials.

To avoid these pitfalls, make the diagnosis-remediation process a constant exploration for the pupil's strengths (1, 3). Try to find ways in which he *does* learn, which then can be strengthened and used even more efficiently to obtain comprehension. Expect variability from one subskill to the next, for this is the normal human pattern, not necessarily an indication of an area of weakness that must be repaired. If he appears to lack a certain skill and it is clear through trials that he is not compensating adequately, and that he can learn this desirable ability, then try to develop it to a functional level. Avoid the a priori judgments regarding the values of any subskill until you have discovered how the pupil functions with or without it, and *whether* he really needs it because he can't compensate for its lack.

5. Diagnosis should be honest. The approach is broad enough to explore almost all possible causes, not just those which the therapist thinks are most likely to be significant. The reading teacher must also recognize that the interrelationship she establishes with her pupils is one of the most important elements in her success and theirs. This implies that she realizes that the teaching materials, the mode of presentation, and her techniques of teaching are of secondary importance. Almost everyone doing remediation claims successes, with about the same supporting statistics, which may again mean that the exact procedure of the program is not very significant, or else some would certainly succeed or fail much more than the others.

The importance of the pupil-teacher interaction also implies a need for self-evaluation of the progress of the teacher in relating to a pupil. None of us can expect to be equally helpful to all our disabled readers, for in some cases we cannot really like them or they do not like and respect us. Remedial teachers must be alert to recognize their own limitations in establishing rapport, in motivating pupils, and in creating an atmosphere of mutual respect. We remember a case in our clinic in which, first an authoritarian male teacher, then a permissive male teacher, and finally a flexible female were unable to stimulate any real progress for the pupil. The problem was not a matter of atmosphere or of sex, as we had thought, but rather a matter of finding something of value to this child that could be related to his reading progress. Quite accidentally, we discovered that the motivating force had to be small amounts of money, which he could use to purchase additional equipment for his sole personal possession, a bicycle. Probably today's behavior modification therapists would have found this solution quicker. But the idea of using concrete rewards to induce reading progress just was not in vogue then. But it worked.

Some clues to this subtle personality interaction may be obtained by such behavior as the pupil's promptness for appointments, response to physical and social contacts between the two, willingness to remain after the appointed time for the session, spontaneity in sharing extraschool and family experiences, making small gifts to the teacher, the reduction of symptoms of tension and anxiety, eagerness to participate in a variety of activities with the teacher such as outdoor games, walks, taking photographs, collecting shells, and so on.

When these or other indications of improving rapport are lacking, the remedial teacher must be honest enough to admit to herself and her supervisor that perhaps the child will make better progress with another staff member.

6. Diagnosis and remediation is temporary, supportive help for the disabled reader. We may improve his feelings about reading, relieve some of his symptoms of maladjustment to school, and improve his reading test scores, for the time being. But as we have pointed out in our chapter on the outcomes of remediation, these are seldom permanent changes that

markedly influence the student's future school progress or life adjustment. The implications here are several: we cannot think of our treatments as curative, but rather as steps we take to help the student's immediate problems in reading and in dealing with school demands. This gives a different viewpoint to the current overemphasis upon reading skill development and shifts our goal toward helping the student meet everyday school demands more effectively. We cannot continue to assume that technical improvement of reading skills is the most important contribution we can make, for the evidence is that these improvements are purely temporary, in most cases.

Second, the temporary effect of remediation implies that we must expect the child to return for more assistance, if we keep our services available. This fact also implies that we should maintain contact with the pupil, even after his reading scores have so improved that he may return to classroom work. We need not meet with him with as great frequency as during the treatment program, but probably can reduce this to weekly or monthly sessions, provided we also schedule brief reevaluations of his progress from time to time.

We could probably expand this list of principles of diagnosis and remediation by pointing out the obvious facts that diagnosis is individualized—a testing not a teaching relationship—while remedial efforts must be interesting and varied, socially approved by the peer group, explained and demonstrated to the classroom teacher who will deal with the student in the future, and scheduled at a time that does not deprive the student of school activities that he enjoys. But we believe these facets are quite apparent to the remedial therapist and need only the barest restatements.

LEARNING PROJECT

Let us assume that a student has been referred to you for diagnosis and treatment because his teacher considers him a retarded reader. Which of the following points would you feel it essential to clarify *before* undertaking a lengthy observation and diagnosis of the student's possible needs for treatment? Be prepared to justify your choices and omissions.

1. **Performances on previous group reading tests or oral reading tests.**
2. **Comparison of reading scores with age.**
3. **Comparison of reading scores with the class medians.**
4. **Comparison of reading scores with M.A.**
5. **Socioeconomic status and the education of his parents.**

6. All previous reading test scores, to determine the probable duration of his problem.

7. Other facts from the school history, such as grades, teachers' comments, attendance record, health history, and schools attended.

8. Results on any diagnostic tests to determine probable areas of difficulty and their severity.

9. Records of I.Q. tests.

10. Performance on his teacher's informal reading inventory.

11. His present teacher's description of her reactions to his reading, her grouping practices, and her method of instruction.

12. The native language of his parents, their fluency in English, and the student's facility in English.

REFERENCES

1. Groesbeck, Hulda G., "Approaches to Diagnosis of Children's Reading," *Reading Quarterly* (Kansas State College) 3 (May 1970), 10–15.
2. Mann, Lester, and Phillips, William A., "Fractional Practices in Special Education: A Critique," *Exceptional Children,* 33 (January 1967), 331–37.
3. Prouty, Robert W., and Prillaman, Douglas, "Diagnostic Teaching: A Modest Proposal," *Elementary School Journal,* 70 (February 1970), 265–70.

part two

DIAGNOSING AND EXPLORING CAUSES

2

Diagnosis: Vision and Visual Perception

Despite the fact that reading is a complex visual act, often little attention is paid to the visual functioning of pupils experiencing reading difficulties. An assessment of the pupil's vision, as complete as possible, is a primary essential for the diagnostician in understanding the disability. Ignoring this diagnostic area, or sampling it only superficially as by the Snellen Test, may result in making remediation completely ineffectual. To promote better diagnosis in the area of vision, basic information regarding the visual functions related to reading, commercial and informal screening procedures, and symptoms of visual problems observable by use of these tests is presented. Several case studies of poor readers who were handicapped by the loss of good binocular coordination are offered. Behavioral and physical symptoms of vision difficulties, as well as classroom training activities to improve visual functioning, are reviewed.

In the discussion of diagnosis in visual perception, common causes of pupil variations are enumerated. Informal diagnosis, rather than the sole use of commercial tests, is emphasized and illustrated in detail. Effective and ineffectual teaching practices in visual perception and discrimination are contrasted. Finally, the interrelationships of this emphasis upon the visual and visual perceptual aspects of reading with the multisensory nature of the act is stressed.

As you peruse this diagnostic area, keep these questions in mind.

1. Can you draw upon your teaching experiences to relate the visual defects and their symptoms to actual reading behaviors that you have observed among poor readers?
2. Do you agree that reading teachers must assume some of the responsibility for using more effective vision screening and visual training procedures?
3. Can you recognize how the perceptual training activities can be also employed as diagnostic screening techniques?
4. Why does the author reject the use of many of the commercial perception tests? Do you agree?

AS ALSO STRESSED in our accompanying book, *Investigating the Issues of Reading Disabilities,* which included a review of the role of visual defects in reading disabilities, assessment of pupil functioning in this area is essential. The various vision screening batteries may not be so reliable and complete as desired; but we shall suggest supplementary tests, both commercial and informal, to strengthen the validity of our observations. To reestablish a background for this discussion, let us first review the terms and definitions of the field and the significance of variations in visual functioning for the reading teacher.

VISUAL FUNCTIONS

Among the visual functions that may be tested are the following:

Acuity Keenness of vision, usually measured at near-point, 14 to 18 inches, and at far-point, 20 feet or more. These distances are simulated in most testing batteries by the size of the target or by placing the test card at stipulated points in the test instrument. Three tests are almost always made, except in Snellen-like letter charts, of left eye, right eye and both, or binocular acuity. Instruments that simulate the Snellen chart testing procedure may omit the binocular test, perhaps under the assumption that reading is done with one eye at a time (1) (?)

Farsightedness Also called hyperopia, it is the condition in which the individual shows better acuity at far-point than at near, in one or both eyes.

Myopia Also called nearsightedness, it implies that the individual is losing or has lost the youthful farsightedness and is beginning to show better visual acuity at near-point than at far (25).

Astigmatism This is a distortion of keenness of vision, often attributed to unequal curvature of the cornea or lens of the eye. The distortion or blurring may be present either at near or far-point, or both, and may be present horizontally, vertically, or obliquely.

Refractive Errors Nearsightedness, farsightedness, and astigmatism are called refractive errors or defects to distinguish them from coordination or motility or other types of difficulties. All involve the individual's ability to discriminate targets clearly at various distances.

Fusion or Phorias

This concerns the ability of the eyes to maintain an appropriate posture with respect to an object so that the images formed in each eye fall on the corresponding points in the retina.

Esophoria—when one or both eyes tend to turn inward in attempting to focus on an object.

Exophoria—when one or both eyes tend to turn outward when focusing.

Hyperphoria—when one eye turns above or below the other when focusing.

Esophoria is often associated with nearsightedness; exophoria, with farsightedness. The effects include inability to get a clear single image of the target or overlapping or double images. The condition may be obvious to the observer, as in strabismus or cock-eye, or discoverable only by testing. If severe, it may result in suspension of the vision in one eye (suspenopsia) or squinting of which the subject may be unconscious.

Stereopsis

Because of the slightly different images received by the two eyes, the subject receives a tridimensional effect; that is, he tends to perceive depth or thickness of objects as well as their height and width. Shading on the object, perspective, and earlier experiences with tridimensional objects enter into the depth perception, of course. In some instances, an individual may show some depth perception on the basis of these other clues even when he is lacking the fusion or good binocular coordination that is usually considered essential for stereopsis or depth perception. A test of stereopsis is perhaps the most objective way of determining binocular coordination, although it may be superficially determined by informal tests or observation.

Accommodation-convergence

There is a coordinated action of the lenses and the posture of the eyes in the act of adjusting to the distance of a target. The eyes separate for distance and converge for near-point focusing. At the same time the lens bulges or flattens to keep the image of the target clear. This is a complex visual function controlled by two separate nervous systems, a function that begins to break down with age (presbyopia) as the lenses lose their elasticity, although this condition may be found in young persons. Measurement of this dual function is really a professional task; however, crude estimates of dysfunction may be made by certain informal tests. The accommodation-convergence reflex is not mature before the ages of five or six, sometimes even later. Because of this relatively late maturation, some vision specialists strongly oppose reading training or other tasks requiring this function for young, preschool children (14).

Color Discrimination The ability to discriminate red, green, yellow, blue colors is significant for reading diagnosis because of the demand for these discriminations in primary reading and seatwork (10).

These are the visual functions commonly sampled in screening batteries or the informal tests that reading teachers can employ. Other defects, such as limitations of the visual field or aniseikonia (different-sized images in each eye), require professional examination; and, in any event, their significance for reading success has not been strongly demonstrated.

From this review of the terminology of the field, we shall move to a consideration of the vision screening tests available to reading diagnosticians and to the supplementary informal tests that may be useful.

VISION SCREENING PROCEDURES

Among the batteries of tests we recommend are the following:

Keystone Visual Survey Tests. Keystone View Division, Mast Development Co, Davenport, Iowa. Several models of this stereoscopic instrument are available, including an abbreviated or short survey test. In scoring the responses, a band of acceptable variation from the ideal is indicated on the record form. This may be too narrow an allowance, for there is some evidence that, when compared with professional examinations, the Keystone tends to overrefer, that is, to indicate defects with which the professionals do not agree, perhaps because of their ability to interpret such test results in the larger framework of a total examination of the interrelatedness of all visual functions (2). But the battery is very popular and is often used by optometrists as part of their preliminary screening.

Ortho-Rater. Bausch and Lomb Optical Company, Rochester, New York. Originally standardized for adult and industrial use to establish desirable visual patterns for various working conditions. Helen M. Robinson restandardized the subtests among intermediate-grade children, and these norms are available for school and clinic use. Referrals among young children may be higher with this instrument but, in general, agree with professional examinations (12).

Professional Vision Tester. Titmus Optical Company, Petersburg, Virginia. Includes the group of tests common to other screening batteries, measuring most of the visual functions enumerated above. Several models varying in price and convenience in operating are offered, of which the Professional and Industrial Model is preferable to the Pediatric Model.

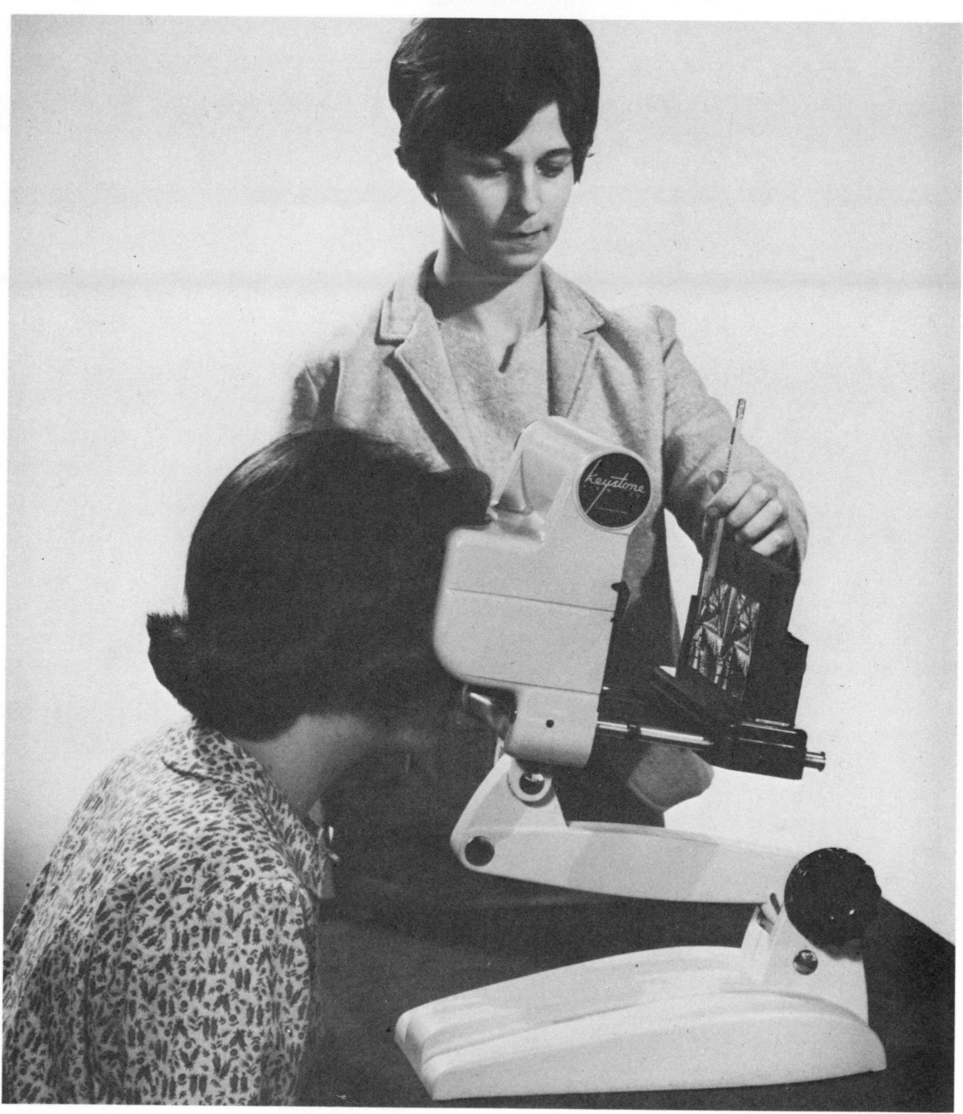

Keystone Visual Survey Test

Titmus Biopter. Titmus Optical Company. An inexpensive battery testing most visual functions. Employs a simple, light-weight stereoscope with the usual lighting, height adjustment, and occluders for administration.

We do not recommend the following because they are simple imitations of the inadequate Snellen procedure.

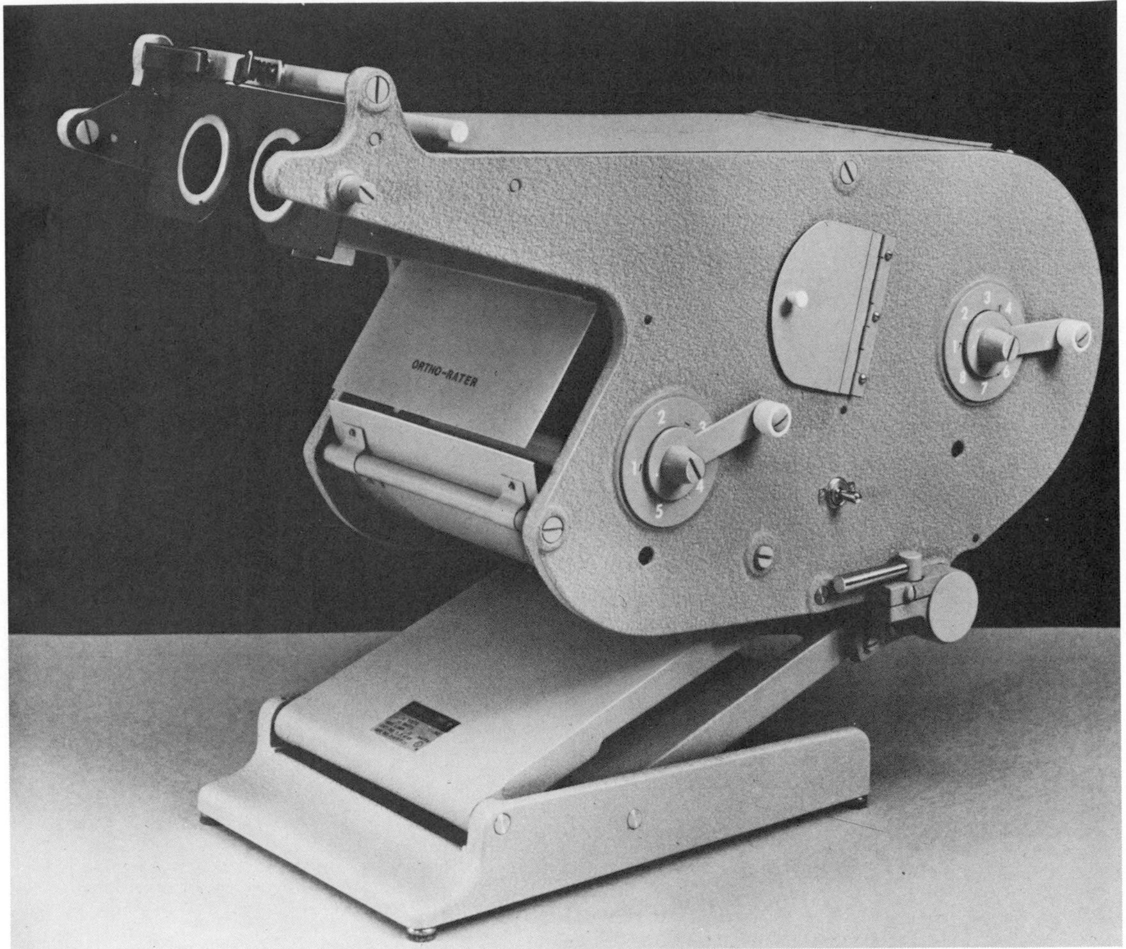

The industrial model of the Bausch and Lomb Ortho-Rater

American Optical School Vision Screening Test.
King Sight Screener.
School Vision Tester, Bausch and Lomb.
School Vision Tester, Titmus Optical Company.

Other tests of this type, such as the Eames Eye Test and the Massachusetts Vision Test, fortunately are no longer available.

If the Keystone or the Ortho-Rater instruments are purchased, they must be supplemented by a measure of depth perception, such as

Titmus Stereo Tests. Titmus Optical Company - includes Stereo Fly for gross stereopsis; Animal Test for minimum stereoscopic requirements; and Stand-Out Circle Test for stereopsis at nine levels of difficulty.

Any of the commercial screening batteries should be supplemented by

Spache Binocular Reading Test. Keystone View Division, Mast Development Company. A measure of the relative participation of both eyes in the reading act. Three levels of the test preprimary, primary, and intermediate grade are available on test cards that can be inserted in any stereoscope, such as the Keystone or Titmus Biopter, or a hand stereoscope. Standardization by the author on students was replicated by independent evaluation by Helen M. Robinson (11, 12, 13). Its manner of testing binocular reading is superior to the similar test using the Gray Oral Check Reading selections offered by the same company (21).

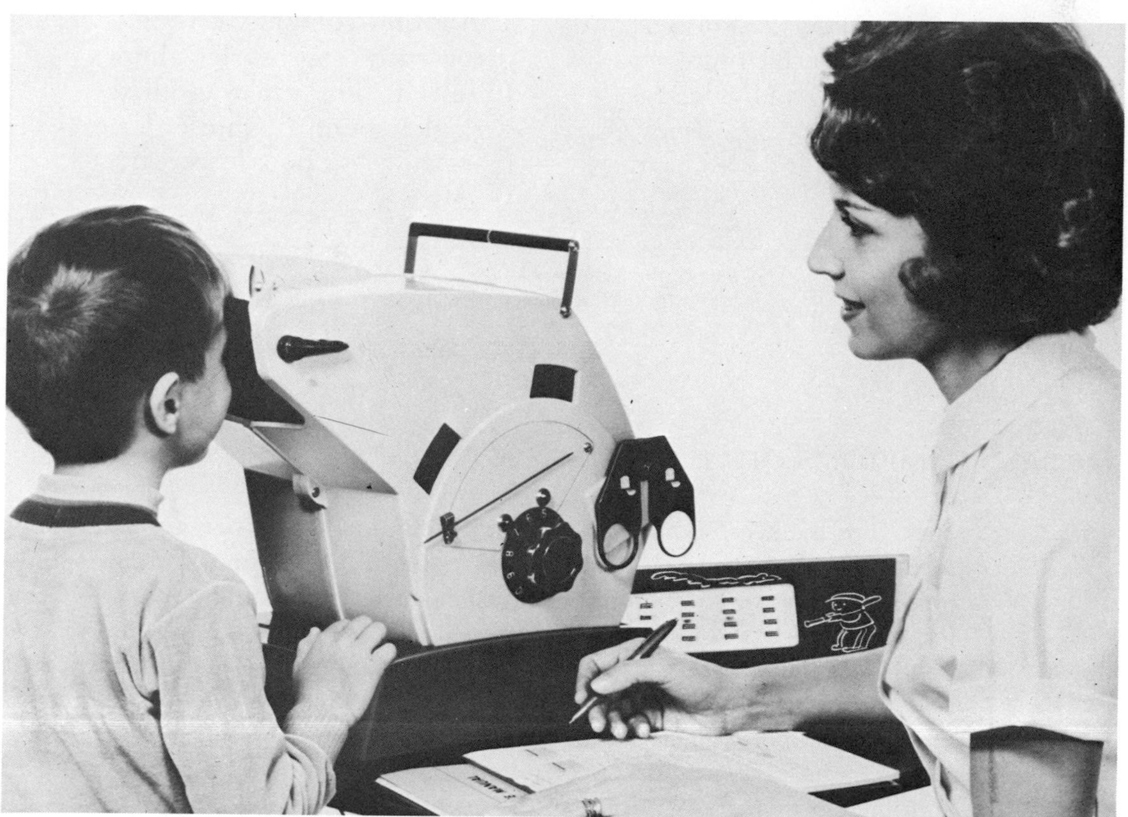

The Titmus Vision Tester

BINOCULAR READING TEST II, A

Once I saw a Queen and her
escorts pass through the
main street of a city. It
was a very sight
because they were dressed
in pretty bright colors. The
men clad in scarlet,
with plumes in their
caps, were the leaders. A
company in yellow, with big blue
plumes, came next in line.
Another company clad in dark
green with scarlet plumes
followed. The air was filled
with music. Cries
from the many people were heard.

I saw a Queen and her
many escorts pass through the
street of a big city. It
was a beautiful sight
because they were all dressed
in colors.
men clad in bright scarlet,
with long white plumes in their
caps, were the leaders. A
company with
plumes, came next
Another company clad in
green with long scarlet plumes
followed. The air was filled
with the sound of music. Cries
from the people were heard.

Part of the Binocular Reading Test
(Keystone View, Davenport, Ia.)

PROBABLE SYMPTOMS OF VISION DIFFICULTIES

These are the symptoms and significant differences between good and poor readers that the research literature has yielded. When present, they should be followed by supplementary or repeated testing and should form the basis for referral of the subject for a professional examination. The referral, we believe, should be to an ophthalmologist who has an extensive child practice, or to an optometrist with similar practice and preferably one who is a member of the Optometric Extension Program, which emphasizes child vision. These facts can be ascertained by consulting the Blue Book of Optometrists, an annotated directory. In using and interpreting the results of the commercial batteries, the reading clinician should watch for these symptoms:

Acuity—any real differences between the measured acuity of the eyes; or if the left eye is poorer.* In either case, check with the Binocular Reading Test (5, 18).

Farsightedness—any in subjects from about fifth grade up; or when linked with phoria deviations; when found with squint; when present in one eye while other is normal or myopic (4).

Myopia—when uncorrected, severe or progressively worse in successive semiannual testings (6).

Astigmatism—when uncorrected or extreme; when present in only one eye.

Fusion or phorias†—esophoria at near or far; any phoria when combined with farsightedness; exophoria at far, particularly for older students. Use Binocular Reading Test to help determine effects of any deviations upon reading.

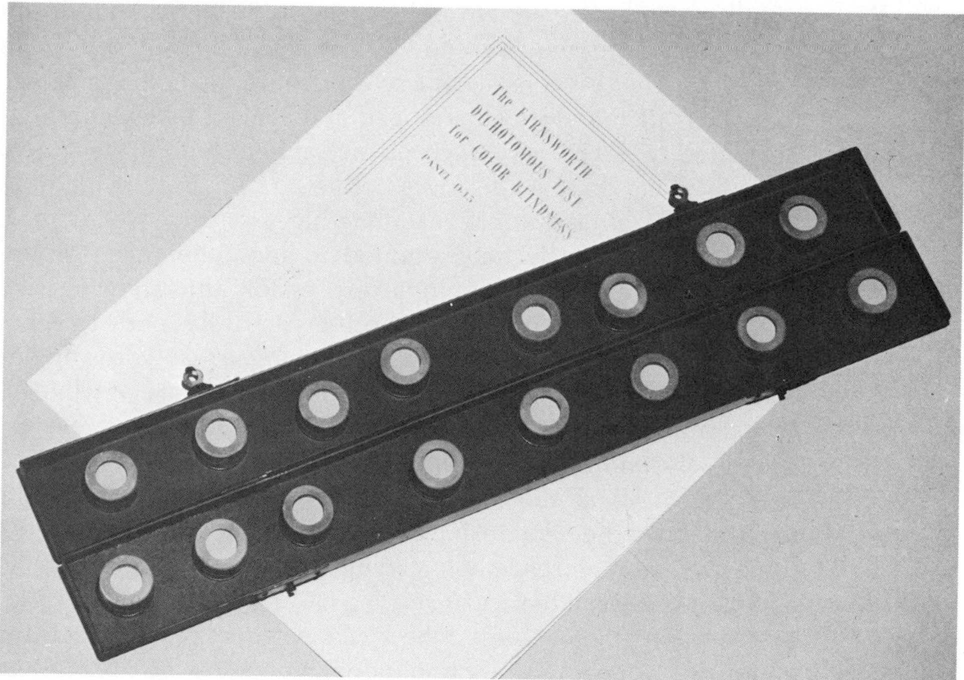

The Farnsworth Dichotomous Test for Color Blindness

*Interestingly, these measurements were the most reliable in the Ortho-Rater battery, according to H. Alan Robinson, "Reliability of Measures Related to Reading Success of Average, Disadvantaged and Advantaged Kindergarten Children," *Reading Teacher,* 20 (December 1966), 203–9.

†Ibid.

Stereopsis—when poor, or linked with exophoria. Use Binocular Reading Test if any deficiency appears in formal or informal tests of binocular coordination (7).

Color blindness—poor discrimination, particularly among primary children (10, 15).

Accommodation-convergence—refer for examination if failure in informal tests.

INTERPRETING THE BINOCULAR READING TEST

We have recommended the Binocular Reading Test as a supplement to any of the screening batteries. It will serve to confirm the diagnosis when responses involving binocular function are variable or doubtful. Moreover, the test because of its greater length and demand upon binocular function in sustained reading is more reliable and discriminative than those of the screening batteries. The test consists of a selection mounted on a stereoscope card with the words of the story so arranged and spaced that a number of words are presented to each eye, which do not appear before the other eye. This is done by using double adjectives before a noun, as "the big red car." Before one eye, the phrase would read "the big. . . . car," while "the. . . . red car" would simultaneously be presented to the other eye. If the child reads binocularly, he reads the complete expression, thus showing that he is reading simultaneously and equally with both eyes. If he tends to suppress vision in one eye, he will, of course, omit some of these test words on one side. "The Big Red Car" selection is best for primary children, while "The Queen" selection is appropriate for those reading at fourth-grade level or above. The latter is also more discriminative in doubtful cases.

We have offered a series of research studies using this instrument in the exploration of the relationships of eye preference to visual acuity differences in the eyes; eye preference and reading ability; validity and reliability of the test; and case studies in binocular reading (16, 17, 18, 19, 20, 21). The test is scored by comparing the percent of the total key words read by each eye. Ordinarily about 73–77 percent of a school population show no great difference in each eye's performance. About 23 to 27 percent definitely read more key words with one eye than the other. Those who read 13 percent or more of the key words with one eye than with the other are exhibiting an eye preference or suppression.

The value of the test lies in its unique measurement of binocular function in sustained reading. No other available test functions quite this way in revealing the almost three out of every ten children who manifest an eye preference. Ordinary reading tests cannot, of course, reveal this visual malfunction. Separate reading tests given to each eye (while the other is occluded or covered) give some indication of the condition; but, since not all children necessarily read better with the preferred eye (only one out of three), the meaning of such a testing procedure may well remain ambiguous. Moreover, in that type of testing some children read better with one eye than when presumably reading with both. In these cases, the Binocular Reading Test often reveals that, in apparently reading with both eyes, the child is often only using one, his preferred eye. Finally, in a sense, the BRT demonstrates exactly what is happening when the child reads in cases of differing visual acuity in the eyes, the phorias or lack of fusion, strabismus, poor binocular coordination, and the like. The test is so easy to understand that many professionals ask the child's parents to observe the effects of visual dysfunctions upon his reading and thus recognize the need for corrective treatment.

A brief résumé of some of the case studies we have reported may serve to indicate some of the clues that may be derived from use of the Binocular Reading Test (19).*

Case of R.J., a fifth grader. Left eye acuity was normal, right eye 50–60 percent of normal. Using the Gray's Oral Check Tests, R.J. achieved a grade score of 5.7 with the right; 6.6 with the left; and 5.5 when presumably reading with both eyes. In both forms of the BRT, there was complete suppression of the right eye. Which reader is R.J., an average fifth-grade reader (with the right eye or both) or an accelerated reader (with the left)? What will happen to the binocular function, to stereopsis, and eventually to academic achievement if this suppression is permitted to continue? As so often happens, will R.J.'s right eye diverge with strabismus or cock-eye? Or should we immediately refer him for efforts to improve his acuity in the poorer right eye and to restore binocular function?

Case of J.G., a third grader who is cross-eyed. In both forms of the BRT he read only with the left eye, omitting all key words offered to the right. Oral reading tests show 3.0 right, 3.0 left, and 3.0 for both (?) eyes. Thus, like many strabismatics, J.G. exhibits no direct association between eye preference and reading ability since, although he now reads only with one eye, he can also read as well with the other. He may never be hindered in his reading by the suppression of the right eye, but he will lose spatial and depth perception and be handicapped by the appearance of the crossed eyes unless he is treated early.

---

*These case studies are abbreviated from the author's original report (19).

Case of D.B., also strabismatic, shows retardation in reading because of preference for the left eye, which was evidenced by complete disuse of the right eye in both of the Binocular Reading Tests. Oral reading was 38 seconds, 1 error or 2.0 with the right; 60 seconds, 1 error or 1.7 with the left; and 67 seconds, 5 errors or 1.6 with both (?). We would expect him to read monocularly because of the crossed eyes, but his preferred eye is much inferior in reading performance to the other. In ordinary reading tests, he would hardly show the potential level possible in his right eye. D.B. is now being given exercises to help the monocular tendency and to regain binocular coordination.

We could cite many other cases of students who manifested suppression or loss of binocular coordination because of poor acuity in both eyes, squint, and other conditions as limited peripheral vision (omitting all key words on one or both edges of the test cards) and retinitis (blank spots in retinal sensitivity) in which the Binocular Reading Test proved a useful screening device.

INFORMAL TESTS AND THEIR INTERPRETATION

These tests should be used as supplementary to a vision screening battery, particularly if the child's responses are ambiguous, if they vary from one test to the next, or if they change while he is taking a test. These informal tests are not more reliable than the screening battery but may be used to confirm its results. Some of the informal tests, as the cover test, are difficult for the inexperienced to judge and therefore should be repeated. In fact, we suggest repeating any of these tests several times at intervals of a day or two, if the child's responses are at all equivocal. Young children have problems in responding correctly when right and left directions are involved. Asking him to point, rather than name, the directions is often less confusing to both the child and the teacher.

Fusion or Binocular Function

Skeffington String Test Hold one end of a 2–3-foot string on the bridge of his nose (without blocking his vision with your hand). Have him focus on a knot in the string 16 inches away while you hold the other end. Ask him, "How many strings do you see?" "What do they do?" and, if necessary, "Show me with your hands what the string does." He should see two strings forming a V at the knot. If he sees two crossing before the knot, he is overconverging (esophoric). If the two strings cross after the knot, he is underconverging (exophoric). If he sees only one string, he is suppressing vision in one eye. If one string is higher than the other, hyperphoria or vertical imbalance is indicated.

Cover Test Hold a card over one of his eyes while he is focusing on a shiny object or small flashlight in your other hand (about arm's distance from him and on a level with his eyes). Lift the card quickly to see whether the covered eye shifts. Repeat for other eye. Repeat tests several times.

Pursuits Test Rotate vertically a small light or shiny object slowly about 16–18 inches from his head, describing a wide circle around his head. Repeat moving object in horizontal and vertical circles and obliquely from right to left and left to right. Tell him to follow the object with his eyes, without moving his head. He should follow smoothly, not jerkily (if your movements are smooth). His head should not have to move, and there should be a reflection of the light in both his eyes at all times.

Binocular Test An additional sample of the child's use of both eyes is recommended by Tole N. Greenstein, a noted child vision specialist. Have the child hold up one finger at arm's length and, looking past the finger, focus on something beyond. He should see two fingers. Cover each of his eyes alternately to see if one of the fingers disappears. Repeat by having him focus on the finger, in the same direction as before. The distant object, if small enough, should now appear to be doubled. This test of teaming of the eyes also indicates whether there is suppression of vision in one eye.

Accommodation-Convergence

Pencil Test Move a small flashlight or pencil slowly horizontally closer to the child's nose, at eye level. Child is to tell you when he sees two. Watch also to determine whether one eye suddenly diverges. Do the test several times. If the object doubles or his eye diverges before you are at 3–5 inches from his nose, score as failure. As the object is gradually withdrawn, the single image should appear again at 5–6 inches away. The normal point of convergence is about 1–3 inches; or some say 4–6 inches.

Point-to-Point Test If the accommodation-convergence function is normal, the individual should be able to jump his eyes from near-point (14–18 inches) to infinity (all the way across the room) with accurate focus at both points. Test by having child move upon signal from a word in his book (previously circled or marked) to a card containing a well-known word on the distant wall of the classroom. Uncover this wall card as you give him the signal to look at it. (Make certain before testing that you have printed the words on the wall cards large enough to be read easily.) Repeat the test in reverse by having him shift back from the wall card to another marked word in the book. Repeat tests several times. He should be able to say aloud the word in the book or on the wall card or alternately without hesitation, in less than a half-second, if he has full control of this visual function.

OBSERVATIONS OF VISUAL SYMPTOMS

A number of vision screening studies have shown that the detection of children with visual difficulties has been markedly improved by the use of planned observations by teachers. A number of long lists of symptoms that teachers are supposed to watch for are offered, but most of these have not been validated against the results of professional examinations. Listed below are symptoms carefully tested for significance in the reports by Knox (9), Wilson and Wold (22,23), Wold (24), and the leaflet "Educator's Guide to Classroom Vision Problems," offered by the Optometric Extension Program Foundation (3). These signs have been compared with, and validated against, professional examinations.

Check List of Vision Problem Symptoms

Appearance of Eyes

- One eye turns in or out at any time
- Eyes or lids sometimes reddened
- Tearing excessively
- Encrusted eyelids, or frequent styes

Complaints from Sustained Close Work

- Headaches in forehead or temples
- Burning or itching
- Nausea or dizziness
- Print blurs after reading a while

Posture and Behavior at Desk

- Squints, closes, or covers one eye
- Tilts head constantly in reading or writing
- Blinks excessively while reading
- Strains forward to see distant objects, as chalkboard
- Frequent errors in copying from chalkboard to paper

Fatigues easily and avoids near-point tasks
Holds head or book in unusual relation constantly
Excessive head movements from left to right while reading

Children with vision problems show a variety of symptoms during the act of reading. The problem in evaluating these is that many of them are also simple symptoms of poor or beginning readers. Perhaps the best we can do is to say that these symptoms may be indicating a vision problem when they are quite frequent, not characteristic of children of the subject's grade level, and not due to the difficulty of the reading material. In other words, these may be other symptoms of undiscovered vision problems if they appear frequently in even easy materials and are not common to the rest of the class:

Losing place on line in reading, needs finger or marker
Moves up or down a line in reading, unknowingly
Writes up or down hill on paper despite lines
Misaligns horizontal or vertical series of numbers
Misreads known or familiar words
Does not like sustained reading, loses interest early
Needs to whisper while reading silently in order to keep place

In addition to these screening batteries, informal tests, and check list of visual symptoms, we believe that the eye-movement camera can be a valuable supplement to diagnosis. Like the Binocular Reading Test, it shows objectively and precisely what the individual is doing visually while reading. It may confirm in a number of ways the effects of the visual deviations upon reading, as no other diagnostic tool can do. It functions in planning a course of remediation and in evaluating the permanent outcomes in terms of eye-movement patterns, which are, after all, the most significant effects that can be produced. Since we discuss the use of eye-movement photography in chapter 11, it will suffice here to reaffirm our belief in its unique values in diagnosis of reading disabilities.

VISUAL TRAINING ACTIVITIES*

Thus far we have stressed only the diagnostic tools for detecting visual problems and implied simply that these should be the basis of referral for professional examinations for children. But there are also training procedures

*For other procedures with visually handicapped, see relevant chapter in our *Investigating the Issues of Reading Disabilities.*

that reading teachers can employ for direct assistance to pupils with these visual problems. We are not suggesting that these treatments should be given to every child who seems to be handicapped in the vision area, however, without professional advice from a specialist who is familiar with these training activities. As part of the use of the professional as a source for estimating the severity and the significance of the deviations found in the testing procedures that we have outlined, the reading teacher should certainly visit with the specialist, at his convenience. Her purpose would be to secure an interpretation of the child's problem and advice regarding the supplementary training that might be desirable in the classroom.

Among the visual training activities of proven merit that teachers can employ are:

1. *The walking beam or rail,* a 2 × 4 about 12 feet long. Supports cut from similar material hold the beam with the 4-inch side up, later with the 2-inch side. Children walk the beam in stocking feet while fixating on a target such as a small Greek cross on the wall directly in front of them. Exercises include Indian Walk—forward or backward, heel to toe; Butterfly Walk—with arms moving like wings and also forward and backward; giant steps; and stepping off distances, as half, one-quarter, or the like. The specific purpose of this training is not body balance, which is incidental, but *control of fixation* while in motion.
2. *The balance disc,* a heavy plywood base 18 inches square balanced on 4-inch square or circular piece of wood glued or screwed to the center on the bottom. Child tries to balance, to move feet apart, or to turn in a circle, stand on one foot, and so on, while fixating on the wall target. (See Evelyn B. Spache, *Reading Activities for Child Involvement,* Boston: Allyn and Bacon, 1974, for more details.)
3. *Swinging ball.* Suspend a small rubber ball from a doorway, light fixture, or other convenient point at child's eye level. Gently swing ball to and fro or, while he is on his back on the floor, in a circle, as he follows the motion with his eyes (without moving his head). Check his concentration by having child try either to catch the ball in a wide-mouthed jar or to touch it with his extended finger as it goes by. The purpose of this rotary pursuit activity is to develop coordinated movements of the eyes.
4. *Finger play.* Have child jump his eyes from the tip of one forefinger to the other with arms extended to about a foot or so from his face, about a foot or two apart. If needed, pace his eyes by swinging your forefinger back and forth to touch his. This is another type of rotary pursuit training.
5. *Flashlight.* Vary the two preceding activities by using a penlight or other bright object in place of his forefingers or the swinging ball. Sometimes hand him the flashlight to be held at his side and then point quickly to various points in a circle of crosses on the chalkboard. As he shows ability to shift quickly and accurately from point to point, move the pencil closer to his face, but not closer than about 6 inches. Repeat training

Several perceptual-motor training activities

at various distances. This is practice in the accommodation-convergence function.

Bean bag or ball throwing and catching with a target or to another child and dart games are supplementary visual training activities readily carried on in the classroom or playground.

DIAGNOSIS IN VISUAL PERCEPTION AND DISCRIMINATION

We feel obligated in beginning this discussion of diagnosis in visual perception to point out that we are *not* concerned here with the subject of brain damage and its effect upon reading. Brain-damaged, as currently loosely used in educational and psychological circles, is a meaningless term. Anyone over thirty is brain-damaged by reason of age in that he has had cell death in the cerebral cortex. Common forms of birth trauma, anoxia, and childhood injuries undoubtedly produce brain damage in 25 percent or more of what are later normal children. Those clearly and demonstrably brain-damaged do produce abnormal scores on certain visual perception tests. But these scores are not usually related to the neurological assessment of the severity of the damage. When such tests are given in an ordinary classroom in which the presence of brain damage is doubtful, the wide range of scores in these tests tells us almost nothing. Longitudinal studies on the validity of these tests in predicting subsequent development of a brain-damaged neurological syndrome are needed—but completely lacking. Most of these visual perception tests recommended for detecting brain damage are based on the hypothesis that *any* type or degree of brain dysfunction will result in inability to reproduce or match forms or complete a gestalt. This hypothesis is hardly credible. Many of the authors of these same perception tests assume that poor scores will necessarily be reflected in any and all types of subsequent learning problems. Our reviews elsewhere of the validity of these predictions, as in *Investigating the Issues of Reading Disabilities,* again refute this naive assumption. In this section, we are not concerned with visual perception and brain damage, but rather with ways of identifying those children whose visual discriminations among shapes and forms are so weak as to interfere with their efforts at word recognition. *We* do not call these children "perceptually handicapped," for there are many reasons for their poor visual discrimination other than actual perception.

What Causes Poor Visual Discrimination?

Sooner or later in the diagnosis of the child's difficulties in visual discrimination, the reading teacher must look for some of the possible reasons for the child's performances. There are a number of contributing factors possible, and in planning remediation or improvement those that appear relevant in each case must be considered. Visual discrimination is not something apart from age, vision, cultural background, and the like, that can be readily improved by using some workbook or other with exercises in copying forms or such, as we shall try to point out. Visual discrimination is not the single behavior of reproducing certain forms from memory, as so many test authors seem to think. Rather it includes many forms or kinds of behavior, with a variety of factors contributing to success in each of these behaviors. Let us first, then, review some of the physical, personal, and sociocultural factors that enter into the child's visual discrimination behaviors.

Poor visual discrimination may be caused by the following:

Visual defects—as astigmatism with its blurring effects; differences in the visual acuity of the eyes with consequent variance in the clarity of the images being received and the inability to achieve a single, clear image; fusional or phoria variations with similar results on images; farsightedness with the subsequent difficulty with near-point tasks; and the accommodation-convergence function defect, which interferes with transposing images from near to far or vice versa.

Body posture in relation to the near-point task—If the child constantly tilts his body or head in viewing images, or if images are presented in a different visual plane than that in which he is trying to reproduce them, distortion in his productions will occur.

Cultural background—Most comparisons of minority and middle-class groups find inferiority in perception test scores for the deprived subjects. It is more logical to assume, not that most such children must be "brain-damaged" or "perceptually handicapped," but that their preschool experiences have probably not prepared them for this kind of behavior. Their experiences with tridimensional objects, and those even with paper and pencil, are inadequate for the test performances. Or, as others have said, these children lack the muscular-tactile experiences with objects in space that would permit them to manipulate shapes and forms visually.

Emotional reactions—Emotional disturbances and anxiety states of many types distort visual discrimination. Children who are threatened by tests or teachers or even school itself may give distorted pictures of their potential for visual discrimination. Children who are rejected by the majority or by the teacher because of differences in race, socioeconomic status, or school adjustment may also give false pictures of their ability.

Directional confusion—Orientation to left and right in space, on paper, in body schema, or in the bodies of others are developmental phenomena influenced by age, intelligence, and cultural background. These abilities are hardly completely developed by primary grade ages for many pupils. Since they can be readily improved by classroom activities, they obviously do not represent a physiological developmental lag, but rather the lack of stimulation and training. Testing children who have not yet reached the developmental stages demanded by the test may well yield inaccurate predictions of their potential for this type of learning.

Cognitive style—Like adults, children approach problem-solving in distinctly different ways. When asked to reproduce certain forms or designs, for example, some must first organize themselves by forming the outlines of the design. Others, who are field-independent, can react to and reproduce, as it were, from the central details outward to the outlines; or, starting in any place, they can move successively from one portion to another without reference to the edges that mark the field. Some children tend developmentally to focus on the details of a complex form, while others seem to perceive wholes, as Piaget and Gesell have shown. Perhaps these approaches reflect the degree of meaningfulness that can be attached to the design, in terms of the child's previous experience with such, for certainly this element, too, influences his production.

It is apparent that performances in visual discrimination tasks can hardly be considered a single behavior attributable to a specific cause. Visual perception is obviously not something the child has or does not have, no matter what the test results imply. We are not antagonistic to the use of all such tests, for we shall point out later some uses that they may have. Rather we are implying that attempting to diagnose the child's difficulties in visual discrimination must take a variety of approaches.

Informal Diagnosis of Visual Discrimination Behaviors

It is our premise that, if we hope to help the pupil who is experiencing severe difficulty in word and letter discrimination or in word recognition, we must explore the many types of behaviors with forms that are related. Only then can we identify precisely what it is that the child cannot seem to do well, consider this in terms of possible contributing factors as outlined above, and then begin to counteract the causes by developmental training. (In reviewing this field, we shall follow the categories of perceptual behaviors used in the chapter on visual perception tests in *Investigating the Issues of Reading Disabilities.*) It will become apparent that we are suggesting many informal, ordinary classroom activities, as well as some standardized tests as alternates, for diagnosis of the visual discrimination behaviors. Experienced teachers will also recognize that many of these sampling procedures will serve as training activities as well.

Part-whole—Matching parts of a whole, as forms cut into pieces, assembling object puzzles, completing partial designs as marble designs, making designs with blocks, and arranging pegboard designs, finishing incomplete drawings (see ditto masters of Continental Press, Elizabethtown, Pa. 17022, for training materials). Thurstone's Pattern Copying Test (from Thelma Thurstone, University of North Carolina, Chapel Hill, N. C.) is relevant here.

Visual memory for designs*—Copying designs. Proceed from tracing first to copying immediately next to the original, to reproducing from memory. Chalkboard activities of these types probably should precede seatwork. The Benton Visual Retention Test (New York: Psychological Corporation) or the Beery Developmental Test of Visual-Motor Integration (Chicago: Follett Publishing) and the Winter Haven Perceptual Achievement Forms (Winter Haven, Fla.: Winter Haven's Lions Research Foundation) are relevant. The Continental Press materials may also be used in this manner, and the templates of the Winter Haven group at chalkboard and desk.

Figure ground—Just what is appropriate testing material in this area is highly questionable. Figure ground discrimination can be assessed in seven or eight different ways. Moreover, its relevance to the act of word or letter discrimination is questionable.

Form discrimination—Matching forms in multiple-choice settings.

---

*See chapter 4 for other possible tests of this function in the ITPA or Detroit Learning Aptitude Tests.

The Thurstone Identical Forms Test (see address for Thelma Thurstone above) is a recognized measure of this ability. It may also be assessed by using cutouts of geometric forms in cardboard or plastic. Commercial training materials at an advanced level are the *Learning to Think Series* by Thelma Thurstone (Chicago: Science Research Associates). Other testing and training activities include sorting and matching parts of large picture puzzles, form boards, pegboards, arranging forms in size or pattern, and the like.

Noting missing parts—as in picture puzzles, designs, pegboard designs, missing part puzzles, dot pictures. Arranging series of pictures in a given sequence is another variant of this skill, or matching parts of a design with the given whole.

Form constancy—The present evidence on the relevance of form constancy or recognizing a shape despite rotations and reversals is weak. Practice in these discriminations with letters is probably more relevant, as described below.

Directional confusion—The chalkboard exercises offered in George D. Spache and Evelyn B. Spache, *Reading in the Elementary School,* 3rd edition (Boston: Allyn and Bacon, 1973), are helpful in promoting orientation to left and right. Briefly these involve having the child connect dots marked on the chalkboard by horizontal, vertical, oblique, horizontal plus oblique, vertical plus oblique, and scattered or mixed lines. Numbers or letters in sequence lead the child from point to point. The child should make a continuous, rapid line from each dot to the next. The lines should be straight and done quickly with a single movement of the hand and arm. A broad-point felt-tip marker with permanent ink is used to place the various groups of dots on the chalkboard for repeated use.

Confusion in body schema may be assessed and helped by such games as Simple Simon Says, exercises with a jointed doll, use of a mirror and rhythmic activities, Angels-in-the-Snow, the moving of hands and legs upon command while lying on the back on the floor, and songs such as "Looby-Loo" and "This Old Man." These activities may be adapted to orientation to the body schema of other bodies also by providing a leader for the game whose motions and verbal directions are to be imitated.

Letter and word discrimination—matching plastic, cardboard, or wooden letters, imitating letter shapes by body position, crossing out letters in mixed or pied material; tracing, copying word outlines, and reproducing from memory are some of the assessment and teaching activities in this area.

Exercises with reversible pictures and later with letters, as *b-d, p-q,* perhaps reinforced with bodily imitation of the letter shapes, are useful here. *Visual Tracking* and *Symbol Tracking* (Ann Arbor, Mich.: Ann Arbor Publishers) are pertinent. These relatively advanced visual discrimination exercises should not be attempted until improvement in the preceding abilities is notable.

Miscellaneous—Testing and training activities in attention span include exercises in recalling the order of presentation of a group of objects (when one has been removed while child is not looking) or pictured objects or meaningful sequences of pictures. Stringing beads to copy a pattern and later to reproduce it from memory are related activities.*

Many more materials suitable for testing and training are listed in this author's *Good Reading for Poor Readers* (Champaign, Ill.: Garrard Publishing, 1974). Good sources of relevant materials are the following manufacturers and publishers:

Creative Playthings Inc., Princeton, New Jersey 08540

Educational Activities Inc., P. O. Box 392, New York 11520

Judy, Inc., 310 N. Second Street, Minneapolis, Minnesota 55401

Webster Publishing Co., Manchester Road, Manchester, Missouri 63011

Teaching Resources, 100 Boylston St., Boston, Massachusetts 02116

Beckley-Cardy, Inc., 1900 North Narragansett Avenue, Chicago, Illinois 60639

There is a hierarchy of skills in visual discrimination of forms, letters, or words. The order of difficulty is tracing, matching, drawing with an aid such as dots, freehand drawing from copy, and freehand drawing from memory. Although the various types of visual discrimination are not arranged above in this hierarchy, this sequence should be observed, in general, in both testing and training to enable the reading teacher to recognize the child's development. If the child cannot match forms or letters or words, there is little point in testing or training him in attempting to draw or write them.

All this testing and training in part-whole relations, visual memory, form discrimination, orientation, and word and letter discrimination has one goal—to help the reading teacher lead the child to greater success in word recognition. So much of the testing and instruction deals with manipulative materials and geometric forms that we sometimes lose sight of the word learning purpose of all of it. In other words, the emphasis upon these preparatory steps, as chalkboard exercises, orientation training, and form discrimination, often becomes an end in itself, rather than a means to an end. Our personal experience and research has convinced us that for economically deprived or culturally different children, or for any that have shown great

*See chapter 4 for relevant tests in this area in the ITPA and Detroit Learning Aptitude batteries.

difficulties in early reading, these preparatory steps may well prove very profitable. At the same time, they must be constantly pointed and shaped toward word and letter discrimination.

Let us try to clarify this point by concrete contrasts of teaching practices:

WHAT WORKS	WHAT DOESN'T WORK
When pupil has demonstrated control, moving from chalkboard exercises to handwriting strokes and letters at chalkboard, then desk	Continuing chalkboard exercises indefinitely
When simple designs or forms can be copied or reproduced from memory, modify by using letters and word outlines to trace, copy, reproduce	Using geometric forms as basic or only material
Recognizing that forms, puzzles, and the like, are preliminary and must be gradually modified to actual letter and word shapes	Expecting transfer from geometric form discrimination to letter and word discrimination
Combining geometric forms to make common shapes, as fish, man, house	Teaching names of forms, as square, triangle
Learning letter discrimination by verbal description; by writing their shapes as directed; by eliciting pupil descriptions or similes (*b* looks like a bat and a ball behind it)	Matching, pairing letters; learning names of letters (a practice that does not contribute to visual discrimination or word recognition)
Reinforcing letter and word discrimination by promoting pupil verbalization, description of distinctive features	Repetitive seatwork in writing, matching, or tracing letters
To avoid confusions and reversals, use contrasting letters (not reversible ones at first) as *b-t, t-d;* then similar letters later.	Using only reversible pictures, forms, or puzzles
Base word discrimination on differences in shapes, that is, ascending and descending letters, noted and pointed out by both teacher and pupils	Matching words as wholes as in common workbooks
Introducing words, use pictures only initially, then drop their use. Substitute associations in meaning and meaningful phrases	Continuing to use pictures to reinforce word recognition

WHAT WORKS	WHAT DOESN'T WORK
Introduce only meaningful words that can be pictured, or demonstrated, drawn from pupil's experiences at first	Emphasizing function words, that is, prepositions, conjunctions because of their frequency
Introduce words in related settings, as *cows* eat *hay, boys* play *ball,* the *rope* is around the *jug,* with picture reinforcement *at first* only. Try to include a verb in these groupings, but avoid teaching two of same visual pattern at same time.	Teaching lists of words justified as basal vocabulary of a reading system
Teach words in small groups related by meaning—*talk, speak, whisper* or by rhyming—*I, eye*	Teaching words by structural relations as *age, ago* or *hat, fat*
When word discrimination level is reached, emphasize grouping or classifying words according to function, rhyme, topic, as action words, color words, farm words, "and" words, moon-night-stars, and so on. Meaningful association, not repetition, is the basis for learning.	Failing to build many associations around words, for example, "teaching words" not meanings

A final caution in using this approach to teaching beginning reading or in correcting reading difficulties is inherent in the recognition that most of these procedures—except perhaps those in overcoming directional confusion—are relevant largely only with primary children. Lateral awareness or right-left discrimination, on the other hand, is not fully established until the ages of eleven or twelve. The research, in general, does not show much relationship of the other procedures or tests to reading success at fourth- and fifth-grade levels, for example. In individual cases of severe retardation, with older pupils reading at very primary levels, these procedures may be helpful. In such instances, they may be given a trial, if the preliminary testing seems to indicate a lack of development for this type of pupil. There will be some progress undoubtedly, if only for the reason that the child is responding to the individualized program. The experience with success in these simple activities will also help restore his self-confidence, a very important component of progress. But, at some time during this trial of these approaches, the teacher must make the difficult judgment as to whether the pupil's apparent progress is really due to the nature of the activities or simply to the Hawthorne effect of her attentions to him. The sophisticated reading teacher shows her insight and wisdom by facing this critical issue, basing her future course on the constant observations that she makes of the pupil's benefit from each type of training and modifying or discarding it as her judgments dictate. She is constantly aware that reading is not just a visual perception act but that it has auditory components and relationships to speech and language development generally.

This recognition of the basic multisensory nature of reading means that, during the remediation program, the teacher will be exploring the values of devices for reinforcing the visual impressions of words. Concretely, this implies that she will try out such auditory training as we describe later, as well as tactile and kinesthetic reinforcements. Among these latter are sandpaper letters, tracing words in sand or water, flocked or magnetic letters on a board, tracing written letters or words with the hand or pencil or both, recognizing letter or word outlines by the hands with an intervening curtain hiding the forms or outlines (in sandpaper, plastic, or wooden letters). In the subsequent discussion of diagnosis in auditory perception and sensory integration, we shall try to show how the choices of training procedures may be made in these areas and combined with the visual and visual perception activities.

LEARNING PROJECT

Several projects are relevant to the concepts offered in this chapter. Your instructor will suggest those that are appropriate for you to complete.

1. Secure one of the commercial vision screening batteries for administering to several retarded readers after you have familiarized yourself with the administrative procedures. Interpret the test results for each pupil and try to determine his needs for professional attention, if any. If the pupils are not your own cases, discuss your findings with their teachers, offering your suggestions regarding their needs for referral to a vision specialist and possible classroom adjustments to lessen the effects of any visual defects upon the pupils' academic progress. (You may need to review the chapter on helping the visually handicapped in the accompanying *Investigating the Issues of Reading Disabilities* to secure ideas for these recommendations.) If the pupils are in your charge, write down the steps that you will take to follow up the implications of the testing in your instructional procedures.

2. Practice the several informal vision screening procedures until you feel confident of your ability to use them. Then screen several poor readers to assess

their visual functioning in those skills tested. Follow up on the indications of the tests in your work with these pupils or in talks with their teachers in the manner outlined in Project 1 above.

3. If an eye-movement camera is available at your college or a nearby clinic, try to borrow the Manual of its administration and interpretation. Arrange to observe use of the camera or, if you are permitted, to test a pupil with it. Use the graph obtained in this testing (or borrow one from the clinic files) and, with the aid of the Manual, score and interpret it. If it has been previously analyzed, compare your scoring and interpretation with the earlier one. With the aid of the Manual (and the chapter on this technique in *Investigating the Issues of Reading Disabilities),* organize a brief statement of the particular values of eye-movement photography in diagnosis and in the evaluation of remedial efforts as you see them.

REFERENCES

1. Ames, Louise Bates, Gillespie, Clyde, and Streff, John W., *Stop School Failure.* New York: Harper and Row, 1972.
2. Crane, Marian M., et al., *Screening School Children for Visual Defects.* Children's Bureau Publications, No. 345, 1954. Washington, D.C.: U.S. Department of Health, Education and Welfare.
3. *Educator's Guide to Classroom Vision Problems.* Duncan, Okla.: Optometric Extension Program Foundation.
4. Grosvenor, Theodore, "Refractive State, Intelligence Test Scores and Academic Ability," *American Journal of Optometry and Archives of American Academy of Optometry,* 47 (May 1970), 355–60.
5. Hirsch, Monroe J., and Wick, Ralph E., *Vision of Children: An Optometric Symposium.* Philadelphia: Chilton, 1963.
6. Holmes, Jack A., "Visual Hazards in the Early Teaching of Reading," in *Perception and Reading,* Helen K. Smith, editor, Proceedings International Reading Association, 13, No. 4, 1968, 53–61.
7. Kelley, Charles R., *Visual Screening and Child Development: The North Carolina Study.* Raleigh: Department of Psychology, College of Education, North Carolina State College, 1957.
8. Kempf, Grover A., Jarman, Bernard L., and Collins, Selwyn D., "A Special Study of the Vision of School Children," *Public Health Reports,* 43, Pt. 2, No. 27, 1713–39. Washington, D.C.: Government Printing Office.
9. Knox, Gertrude, "Classroom Symptoms of Visual Difficulty," Master's thesis, University of Chicago, 1951.
10. Krause, Irl Brown, Jr., and Thomas, Isabella Dodson, "The Use of Colour Contextual Clues in Reading," *The Slow Learning Child,* 16 (March 1969), 44–50.
11. Robinson, Helen M., Visual Efficiency and Reading," in *Clinical Studies in Reading I,* Supplementary Educational Monographs No. 68. Chicago: University of Chicago Press, 1949.

12. Robinson, Helen M., "Visual Efficiency and Reading Status in the Elementary School," in *Clinical Studies in Reading III,* Helen M. Robinson, editor, Supplementary Educational Monographs No. 97. Chicago: University of Chicago Press, 1968, 49–65.
13. Robinson, Helen M., and Huelsman, Charles B., Jr., "Visual Efficiency and Learning to Read," in *Clinical Studies in Reading II,* Helen M. Robinson, editor, Supplementary Educational Monographs No. 77. Chicago: University of Chicago Press, 1953, 31–63.
14. Rutherford, W.L., "Vision and Perception in the Reading Process," in *Vistas in Reading,* J. Allen Figurel, editor, Proceedings International Reading Association, 11, 1966, 503–7.
15. Shearron, Gilbert F., "Color Deficiency and Reading Achievement in Primary School Boys," *Reading Teacher,* 22 (March 1969), 510–12, 577.
16. Spache, George D., "A Binocular Reading Test," *Journal of Applied Psychology,* 27 (February 1943), 109–13.
17. Spache, George D., "Eye Preference, Visual Acuity and Reading Ability," *Elementary School Journal,* 43 (May 1943), 539–43.
18. Spache, George D., "A Binocular Reading Test," *Journal of Educational Psychology,* 30 (September 1943), 368–72.
19. Spache, George D., "Case Studies in Binocular Reading," *American Journal of Orthopsychiatry,* 13 (October 1943), 723–26.
20. Spache, George D., "One-Eyed and Two-Eyed Reading," *Journal of Educational Research,* 37 (April 1944), 616–18.
21. Spache, George D., "The Validity of the Binocular Reading Test," *Journal of Educational Research,* 41 (February 1948), 461–66.
22. Wilson, W.K., and Wold, R.M., "School Vision Screening Implications for Optometry," *Optometric Weekly,* 61 (1970), 488–93.
23. Wilson, W.K., and Wold, R.M., "A Report on Vision-Screening in the Schools," *Academic Therapy,* 8 ((Winter 1972–73), 155–66.
24. Wold, R.M., "The Santa Clara County Optometric Society's Perceptual-Motor Survey," *Optometric Weekly,* 60 (1969), 21–26.
25. Woodruff, M. Emerson, "Observations on the Visual Acuity of Children During the First Five Years of Life," *American Journal of Optometry and Archives of American Academy of Optometry,* 49 (March 1972), 205–14.

3 Diagnosis: Auditory Perception and Sensory Integration

Despite the lack of strong supporting evidence of its essentiality, training in auditory discrimination has long been included in early reading programs. The relationship of such training to the common phonics program of these school years is so apparent that the true values of auditory discrimination and their limitations for some children have not been questioned in the past. But recent exploration of other auditory abilities, of intersensory integration, and of the learning modalities of youngsters have brought new viewpoints about auditory discrimination. In this chapter, possible steps in diagnosis of a number of auditory abilities that may be related to progress in reading are contrasted. Related classroom adjustments to pupils' auditory deficiencies and some training procedures are suggested. The validity of various methods of exploring intersensory integration and learning modalities is also examined. While reading these suggestions, use these questions to crystallize your understandings of this area.

1. What are some of the reasons for the divergence of opinions and research reports on the significance of auditory discrimination?

2. Which of these auditory abilities seem logically related to learning to read? Does the research support this logic? For what types of pupils and under what conditions are these various abilities significant?

3. What seems to be the justification for the research in intersensory integration and learning modalities? Is this research really significant for reading instruction? If you think so, how would you apply it in diagnosis and instruction?

AS IS TRUE OF VISUAL PERCEPTION, we are not speaking of a unitary trait when we discuss auditory perception. Among the components of interest to reading teachers are auditory acuity, auditory discrimination, auditory memory of several types, and auditory synthesis of sounds. Although most of these elements are spoken of as though they were independent auditory abilities, and many training programs are so planned, there is probably considerable overlap among them. These interrelationships will appear as we consider each auditory trait.

Auditory acuity is commonly called "hearing"; its lack is termed deafness or partial deafness. In reality, it is not a general measure but rather the specific testing of pitches of sounds at various levels of loudness. These pitches within a certain range correspond to those of the human voice, or in a wider range to the variation in pitches possible in Western music. Thus it is apparent that testing of auditory acuity is, in effect, the assessment of the individual's power to hear speech and music, as well as noises.

TESTING AUDITORY ACUITY

While deafness can be general or complete, it is more common to find that the acuity loss is present in a relatively narrow band of pitches somewhere on the complete scale. Thus the individual is more likely to be deficient in hearing low- or high-pitched tones of ordinary loudness. Other methods (as using a loud-ticking watch or measuring the distance at which the subject can hear a whisper) are possible, but these obviously unstandardized techniques have generally been discarded in favor of testing by an instrument called an audiometer. This is an instrument that produces pure tones of specific vibration rates, usually from 125 to 8000 cycles per sound. The instrument is relatively simple to learn to use, for one dial usually controls the pitch of the sound, while another affects the loudness with which that pitch is produced. Ideally the testing should be done in an isolated or even soundproofed room into which no extraneous sounds can enter. Individual screening is preferable to group, although group tests (as from an audiometer or a record player or cassette player) are available. Because there is almost always some extraneous sound around us, the loudness of the pitches that the normal person is expected to hear begins at a base level slightly above the softest reproduction possible.

Testing usually involves placing the headphones on the subject, seating him where he cannot see the dials being manipulated, and giving him a buzzer or other signal device to use in indicating when he can hear a sound. As testing proceeds at each pitch level through the range of loudness back and forth from loud to soft and reverse, an interrupter switch is intermittently employed. This cuts off the tone and thus permits the examiner to determine whether the child is simply perseverating in signaling or whether he is really attending to the duration of the tones that he is hearing.

As the examination continues, the teacher marks the lowest level of loudness at which the subject can hear each pitch on a chart called an audiogram. When finished, these points are joined by a line and a graph of the hearing thus recorded. Complete testing by a professional includes three or four types of assessment as by tones, by calibrated human voice, by bone or air conduction, and the like. Audiometric screening by the teacher or nurse is preliminary and is intended only to establish whether or not there is a loss in auditory acuity and a basis for referral to a hearing specialist.

At the hands of the teacher this screening procedure is, of course, not perfectly reliable, for testing conditions are seldom well controlled. Moreover, temporary conditions such as any type of upper respiratory infection may well detract from the accuracy of the assessment. Group testing is even more

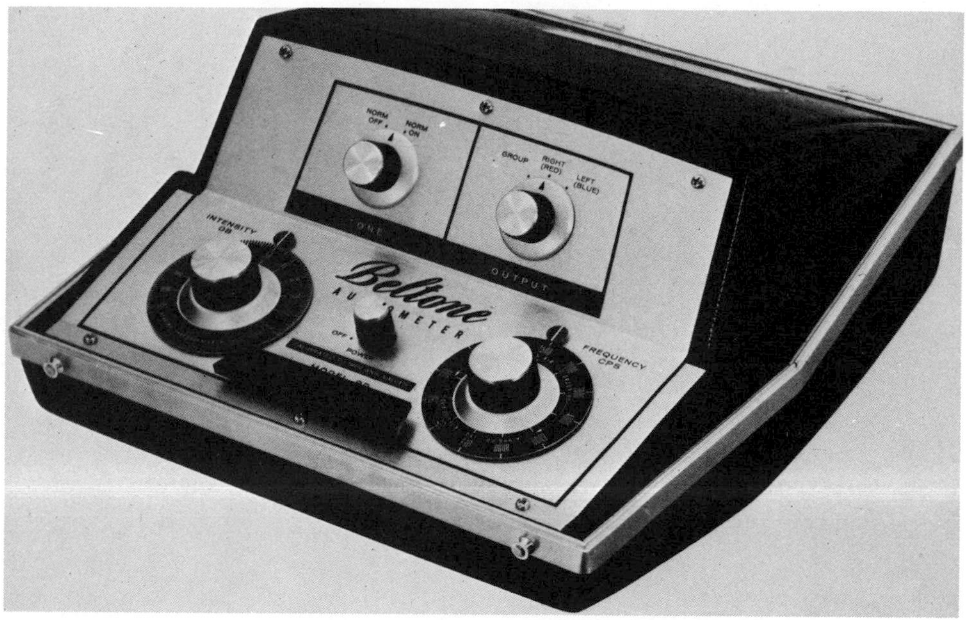

Beltone Audiometer

fallible, as the present author once discovered in testing a small school population. Because of the incidence of winter colds and the intrusion of extraneous noises in the environment, follow-up testing some months later indicated, to his embarrassment, that most of the original diagnoses of hearing losses were false. In our experience, teachers have learned to give the testing efficiently and properly, but they need to be reminded that the screening is a dichotomous way of identifying those who may or may not have a significant loss in auditory acuity, not a diagnosis as a basis for classroom treatment of the hearing difficulty.

There are a number of audiometers of varying types and prices available, as the following*:

Beltone, Model 9D, a portable instrument of average cost.

Zenith, Model ZA-100T, a more expensive instrument available as a portable.

Maico, Model MA-19, a portable that can be integrated with multiple headphones for small-group testing.

Eckstein, Model Tetra-Tone 46, which tests in the narrower range from 500 to 4000 cycles in four steps. The manufacturer offers some evidence that this range is sufficient and economical of testing time for the sweep check screening. Less expensive.

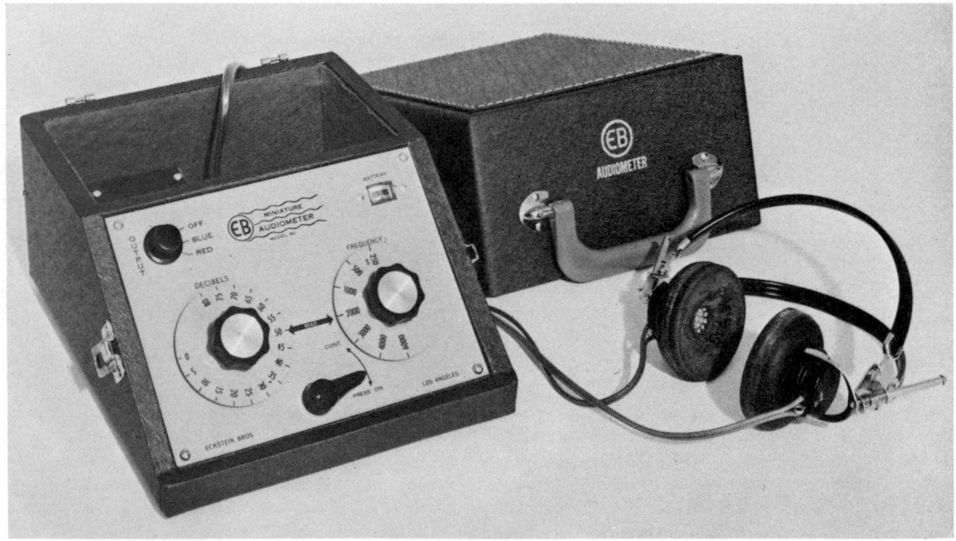

EB Audiometer

*See references at end of chapter for addresses of these manufacturers.

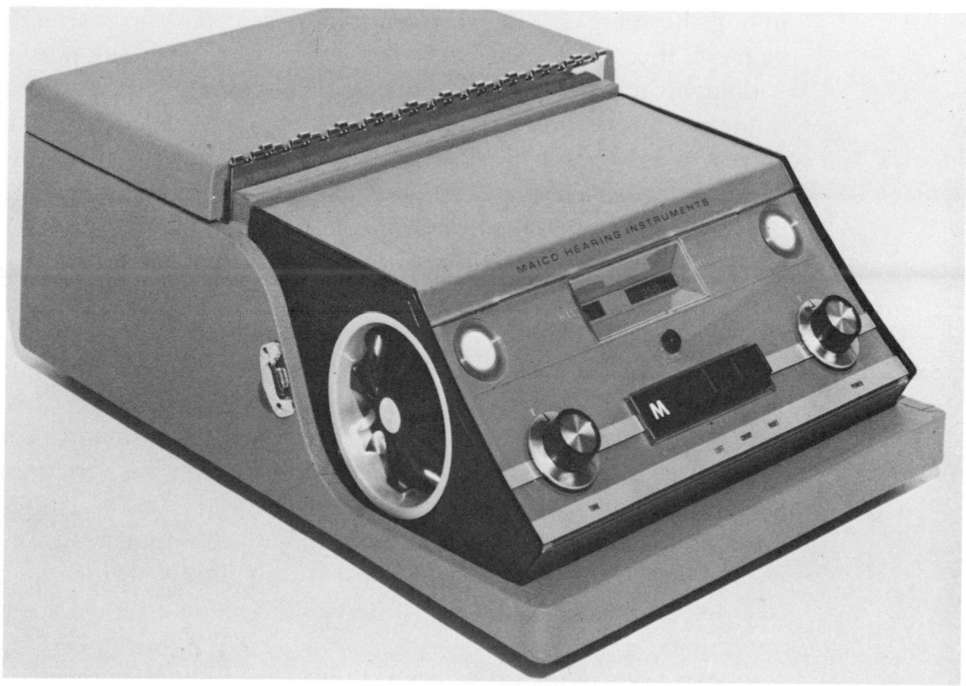

Maico Audiometer

Audivox, Model 7BP, a portable for individual or group use. A more expensive instrument.

Eckstein, Model 60, tests at seven frequencies from 250 to 6000 cycles. Less expensive than most of the others.

Maico, Model MA-12, testing in five steps from 250 to 8000 cycles. Medium priced.

Classroom Adjustments

If a hearing loss is discovered, the subject should be referred for the thorough assessment of a medical hearing specialist, an otologist, or, perhaps, to the speech and hearing clinic of a nearby college, if such is available. Complete treatment may be a medical problem, but the university-trained speech and hearing personnel, because of their frequent relationships with schools, can be very helpful. They can assess the severity of the loss, the need for medical referral, and the extent of the effects upon speech, articulation, and other auditory abilities. They may also suggest classroom adjustments.

Losses in acuity at the upper end of the pitch range, the high tones, affect the subject's ability to deal with some consonant sounds and blends.

Among these are *s, l, t,* and their combinations. Vowel sounds are lower in pitch and thus are not usually affected. Since English and particularly primary reading vocabularies are distinguished by their consonant sounds rather than by their vowel sounds, as in French, Chinese, and certain other languages, high-tone losses are a real handicap in learning to read. The beginning emphasis upon consonant sounds, blends, and digraphs in the early work in phonics imposes a difficulty for these high-tone loss children. The muffled, indistinct way in which these children hear words is generally recognized as a distinct handicap to learning to read in the usual program, and even more so in programs emphasizing isolated phonemes.

In low-tone losses, vowel sounds are not heard clearly, nor are the consonants *m, g, b, h,* and their blends. As we remarked, vowel sounds are not very distinctive features of our enunciation, for in many instances they are interchangeable, indefinite, or indistinct. Though the variations in American dialects are largely present in the sounds given the vowels, this is no barrier to our communication. Similarly the child with low-tone losses may be inaccurate in some of his pronunciations of vowels, but we understand him and he, us. His reading progress is not particularly affected if we are tolerant of his difference.

For both types of children, there should be a referral for professional evaluation and a consultation with the specialist to seek advice regarding ways of helping the child in the classroom. For example, a hearing aid may be prescribed and fitted, but the teacher will need to supervise the child's use of it if he is to receive its full benefits. Children are prone to forget to adjust the volume of their aids, to replace the worn-out batteries, and even to turn the aid on. They must learn to watch the face of the speaker in a two-way conversation to use his facial expressions and gestures as a contextual aid to understanding his ideas. We no longer emphasize reading the lips of the speakers as a basic aid for the hard-of-hearing, since hearing aids have improved greatly. But direct attention to the speaker is an essential for these pupils, and teachers can help these children acquire it. Unless the hearing loss is similar in both ears, which is not usual, the child experiences difficulty in localizing sound—in recognizing the direction from which it emanates. This is another reason for securing his direct attention before speaking to him. Other classroom adjustments can be made in the seating of the child near the teacher, in securing his direct attention when he is being addressed, and in being certain that he understands general directions or announcements made to the class.

For many of these children with hearing losses, extraneous noises and other voices tend to mask or to cloud the clarity of reception of a speaker. On a noisy playground, in the street, or even in a small group, they cannot sort out the voice of someone speaking to them from the other noises or voices, even when wearing a hearing aid. The hearing aid usually simply increases the loudness of sounds, all of them in the environment, rather than making it easier to hear just voices in a noisy setting. For this reason, we emphasize that hearing-loss children be trained to look directly at the speaker to secure as many meaning clues as possible, and that teachers address the child directly in a face-to-face manner as often as possible. Teachers may also employ some sort of signal to secure relative quiet in the classroom, when they are about to address a direct question to this type of children. In some cases, nothing of an educational nature can be done to restore the child's hearing of low tones or high tones, for this is really a medical problem. But these simple classroom adjustments will aid the child to make a better adjustment to school life.

A very pertinent question in teaching reading to these children is the approach to sound-symbol relationships. If the hearing loss appeared early in life or is congenital, it is possible that it affected the child's articulatory development. Not hearing certain letter sounds as others do, he may not have ever learned to enunciate them in the usual manner. Substitutions for letter sounds in the pitches he does not discriminate well will be present. How, then, does the teacher train him in using letter sounds to unlock the pronunciation of common words, particularly in the use of initial consonants and consonant blends as a word recognition technique, when he hears and/or says them incorrectly?

Actually this is not as great a problem as it seems at first thought. In the case of low-tone losses (where mainly vowel sounds are involved), much of the early phonics training can be given these children if their enunciation of the medial vowels—so common in the many monosyllables of a beginning reading vocabulary—is accepted. With children of high-tone loss, who lack many consonant sounds, such training is somewhat more difficult but often still possible. After all, the letters we use to represent spoken sounds are simply conventional symbols. The same letters have different sounds in various languages as well as different symbols. Even within one language with one set of conventional symbols, the speakers of that language vary in their enunciation of sounds and pronunciation of words. Dialects, as they are called, are present in practically all languages, yet usually users of different dialects can communicate.

Even though a child may misarticulate sounds or mispronounce them from printed symbols, if he has a constant association or enunciation for each symbol, he can read and he can use phonic clues reasonably effectively. His exact enunciation of the sound for a consonant or blend does not really matter, if he uses that sound-symbol association consistently. For example, he may constantly say *breaf*—for *breath*. Provided he has established a meaning for the word, his pronunciation does not interfere with his sight recognition of it. Consider the fact that black dialect speakers and Spanish-speaking children often vary in their enunciation of a variety of letter sounds from what is considered standard. Yet they learn to read standard English texts in their own inflection patterns when reading orally, and they progress in reading under empathetic teachers. If we accept and help him to stabilize his responses to sound-symbol associations, these hearing-loss children can learn to read.

When the hearing-loss is accompanied by misarticulation, it may be desirable to seek assistance from the speech-correction specialists. They will decide whether the child can progress in improving his articulation and will provide the appropriate training. Often this specialized help can be supplemented by teacher efforts. When a child is accepted for corrective training in speech, the concerned teacher will consult with the special teacher, asking for suggestions that she may follow in the classroom.

In chapter 8, on analyzing and teaching word analysis skills, we speak of alternatives to phonics to be used when the student has great difficulty in employing this aid to word recognition. Among those suggested were use of the cloze procedure and other types of contextual analysis. For some, kinesthetic reinforcement in tracing and writing words will be helpful. Or employing the child's own oral vocabulary as the written material may be a viable alternative to phonics training. Further details about these procedures are given in chapter 8 and later in chapter 10, in the discussion of remedial approaches.

AUDITORY DISCRIMINATION

This auditory ability may be defined operationally, as it is commonly tested, as skill in hearing the differences in letter sounds, words, or nonsense syllables. It is usually measured by asking the listener to indicate whether two words, often varying only in a single letter sound, are the same or different. It is obvious from the preceding discussion that, in some cases, poor performance in measures of auditory discrimination may be due to high-tone or low-tone losses in acuity. But more commonly we find relationships between the errors in auditory discrimination and the individual's dialect and articulation.

The significance of poor auditory discrimination is debated by various authorities. Some claim it to be highly important for early success in reading, while others point out the relatively low statistical relationships between auditory discrimination and reading test scores. Another source of disagreement in this area is found in the question whether auditory discrimination is a simple auditory ability or actually a complex behavior related to other auditory abilities and to a variety of factors in the testee's background. Price (32), for example, distinguishes three explanations for poor auditory discrimination: (a) central nervous system dysfunction that requires specialized treatment; (b) lack of familiarity with standard English sounds, as in lower-class or some black children; and (c) inattentiveness, which leads to a variable performance from test to test.

Belle Ruth Witkin (49), administering a number of auditory tests to young adults, found considerable interrelationships among auditory discrimination, span, and synthesis. The overlap among these supposedly independent auditory abilities led Witkin to question just what auditory discrimination tests were measuring, since performances were obviously influenced by the status in the other skills. Witkin also makes the point that some of the various auditory skills that we test are obviously related to intelligence, especially so in the case of auditory span, and probably so in auditory discrimination.

Morency, Wepman, and Hass (29, 45) emphasize the interrelationships among articulation, auditory discrimination, and reading. Children of all classes show a gradual development of correct articulation (and accurate hearing or perception of?) speech sounds. Some sounds are not fully developed in the average primary child's speech, although they do gradually improve during this period. Are auditory discrimination tests given in the early school years, then, really measures of speech development in many cases? Are auditory discrimination tests really valid and reliable in measuring what they claim to measure at beginning school levels?

Since the child gradually improves in articulation and auditory discrimination, it seems that measurements of these abilities may well vary in their relevance to reading progress at various times during this development. Wepman (45) showed, in a sample from the first two grades, that those with adequate performance in articulation and inadequate discrimination did as well in reading as did the group that was good in both traits. This seems to imply that development in articulation is more significant for reading success and that, if this development is present, poor auditory discrimination is of minor importance.

H. Alan Robinson (36) further complicated our consideration of the significance and meaning of auditory discrimination measures in demonstrating the marked variability of the reliability in different populations. In contrasting average, disadvantaged, and advantaged children, he found reliability of a common test much lower for average and disadvantaged children than for the middle or upper class. This type of comparison raises real doubts about the supposed inferiority of dialect-speaking children in this auditory ability that many studies seem to show. Venezky (44) further questions the reality of this class difference on the basis of the standard English distinctions demanded in the very items of most such tests, distinctions not learned by dialect users. The test created by Norman A. Buktenica (7) avoids this cultural bias, the author says, by using tones to test pitch discrimination, a procedure probably equivalent to testing discrimination of letter sounds. In his monograph Beery (3) claims that this pure tone discrimination test was more discriminative than the common paired word test of Wepman (46) in a middle socioeconomic group but merely equal in discrimination to that test in a low socioeconomic population. The relationships of the pure tone test to reading and spelling achievement were very similar to those for the Wepman test.

In his comparative study of seven tests of auditory discrimination, Dykstra (11) reminds us that varying tests are not equivalent in predictive ability or in their relationship to reading. All are related to reading achievement—but none very high—and even combinations of five or six of these tests give only a moderate total relationship, no better than an intelligence test. The relationships with reading were similar for boys and girls, even though, as usual, boys tested poorer in both auditory discrimination and reading. That test requiring matching of picture with a spoken word beginning with the same sound as the picture object was the most effective for predicting reading.

Testing Auditory Discrimination

In administering an auditory discrimination test, the need for privacy and quiet is apparent. The child is usually placed with his back to the examiner so that he cannot see the examiner's mouth. Then, as pairs of words are read to the subject, he is to indicate whether they are the same word or different words.

Among the tests most commonly used are the following:

Boston University Speech-Sound Discrimination Test. Boston: W. Pronovost, Department of Speech, Boston University. Thirty-six pictures are presented, the names of which are identical or present a contrast of a single sound as *cat–rat.* This is really a measure of the child's articulation of letter sounds, rather than of his auditory discrimination. But because of the interrelatedness of these elements, the test is pertinent here for supplementary use (5).

Norman A. Buktenica, *Tenvad.* Chicago: Follett Publishing. A nonverbal test of auditory discrimination by pure tones. Includes measures of the related auditory abilities of loudness, rhythm, duration, and timbre of sounds. Administered by a record (7).

Goldman-Fristoe-Woodcock Test of Auditory Discrimination. Circle Pines, Minn.: American Guidance Service. Uses taped directions for pupil to respond to by pointing to pictures (12).

Haspiel, George, and Bloomer, Richard, "Maximum Auditory Perception (MAP) Word List," *Journal of Speech and Hearing Disorders,* 26 (May 1961), 156–63. Offers groups of words requiring discrimination among phonic elements. Offered for testing and auditory and phonics training in reading problem cases (16).

Kimmel, G.M., and Wahl, J., "Screening Test for Auditory Perception," *Academic Therapy,* 5 (1970), 317–19. Battery includes test of paired words differing in single phonic element and measures of memory for rhyming words and for rhythmic patterns. Reliability of total test .80 in second grade but only .67 in third (21).

Wepman, Joseph M., *The Auditory Discrimination Test.* Chicago: Language Research Associates, 1973. The newly revised version of the best-known test in the field. Score now recorded in number correct rather than errors, on a five-point rating scale. Normed for ages five to eight. Author reports reliabilities of .91 to .95 in test-retest; .92 Form A vs. Form B. This is basically the same test first offered in 1958 and evaluated for reliability by Robinson and many others, as reported above (46). Morency et al. (28) reports that first-grade use of this test predicted reading and word knowledge in grades four, five, six by correlations of .20 to .29. In the first grade, validity coefficients ranged from .235 to .348.

Lindamood Auditory Conceptualization Test. Boston: Teaching Resources. Includes measures of discrimination of speech sounds, number and order of sounds in sequences of syllabic and nonsyllabic patterns. Child uses colored blocks to show distinction of same and different sounds in answering. Offered for all ages (23).

Katz, Jack, *Kindergarten Screening Test.* Chicago: Follett Publishing. A kindergarten–first grade test of discrimination of word pairs, blending sounds into words, and listening for speech against a noisy background (19).

There are undoubtedly other auditory discrimination tests that we have failed to discover in the literature. Still others are part of various individual diagnostic reading batteries and are discussed in chapter 7. Because it seems so simple to arrange pairs of words that differ in a single sound or to match a set of pictures with words beginning or ending with the same sound, we may well expect that many of these types will continue to appear, despite Dykstra's comments on their validity.

Interpreting Auditory Discrimination Tests

The use of one of the tests listed above will yield a score that indicates whether the child lacks good auditory discrimination. Just what this result means, however, is not always as apparent. We believe that the test score of auditory ability should be interpreted in the light of these facts:

1. Poor discrimination of vowels in the test may reflect low-tone hearing loss.

2. Poor discrimination of certain consonants may reflect high-tone hearing loss. Was an audiometric screening test done? What were its indications?

3. The test result is related to the child's articulatory development. What were the indications of screening by an articulation test? Is this speech development similar or farther advanced or relatively worse than the auditory discrimination? If it is equally poor or less advanced than the auditory discrimination, shall we give training for the auditory skill? Would he be likely to learn to hear differences in sounds that he cannot articulate properly yet? Auditory discrimination is probably not highly related to reading progress, if articulation is well developed, but in this case training might be helpful.

4. How old is this child? If older than primary grades and of average intelligence, he has passed the ages during which auditory discrimination usually develops. Few tests show any significant growth in this auditory skill after the ages of eight or nine. Nor is his poor performance probably affecting his reading.

If he is of primary age and engaged in a reading program that makes strong demands for phonic knowledge, auditory training may be desirable if articulation warrants it.

5. What is the extent of his auditory deficit in parallel tests of span and synthesis? Should any training include these related skills?

6. The test score is affected by intelligence and use of dialect. Could either of these be responsible for his performance? If he speaks in dialect and tests poorly, the auditory discrimination skill can probably be improved. But is it essential for the reading program, and will its improvement really accelerate reading ability? Moreover, testing with these children is not very reliable, and probably should be repeated, perhaps using another type of test than the paired words version.

7. With beginning readers or kindergarten children, and particularly disadvantaged children of these ages, testing is difficult and not very accurate. Final diagnosis should probably be based on repeated testing. Also, at these ages and with these types of children, a pure tone test may be more easily administered than the usual.

8. The auditory discrimination tests included in readiness batteries vary considerably in validity. The best seems to be that of matching a picture with a spoken word beginning with the same sound as the pictured object.

It is apparent that the results of an auditory discrimination test do not simply divide pupils into two categories—those who need training and those who do not. As we have suggested, the decision must also consider the factors of age, intelligence, use of dialect, other auditory deficits, and the child's basic articulatory development, as well as the possibility of a basic cause in hearing loss.

Training in Auditory Discrimination

The lack of close relationships between auditory discrimination and reading success and the general results of training programs do not argue strongly for intensive training in this area for most pupils. On the other hand, some reading programs at primary grades are highly phonic oriented, and, in these instances, auditory discrimination skill is almost essential for success. Alternative methods of word recognition could be taught some of the children who do not appear likely to profit from this type of auditory training. But many teachers are not flexible enough to vary their method according to pupil potential. We often see pupils receiving such training regardless of their needs or potential for profit from it, as in the use of readiness workbooks, for example. Moreover, we observe that teachers do not see the direct relationship between auditory training and phonic discriminations. Each is practiced or taught as though unrelated to the other, rather than as a stage of a continuous development toward handling sound-symbol relationships.

Auditory discrimination is also often treated as an independent hearing skill, unrelated to auditory awareness, auditory experiences, and perception and auditory memory. We see children who lack basic auditory discrimination of sounds and noises offered a training program that begins with letter-sound discriminations, which are really an advanced auditory skill, with, of course, negligible success or effect upon reading.

There is no research evidence to indicate the exact training sequence that should be followed. But our logic dictates this sort of sequence:

Auditory Awareness*

Practice in hearing, naming, and discriminating among sounds in the environment, of the street, of the classroom, of the weather, of the sea. (See References for instructional materials.)

Practice similarly with the sounds of animals and manmade sounds, such as a bouncing ball, crumpling paper, planes, trains, and bells.

Practice hearing variations of these sounds in terms of loudness, pitch, duration, and sequence. Help children verbalize the descriptive terms implicit in these discriminations, for example, loud-soft, high-low, slow-fast.

Move gradually toward exercises involving discriminations among words, such as voices implying pleasure and anger; detecting where accent

*For further details of this training, see George D. Spache and Evelyn B. Spache, *Reading in the Elementary School,* 3rd edition (Boston: Allyn and Bacon, 1973).

is in polysyllabic words; recognizing other children's voices in various games; recognizing rhythm and rhyme in children's stories and poetry, limericks, and jingles.

Auditory Perception

Provide opportunities for children to express the way sounds affect them in dances, rhythmics, tapping, and the like.

Provide experiences in specific extraschool sites for listening to and describing sounds, such as a farm, factory, garage, playground, home, ball game.

Arrange experiences with alliteration with jingles, such as Lucy Lockett, Baa-Baa Black Sheep, Hickory, Dickory, Dock, and the like. Promote attention to beginning sounds by picture arrangements, a picture dictionary, and games in thinking of words beginning with a specific letter sound.

Auditory Memory

Provide experiences in following and imitating sound sequences, such as tapping, musical notes, directions, numbers, and words. Play games in repeating phrases, sentences, and directions from one child to another around the circle.

Auditory Discrimination

Precede such training by those listed above. Use children's names, common objects, polysyllabic words for children to identify number of separate sounds. Emphasize beginning sounds of classroom objects, names, pictured objects, and the like, to games in classifying words by initial sound. Discuss with children the similarities and differences among these sounds.

Identify such letter sounds not by the name of the letter but as the "*M* sound as in the beginning of *Mary*." Avoid sounding letter in isolation, such as "Mah."

Introduce blends by analogy with common sounds, as *drip, splash, g-r-r.* If needed, use commercial materials as listed in the References.

Ask children to discriminate among words with similar sounds in initial, medial, or final position in words, again using names of children and familiar objects for examples. Move gradually from initial sound to other discriminations as children's development of skill dictates.

Use the McKee-Harrison combined context–initial sound technique of reading stories to children containing a number of words with the same beginning sound. With this sound in mind, have children try to identify each such word when it appears in the story, before you pronounce it.

Auditory Synthesis*

In a sense, the hearing of words does require attention to order of sounds and a blending of these, which is termed *auditory synthesis.* This

*See chapter 4 for additional tests of this function in the ITPA battery.

auditory ability is developmental in that accuracy in pronouncing all the elements of a word can be observed to mature as children grow in speech. There is also an element of auditory synthesis in listening to sentences and paragraphs in the perceiving of relationships among ideas. This latter type of synthesis is more often called auditory comprehension, however. A third type of synthesis is present in blending the sounds of a word as designated by printed symbols into the pronunciation of the whole word, as in the task of phonic analysis. This type of synthesis of sounds also occurs in attempting to spell a spoken word.

Because of these facets of auditory synthesis and the lack of research indicating the true nature of auditory synthesis, we find wide divergences in the testing approaches. For example, among tests purported to measure auditory synthesis, there are these examples:

> A test of two to four sounds, which one by one, form words; plus rearranging given vowel and consonant sounds to form a written word, as *s-t-e-a = eats* or *east;* given a word, the child must reverse the sound sequence to form another word, as *some = muss;* and anagrams, or forming words from given letters. These were used in a study of young adults by Witkin (49).
>
> Marking a picture corresponding to unblended spoken sounds that form the appropriate word is part of a battery formed by McNinch et al. (25) and also appeared in the old Monroe Reading Aptitude or readiness test. Chall and Roswell offer a test, *The Roswell-Chall Auditory Blending Test,* in which the child is to blend mentally the spoken sounds of a word and match it with a printed word. Similar tests occur in a number of the word analysis skills tests evaluated in the relevant chapter. The assumption in the Roswell-Chall is that the child is synthesizing mentally the sounds given him and matching them with the printed word. Since the words dealt with are very common and might well be in the child's sight vocabulary and thus require no real blending, the validity of this test is questionable (8).
>
> Rosner and Simon (40) have offered a test in which the child is asked to repeat a given word and then say it again without a certain portion, as the final or beginning sound. The authors offer some evidence of the relationship to reading, particularly among primary children from a middle-class suburban population only.
>
> Turaids, Wepman, and Morency (42) report on the standardization of a new perceptual test battery that includes a measure of memory for digits as its sample of auditory sequencing or synthesizing. This approach by the measurement of span for numbers, object, or words has long been considered a measure of memory rather than sequencing or synthesis, although, of course, the child must attend to the order of items, which might be thought as a synthesizing act by some. We shall discuss tests of this type later in this chapter as measures of auditory memory span.

The lack of clear definition of auditory synthesis is marked in these various approaches to its measurement. Some of the behaviors sampled probably do occur in reading and spelling, and difficulties in performing them might conceivably interfere with success in these fields. But we do not know which of these behaviors are really significant or how to measure them. And we do not know what the components of auditory synthesis are, or the best methods of assessing pupil skill in these elements. Training programs in sequencing or synthesizing have been outlined by Rosner (39) and Kottler (22); these may possibly contribute to reading success, although in the present state of our knowledge we cannot say how or why they may help.

Auditory Span Although memory span measures have been in use in intelligence and reading tests for over half a century, the evidence that, except in extreme cases, they are very significant for reading success is still quite weak. But we still see emphasis upon one such memory span test for digits, as in the WISC, constantly referred to as a significant symptom of reading disability. (We discuss this WISC test at length in chapter 4 on intellectual factors and again in chapter 10, our discussion of dyslexia.) Our review of twenty-seven studies of WISC patterns did show that, when a group of poor readers differed significantly from good readers in this behavior, their performance was uniformly inferior. Apparently poor readers do tend to perform badly in this auditory memory ability. But the questions remain whether this ability is really significant to reading and is amenable to training, or whether performance in this area is really a measure of attention or distractibility. There is the related problem that the memory span can be tested with words, syllables, digits, and sentences, or even tapping patterns. Which of these approaches measures auditory memory span in a manner significant for reading?

The evidence in answer to these questions is neither large nor entirely conclusive. In various samples, we find correlations with reading of the usual digit span test of .634 (13) in a small fourth-grade group; .162 with a first-grade reading test and .282 in the second grade; and again of .242 in the third grade (47); of .58 for the WISC span test in the first grade (24). A correlation of the test score in the first grade with reading achievement in the fourth, fifth and sixth grades yielded *r*'s of .23, .25, and .23 respectively, and with vocabulary, .23, .25 for fourth and sixth graders (28).

A factor analysis of some seventeen visual and auditory abilities of poor readers (14) identified an auditory factor composed of tests for memory for words, related syllables, and digit span; but this factor was not related to the reading factor in this third-grade study. The authors did feel that auditory memory might be more significantly related to reading, however, at the first-grade level. Similarly, in a population referred for diagnosis of reading difficulties, Rose (38) found the digit span of the Stanford-Binet apparently related to reading, but one-third of the poor readers did as well in this test as average readers.

Keogh and Macmillan (20) contributed to another aspect of this testing of auditory memory span in pointing out that middle-class white children did not differ from lower-class black provided both were of normal intelligence. Mentally retarded pupils of either race were, of course, poorer in this performance.

We could assume that, in general, there does seem to be relationship between auditory memory span for various kinds of material and for reading. We are not certain whether this relationship is more significant at primary or later grades. Perhaps the strongest evidence is that found in the comparisons of good and poor readers in the WISC studies and our review of the ITPA. A factor analysis of the ITPA tests did identify an integrative-sequencing factor composed in part of the digit span tests of that battery and of the WISC, a factor related to reading. Other studies indicate that this auditory processing factor may be present only in samples of lower-class children and may reflect their problem in understanding the dialect of the examiner. But, as in the WISC studies, comparisons of good and poor readers on the ITPA digit span test indicate inferiority of the latter.

This conclusion that auditory memory span is somewhat related to reading must be modified by the observation that this relationship is dependent upon the nature of the reading program. Like auditory discrimination, memory span interacts with method, assuming greater significance in a phonics-oriented program than in many basal reading programs. Emphasis upon listening to the teacher read before reading aloud or silently also was interrelated with span, according to Neville (30), thus reemphasizing the significance of this auditory ability in a reading program with an auditory demand.

A test that will serve in this assessment is the *Auditory Memory Span Test,* by Joseph M. Wepman and Anne Morency (Chicago: Language Research Associates, 1973). The task for the child is to repeat unrelated words in series from two to six in number. He is given three trials and his score summed for all three. The test is normed for ages five to eight. A reliability of .92, Form A vs. Form B, is cited by the authors (47). Relevance to reading was .216 to Word Knowledge, .299 to Word Discrimination and .242 to reading in a third-grade population. Some appropriate training procedures have been mentioned

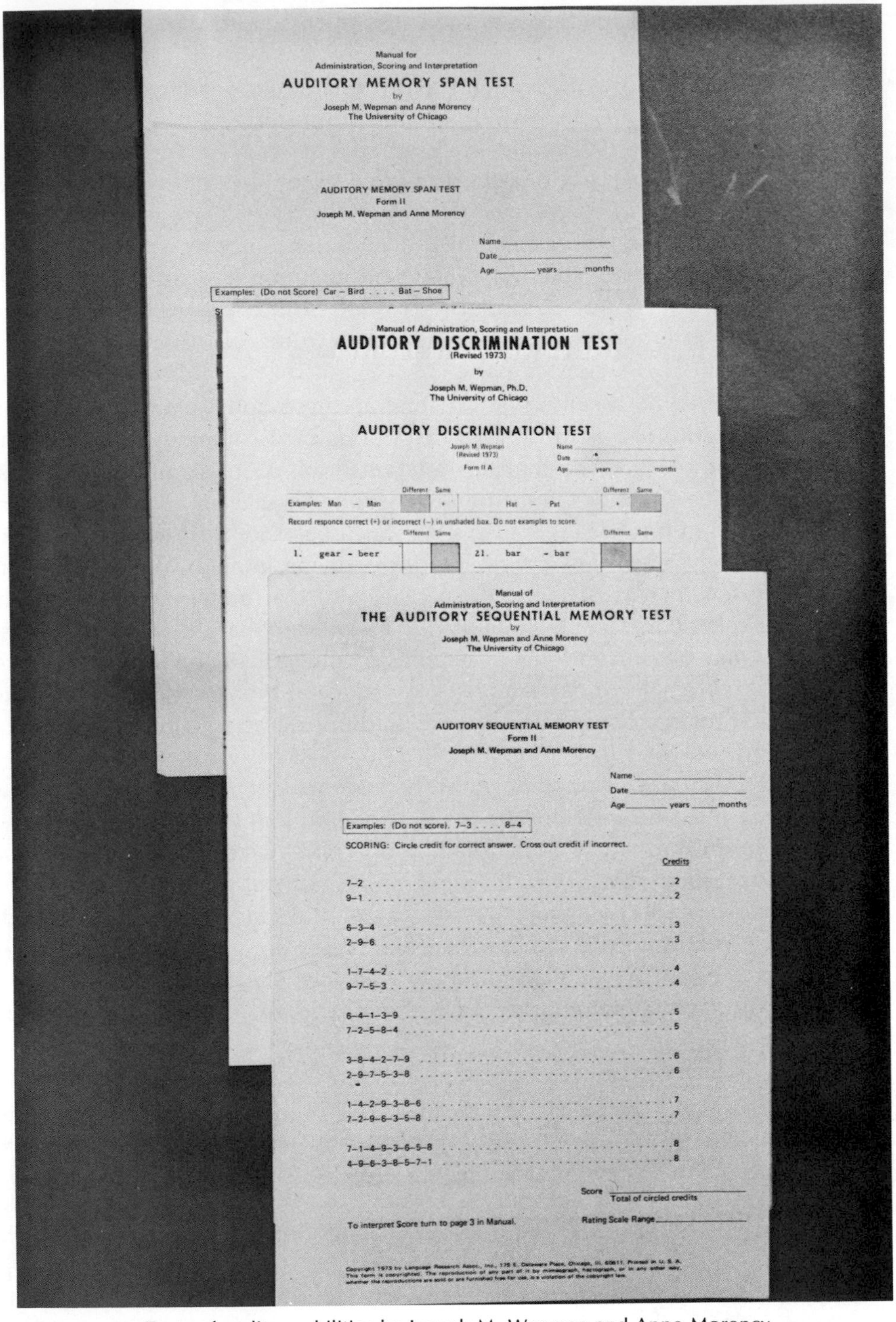

Manual for
Administration, Scoring and Interpretation
AUDITORY MEMORY SPAN TEST
by
Joseph M. Wepman and Anne Morency
The University of Chicago

AUDITORY MEMORY SPAN TEST
Form II
Joseph M. Wepman and Anne Morency

Name ______
Date ______
Age ______ years ______ months

Examples: (Do not Score) Car – Bird . . . . Bat – Shoe

Manual of Administration, Scoring and Interpretation
AUDITORY DISCRIMINATION TEST
(Revised 1973)
by
Joseph M. Wepman, Ph.D.
The University of Chicago

AUDITORY DISCRIMINATION TEST
Joseph M. Wepman
(Revised 1973)
Form II A

Examples: Man – Man + ... Hat – Pat +

Record responce correct (+) or incorrect (–) in unshaded box. Do not examples to score.

1. gear – beer
21. bar – bar

Manual of
Administration, Scoring and Interpretation
THE AUDITORY SEQUENTIAL MEMORY TEST
by
Joseph M. Wepman and Anne Morency
The University of Chicago

AUDITORY SEQUENTIAL MEMORY TEST
Form II
Joseph M. Wepman and Anne Morency

Name ______
Date ______
Age ______ years ______ months

Examples: (Do not score). 7–3 8–4

SCORING: Circle credit for correct answer. Cross out credit if incorrect.

	Credits
7–2	2
9–1	2
6–3–4	3
2–9–6	3
1–7–4–2	4
9–7–5–3	4
6–4–1–3–9	5
7–2–5–8–4	5
3–8–4–2–7–9	6
2–9–7–5–3–8	6
1–4–2–9–3–8–6	7
7–2–9–6–3–5–8	7
7–1–4–9–3–6–5–8	8
4–9–6–3–8–5–7–1	8

Score ______ Total of circled credits

To interpret Score turn to page 3 in Manual. Rating Scale Range ______

Tests of auditory abilities by Joseph M. Wepman and Anne Morency earlier, and other sources are listed in References*, if deemed essential for a particular reading program.

Auditory Comprehension

We discuss this auditory ability as a measure of potential for improvement in reading in our accompanying book, *Investigating the Issues of Reading Disabilities.* It is appropriate to mention auditory comprehension again here since, first, it is an auditory ability; second, it is related to reading success. Measures of listening or auditory comprehension appear in a number of the individual diagnostic batteries for assessment of reading skills. Most of these are offered without any evidence of their validity in predicting reading growth or their reliabilities. Commercial tests for listening comprehension are listed in chapter 7 and, for the most part, are somewhat better defended by their authors. Of the diagnostic individual reading test batteries reviewed in chapter 7 of this book, only the Spache Diagnostic Reading Scales support the use of their measure of listening comprehension with sufficient information.

In two samples acquired in the course of standardizing the Spache Diagnostic Reading Scales, the correlation of listening comprehension and WISC verbal I.Q. was .75 in each group. Those reviewing a large number of such comparisons find an average *r* of .61. In other words, there is a definite relationship between listening comprehension and verbal intelligence. This would be expected, for both auditory and silent reading comprehension place demands upon the intellectual factors of reasoning, vocabulary, and perception of relationships. This interaction between intelligence and this auditory ability does not imply, as some might assume, that improvement is almost impossible because the performance depends heavily upon the child's intellectual capacity. Both intelligence and auditory comprehension can be improved by careful training. Both are really ways and skill in thinking, and (as outlined in chapter 9 in the section on improving silent reading comprehension), they can be modified.

Testing of ability in auditory comprehension may be approached on a group basis with one of the commercial tests listed in chapter 4 on intellectual factors. Or it may be assessed by using that test as included in the Spache Diagnostic Scales battery. Another simple method is to administer a group reading test to the pupils in the usual fashion, and a few days later to administer a second form of the same test as a measure of auditory comprehension, that is, by reading the selections and the questions to the children, with ample time to answer in writing on the record form for the test.

---

*See chapter 4 for additional tests of this function in the ITPA and Detroit batteries.

When the two reading test scores are compared, consider a difference of two stanines as significant. Stanine scores are usually available in the Manual or from the publisher. If not, consider a difference of two years at intermediate grades and a year or more in primary grades as significant (provided such differences are twice the standard error of the test score. See the Manual for this information). At intermediate grades the average middle-class child will probably test about two years higher in auditory comprehension than in silent reading. This, in general, is about the average difference found. Disadvantaged children or others with a language-deprived background will probably not show this difference as frequently. Mentally retarded children will not usually test much higher in auditory than in silent reading.

When the auditory test score is above the silent reading, we cannot consider that poor auditory comprehension is, in any sense, retarding the child's reading development. When silent reading yields the higher score, there is reason to consider training in auditory comprehension. Even if these two abilities are not causally interlinked and inadequate auditory comprehension could not be shown to retard general reading development, such training could be justified. There is ample evidence that training programs in auditory comprehension tend to increase reading ability. After all, they are simply stimulation of the same types of thinking that compose silent reading with the practice being in a parallel medium. (We outline our concepts of appropriate training of comprehension in chapter 9, on silent reading abilities, and need not repeat them here.) A few commercial materials that offer programs related to auditory comprehension are listed in the References. If these programs for reading to children are employed, we certainly recommend reinforcing them with the use of the questioning strategies outlined for training in silent reading.

INTERSENSORY INTEGRATION

Simply stated, intersensory integration is the ability to translate stimuli from one sensory channel into a response involving another channel. Among the types most commonly explored are the following:

Audio-Visual—matching tapping or pure tone patterns to printed dot arrangements.

Visual-Auditory—matching light flashes to pure tone patterns.

Visual-Visual—matching light flashes to dot patterns.

Auditory-Auditory—tapping patterns to pure tone arrangements.

Some of these patterns can be conceptualized somewhat differently, as these:

> Temporal-Spatial—for Visual-Visual or for Auditory-Visual.
> Visual-Temporal—light flashes.
> Auditory Temporal—tapping or pure tone patterns.

From this terminology, it appears that intersensory translation of stimuli involves elements of the channel employed—the visual or auditory—plus characteristics of the stimuli, as temporal arrangement of sounds and spatial arrangement of visual stimuli. Both temporal and spatial sequences, in turn, involve auditory sequence perception and visual sequence perception.

In terms of analogy to reading, reading a word silently demands recognition of a spatial arrangement and of the visual sequence, as of ascending and descending letters. Reading a word aloud may add the temporal sequence of the sounds to the recognition procedure. The hypothesis on which the research in intersensory integration is based is that the tests parallel, in a sense, these sensory processes in silent and oral reading.

Apparently the tests employed do not sufficiently simulate the sensory processes in reading, for a great many fail to show differences in their test results for good and poor readers. The dissimilarity of the test tones, light flashes, dot patterns, and so on, to letter and word recognition may be a partial explanation of this failure of many research studies to show relevance to reading. Another difficulty encountered is the fact that these various sensory tests are, in effect, measures of intelligence. In many of the studies, any real relationship to reading has been due to the intelligence factor that operates both in reading and in these intersensory measures. A third factor militating against finding marked relationships with reading is that the kinesthetic element of learning in reading is being ignored in these experiments. The processing of visual stimuli is markedly influenced by visual-kinesthetic perception. Visual-kinesthetic responses may occur in the reinforcement of visual recognition of an object, such as a ball, by the recall of muscular sensations of weight, roundness, hardness, and so forth, previously experienced in handling a ball. These kinesthetic reinforcements are readily observed when a subject is asked to describe a circular staircase or a stovepipe hat, for many must gesture with their hands to illustrate their verbal explanation.

What we are saying is that response to a printed word is not just a visual stimuli, for in the mediating process many more sensory impressions or associations may be called upon. In this sense, none of the sensory tests described above parallels completely the mental and sensory processes involved in recognition of a word. It is probably true that, as some authors say, the visual processing of such stimuli as words eventually predominates the other senses, and auditory or kinesthetic or multisensory memories formed in early experiences with the word become less and less significant.

Van Mondfrans et al. (43), for example, found that single-channel presentations did not differ from dual-channel at the college level. And other studies indicate that, even by fourth grade, there is not much difference in ease of learning by single or dual channels. But most of the experiments have concentrated on young school children who may not have reached this later developmental stage and who may still be at least partially dependent upon the kinesthetic element in word recognition, which is ignored in the common intersensory integration studies.

Further evidence of the lack of parallelism between intersensory testing and the act of reading is evident in the fact that, when such tests do show relevance, it is most frequently to word recognition but not to comprehension. To us, this is further evidence that there is more to the act of reading than just the translation of a visual symbol to an auditory response, or vice versa, or of cross-translation of temporal or spatial arrangements.

Finally, there is a question in the minds of some writers whether there is not an independence of sensory impressions such as the visual and auditory. Some go so far as to say that instruction in reading should even avoid emphasis upon multisensory impressions. Several factor analyses of groups of visual and auditory tests would seem to support this belief. Guthrie et al. (14), for example, found auditory memory a separate factor from another in which visual attention span and reading were combined. Measures of visual memory for designs was a third separate factor, while oral vocabulary formed a fourth. This identification of visual and auditory abilities as relatively separate and distinct is confirmed in several other factor analyses cited in the chapter on auditory abilities in our *Investigating the Issues of Reading Disabilities.* It is also present in the relatively low intercorrelations between the auditory and visual components of batteries of both types of tests mentioned earlier in this chapter. In the McNinch et al. battery for screening auditory perceptual abilities (25), even the auditory-visual integration test of marking dots corresponding to oral speech patterns has low intercorrelation with the other auditory tests.

All this conflicting evidence regarding intersensory behavior in reading—and the doubts that it even exists in the act of reading—leaves us without much information that can be applied to reading instruction. We have not yet devised intersensory tests that sample this function as it occurs in reading, even assuming that it does function. It may be that learning the meaning of words is in part dependent upon visual recognition, auditory memories, and kinesthetic associations, with varying predominance of these systems at different stages of reading development. It may also be true that some children are deficient in reception or processing in one of these channels and that this may interfere with learning to read, particularly at beginning stages. It may be that each of the auditory abilities previously discussed may, independently, be deficient in some children and, if related to reading, may thus interfere with the child's progress. But, for the most part, these are all still hypotheses without definitive evidence. Perhaps there may be greater significance for the reading teacher in the later discussion of learning modalities and their interpretation in reading instruction. At this stage of development in our knowledge of intersensory integration, we do not feel it essential to recommend attempts to diagnose intersensory differences in children.

LEARNING MODALITIES

Attempts to determine the channel or modality through which children would learn best have waxed and waned in popularity during the past decades. At one time, educational psychologists were prone to identify visual, auditory, or motor-minded learners quite freely. The subjects were supposed to vary in the type of imagery that they had, this fact determining whether they were "eye-minded, ear-minded, or motor-minded." Some remnants of this type of thinking persist in some quarters, as evidenced by the presence of a sample of imagery in the Durrell Diagnosis of Reading Kit and in the Robbins Speech-Sound Discrimination and Verbal Imagery Type Test (35). As more scientific techniques of investigation appeared, doubts arose about this categorizing of individuals in terms of their imagery predilections. Imagery proved to be almost too ephemeral for critical examination, and investigations of this area virtually disappeared.

The belief that there might be a preferred, more efficient channel for learning for some children has persisted, however, receiving considerable attention in the past decade. Most investigators acknowledge that reading, and especially word recognition, is probably a multisensory act involving both visual stimuli and auditory memories for words, and possible kinesthetic experiences that enrich the meanings. But (as almost any adult who once attempted to learn a foreign language will probably recall), as individuals we tend to differ somewhat in our use or need for different types of sensory stimuli in this learning. Some of us can learn another language simply by listening and imitating. Others must reinforce the auditory with the printed word before attempting to use them in their own speech. Some of us learned a foreign language and can still read it, but cannot converse; while others can converse better than they can read. Thus, even though both visual and auditory modalities may be inherent in reading, they are not indivisible, as Blanton (4) and others argue.

It is true, as we have remarked earlier, that attempts to determine the role of separate auditory or visual abilities in reading or intersensory integration, as we currently are measuring it, have not been resoundingly successful. There may be relationships with reading at certain developmental levels for auditory discrimination, auditory memory span, auditory acuity and comprehension, and, perhaps, auditory synthesis. There may be some relationship with reading in intersensory integration once we learn how to assess it in a relevant manner. This is, in a sense, separating out the auditory components of reading; the justification lies in the fact that special training keyed to this analytical diagnosis does help reading progress for some children. We could say much the same things about our experiences in diagnosing the visual perception components of reading and the outcomes of special attention to them. The visual, auditory, and kinesthetic elements of word recognition are not so complexly interlinked that we cannot observe and treat them separately. In fact, we have not been very successful at all in considering them jointly and studying their integrated nature.

Having recommended continuing this treatment of learning modalities, we now look at the outcomes of some of the relevant research. We do not do this in the hopes of finding a "best" approach (as Blanton (4) criticizes us for doing), for there is no hope of such a result. A group of children is no more homogeneous in learning modality than in any other number of traits. Our goal is, rather, to determine whether identifying what appears to be the child's most efficient channel or his preferred modality, and then addressing our instruction in reading to this channel, is a particularly efficient way of teaching reading for some children.

OUTCOMES OF MODALITY TESTING AND TEACHING

There are three ways of attempting to identify a learner's preferred modality: (1) comparing his performances on tests of visual versus auditory abilities; (2) actually teaching him word recognition by contrasting methods emphasizing either the visual, auditory, or kinesthetic element or a combination of all these; and (3) simply contrasting learning by a presentation in one modality with that in another. Among the first type of approach are the reports of

Bruininks (6) with disadvantaged children, Robinson (37) with average children, and Sabatino (41) with learning-disabled pupils. All three investigators identified the apparently preferred or more efficient modality of their subjects; they then contrasted the effectiveness of a certain method or methods with the types of children. Bruininks found no differences in the learning by a visual or auditory approach for high-visual, low-auditory, or the reverse type of pupils. Robinson contrasted a basal and a phonic approach for the four categories of pupils, high in one modality and low in the other, and low or high in both modalities. No differences in learning to read appeared except for the low-visual–high-auditory, who did better under a phonics-oriented program. Sabatino, in offering a training program featuring word form configuration, discovered, as we would expect, that learning for the visiles was greater than for the audiles. While these three studies are not in complete agreement, there does appear to be some point in relating method of approach to modality, particularly in the auditory channel. The results of these experiments seem to indicate that when a method is specifically related to the child's modality (as phonics to the auditory channel or word form to the visual), results are clearer than when the method is mixed, as in a basal. Bruininks's study may have failed to make these distinctions because of its brevity, for he compared results in the learning of only thirty words.

Bateman (2) and Harris (15) were, like Bruininks, unsuccessful in finding a relationship between teaching to a child's apparent modality and his reading progress. Using their own modality test, Ringler et al. (33) had similar results, also with first-grade children. We shall offer some explanations of these conflicting results later.

Several studies contrasting pupil actual learning under different modality emphases, without previously testing their relative modality strengths, are available in the literature. Among these are the original study by Mills (26), who devised a testing-teaching kit for this type of study and a replication of his study in the dissertation of Rivkind (34), who demonstrated the applicability of the idea in a group situation, in addition to the individualized procedure designed by Mills. Mills's testing-teaching-testing procedure is involved with alternation of methods from visual to auditory to kinesthetic to combination with groups of graded and equated words. Learning by each method is compared by a posttesting one day after each lesson. Using Mills's technique, Arnold (1) found no real differences among retarded readers in terms of words learned after sixteen sessions. Learning was apparently more dependent upon initial reading level than upon method. For this group, the kinesthetic was the least effective. Cooper (10) followed the same technique in teaching good and poor first-grade readers to learn nonsense syllables rather than words. He found, as Mills demonstrated in his initial studies, that modality preference was an individual matter, not a group phenomenon and that, under most circumstances, these individual differences cancel each other; therefore, for a group, no method appears more efficient than the others. Modality seemed less significant for good readers, according to Cooper, for they learned better in all modalities than poor readers, except in the visual. They also retained more from the combination and kinesthetic modalities than the poor did in the postlearning test. Poor readers, as we might expect, varied more in learning in daily lessons and in retention than did good.

Others who have followed the Mills technique are Coleman (9) and Jones (18). These and other studies of this type are also mentioned in J. P. Jones's review of this area (17). In toto, these studies seem to indicate that the Mills test can function in identifying preferred modality for some children's learning in typical word recognition lessons that vary in emphasis upon a modality. One serious lack in the evidence for this procedure is the absence of follow-up studies indicating whether long-term learning is better for the individual child if approached through his preferred modality. We can readily show that differences in short-term learning, as in a single lesson of a certain type, seem to be related to a modality. But long-term experiments, such as that of Arnold and Cooper or Coleman and Jones, are not all in agreement that following the indications of the Mills procedure makes a great difference. Thus far, the best we can say for fitting method to children's modality, as determined by tests or the Mills procedure, is that it works logically in some instances and is apparently fruitless in equally as many.

A third type of approach to teaching to modality employs no pretesting or modality sampling but offers only a comparison of the results of one modality emphasis versus another in various samples of children. For the most part, these are isolated experiments that would be very difficult to generalize. We shall not review the details, but rather their implications. Both Otto (31) and Morency (27) conclude from their reviews that children vary in their patterns of learning aptitude, perhaps even changing through the years, whether they are good or poor readers. Apparent modality preferences can be ascertained for many children but not all, for among brighter children or more successful readers (as in the Mills and Cooper studies), modality preferences are not frequent.

There are a number of reasons that may account for our difficulty; first, in establishing whether children have modality preferences that are significant for their learning, and, second, whether addressing our reading instruction to this modality actually facilitates faster learning. Many factors affect the attempts to establish pupil modalities, such as their age; their previous exposure to a mode of instruction; the meaningfulness of the instructional material (as words in general versus nouns versus nonsense syllables); the relevance of the tests used to clarify modalities to reading (dot patterns, light flashes, pure tones, and the like). Moreover, we cannot really be certain that the pupil is utilizing the channel through which we think we are teaching or testing him. As Wolpert (50) and others have pointed out, he may actually translate or process in channels different from what we expect. His mediating or associative thinking about the words, for example, may be more significant in their learning than the medium through which they are being presented. Compare, if you will, common teaching procedures in presenting nouns, action words, and prepositions—without any real differentiation in the manner of presentation—with the learning that usually occurs in this type of situation. Although these types of words are presented in the same manner, nouns and action words are almost universally learned more readily, no matter what modality is emphasized in the teaching. Whether we call this a response of the child to the meaningfulness of the words or say that the difference in retention reflects the associative thinking that can be done with various words is immaterial. The point is that a modality emphasis does not necessarily produce use of that channel for the children. Finally, as Wolpert has suggested (and we have repeated several times elsewhere), learning of a word is not a unimodal experience, as simply a visual memory, an auditory memory, a kinesthetic gestalt, or a tactile sensation. Hence it is highly questionable whether we can isolate a reception channel in our "unimodal" teaching experiments and be at all certain that this is the only medium the child is employing.

Our inconclusiveness about determining pupils' modalities—and even that regarding the variable results from modality teaching—should not prevent teachers, however, from exploring this area. The Mills technique can ascertain the kind of word recognition lesson that seems to work best for each pupil. If distinctions appear for certain pupils, we recommend using the appropriate kind of lesson for each pupil, preferably in small-group arrangements. The Mills technique is reliable in indicating modality preference for certain types of word recognition training, for retests within a six-months' limit tend to give precisely the same results. Since this reliability is present, it will be profitable to use the approaches indicated by the children's responses. Even if no other justification were possible, we could defend this logical approach on the basis that it will probably, even if only temporarily, produce a modicum of success for the child. This motivating effect is extremely desirable, especially if he has had difficulties previously. If he later falters in maintaining his progress, the approach can readily be broadened to include other modes of learning, not just because multimodal presentations are better, for this has hardly been proven. Rather, introducing an element of newness or a variation in the previous procedures will, again, give a lift to his progress and provide the motivation inherent in self-recognition of success.

Following the indications of the Mills diagnostic procedure is not a panacea for cases of word recognition difficulty—we have no such illusions—but we do know that the impetus given by the usual success of the child in at least a month or more of trials with this procedure may alleviate the discouragement and anxiety that the pupil feels. As these deterrents are relieved, his actual potential for learning manifests itself; and, in believing for the first time that he can really learn to read, his capacity for learning will monitor his progress. We have a very strong respect for the effect of the child's self-concept as a reader and have seen this approach succeed frequently in that fashion.

LEARNING PROJECT

Outline a diagnostic testing program that you believe reveals the needs for training in the auditory abilities touched upon in this chapter. Include also your plans regarding diagnosis in intersensory integration and learning modalities if you believe these areas to be significant.

Plan your testing program for specific ages or grades with which you are familiar. Include in your outline the following items:

1. The specific testing instruments you would employ and your reasons for their choice.

2. A brief explanation of the relevance of each ability you would test for the act of reading; that is, how does this ability function in or affect the child's reading?

3. Your reasons for omitting diagnosis in certain areas, if you so choose.

4. Some description of the way in which remedial training for any of the auditory deficiencies that you think significant could be integrated into the usual reading instructional program.

REFERENCES

1. Arnold, R.D., "Four Methods of Teaching Word Recognition to Disabled Readers," *Elementary School Journal,* 68 (1968), 269–74.

2. Bateman, Barbara, "The Efficacy of an Auditory and a Visual Method of First Grade Reading Instruction with Auditory and Visual Learners," *Curriculum Bulletin* (School of Education, University of Oregon) 23 (1967), 6–14.
3. Beery, Keith E., *Visual-Motor Integration Monograph.* Chicago: Follett Publishing, 1967.
4. Blanton, Bill, "Modalities and Reading," *Reading Teacher,* 25 (November 1971), 210–12.
5. *Boston University Speech-Sound Discrimination Picture Test.* Boston: W. Pronovost, Department of Speech, Boston University.
6. Bruininks, R.H., "Teaching Word Recognition to Disadvantaged Boys," *Journal of Learning Disabilities,* 3 (1970), 28–37.
7. Buktenica, Norman A., *Tenvad.* Chicago: Follett Publishing.
8. Chall, Jeanne, and Roswell, N., *The Roswell-Chall Auditory Blending Test.* New York: Essay Press, 1963.
9. Coleman, James C., "Learning Method as a Relevant Subject Variable in Learning Disorders," *Perceptual and Motor Skills,* 14 (April 1962), 263–69.
10. Cooper, J. David, "A Study of the Learning Modalities of Good and Poor First Grade Readers," in *Reading Methods and Teacher Improvement,* Nila B. Smith, editor. Newark, Del.: International Reading Association, 1971, 87–97.
11. Dykstra, R., "Auditory Discrimination Abilities and Beginning Reading Achievement," *Reading Research Quarterly,* 1 (Spring 1966), 5–34.
12. *Goldman-Fristoe-Woodcock Test of Auditory Discrimination.* Circle Pines, Minn.: American Guidance Service.
13. Green, Richard B., and Rohwer, William D., "SES Differences on Learning and Ability Tests in Black Children," *American Educational Research Journal,* 8 (November 1971), 601–9.
14. Guthrie, John T., Goldberg, Herman K., and Finucci, Joan, "Independence of Abilities in Disabled Readers," *Journal of Reading Behavior,* 4 (Spring 1972), 129–38.
15. Harris, Albert J., "Individualizing First-Grade Reading According to Specific Learning Aptitudes," *Research Report,* Office of Research and Evaluation, Division of Teacher Education of the City University of New York, 1965.
16. Haspiel, George, and Bloomer, Richard H., "Maximum Auditory Perception (MAP) Word List," *Journal of Speech and Hearing Disorders,* 26 (May 1961), 156–63.
17. Jones, John Paul, *Intersensory Transfer, Perceptual Shifting, Modal Difference and Reading.* ERIC/CRIER and International Reading Association Reading Information Series. Newark: International Reading Association, 1972.
18. Jones, Ruby D., "Learning Mode Preference of Educable Mentally Retarded Children," Doctoral dissertation, University of Missouri, Columbia, 1967.
19. Katz, Jack, *Kindergarten Auditory Screening Test.* Chicago: Follett Publishing.
20. Keogh, Barbara K., and MacMillan, Donald L., "Effects of Motivation and Presentation Conditions on Digit Recall of Children of Differing Socioeconomic, Racial and Intelligence Groups," *American Educational Research Journal,* 8 (January 1971), 27–38.
21. Kimmell, G.M., and Wahl, J., "Screening Test for Auditory Perception," *Academic Therapy,* 5 (1970), 317–19.
22. Kottler, Sylvia B., "The Identification and Remediation of Auditory Problems," *Academic Therapy,* 8 (Fall 1972), 73–86.

23. *Lindamood Auditory Conceptualization Test.* Boston: Teaching Resources.
24. McNinch, George, "Auditory Perceptual Factors and Measured First-Grade Reading Achievement," *Reading Research Quarterly,* 6 (Summer 1971), 472–92.
25. McNinch, George, Palmatier, Robert, and Richmond, Mark, "Auditory Perceptual Testing of Young Children," *Journal of Reading Behavior,* 4 (Spring 1974), 120–28.
26. Mills, Robert E., *The Learning Methods Test Kit.* Fort Lauderdale: The Mills Educational Center, 1970.
27. Morency, Anne, "Auditory Modality, Research and Practice," in *Perception and Reading,* Helen K. Smith, editor, Proceedings International Reading Association, 12, No. 4, 1968, 17–21.
28. Morency, Anne, and Wepman, Joseph M., "Early Perceptual Ability and Later School Achievement," *Elementary School Journal,* 73 (March 1973), 323–27.
29. Morency, Anne, Wepman, Joseph M., and Hass, Sarah K., "Developmental Speech Inaccuracy and Speech Therapy in the Early School Years," *Elementary School Journal,* 70 (January 1970), 219–24.
30. Neville, Mary H., "Effects of Oral and Echoic Responses in Beginning Reading," *Journal of Educational Psychology,* 59 (1968), 362–69.
31. Otto, Wayne, "The Acquisition and Retention of Paired Associates by Good, Average and Poor Readers," *Journal of Educational Psychology,* 52 (October 1961), 241–48.
32. Price, Landon Dewey, "The Trouble with Poor Auditory Discrimination," *Academic Therapy,* 8 (Spring 1973), 331–38.
33. Ringler, L.H., Smith, I.L., and Cullinan, B.E., "Modality Preference, Differentiated Presentation of Reading Tasks, and Word Recognition of First Grade Children," paper presented at the International Reading Association Convention, 1971.
34. Rivkind, Harold C., "The Development of a Group Technique in Teaching Word Recognition to Determine Which of Four Methods Is Most Effective with Individual Children," Doctoral dissertation, University of Florida, 1958.
35. *Robbins Speech-Sound Discrimination and Verbal Imagery Type Tests.* Magnolia, Mass.: Expression Company.
36. Robinson, H. Alan, "Reliability of Measures Related to Reading Success of Average, Disadvantaged and Advantaged Kindergarten Children," *Reading Teacher,* 20 (December 1966), 203–9.
37. Robinson, Helen M., "Visual and Auditory Modalities Related to Two Methods for Beginning Reading," *AERA Paper Abstracts,* 1968, 74–75.
38. Rose, Florence C., "The Occurrence of Short Auditory Memory Span Among School Children Referred for Diagnosis of Reading Difficulties," *Journal of Educational Research,* 51 (February 1958), 459–64.
39. Rosner, J., *Phonic Analysis Training and Beginning Reading Skills.* Learning Research and Development Center, University of Pittsburgh, 1971.
40. Rosner, J., and Simon, D., *The Auditory Analysis Test: An Initial Report.* Learning Research and Development Center, University of Pittsburgh, 1970.
41. Sabatino, David A., and Streissgurth, W.O., "Word Form Configuration Training of Visual Perceptual Strengths with Learning Disabled Children," *Journal of Learning Disabilities,* 5 (August-September 1972), 435–41.
42. Turaids, Dainis, Wepman, Joseph M., and Morency, Anne, "A Perceptual Test Battery: Development and Standardization," *Elementary School Journal,* 72 (April 1972), 351–61.

43. Van Mondfrans, Adrian P., and Travers, Robert M.W., "Paired-Associate Learning Within and Across Sense Modalities and Involving Simultaneous and Sequential Presentations," *American Educational Research Journal,* 2 (March 1965), 89–99.
44. Venezky, R.L., *Nonstandard Language and Reading.* Madison: Wisconsin Research and Development Center for Cognitive Learning, 1970.
45. Wepman, Joseph M., "Auditory Discrimination, Speech and Reading," *Elementary School Journal,* 60 (1960), 325–33.
46. Wepman, Joseph M., *The Auditory Discrimination Test.* Revised 1973. Chicago: Language Research Associates, 1973.
47. Wepman, Joseph M., and Morency, Anne, *Auditory Memory Span Test.* Chicago: Language Research Associates, 1973.
48. Wepman, Joseph M., and Morency, Anne, *Auditory Sequential Memory Test.* Chicago: Language Research Associates, 1973.
49. Witkin, Belle Ruth, "Auditory Perception—Implications for Language Development," *Journal of Research and Development in Education,* 3 (Fall 1969), 53–71.
50. Wolpert, Edward M., "Modality and Reading: A Perspective," *Reading Teacher,* 24 (April 1971), 640–43.

Sources of Audiometers

Ambco Electronics Inc., 1222 Washington Boulevard, Los Angeles, California 90007.
Audivox Co., 123 Worcester Street, Boston, Massachusetts, 02118.
Beltone Electronics Corp. 4201 West Victoria Street, Chicago, Illinois 60646.
Eckstein Bros. Inc., 4807 West 118th Place, Hawthorne, California 90250.
Maico Electronics Corp., 21 North 3rd Street, Minneapolis, Minnesota 55401.
Zenith Hearing Aid Sales Corp. 6501 West Grand Avenue, Chicago, Illinois 60635.

AUDIO-VISUAL AIDS

Tapes and Records

Auditory Perception Training. Chicago: Developmental Learning Materials. Tapes and ditto masters for training in auditory memory, auditory motor, auditory figure-ground, auditory discrimination, and auditory imagery. Nine to seventeen tapes for each, eighteen to thirty-six ditto masters.

Auditory Training. Chicago: Developmental Learning Materials. A single tape for sound identity and discrimination.

Auditory Training. Chicago: Greystone. Offers a group of records for auditory training.

Happy Time Listening. Freeport, N.Y.: Educational Activities. An album to promote auditory perception and sound discrimination. For kindergarten through grade three.

Gateway to Good Reading. Kankakee, Ill.: Imperial. A tape-centered program in auditory discrimination and visual perception. Includes student work sheets and teachers' manuals.

Sound, Order, Sense. Chicago: Follett Publishing, 1970. A two-year program with 160 daily lessons for each year. Suggest twenty minutes daily in listening for sounds, listening for sequences of sounds in words and words in groups, associating meaning with the words. For grades one–two or remedial.

Scagliotta, Edward G., *Auditory Perception Records.* San Rafael, Cal.: Academic Therapy. Three records to aid children in differentiating sounds or in understanding speech elements.

Wilson, Robert H., Humphrey, James H., and Sullivan, Dorothy D., *Teaching Reading Through Creative Movement.* Freeport, N.Y.: Educational Activities, 1970. Manual for use of two records and eight workbooks for beginning reading. Uses A (audio–story), M (movement–act out story), A-V (audio-visual–children read while listening to story).

Filmstrips

General Electric/Project Life Program. Schenectady: General Electric. Offers filmstrip projector with response buttons—*programmed language* (grammar); *perceptual training*—size, shape, color, figure-ground, inversions, rotations, etc.; *thinking activity*—visuals not words at primary level: memory, sequencing or seriation, pattern analysis, picture absurdities, shape disc. Intermediate level—words and pictures. Higher—largely words.

Reading Readiness. Chicago: Eye Gate. Set of ten strips includes some on visual and auditory discrimination.

System 80. Niles, Ill.: Borg-Warner. A combined filmstrip projector and records for individual use in programs in letter names, letter sounds, words in context, and the like.

Miscellaneous

Auditory Discrimination in Depth. Boston: Teaching Resources. Program of training in gross listening, speech sounds, and sound-symbol relationships.

Auditory Perception. Troy, Mich.: Education Corp. of America. Offers tapes and worksheets for programs in figure-ground, auditory imagery, auditory memory, and discrimination.

KELP. St. Louis: Webster Publishing. Kit includes a number of spatial, form discrimination, and auditory perception materials for kindergarten and first grade.

Klasen, Edith, *Audio-Visual-Motor Training.* Freeport, N.Y.: Educational Activities. Manual for audio-visual training.

LBB Learning Associates of Miami offer a wide collection of auditory and phonic games.

McLeod, Pierce H., *Reading for Learning.* Philadelphia: Lippincott, 1970. Outlines a six–ten weeks' program for visual and auditory training, plus advanced tasks.

Maney, Ethel S., *Reading Fundamentals Program.* Elizabethtown, Pa.: Continental Press. Includes a number of ditto masters for training in prereading auditory skills.

Rosner, J., *Phonic Analysis Training and Beginning Reading Skills.* Pittsburgh: Learning

Research and Development Center, University of Pittsburgh, 1971. An auditory skills-phonics program.

Slepian, Jan, and Seidler, Ann, *Listen-Hear Books.* Chicago: Follett Publishing. Story collections to develop auditory discrimination of speech sounds among primary pupils.

Sounds Around Us. Evanston, Ill.: Scott, Foresman. Records for training in auditory discrimination for primary use.

Sounds for Young Readers. New York: Educational Record Sales. An album of three records for auditory discrimination training.

4 Diagnosis in the Intellectual Area

A major area of diagnostic significance, the measurement of intelligence, is explored in this chapter. The values, limitations, and interpretation of a number of intelligence tests are examined in detail. Some of these tests, such as the WISC, can be given only by certified examiners in some school systems. But their results can be and are interpreted by reading specialists in many centers. Thus, even when administration of a test may be proscribed or impossible because of lack of special training, the significance of the results for a reading disability may be realized.

A number of alternative tests, which are feasible for the reading specialist with some experience in individualized testing, are also reviewed in detail. In each instance the possible relationship of the test to reading success, the evidence regarding its cultural bias, and its values for difficult testing situations are pointed out.

As you read this chapter, consider these questions:

1. The author rejects the idea of using the intelligence test as a measure of expected reading level or of potential. What other kinds of information does he suggest may be obtained from such testing?
2. What values do you see in using an intelligence test in a case of reading disability?

THE PRIMARY PURPOSE in assessing the intelligence of each case of reading disability is usually to permit comparison of the mental level with that in reading. As we show in the related chapter on the intellectual factor in *Investigating the Issues of Reading Disabilities,* this is not a simple comparison for many reasons.

To reinforce this viewpoint, let us summarize the evidence already cited against a direct comparison of mental age and reading level.

1. Intelligence tests do not show a very close relationship to reading tests, even when they are group tests of intelligence that actually involve reading. Individual tests show even less relationship.
2. At primary grades, particularly, the similarity between mental and reading test results is very moderate. This relationship increases somewhat as the age of the pupil increases and reading tests become stronger measures of the reasoning factor. But the parallelism is never great enough to permit individual predictions.
3. Mental tests vary in their content: some measure elements important in the reading act as vocabulary and reasoning; others stress quantitative and spatial thinking that is irrelevant. Hence different tests vary greatly in their relationship to reading performance.
4. Reading success is more dependent upon instructional method and the degree of personalized attention than upon mental age. Pupils with similar mental ages will not necessarily make the same progress under the same method or organizational pattern.
5. Since human beings normally vary in their development of cognitive processes or reading skills, we cannot expect the mental age to predict performances in a variety of areas, as vocabulary, word analysis, comprehension, and rate.
6. The only level at which mental ages and reading levels tend to be similar is in the I.Q. range from 90 to 110. Above this range, reading tends to be significantly lower; while below this range, reading tends to excel mental age.
7. Both mental and reading test scores have sizeable errors of estimate that are often ignored in these comparisons. Differences in some cases should be greater than a year or even two before they can be considered real.
8. Since intelligence and environment interact to determine the individual's functioning, no simple comparison or predictive formula can work for any sizeable number of pupils, for it ignores all the environmental, linguistic, socioeconomic, and personality factors present in each case.

The relation of mental and chronological ages that yields the I.Q. does not necessarily reflect the learning rate of the subject or the rate at which he will progress. Learning rate is affected by sex and socioeconomic status as well as by cognitive style and personality, not only by I.Q. The corollary of these common interpretations of mental level and I.Q. are the judgments as to whether the subject is really retarded in reading and whether he will respond well to remediation. In chapter 1 we offered what we believe is a much better group of criteria for making these judgments. Here we would like to show that, although the criteria may not yield the definitive facts needed for these judgments, they will make other contributions to the total diagnosis.

INTERPRETING WISC INTELLIGENCE TEST RESULTS

The WISC (Wechsler Intelligence Scale for Children*) and its adult counterpart, the WAIS, have become almost the standard instruments for individual testing in reading centers, clinics, and schools. This widespread use is certainly justified by the relative ease of administration and the variety of clues yielded.

The Wechsler Scale is composed of eleven tests of items of increasing difficulty. Five Verbal tests of Information, Comprehension (social situations), Arithmetic (oral problems largely), Similarities (common properties), Vocabulary (oral definitions), and Digit Span (repeating digits forward and backward) form one scale. The Performance Scale is composed of Picture Completion (finding missing parts), Block Design (assembling according to a given design), Object Assembly (four wooden puzzles), Coding (associating symbols with numbers), Picture Arrangement (arranging series logically), and an alternate test, Mazes (pencil and paper mazes). The scores on each test are translated into scaled scores, which are then summed to find a Verbal and a Performance, as well as a Total Scale, I.Q.

Several types of interpretation are made of the results of the WISC. One of these is the comparison of the Performance and Verbal I.Q.'s. When the P is higher than the V, it is considered by many examiners to be a basic symptom of a reading disability. Moreover, the higher P I.Q. is thought to indicate the true potential of the subject. But unfortunately for these beliefs, variations between these measures in either direction are quite common, and exact equality is probably rare, according to Beck (3). As Reed (16) and other studies show, when a group of tests of various reading and motor skills is given to poor readers who are matched in Verbal I.Q., their performances equaled those of good readers. When matched in Performance I.Q., the test differ-

*These suggestions refer to the 1949 edition of the WISC, not the 1974 Revision.

Object Assembly Subtests of the 1974 WISC-R
(Courtesy of the Psychological Corporation)

ences were quite small but favored the good readers. In other words, the identification of poor readers was determined by the I.Q. used and its relationship to the other tests, not by a difference between the P and V I.Q.'s of the WISC. In twelve of fifteen studies we have reviewed, including one of our own (18), the WISC P I.Q. exceeded the V for either poor or good readers. In fact, there is reason to believe that this difference was present in the original standardization population.

A second popular interpretation of the WISC is in terms of the patterns of high and low scaled scores in the various subtests. (We summarize the patterns found in twenty-six studies in *Investigating the Issues of Reading*

Disabilities.) As a group, it appears that poor readers tend to perform badly in the Information, Arithmetic, Digit Span, and Coding tests, and sometimes on the Vocabulary subtest. In contrast, poor readers tend to achieve relatively high scores in Picture Completion, Block Design, Picture Arrangement, and, sometimes, the Object Assembly and Comprehension tests. Some of the authors are quite positive of the meanings and interpretation of the subtest patterns. They claim to identify poor readers by the pattern of their low scores in such subtypes as the dyslexic, the normal, those with a specific language disability, and the neurologically impaired. Another author groups test scores and pupils into three categories—spatial, conceptualizing ability, and sequencing abilities—and prescribes remediation according to his diagnosis.

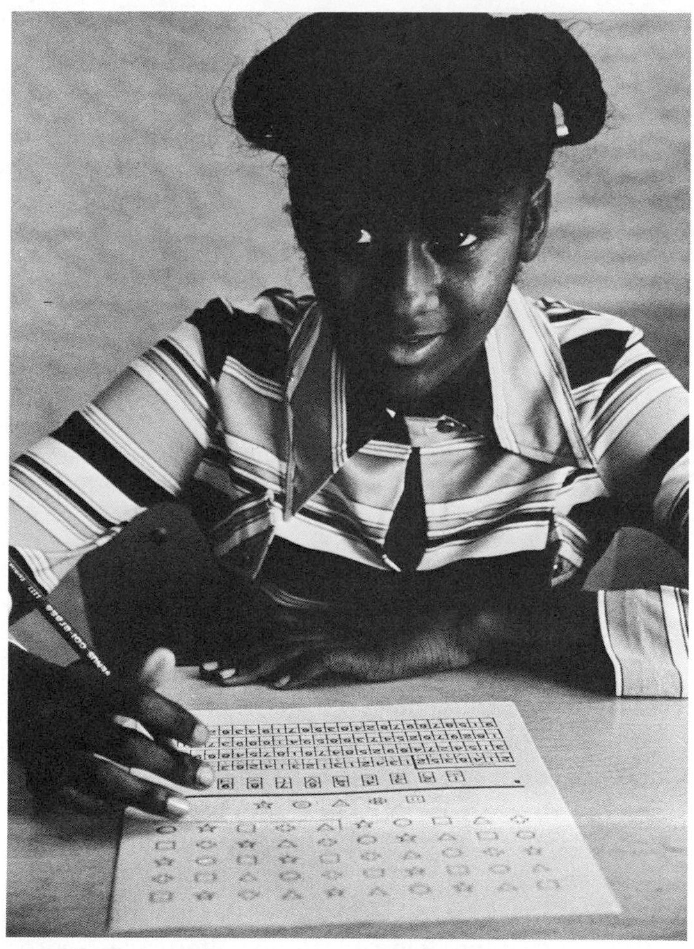

Coding Subtests of the 1974 WISC-R
(Courtesy of the Psychological Corporation)

These are but a minute sample of the types of pattern analysis that have been proposed ever since the test was first offered.

This interpretation of subtest patterns has been severely criticized on a number of grounds. First of all, it involves a comparison of single tests of not very high reliability, without attention to the statistical significance of the differences between scores. Second, many of the so-called patterns were based on clinical populations rather than on true samples of the entire population. The patterns supposed to characterize poor readers, for example, can be faulted for selecting cases from different schools, social classes, and ages, rather than homogeneous groups.

More defensible interpretations of the WISC may be based on factor analysis of the scales in our opinion. We begin our interpretation by comparing the subject's performances in the groups of related tests indicated by Cohen's factor analysis, somewhat in this fashion (4).

FACTOR	PROBABLE SIGNIFICANCE AND RELATED ADJUSTMENTS
Verbal Comprehension I *(School Learning)* Information Arithmetic Similarities (Vocabulary)	These tests may reflect the quality and other characteristics of the child's schooling. Trace the school history to find whether there are excessive absences, frequent school changes, changes of teachers, previous marks, and teacher comments in the records. Secure these by correspondence or interviews, if necessary. Consider also the effect of cultural background upon these tests. Consider also the quality or maturity of the responses in the vocabulary test, as indicative of verbal facility.

Assembling these facts helps give the picture of the child's previous school experiences, the successes and failures he has met, the teacher-pupil relationships he has encountered, and perhaps some indication of the inception and duration of his reading difficulty. These life experiences have undoubtedly influenced his attitudes toward school and teachers, as well as his self-concept as a reader. Some of these attitudes may well be transferred to the reading teacher, for in the child's eyes she is just another teacher. If they are negative, suspicious, or resentful, somehow or other the reading teacher will have to project an image different from that created by previous teachers; otherwise her remedial efforts will be in vain. We shall treat this point in greater detail later in chapter 5 discussing teacher-pupil relationships, and again in chapter 10 in considering alternative approaches to remediation.

Verbal Comprehension II (Verbal or Social Judgment) Comprehension Picture Completion	These tests may reflect the child's recognition of, or judgment in, social situations and the ordinary objects in life. They are not usually poor among retarded readers, for they are not determined by his school-related experiences. In a sense, they indicate his knowledge of the appropriateness of certain social behaviors.

Poor readers may have the judgment needed for acceptable social behavior, an understanding of the way things ought to be. Yet many seem to fail to use this judgment to achieve good relations with their peers, their teachers, and even their families. Their knowledge and judgment is on a verbal rather than an operational level (they can tell you what should be done, but we may find that they do not handle the situations that way). Evaluation of performances in this factor should be the first step in exploring the child's social relations, as emphasized in the later discussion of personality factors in chapter 5.

Perceptual Block Design Object Assembly (Picture Arrangement)	These tests reflect the child's understanding of spatial relationships under time limits. A poor performance in this area may suggest the need for exploration of developmental behaviors that appear earlier than these relatively high-level tasks, as hand-eye coordination or visual motor skills. Consider also the possibility that these performances are affected by cultural background (17). If we watch carefully his execution of the larger block designs, we may see some manifestation of his cognitive style, as in field dependence in setting up corner and outer blocks first.
Perceptual Speed Coding	This test may or may not sample associative learning. Check by having the child reproduce next to each number on a separate piece of paper the associated symbol used in the test. If he can remember only two or three, we have tested speed in transcribing, not learning. If performance in speed is poor, explore hand-eye coordination or small muscle coordination as in handwriting and writing at dictation. If performance reflects learning, explore by Mills's testing procedure or paired associate learning tasks. Tests of this nature are usually free of cultural bias.

Do not classify the child as "perceptually handicapped" or probably "brain-damaged" if he does relatively poorly in these perceptual factors. The terms are meaningless. Rather, establish his specific strengths or weaknesses in form comparison or reproduction, ocular motility, hand-eye coordination, and the like, perhaps as outlined in our discussion of that area in the second chapter. Rather than labeling him, try to discover what perceptual skills relevant to reading success he has or lacks, as these facts are related to the remedial plan.

Freedom from Distractibility Digit Span Arithmetic	Consider this performance as a measure of the child's attention, concentration, or freedom from anxiety. Consider their implications in planning the remedial program in terms of small group versus pupil teams versus individualized; need for quiet and privacy; duration of sessions; possibilities of distraction in using a large, cluttered room; and the effect of frequent variation in tasks.
Performance I.Q. versus Verbal I.Q.	Although poor readers tend to perform better in the Performance than in the Verbal tests, so do many children (3). The difference may well be reversed among the children of middle- and upper-class status because of their favorable verbal environment. The difference may also reflect the individual's gradual compensation for weaknesses, in emphasizing and thus improving his strengths.

Per se, P greater than V is not a primary proof that the child is a poor reader or will be soon. It is an indication again of strength and weakness, of background, or of unconscious compensation in seeking a more positive self-concept. In the presence of a lower V performance and poor reading, do not consider the P as an indication of the child's potential for improvement (16). Tests like these, which make less demand upon verbal ability, seldom show much more relationship with reading than .20 to about .50. In other words, the interrelationship may account for 4 to 25 percent of the variation in reading performance in the average sample. This hardly permits an accurate prediction of the outcomes of remediation. Lower P than V, the reverse of the usual "symptom," might well be a favorable sign for improvement and give a better prediction than the P performance.

Significance of Differences

Newland and Smith (13) have supplied a table of the statistically significant differences between the subtest scaled scores of the WISC. Consult this table in comparing performances in the various factors outlined above.

MEDIAN SIGNIFICANT DIFFERENCES BETWEEN SUBTEST SCALED SCORES (AFTER NEWLAND & SMITH [13])

AGES	BELOW 9	9–12	OVER 12
Intraverbal	5	4	4
Intraperformance	5	4	4
Verbal versus performance	5	4	4

These data, based on the information in the WISC manual, represent differences in scaled scores that are significant at the 5 percent level. At the 1 percent level, the differences must be as great as 6–7 scaled score points for significance.

Variability among scores is a normal phenomenon that probably increases with age as environment, schooling, and other factors modify intellectual development. There is no real evidence that one or two subtest scores well above or below most of the others indicates (as some seem to think) that the child is "emotionally disturbed" or "brain-damaged." In one of our own studies of 100 retarded readers drawn at random from clinic files (18), 90 percent showed marked deviation from their own average scaled score in at least one test in Verbal; 88 percent in the Performance scale; and 97 percent from the Total mean score. Increasing variability among a body of physical or intellectual tests is characteristic of ordinary human development, not usually a symptom of some abnormality.

Other Cautions

Do not ignore the possibility that your race or sex has influenced the test results; because you differ from the child and may, hence, be a threatening figure, his response level may be depressed. Remember also that you may be conducting the entire test in a dialect (for you probably use one) that is unfamiliar to the child. It may help the situation to have a familiar figure such as the mother in the case of young children, or a teacher or friend of the same sex or race as the testee present during the testing. Make certain that this third person understands his or her role and, when you suggest it, makes only positive, encouraging remarks to the child.

If you cannot make positive adjustments to counteract these possible conflicts, and if you have reason to believe that your test results may have been depressed for lack of rapport with the child, consider comparing the results with another sampling of the child's intellectual behavior. Among the alternatives possible are a group test not involving reading given by a very familiar teacher, or a second testing using the Goodenough-Harris drawing of a man, the Raven Matrices, or some other instrument relatively free from the demand for much personal interaction with the testee. Recognize that no matter how experienced or confident you are, there will be instances in which you are not the most appropriate person to assess formally a child's abilities.

In attempting to work with pupils of a lower socioeconomic status than your own, remember that they are apt to be less verbal, less self-confident, less motivated to academic achievement, less conforming in behavior. They are also not attuned to follow time limits, or to try to do the greatest amount possible in the shortest time, or to try to please the examiner by making their greatest effort. Their motivation in taking the test may well differ greatly from the attitude of middle-class children. Moreover, long-range predictions based on intellectual measurement of lower-class pupils are not highly accurate. And, in many comparisons, lower-class children test lower in the WISC because of the cultural bias of the test items. Thus your test results, for these many reasons, may not predict the pupil's potential for learning or his probable academic achievement. Apparently, however, this instrument does not discriminate against rural children, as it does against ethnic, racial, or linguistic minority groups (6, 9).

ALTERNATIVE TESTS

As we have summarized in chapter 6 of *Investigating the Issues of Reading Disabilities,* the Stanford-Binet is a highly verbal test that yields depressed ability estimates for poor readers and minority groups. These limitations hardly justify its use in reading diagnosis. Other alternative individual intelligence tests include the PPVT, the Raven Progressive Matrices, the Goodenough-Harris, and several others we shall discuss.

The Peabody Picture Vocabulary Test shows reasonable validity, reliability, and relationship with reading success. If both forms are administered, the testing time still does not extend beyond a half-hour, and reliability of the estimate is improved. Since the test is one of verbal intelligence, it may be influenced by socioeconomic or linguistic handicaps, although this effect is not great. Ali and Costello (1) have offered an abbreviated version that they believe eliminates the cultural bias. If the test is being used in such a population, it would be wise to consider this revision. In our reviews of other picture vocabulary tests (see *Investigating the Issues of Reading Disabilities),* such as the Full Range or the Quick Test, we feel that the Peabody is a preferable choice, because of its greater similarity to the WISC and the Binet, its shorter testing time, and its greater discrimination especially at lower age ranges.

For those who are unfamiliar with its nature, the PPVT, as it is known, consists of a spiral-bound book of 150 plates of four drawings each. When the examiner names one of the four objects or the action depicted, the pupil points to the corresponding drawing. This measure of verbal intelligence may be used from two years, six months to eighteen years of age and is available in two forms that use the same set of plates. Each form requires about ten to fifteen minutes to administer. The PPVT has been found to give reasonable correlations with the Binet and the WISC, although there is a trend toward higher I.Q.'s on it.

The test offers the advantages of a verbal intelligence measure, free from the depressing effects of the pupil's reading ability. The manual cites correlations with reading for several atypical groups in which the PPVT

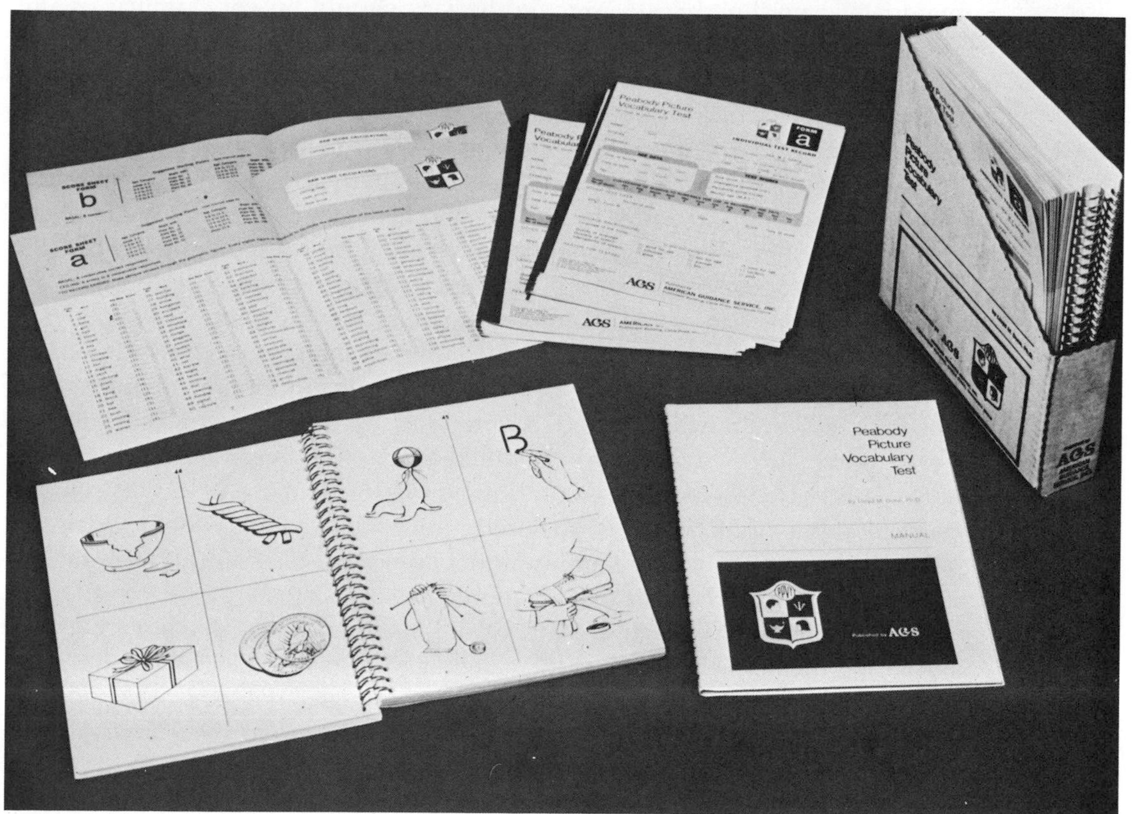

Peabody Picture Vocabulary Test

compared quite favorably with other similar intelligence tests, but tended to be lower than those found for the WISC. Moreover, since it is almost purely a measure of vocabulary, recognized as a good sample of verbal intelligence, the PPVT may be influenced by bilingualism or other linguistic handicaps. This limitation has been noted in the revised version offered by Ali and Costello (1).

The Goodenough-Harris drawing of a man, a woman, and the self is a much improved instrument in comparison with the original Goodenough test (8). The test is very simple to administer, yields good reliability, is reasonably related to reading achievement for a nonverbal test, and may even be used as a group test. At primary ages it may yield lower scores for disadvantaged children (7) but, on the other hand, is a strong choice when rapport between examiner and child is difficult to obtain. There does not appear to be a sex difference in the scores, although the test does seem somewhat more reliable for testing of boys (10). The test may be repeated after intervals of several weeks, if it seems desirable, without any material practice effect. The materials given the child to execute the task should be very familiar to him, such as the pencil (stubs?) and paper commonly used in his classroom (11). As in other art activities, if rapport is good, the child may be led to talk about his drawing: to describe it, its feelings, and its activities. In this fashion, the relationship with the pupil becomes more personalized, and we may gain some insights into his feelings and activities. In all probability, there is a relation between his manner in drawing and his cognitive style. We may gain some insights into his field dependence or need for setting limits, as perhaps in executing the outer outlines of the figures before putting in details in any one segment instead of his complete execution part by part.

The pupil's drawings of a man and a woman are scored for various details and the scores averaged for greater reliability in finding an intelligence quotient. The drawing of self is intended as a device for the study of personality, not as a measure of intelligence. The basic simplicity of the administration and scoring has contributed to extensive use of this instrument, particularly at primary levels. There is no evidence that it is more closely related to reading success than are most nonverbal tests, but it is a practical choice in many difficult testing situations.

The Raven Progressive Matrices are a series of British nonverbal tests requiring the subject to choose matching designs or design parts, or to recognize an analogy or logical sequence of designs. The tests have had wide use in European countries and Canada because of their ease of administration. Comparative testing of Eskimo, Indian, and white groups in Canada of varying socioeconomic groups, and of white and black children in this country indicate that the tests are not influenced by the experiential background of the testees.

Another study indicated that the tests measure general rather than verbal intelligence. Three series, the Standard for ages eight to sixty-five; the Coloured for ages five to eleven, and the Advanced for gifted adolescents and adults are available (15).

The Raven Progressive Matrices present several problems in applying the norms to American children (15). On the other hand, they are apparently free from cultural bias, compare reasonably well with validity criteria such as the WISC or Binet except for mentally retarded, and demand very little interaction of examiner and testee (9, 17). If available, this instrument may be a good selection for difficult testing situations. Its relevance for reading has not been widely reported, but is probably as great as most tests that sample general intelligence, as this one does.

The Porteus Maze Test, though not widely known in reading and school testing, has certain unique advantages (14). In addition to the general measure of mental ability, it can be scored in terms of social competence or adjustment to life demands (5). Moreover, it is entirely culture-free and not affected by the reading ability of the testee. Boys do tend to score higher in solving the mazes than do girls, and its relevance to the type of intelligence of significance in reading is probably not very great. It may be considered for retesting or supplementary testing or for difficult testing situations.

The Pintner-Cunningham Primary Mental Test is suitable for group or individual kindergarten to primary grades. Its reliability, validity in comparison with the Binet, and measurement of verbal intelligence largely recommend its use. On the other hand, the tasks involved require the comprehension of oral directions, the recognition of the properties of objects, and one visual motor task. All these are conceivably culturally biased, for they require good communication between the examiner and the children, who may be of different dialectal backgrounds. The visual motor task of copying designs is one not easily done by lower-class children. In middle-class populations, however, the test will function well.

The Slosson Intelligence test, a brief verbal measure of good validity, is easy to administer and to score. It is suitable probably in middle-class schools and for good or average readers. Like the Stanford-Binet, which it was built to emulate, the test is basically a question-answer interaction between examiner and subject. As Neville (12) and others have shown, tests of this highly verbal type certainly penalize and underestimate the probable ability of poor readers.

The Detroit Tests of Learning Aptitude are, as we have said, a series of scales measuring a number of intellectual behaviors (2). Since each scale is independent of the others, the reading teacher may choose to use any one or several for supplementary testing. The individual scales, of course, are not highly reliable, but they are probably as accurate as most others of these types. Certain of the scales are pertinent in reading diagnosis, such as the motor speed and precision; the visual attention span for letters and for objects (for a measure of visual memory); the memory for designs (for form discrimination); and the attention span for unrelated words and for syllables (for a sample of auditory attention span). In the absence of knowledge of the factorial content of the Detroit tests, we are assuming—at least in those we have just named—that they measure what they appear to sample. Since they resemble many other widely accepted tests, this assumption is reasonable.

Another approach to intelligence measurement is in the use of a test of listening comprehension. Such tests certainly sample the reasoning factor of intelligence and probably also reflect the verbal background of the pupil. Their use will aid in evaluating the pupil's abilities in these areas and hence give some clue to his potential for improvement, when they are employed in conjunction with other such measures.

A number of the individual diagnostic tests that we review in chapter 7 suggest the use of part of their batteries as a measure of listening comprehension—or a measure of potential for achievement in reading. Group measures of listening comprehension are also available. Of all these tests, only the Diagnostic Reading Scales offer any data supporting this assumption. From these data, it is apparent that predictions are variable from one population to another (perhaps because of the method of instruction), and they vary in predicting different reading performances such as oral or silent reading or word recognition. Intensive instruction, as that in remedial tutoring, also influences the accuracy of prediction from pretraining to posttraining testing.

Listening comprehension is not highly correlated with silent reading, as evidenced in a median *r* of .61 in a number of studies. Nor can we necessarily assume that (as most test authors claim) a higher listening performance than that in silent reading is prima facie evidence that the pupil will show the same degree of progress when given appropriate training. Some do gain, while others do not show more than normal progress, and others may actually show losses on retests, even though they tested significantly higher in listening than in reading, according to Crowley and Ellis.* In other words, if another measure of verbal intelligence and language background of a pupil is desired, a measure of listening comprehension may give tentative clues, but not highly accurate estimates.

---

*H. L. Crowley and Bessie Ellis, "Cross Validation of a Method for Selecting Children Requiring Special Services in Reading," *Reading Teacher,* 24 (January 1971), 312–19.

Some—and that probably includes the authors—would object to our suggesting that only certain parts of the Illinois Test of Psycholinguistic Abilities be employed in reading diagnosis. But (as we demonstrate in our intensive review of the literature in *Investigating the Issues of Reading Disabilities*), there is ample support for this attitude. In his review of the test, in the *Seventh Mental Measurements Yearbook,* John B. Carroll severely criticizes the rationale of the ITPA. He doubts that it is truly a measure of psycholinguistic abilities, since only half of the tests involve the use of language by the testee or examiner. He cites several analyses of the test indicating that it is probably a measure of only three factors: verbal intelligence, immediate memory span, and auditory processing. Hence the labeling and grouping of the subtests by the authors are questionable. Carroll also decries the standardization of a test intended for use with language-handicapped or mentally retarded children on a middle-class group of average mental and school achievement, almost exclusively composed of white children.

These and other criticisms of the ITPA raise serious questions regarding the author's suggestions for the identification of various deficits by comparison of the individual subtest scores or the Profile. In an attempt to solve this dilemma, a number of researchers have attempted to identify patterns of ITPA subtest scores that are characteristic of poor readers. We tabulated the results of thirteen such studies in the parallel chapter in *Investigating the Issues of Reading Disabilities.* The consistency of any pattern of scores was not found to be marked. Only the Auditory Sequential Memory (a digit span test) appeared to be present among poor readers in about half of the reports. Other tests appearing in a number of studies were the Grammatic Closure Test (a task in completing a sentence depicting the action in a picture), Visual Sequential Memory (reproduction of a sequence of symbols), and Auditory Association (completing an analogy read to the testee).

McLeod* found these tests, excepting the Auditory Association, to form a related factor in his analysis of the series, a factor related to reading achievement in that poor readers tend to perform poorly in these elements. Other studies reaffirm the relationship of the Grammatic Closure and Auditory Association with reading success, and with readiness tests.

It should be noted, however, that the Auditory Sequential Memory (digit span) has long been identified as a measure of intelligence, while other studies indicate that performance on the test is significantly related to the

---

*John McLeod, *Dyslexia in Young Children: A Factorial Study with Special Reference to the ITPA.* (University of Illinois IREC Papers in Education, 1966).

particular method of reading instruction. Auditory span was found to be negatively related to word recognition success, for example, when silent reading was the medium of instruction, but irrelevant to a basal reader system.

Moreover, a large-scale study of disadvantaged children indicated that they were below average on all the ITPA tests except the Visual Sequential Memory, and Auditory Sequential Memory, implying that the remainder of the tests were culturally biased. In other words, only certain portions of the ITPA appear related to reading, and even these must be used cautiously.

Those we suggest using, again as supplementary aids, are the factorially related group of Grammatic Closure, Visual Sequential Memory, and Auditory Sequential Memory; possibly also the Auditory Association. Respectively, these sample reasoning in reading, visual memory span, auditory memory span, and reasoning in reading. Alone, they are probably not reliable enough for conclusions but, when used as parallel tests, can add weight to the validity of the diagnosis.

Some will question whether there is real need for or value in a measure of intelligence in a reading diagnosis. This argument seems particularly cogent when we admit that the mental age derived from such a test is not a good predictor of future reading performances and that the I.Q. alone is not highly valid for predicting the rate of learning. Furthermore, neither listening comprehension measures nor the ITPA will add much to the estimate of the pupil's potential for improving in reading. The question seems to be, "Why bother with such testing?"

Yet, pragmatically, there is a necessity for the reading teacher to make gross estimates about pupils' potentials. She must formulate some criteria for selecting pupils for remediation who will profit therefrom and for eliminating others (or her case load becomes impossible). She must estimate the probable duration of the remediation in order to maintain a schedule and to control the flow of cases she treats. She must make plans for the pupil in terms of small-group, individualized, or pupil team work; frequency and duration of remedial sessions; and possible effect of attention span and perseveration on the length and variety of tasks engaged in by the pupil.

It is true that some of those decisions can be made on a trial-and-error basis during the first few weeks of remedial training. But this process can be abbreviated by careful observation and interpretation of the pupil's performances in many of the tasks inherent in a diversified testing of intelligence and listening comprehension. Through careful attention to the pupil's behaviors during the testing, the reading specialist may be able to identify his cognitive strengths and weaknesses, as in visual and auditory memory span, verbal reasoning, vocabulary, attention or concentration, persistence in tasks of varying difficulty, and his tendencies to perseveration. Thinking disorders such as weak conceptualization, overconcreteness, poor judgment, and verbalism may be observed. Test anxiety or tension, general informational background, and perhaps clues as to the quality of his previous schooling may also be obtained from the intelligence testing. While these significant facts could be obtained, in a gross sense, by observation during remediation, they are more quickly and accurately noted in a diversified intelligence testing, for many of these traits are being sampled in a standardized fashion.

LEARNING PROJECT

Several worthwhile projects in the application of the procedures suggested in this chapter are possible. Your instructor will suggest those of greatest value for your learning.

1. Analyze the results of a WISC test in the manner proposed by the author. Consider the implications of the pupil's performances in each major factor of the test. Show how these implications would direct remedial planning and treatment of this pupil. If social and school history data are available, relate your deductions from the WISC to this information.

2. Administer the Peabody Picture Vocabulary Test or the Goodenough-Harris to several of your pupils for whom other intelligence test results are recorded. Compare the results on this new testing with the earlier figures for mental age and I.Q. Are the I.Q.'s relatively similar? If not, are the differences in I.Q. a reflection of the content of the different tests or of their emphasis upon verbal or nonverbal ability? Which test agrees most closely with your estimates of the pupils' intelligence?

REFERENCES

1. Ali, Faizuniza, and Costello, Joan, "Modification of the Peabody Picture Vocabulary Test," *Developmental Psychology,* 5 (July 1971), 86–91.
2. Baker, Harry J., and Leland, Bernice, *Detroit Tests of Learning Aptitude.* Indianapolis: Bobbs-Merrill, 1968.
3. Beck, Frances, "Performance of Retarded Readers on Parts of the Wechsler Intelligence Scale for Children," in *Clinical Studies in Reading III,* Helen M. Robinson, editor, Supplementary Educational Monographs No. 97, 1968, 91–103.
4. Cohen, J., "Factorial Structure of the WISC at Ages 7-10, 10-6 and 13-6," *Journal of Consulting Psychology,* 23 (1959), 285–99.

5. Cooper, G. David, et al., "The Porteus Test and Various Measures of Intelligence with Southern Negro Adolescents," *American Journal of Mental Deficiency,* 71 (March 1967), 787–92.
6. "Guidelines for Testing Minority Group Children" *Journal of Social Issues,* 20 (April 1964), 127–45.
7. Hanson, E., and Robinson, H. Alan, "Reading Readiness and Achievement of Primary Grade Children of Different Socio-Economic Strata," *Reading Teacher,* 21 (1967), 52–56.
8. Harris, Dale B., *Goodenough-Harris Drawing Test.* New York: Harcourt Brace Jovanovich, 1963.
9. Littell, William M., "The Wechsler Intelligence Scale for Children: Review of a Decade of Research," *Psychological Bulletin,* 57 (1960), 132–56.
10. McGilligan, Robert P., Yater, Allan C., and Huesing, Ralph, "Goodenough-Harris Drawing Test Reliabilities," *Psychology in the Schools,* 8 (October 1971), 359–61.
11. McWhinnie, Harold J., "Review of Recent Literature on Figure Drawing Tests as Related to Research Problems in Art Education," *Review of Educational Research,* 41 (April 1971), 131–42.
12. Neville, Donald, "The Relationship between Reading Skills and Intelligence Test Scores," *Reading Teacher,* 18 (January 1965), 257–62.
13. Newland, T.E., and Smith, P.A., "Statistically Significant Differences between Subtest Scores on the WISC and the WAIS," *Journal of School Psychology,* 5 (1967), 122–27.
14. Porteus, Stanley D., *The Porteus Maze Test.* New York: Psychological Corporation, 1965.
15. Raven, J.C., *Progressive Matrices.* New York: Psychological Corporation, 1938.
16. Reed, James C., "The Deficits of Retarded Readers—Fact or Artifact?" *Reading Teacher,* 23 (January 1970), 347–52, 393.
17. Semler, Ira J., and Iscoe, Ira, "Structure of Intelligence in Negro and White Children," *Journal of Educational Psychology,* 57 (December 1966), 326–36.
18. Spache, George D., "Intellectual and Personality Characteristics of Retarded Readers," *Psychological Newsletter,* 9 (1957), 9–12.

5 Understanding Pupil Personality and Pupil-Teacher Interaction

Various approaches to understanding pupil feelings and attitudes, such as projective devices, drawings, children's stories, rating scales, and the sentence completion technique are presented. Peer relationships are explored by sociometric analysis. Ways of sampling pupil self-concepts through tests, parent contacts, and teacher observation are mapped out for the reading teacher. The insights thus obtained are integrated into the discussion of pupil-teacher relationships, while specific suggestions for pupil management and for building their self-concepts are offered.

The reading teacher desiring to improve professional skills in these diagnostic areas and to foster favorable pupil-teacher relationships will probably want to read this chapter again and again, together with the related background materials in *Investigating the Issues of Reading Disabilities.*

For the first reading, consider these questions:

1. Why does the author place so much stress upon the study of pupil personality and self-concepts as significant for pupil-teacher interaction?

2. What ideas about pupil-teacher relationships, group dynamics, and self-concept building can you contribute from your own experiences?

THERE IS LITTLE QUESTION of the significance of the interaction of teachers' and pupils' personalities and the consequent effect upon the pupils' learning. But recognition of this fact immediately raises several questions. Are teachers or reading specialists competent in studying pupils' personalities objectively? Can they discern the traits and motivations of each individual child? And, more significantly, can or will they adapt their treatment and approaches to different children accordingly?

It is true that the study of personality has become a technical matter, with esoteric tests and theories of personality structure dominating the field. Yet we see many teachers dealing successfully with pupils who present a wide variety of adjustment problems, helping them to overcome these handicaps and to progress academically. Our purposes in this chapter are to support this kind of effort by mentioning a number of tools that teachers and reading specialists may employ in their efforts to understand pupil personalities and self-concept. Simple treatment approaches to maladjustments and supportive steps to strengthen pupil self-concept are also offered.

In dealing with the majority of retarded readers, the reading teacher must deal frequently with personality deviations and low self-concepts. Among the feelings and behaviors that seem to be fairly common are aggressiveness or hostility toward both adults and peers, especially among boys; a tendency to social conformity among girls; negativeness to adult suggestion; withdrawal from active social or personal relationships; anxiety and tension about reading; as well as poor social acceptance by classmates. The attempt to determine whether these obstacles to academic achievement and interferences with establishing good working relations with the child are present is an essential part of diagnosis. It is true that many reading teachers and clinics do not bother to explore this facet of remedial work. Their reasons are often offered that either teachers are not really competent or trained in understanding or diagnosing personality difficulties or that the proportion of disturbed disabled readers is very small (the usual conclusion of clinics that literally make no attempt to assess the problem). Another rationalization given is that, after all, the purpose of remedial reading is to repair the child's reading skills and that, if this is done, personality or adjustment problems will probably be improved or disappear (20). We disagree completely with these beliefs, for we do not believe that any of them is true.

Teachers can learn to secure insights into a pupil's feelings and attitudes and to attempt to manipulate their relationship with the poor readers to alleviate these negative influences. The proportion of emotionally disturbed poor readers—using that term to indicate children who show feelings and attitudes that are self-defeating—is very large, perhaps as great as three out of every four (29). Finally, since personality maladjustments often precede and contribute to reading failure, they are not likely to be dissipated when the child is temporarily successful because of intensive remedial assistance.

Our purpose in this section is to suggest ways and means of approaching pupils' personality problems that is well within the capabilities of the average teacher who is willing to learn them. No special competencies other than the recognition that a successful pupil-teacher relationship is *the* most important element in the pupils' learning are needed. In achieving this relationship, it is obvious that the personalities of both teacher and pupil and their interaction are the core of successful remediation. If we have learned nothing else from the major research of the past decade, it is certainly that teacher-pupil interaction is preeminently important; it is above all consideration of methods, materials, and the like in both classroom and remedial situations.

APPROACHES TO DIAGNOSIS OF PUPIL PERSONALITY

Projective Techniques

There are a number of technical tools that, without specialized training, the classroom teacher cannot use. Among these are the Rorschach, the C.A.T. (Children's Apperception Test), the T.A.T. (Thematic Apperception Test), to mention only a few (18). These require preparation in personality theory and in the techniques of administration, scoring, and interpretation. To overcome the difficulties inherent in the use of these instruments, a number of questionnaires, check lists, and group tests of personality have been offered. While the apparent validity and reliability of some of these is acceptable, such an approach makes a number of questionable assumptions. To accept the respondent's answers at face value, we must believe that he has not recognized the personal nature of the test and, therefore, does not censor or modify his answers to give a good impression. Second, we must believe that, in answering, he understands his own behavior sufficiently to know what are the correct answers he should give about himself, and that he is willing to give these revealing answers. He may have to, in effect, deny his self-concept and answer realistically and honestly to questions that present him in a negative view. Third, we must assume that the questions are interpreted precisely as the author intended, without varying interpretations from pupil to pupil.

These assumptions are hardly ever true for a group of testees, particularly adolescents and young adults. If one of these commercial group personality tests must be used for preliminary identification of areas of difficulty of adjustment, their results will have to be verified with observations and other instruments. We prefer to initiate the exploration of pupil personality with the latter.

To avoid the untenable assumptions in most group personality instruments, the approach through projective devices that presumably elicit responses more accurately, reflecting the individual's feelings and attitudes, has been devised. By responding to, and giving his interpretation of, pictures of people, animals, inkblots, ambiguous classroom situations, or a child and an adult in a disagreement, he is expected to project his concepts of social relations. Since there are no choices between acceptable and unfavorable answers, he cannot choose to hide his own interpretations, but must express in his own words what the subjects in the test are trying to, or should, do. Projective tests are usually standardized in terms of the personality mechanisms displayed by various categories of answers. Thus those facets of personality emphasized in the theory of personality structure of the author can be uncovered.

We have used a test of this nature, the Rosenzweig Picture Frustration Study (19), with disabled readers in a clinic and in practice as a school psychologist. Our observations have been reported in a number of articles and are summarized in the parallel chapter (in *Investigating the Issues of Reading Disabilities*) on personality and self-concept (29, 30). This instrument is relatively easy to administer and to score, and we have introduced it to many of our graduate assistants and in-service teachers preparing to function in remedial reading. In our opinion, it tends to reveal the basic feelings and attitudes of the testee, in most cases, toward the adult figure or teacher and toward his peers. After some use, we devised a dual scoring scheme that distinguishes adult-child from child-child relationships (28). It is true of this test, as reviewers have said, that we do not know whether the child's responses indicate what would be his behavior or his opinion on how to behave. We do not think that this is an important criticism, for we are not concerned with his acting out of his feelings but rather to know what these attitudes are. His acting out of his feelings would be apparent in our contacts with him and in his classroom. The comment that the test pictures boys versus an adult more often than girls, and in all has twice as many pictures involving boys, is not a handicap in reading diagnosis, for most of our subjects are boys. Besides there are no differences in the reactions of boys or girls that could have been due to the sex of the child in the picture except in one drawing, according to our data. Our recommendation of this test to those who are willing to take the time to read the research about it and to study its use reflects, of course, our personal experiences with the instrument. As Gabriel Della-Piana has suggested, the reading teacher searches for an instrument that helps her understand the underlying feelings and attitudes of her cases. Her selection is based on the successful use of whatever she finally adopts in clarifying her insights. For us, this was the Rosenzweig Picture Frustration Study. But there are many others from which to select.

Drawings of school-related situations that evoke significant pupil responses are a logical approach in reading work. Margaret LaPray and Joan Owen offer a *Reading Attitude Dialog* (San Diego: San Diego State College, 1971) for the first four grades. The child's responses tend to agree with teacher's judgment of his attitude toward school, and responses were definitely related to interest in reading as shown by library use. Irving L. Solomon and Bernard D. Starr have carried this idea farther in their *SAM-School Apperception Method* (New York: Springer Publishing Co., 1972). Twenty-three pictures are offered for kindergarten to ninth grade, and scoring is done in nine areas of feelings and attitudes. Like the LaPray-Owen instrument, this is a preliminary study, for no validity or reliability data have been offered. Another such instrument has been devised by Hake (11).

Children's drawings of the human figure have been interpreted for indications of emotional disturbance by a number of researchers. Some say that abnormalities in the drawings are signs of this condition, while others do not always find that the signs are valid (9). Robert C. Burns and Howard S. Kaufman offer a collection of *Kinetic Family Drawings* (New York: Basic Books, 1972) in which the child represents his "family doing something." In all probability, children do project their concepts of the family constellation; thus we may achieve some insights into this family pattern and its impact on the child. Validating precise signs of this or that relationship, feeling, or attitude is a very difficult task influenced often by the subjective opinions of the scorers. But these drawings can be useful if their implications are confirmed by interviews and observation. Even if not always accurate, the signs can suggest areas to be explored and evaluated.

Rating Scales

Rating scales applicable in reading disability cases are numerous and, if used to collate the observations of previous teachers, can also help to focus our attention on certain attitudes and behaviors. Among those available are the following:

AML Behavior Rating Scale, by R. Brounbridge and D. Van Fleet. San Francisco: Pace ID Center. Ratings in aggressiveness, moodiness, and learning ability.

Burke's Behavior Rating Scale for Organic Brain Dysfunction.: Arden Press. Yields four scores reflecting areas of behavioral difficulty. (Is not a test of brain damage.)

Child Behavior Rating Scale, by Russell N. Cassel. Los Angeles: Western Psychological Services. A seventy-eight item scale for rating child's adjustment in self, home, social, school and physical activities.

Children's Rating Scale, by James Gallagher. In his book *The Tutoring of Brain-Injured Mentally Retarded Children,* pp. 185–87. Springfield, Ill.: Charles C. Thomas, 1960. Ratings on descriptive statements of independence of action, self-regard, socialization, hyperactivity, attention, and five other behaviors.

Devereaux Elementary School Behavior Rating Scale. Devon, Pa.: Devereaux Foundation Press. For kindergarten to grade six. In eleven scales of behavior we do not share the viewpoint of the author of this scale, which interprets any behavior that indicates the child is not meeting the demands of the school as undesirable problem behavior.

Pupil Rating Scale for Learning Disabilities, by Helmer R. Myklebust. New York: Psychological Corporation. Five point rating scales in auditory comprehension, language, orientation, motor coordination, and personal-social behavior, for ages seven to ten.

Walker Problem Behavior Identification Checklist, by Hill M. Walker. Los Angeles: Western Psychological Services.

We have found the Gallagher scale serviceable in collating the observations by teachers of children being seen in the clinic. Although validated with brain-injured children, like the Burke scale, it samples many of the child's behaviors pertinent to remedial reading work. Like the other scales, it serves as an information-gathering tool and a screening instrument to indicate areas that we should carefully observe and relate to our handling of the child.

Sociometric Testing

In sampling peer relations among pupils, an approach using children's expressions of their liking for other pupils is a valuable technique. The pupils are asked to list the two or three other pupils they would most like to play a game with, read with, sit next to, or have as their best friends. These choices are collected and translated into a diagram called a sociogram in which the children are represented by a named circle and their choices by arrows connecting the circles. The arrows lead to or from circle to circle as indicated by the children's choices. The nomination of leaders or popular figures is easily observed in the frequency of arrows leading to the circles representing these children. Rejected children who are not often chosen by the others, and whose choices are often not reciprocated by those they choose, are also identified. As Holliday's master's thesis (12) indicates, these socially isolated children are often the poorest readers of the class. The information obtained may serve to guide the teacher (or the remedial teacher who uses sociometric testing in her groups) in her handling of group relationships, of leaders and followers, of pupil teams, and the like. The information may be relevant to her promotion of the self-concept of certain children, or of better peer relations and similar efforts (10, 13, 17, 24). The articles by Mann (13) and Shaw and Shaw (24) will convey some concepts of the significance of group relations.

Sentence Completion

Although it is really a projective technique that presumably elicits pupil responses free from censorship or imitation of a proper social mode, we have chosen to present this approach in a separate segment of this chapter. The sentence completion format was long known in the psychological testing of the early part of this century as a measure of language facility, sentence structure, reasoning in reading, and the like. The task is to complete a given word or few words with a spontaneous addition to form a complete sentence. Its use in sampling feelings and attitudes has gradually been recognized, and a number of prototypes for use in school and industry are now available (3, 27, 32).

The sentence completion technique can be adopted to the particular situation in which it is to be used. For example, it may be devised to sample ego development, attitudes toward school, feelings about self, or, in our case, attitudes toward reading. The version we have employed (see Appendix) was designed by Faye Huskins while a staff member of our reading clinic. It is specifically designed to sample the intermediate and upper elementary pupils' attitudes and feelings about reading. It may also be used with primary children with whom good rapport has been established, using the directions suggested. With the older pupils, the directions can simply ask that the children finish each sentence with the first idea that comes to mind. Doing the first item or two aloud with the pupil may be necessary to clarify the task.

Our incomplete sentence test for elementary children has not been standardized in the way that some commercial versions are constructed by stipulating that certain answers are correct or indications of poor adjustment or whatever. Answers to such an instrument cannot be determined by norms or a priori judgments of what are proper answers. In fact, such scoring destroys the unique value of the instrument in reflecting the individuality of each respondent's feelings and attitudes. In other words, there are no correct answers to be sought for. The test offers a summary sheet for collating the responses in six areas in which the reading teacher would be interested. The items in which responses may be related to each area are indicated. When a response clearly reflects feelings or attitudes in an area, she writes the response in that category. But since we cannot predict just how a child will interpret each item, the teacher will have to be alert to assign a response to a different problem area when it is pertinent. As familiarity with the technique grows, teachers will probably identify new problem areas that seem to be sampled in children's responses and can add these categories to the suggested summary. In effect, this approach will yield specific as well as overall impressions of the reactions of children toward situations involving reading and reading instruction. They may or may not act out these feelings in their relations with teachers and peers, for there is often a real tendency for these children to be anxious about their feelings, to conceal them in what Dudek and Lester (8) have called the "good child facade" of passivity, depression, and apparent compliance with adult demands. Thus, when overt behavior and the impressions gained from this instrument are not consistent, the value in probing behind the behavioral facade is demonstrated. The behavioral manifestations of agressiveness, hostility, or negativism are readily observed by the teacher; but when these are concealed, instruments of this type are particularly valuable in helping us understand some of the reasons for the child's reading failure.

Children's Stories

As in the sentence completion technique, children's spontaneous verbalizations in the form of stories can be structured to yield significant information about them. Carolyn Hendrix, a former graduate student, evolved a number of story titles for her children and found these extremely useful in understanding them better. Among her titles are these:

"What I Think Heaven Is Like"—often draws out the child's wants and needs, and what he misses in his home life.

"The Way I Feel on Dark, Rainy Days"—used on such a day this evokes mood responses.

"The First Thing I Remember"—what seems important or dramatic according to the child's memories.

"The Reason I Like My Best Friend"—often brings forth the implicit comparison between self and other, thus giving clues to the child's self-concept.

"Why I Am Happy"—may reflect peer or home relations.

"Why I Am Sad"—may reveal tensions or anxieties.

"Ten Rules for Mother and Daddy"—what the child wants, behaviorally speaking, of his parents and perhaps the contrast with what they expect of him.

"What I Want Most to Do When I Grow Up"—may offer a picture of the hopes and aspirations as well as of the self-ideal.

"What Makes Me Bad"—giving clues to parent relations, self-concept, and perhaps the self-ideal.

"The World I Live In"—when related to class discussion of space or other lands, or as an imaginary conversation with a child from outer space or another country, this title may lead to insights into the child's world.

Other story starters are:

"If I Were a Turkey"—used at appropriate holiday to reflect child's needs and feelings

"If I Were Santa Claus"

"If I Were the Christ Child"

"People Should Remember That"—relations with peers or adults

"If I Could Go To——I Would Take"—may reflect wants, peer or family relations

"If I Had Three Wishes"—what he needs or wants in his life.

"If I Had Only Known"—usually evokes the recounting of an embarrassing or guilt-laden incident.

To illustrate how one or the other of these story-provoking titles may work, here is an account of one such experience of Miss Hendrix.

Edna, a child in my room, was reading, but without comprehension. Answers to questions on anything read were written with combinations of letters that did not even resemble words. She had no concept of what she was doing. I had her tested for the special education class in our school and found her I.Q. to be about 80, which was surprisingly high to me. Much background should be given to give an accurate picture of what took place in my room with this child, but to make a long story short, we had a writing period one day on the subject What I Think Heaven Is Like. I had let Edna dictate some of her papers to me, but decided to see what she would do with the art illustration of heaven. Her paper came in with every word spelled correctly and written in a fairly neat hand. No one had helped her, as I had been observing her, and her picture was good, too. She had written, "I can't wait to get to heaven where there are pretty little angels, and I can play and play and play with them forever." I talked with her after school and asked her why she handed in her assignments written in an unreadable fashion when she could write and spell as nicely as she had done in this art work. She told me that she didn't have time to do it at

> home. I explained, as she knew, that I gave time in class to do assignments so that I could help, and that taking it home was unnecessary. Edna said that she could not get her mind on working at school. Noticing that her desire in heaven was to play forever, I asked if she ever played with anyone at home. The mystery then revealed itself. I knew there were nine children in this family besides Edna, and she told me, in tears, that she had to do all the cleaning, cooking and dish washing at home and that her mother wouldn't make the other children help her. She said her only opportunity to play at all was at recess while at school, and then I understood her talkative record within the classroom. Edna and I have worked together, now that I know her problem and she is reading with more comprehension and some improvement in attention span. The attendance department was contacted and told her frequent absences were due to the mother keeping Edna home to work, and this stopped. The school nurse visited the home for me and told the mother that over-work was ruining Edna's health, school work and general outlook on life. The mother agreed, and Edna tells me that she is now allowed more time for play at home and children help her with the work. The mother seems to resent Edna, although I haven't reached any conclusions about this, but she was literally working the child beyond her own capacity as a result of this.
>
> I feel that such a brief report on this case is doing it an injustice, but it does give a concrete sample of my work with creative writing in solving emotional and scholastic problems of children.

We have tried to supply some clues and tools for the teacher's approach to understanding pupil personality because, in our opinion, the success and permanence of the effects of remedial work depend upon her implementation of these insights. We shall postpone the discussion of activities for the teacher in the presence of pupil personality problems until we have considered the self-concept.

APPROACHES TO UNDERSTANDING PUPIL SELF-CONCEPT

The relatively recent emphasis upon the importance of pupil self-concept has led to the publication of a number of diagnostic instruments in this area. Among these are the following:

How I See Myself, by Ira J. Gordon. Gainesville, Fla.: The Author. A forty-item individual or group measure for elementary grades. Pupil is to rate two opposing statements on a five-point scale.

Piers-Harris Children's Self-Concept Scale. Nashville: Counselor Recordings and Tests. An eighty-item first-person series of statements to be responded to in grades three to twelve or read to younger children. Construct validity is acceptable, but retest reliability is only moderate.

Self-Concept as a Learner, by John K. Fisher. Edinboro, Pa.: Edinboro State College: The Author. For grades three–six, sample self-views as a class member, task-oriented individual, a problem solver, and a motivated individual.

Self-Perception Inventory, by Anthony R. and Louise M. Soares. See *American Educational Research Journal,* 6 (1969), 31–44, and our earlier discussion of this instrument in chapter 5 of *Investigating the Issues of Reading Disabilities.*

Tennessee Self-Concept Scale, by William H. Fitts. Nashville: Counselor Recordings and Tests. A form offered for counselors gives fifteen profile scores in self-criticism, self-esteem, and so on. Consists of 100 self-description items to be ranked on a five-point scale. Reliability of total score in the .80s, but subtest scores are highly related. Validity with other tests is only moderate. For ages twelve and up.

The Thomas Self-Concept Values Test, by Walter L. Thomas. Rosemont, Ill.: Combined Motivation Education Systems. Offered for ages three to nine, with nineteen scores in happiness, size, sociability, sharing, male acceptance, fears, and so on. Child is supposed to respond first in terms of own perceptions, and then in terms of others' perceptions of him, that is, his mother's, peers', and teacher's concepts. Reliability of most subtest scores is relatively low, and these scores show substantial overlap, as we might expect.

There are problems, of course, in this sort of measurement of aspects of the self-concept. Blacks tend to rate themselves very high or very low, and low socioeconomic whites vary similarly. Most of the tests assume that the child can verbalize his feelings about his abilities and disabilities and that he is perfectly willing to. These instruments could be useful in preliminary screening to detect probable areas of further investigation, but the subscores very frequently offered are hardly valid and meaningful. In our opinion, the teacher will probably be better served by some of the diagnostic techniques mentioned earlier, as the sentence completion, the ambiguous school-related pictures, the rating scales, the sociometric testing, and children's stories.

In our discussion in *Investigating the Issues of Reading Disabilities,* we suggested that the pupil self-concept is modified by such factors as his family, his search for sex identity, his peer relations, his race, and his relationship with his teachers. Each of these areas should be probed in the total attempt to understand the child's feelings and attitudes. This implies visits to the child's home at times when both parents are present and agreeable to the interview. Among the questions the teacher will need to answer as a result of these interviews are these:

What are the attitudes of the parents toward the child and his reading difficulty?

What are their aspirations for him, if any?

How do they see him in comparison to the siblings?

What problems do they have with him, as in behavior, attitudes?

> What are their own reading habits, use of the library, and provisions for his recreational reading?
>
> How does he act toward his siblings?

Other facets to be explored will, of course, be suggested by the nature of individual cases, for this is just a beginning of the teacher-parent relationship. Other information regarding the family relations and the child's place in the family constellation will be available in the child's structured stories and, as in other areas to be explored, will be added to the overall impressions of the child.

The questionnaire (given in chapter 13, on organization of remedial work) that is sent to the parents before they come to the school, and then discussed with them, is another important source of information.

The child's search for sexual identity and for an adult model for his behavior and aspirations may also be explored with the family in terms of his relations to each parent, of his activities with either parent, and in accounts of family or parent-child activities. This information may be gathered from interviews with the child, with the family, and from his family drawings and creative stories.

Peer relations are readily observed in the classroom, in sociograms, in interviews with the child in terms of his leisure-time activities and friends, in such instruments as the Rosenzweig, and in his creative stories. The teacher is trying to discover answers to these questions:

> Does he have any close friends, or does he just think that he has?
>
> How does he see himself in comparison with the rest of the class, as a reader, as a leader or follower?
>
> How do the other children accept or reject him? How do they show these feelings?
>
> Are his friends of similar age, or is he trying to follow older children, or to compensate for lack of friends of his age by choosing a much younger child?
>
> Are his friends outside of school drawn from his classmates or elsewhere? What are their activities?

We have seen much evidence of the racial differences in self-concept and should explore this area when the pupils differ from the majority of their classmates (31). If the teacher is of a different race than the child, obtaining frank responses may be very difficult. If this is the case, perhaps indirect approaches through observation, the sociogram, and the child's drawings and stories may be the most feasible. Racial identity can be explored by talks with the child, sampling his knowledge and feelings about prominent figures of his race in the community and the country. There seems little point in trying to determine whether he feels discriminated against, for, if he is a minority member in a group of another race or another ethnic nature, the discrimination is real and he is undoubtedly aware of it. Our emphasis in this area should be on how the recognition of discrimination has affected his self-concept as manifested in his hopes and aspirations. Are these still positive? Does he have realistic estimates of his abilities and what he could accomplish with these? Who are his models, his ideal figures, and does he hope to emulate them?

TEACHER-PUPIL RELATIONSHIPS

The whole purpose of this exploration of pupil personality and self-concept is, of course, to gain information that will guide the teacher in her handling of the pupil. We must assume that the reading teacher is sincerely interested in basing her relations with the pupil on the information that she gathers about him as a person. We must assume that she will modify her instructional procedures in terms of the needs she sees, rather than her predilections for certain methods. And, in the same fashion, she will approach the child in the ways her diagnosis of his personality and self-concept indicates he will respond to most positively.

The research on teacher-pupil interaction tells us a number of significant facts.

Pupils differ in their need for, and profit from, teacher direction. Some who see the outcomes as the result of their own efforts gain more when self-directing; that is, selecting materials, checking and scoring, and returning materials (14). Others who are more anxious, and not as well organized, need a program in which direction of the teacher is obvious. Similarly those who are dependent need structuring and detailed planning by the teacher (26).

Some who are aggressive or hostile to the adult need the stability of limits, consistently applied; for example, time for work versus that for play; time of arrival and departure; returning or filing materials; restricting child's selection to one of the given choices, as in selecting a book or a game, and so forth. Structuring the remedial time, as "first we will , later we will . . . ," helps to set definite limits and to stabilize the relationships. We are not suggesting an authoritarian tone, but rather one in which the requirements are clearly stated and ever-consistent, but not punitive. Definite short-range goals, perhaps even day by day, should be set at first by the teacher; then gradually by the child as he begins to identify with the training and to meet it with effort to accomplish rather than resistance. The use of a behavior modification approach of systematic rewards for improvement in a specific type of behavior is very relevant in these more difficult cases. We shall clarify this technique in chapter 10, on various approaches to remediation. In these cases, if remedial work is undertaken, the routine and choice of materials should be explained impersonally, as though his compliance were expected. Any suggestion by the child should be evaluated frankly with him and adopted, if feasible. Learning materials must appeal to their interest levels, not appear obviously immature or easy, and present some challenge to their abilities (30).

Morrison (15) has pointed out some of the differences in teacher-pupil interaction as teachers move from a stereotyped basal or programmed approach toward greater individualization. As the variety of materials and activities increases, so do closer teacher-pupil planning, pupil demonstration of self-directing efforts, more positive verbal and physical behavior by pupils and between pupils, more positive teacher behavior, and less need for punitive behavior.

As we implied above, some pupils hampered by anxiety, negativism, or resistance to adult suggestion are not initially ready for the ideal program suggested by Morrison. Pupil-teacher planning may have to be delayed until a carefully defined, stabilizing climate has been established with much teacher direction and clarification of short-range goals. Later, as the pupil's resistance or emotional feelings about reading diminish, new activities and materials may be introduced; then pupil responsibility for use of these, as well as for their selection, should be promoted.

Eventually we hope to reach the type of program that has the obvious advantages outlined by Morrison. Ideally speaking, we should gradually move toward the atmosphere that will permit us to greet the pupil with such remarks as, "What do you want to work with today that will help you read better?" In our opinion, permanent improvement can be achieved only when this level of self-insight and self-direction is achieved.

It might be pertinent to note here the apparent goals and techniques that remedial teachers claim. Olive C. Sampson (21) queried 675 such teachers regarding the incentives that they employed. The pupils' experience of success was considered of primary importance, while praise and encouragement was of secondary significance. Of lesser importance, in these teachers' minds, were the relationship and atmosphere; the child's interests, rewards and privileges; competitive activities; and the pupils' ambitions. The concept that remediation is teacher-dominated, teacher-planned, and teacher-directed seems to permeate these responses, unfortunately, in our opinion. There is the implicit impression that remedial reading is something that the teacher does to pupils, rather than that improvement is something coming from within the child in utilizing his capabilities to their fullest to fulfill his own needs.

It is our impression that the field of remediation is laden with this concept of "teacher treating pupils." Our standards in selecting pupils according to the similarity of their achievement to some static standard as mental age or grade level; our overconcern with finding ever-new materials of instruction that will effect "cures"; our overemphasis upon identifying the specific picayune defect that is entirely responsible for his failure and then expecting the whole problem to disappear after the apparently appropriate training; and, finally, our methods of release from remediation based on the equivalence of his posttraining performance to our hypothetical standards for his mental age or grade level. Where is the recognition in all this of the fact that we are dealing with a personality with certain backgrounds and self-identifications, one who is fundamentally different from each other case in goals, needs for identity, and self-realization?

We, too, have had to learn this new frame of reference the hard way, if we may be permitted a personal reference. After several months of intensive work with an adult illiterate mother of one of our clinic cases, we had helped her to progress in reading and writing to about fourth-grade level, then released her for the between-semester break. When the clinic reopened, we made several attempts to contact her by telephone and to resume her tutoring schedule. She politely declined with the explanation, when pressed, "I'm happy. I can read the labels on cans now and go shopping. I can read my daughter-in-law's letters and thus learn about my son's activities. I can now read the hymnbook in church and enjoy the singing. What do I want with more training?" With her life enriched by these new capabilities, what indeed did she need from the clinic? A higher level of performance commensurate with her adult status and basic mental ability?

BUILDING SELF-CONCEPT

It is apparent that our concept of the true goal of remediation is the creation of a positive self-concept as a reader for the individual. In keeping with this view, we shall emphasize ways and means that the reading teacher can employ to approach this goal.*

---

*See also George D. Spache, *Good Reading for the Disadvantaged Reader* (Champaign, Ill.: Garrard Publishing, 1974).

In Verbal Behavior

The teacher's verbal relationships with the pupil should be characterized by a positive tone to convey these impressions: she believes that he is capable of improving his reading; she respects his feelings, both positive and negative, and even helps him express these on a verbal level and thus diminish or increase their intensity; she shows respect and acceptance of his judgments and of him as a person. She praises his successes and helps him tolerate, but plan to overcome, his weaknesses. As one writer has entitled his series of suggestions for promoting more positive self-concepts, "The Content Is the Medium: The Confidence Is the Message."

In Activities

The remedial teacher fosters the child's belief in his own worth by selecting challenging but possible tasks; by helping the pupil maintain records of his own progress; by providing opportunities for self-expression and verbalization of feelings, as in puppetry (4) and spontaneous dramatization of and discussion of the motives and feelings of characters in his stories or those in the books used (5, 6); by using role-playing in imitation of book characters or in spontaneous enactment of common interactions of pupils, teachers, parents, and so on (7, 22, 25); by perhaps using the picture stimuli organized by Black (2), Schaftel (23), and others; by selecting the content or nature of the instructional or reading materials in terms of his interests rather than their emphasis upon this or that particular skill. Finally, she arranges for constant application of his reading in related activities that give opportunity for leadership and demonstration of competence, as in a student newspaper circulated throughout the school, reading to younger children, tutoring younger poor readers, working with a weaker pupil in a pupil team and the like.

In Physical Relations

In all types of relations with others, we are implementing our verbal messages by body signals and signs as part of the message. We reinforce our speech with gestures, with physical contact with the listener, with facial expressions, and with bodily movements (1, 16). We can also negate our verbal expressions by contradictory physical behavior or by delivering them with a lack of facial confirmation. We are saying that verbal praise must be accompanied by physical action as a smile, a pat, a hug, or all of these. Pupil failure should be greeted with impersonal acknowledgment but followed immediately with such action as sitting down with the child to join in correction and thus demonstrating beyond doubt our concern and identification with the pupil. If we do not demonstrate enthusiasm *both verbally* and *physically* for the pupil's efforts, how can we expect him to be concerned with their outcomes? In pupil-teacher interaction, we must constantly be aware that remediation is not something we are doing to or for the pupil but something we are trying to do *with him* for his own self-realization.

If teachers feel the need for guidance and direction in building self-concepts, these programs will be pertinent.

About You. Chicago: Science Research Associates. A program for grades nine to twelve.

Clayton, Thompson, *What It Takes.* Belmont, Cal.: Fearon, 1972. Addressed to high school students to help improve their self-concepts, at primary reading level.

Developing Understanding of Self and Others. Circle Pines, Minn.: American Guidance Services. Program for elementary pupils.

Dimensions of Personality. Dayton: Pflaum-Standard. A text-workbook addressed to secondary pupils.

Dinkmeyer, Don, *Developing Understanding of Self and Others.* Circle Pines, Minn.: American Guidance Services. A kindergarten-primary kit for developing self and other concepts. Involves role-playing, puppetry, group discussions, pictures, and the like.

Discovering Yourself. Chicago: Science Research Associates. A program for grades seven to nine.

Emotions Identification Program. Chicago: Children's Press, 1974. Simple stories emphasizing the reader's emotions in such situations as: a new baby, friends can help; big sister, little brother; being alone, being together. Each of these books is accompanied by a parallel cassette. For primary children.

Experiential Development Program. Chicago: Benefic. Pictures and activities to stimulate the child's self-concept and concepts of his role in family, peer, and community relationships. For preschool and primary grades.

Feelings Self-Identification Program. Chicago: Children's Press, 1974. Relations between brothers and sisters, with friends, with grown-ups and children, and with parents and children are presented in separate story books. Questions appended to each story emphasize the readers' feelings. For primary pupils.

Focus on Self-Development. Chicago: Science Research Associates. Programs are offered for kindergarten to second, second to fourth, and fourth to sixth. As in the other programs by this publisher, pictures and activities, group discussions, and teacher's guide are the basic content.

Grimm, Gary D., *It's Me—You'll See.* New York: D.O.K. Publishers, 1973. Half of the book is devoted to ideas for promoting self-concept. The other half is a set of ditto masters to permit implementing these ideas.

Here I Am. Chicago: Science Research Associates. Pupil activity books in self-concept building for kindergarten to second, second to fourth, and fourth to sixth grades.

Thoburn, Tina, and Hedges, Betty Lou, *My Story About Me.* New York: Western, 1970. Through his own drawings, the child is led to a deepening of his self-concept.

Audio-Visual Resources

Children of the Inner City. Chicago: Society for Visual Education. Six strips and parallel records with teacher's guide. Each stresses the difficulties of a different ethnic group in adjusting to inner-city life.

Guidance Associates. Pleasantville, N.Y.: Guidance Associates. Five strips and records for exploring self-concepts and human relationships.

Just Like You. Malibu, Cal.: Bosutow Productions. A six-minute 16 mm film on similarities among racial and ethnic groups.

Kindle. Englewood Cliffs, N.J.: Scholastic Book Services. Units on "Who Am I?" and "How Do I Learn?", each of five strips, records and manual, for grades four to eight.

Personal Feelings About Yourself. Troy, Mich.: Educational Corp. of America. Seven strips with records on self-evaluation. Other similar units on family relationships and responsibilities to self and others. For junior-senior high school pupils.

Teacher's Guides

Gateway English: Identification and Image Stories, by John J. Marcatante. New York: Hunter College. A guide to writing stories for and about pupils.

Magic Circle. San Diego: Human Development Training Institute. Guidelines for a program in development of self-awareness.

Self-Enhancing Education, by Norina Randolph and William Howe. Palo Alto: Stanford Publishers.

A Teaching Program in Human Behavior and Mental Health, by Ralph Ojemann. Cleveland: Educational Research Council of America.

In our discussion of tests and other instruments in this area of personality and self-concept, we have not attempted to supply an all-inclusive list. Actually we have mentioned only a few of the available devices, stressing those that have been reported as pertinent in a number of published studies. There are a great many formal and informal measures of personality and self-concept about which little has been published. Some of these are listed in *Improving Educational Assessment: An Inventory of Measures of Affective Behavior,* Walcott H. Beatty, editor, Washington, D.C.: Association for Supervision and Curriculum Development, 1969. Those reading teachers who enjoy trying new instruments, in the search for devices that may prove personally useful, may find this inventory helpful.

LEARNING PROJECT

1. Administer and interpret the sentence completion test given in the Appendix. Do this with several pupils in order to contrast the insights you obtain regarding each pupil. Comparing the similarities and differences among the answers, relate your deductions to your observations of their behavior and apparent attitudes and

feelings. Does this approach seem to confirm some of your observations or knowledge about these pupils; does it also suggest areas to be explored that you had not thought of previously?

2. Collect samples of the various self-concept tests or the rating scales; compare and evaluate them in terms of your situation. Analyze the data given by the author with the relevant questions of the Check List for Evaluating Tests offered in the accompanying background materials textbook, *Investigating the Issues of Reading Disabilities*.

3. Follow the sociometric approach to studying peer relationships among a class of pupils. Collect the pupils' choices and, representing each pupil by a labeled circle, construct a chart of the interpupil relations. How does the chart aid you in identifying leaders, followers, isolates, small groups with good interrelations, and the like?

REFERENCES

1. Birdwhistell, Ray L., *Kinesis and Context.* New York: Basic Books, 1970.
2. Black, Millard J., et al., *Visual Experiences for Creative Growth.* Columbus: Charles E. Merrill, 1967.
3. Boning, Thomas, and Boning, Richard, "I'd Rather Read Than . . ," *Reading Teacher,* 10 (April 1957), 196–99.
4. Carlson, Ruth K., "Raising Self-Concepts of Disadvantaged Children Through Puppetry," *Elementary English,* 47 (March 1970) 349–55.
5. Carlton, Lessie, and Moore, Robert H., "The Results of Self-Directive Dramatization on Reading Achievement and Self-Concept of Culturally Disadvantaged Children," *Reading Teacher,* 20 (November 1966), 125–30.
6. Carlton, Lessie, and Moore, Robert H., *Reading, Self-Directive Dramatization and Self-Concept.* Columbus: Charles E. Merrill, 1968.
7. Chester, Mark, and Fox, Robert, *Role-Playing Methods in the Classroom.* Chicago: Science Research Associates, 1966.
8. Dudek, S.Z., and Lester, E.P., "The Good Child Facade in Chronic Underachievers," *American Journal of Orthopsychiatry,* 38 (1968), 153–59.
9. Fuller, Gerald B., Preuss, Michele, and Hawkins, William F., "The Validity of the Human Figure Drawings with Disturbed and Normal Children," *Journal of School Psychology,* 8 (1970), 54–56.
10. Gronlund, Norman E., *Sociometry in the Classroom.* New York: Harper and Row, 1959.
11. Hake, James M., "Covert Motivations of Good and Poor Readers," *Reading Teacher,* 22 (May 1969), 731–38.
12. Holliday, Kathleen M., "Values of Combined Remedial Reading Techniques and Certain Types of Psychotherapy for Emotionally Disturbed and Normal Pupils," Master's thesis, University of Florida, 1968.
13. Mann, Richard D., "A Review of the Relationships Between Personality and Performance in Small Groups," *Psychological Bulletin,* 56 (July 1959), 241–70.

14. Mathis, William R., "Personality Differences and Learning Styles in Reading," in *Reading: Process and Pedagogy,* 19th Yearbook National Reading Conference, 1971, 221–25.
15. Morrison, Virginia B., "Teacher-Pupil Interaction in Three Types of Elementary Classroom Reading Situations," *Reading Teacher,* 22 (December 1968), 271–75.
16. "Let Your Body Do the Talking," *Reading Newsreport,* 6 (1972), 44–45.
17. Northway, Mary L., and Weld, Lindsay, *Sociometric Testing.* Toronto: University of Toronto Press, 1957.
18. Rabin, A.I., *Projective Techniques in Personality Assessment.* New York: Springer Publishing, 1971.
19. Rosenzweig, Saul, *The Rosenzweig Picture Frustration Study.* St. Louis: Washington University, the Author, 1960.
20. Rutherford, William L., "From Diagnosis to Treatment of Reading Disabilities," *Academic Therapy,* 8 (Fall 1972), 51–55.
21. Sampson, Olive C., "A Study of Incentives in Remedial Reading," *Reading,* 3 (March 1969), 6–10.
22. Schaftel, Fannie R., *Role-Playing for Social Values.* Englewood Cliffs, N.J.: Prentice-Hall, 1967.
23. Schaftel, Fannie, and George, *Words and Action: Role Playing.* New York: Holt, 1967.
24. Shaw, Marvin E., and Shaw, Lilly May, "Some Effects of Sociometric Grouping upon Learning in a Second Grade Classroom," *Journal of Social Psychology,* 57 (August 1962), 453–58.
25. Simmons, John, "Role Playing as a Method of Teaching Psychology in the Elementary School," *Journal of School Psychology,* 4, (Autumn 1965), 13–15.
26. Smith, Donald E.P., et al., "Reading Improvement as a Function of Student Personality and Teaching Method," *Journal of Educational Psychology,* 47 (January 1956), 47–59.
27. Spache, George D., *An Incomplete Sentence Test for Industrial Use.* Gainesville: Reading Laboratory and Clinic, University of Florida, 1949.
28. Spache, George D., "Differential Scoring of the Rosenzweig Picture-Frustration Study," *Journal of Clinical Psychology,* 6 (October 1950), 406–8.
29. Spache, George D., "Personality Characteristics of Retarded Readers as Measured by the Picture-Frustration Study," *Educational and Psychological Measurement,* 15 (1954), 186–91.
30. Spache, George D., "Appraising the Personality of Remedial Pupils," in *Education in a Free World.* Washington, D.C.: American Council on Education, 1955, 122–32.
31. Spache, George D., *Good Reading for the Disadvantaged Reader.* Champaign, Ill.: Garrard Publishing, 1974.
32. *Washington University Sentence Completion Test.* San Francisco: Jossey-Bass, 1970.

part three

DIAGNOSIS OF READING SKILLS

6 Analyzing Oral Reading

Since the early days of diagnosis and remediation in reading in the 1930's, the analysis of oral reading has been a standard procedure. Oral reading errors formed the basis for most remedial efforts in phonics, word recognition, vocabulary and even comprehension. Only recently have some raised questions about the detailistic counting of letter-sound and word errors as meaningful for the understanding of a pupil's reading behaviors. Whether oral reading is really a clue to what happens in silent reading or to the degree of the reader's comprehension is now also being challenged. And whether the tabulation of letter-sound errors is truly indicative of the reader's efforts to deal with reading matter is another matter being debated.

To give the picture of the development of these trends in analyzing oral reading, we have reviewed the error types emphasized by most diagnosticians and their probable meanings for understanding the reader's development. The newer systems of error classification that emphasize the graphic similarity of the printed word and the miscue and that stress the grammatical, syntactic and semantic nature of the miscues are contrasted with the earlier systems. These new systems are critiqued and evaluated in terms of their apparent usefulness in guiding remedial training. The conditions inherent in the reading selections, the reading, the mode of instruction, and their influence upon oral reading errors are examined in detail. Finally, a system of classification of oral reading miscues which attempts to combine the diagnostic values of the old and the new approaches is proposed.

In reviewing this brief historical survey of systems of oral reading analysis, try to answer these questions:

1. Do you see any way in which the question of the validity of an oral reading test in predicting silent reading behaviors can be resolved?
2. What was the apparent concept of the process of learning to read among early diagnosticians?
3. Each specific error type in oral reading is apparently defined differently by

different authors. How would you attempt to reconcile these variances and achieve workable definitions?

4. What are some of the concepts of the reading process and the reasons for oral reading miscues that recent writers are emphasizing?

MOST USERS OF ORAL READING TESTS, whether informal or standardized, seem to have certain goals in mind. By observing oral reading habits and errors, both teachers and clinicians believe that they are analyzing the child's typical behaviors in both silent and oral reading. Thus, by the testing of oral reading, plans can presumably be made regarding the level of reading materials that should be used in instructing the child, as well as the retraining steps that should be undertaken to repair the pupil's weaknesses in such areas as sight vocabulary, word recognition skills, and word analysis skills.

If the reading program was exclusively practice in oral reading, there could be little objection to frequent use of oral reading tests to guide the teacher's or clinician's efforts. But the program includes a proportion of silent reading that markedly increases as the pupil progresses in school. Therefore, those who use oral reading tests to diagnose pupil needs must be assuming that silent and oral reading are closely parallel and that the child uses his various reading skills in exactly the same manner in either type of reading. We shall examine the evidence regarding this questionable assumption later.

In contrast to those who use oral reading to discover errors and skill deficiencies, another group of experts is suggesting that the testing should be used largely to observe the gradual development of word recognition and word analysis skills among normal or good readers. In this interpretation of the purpose of testing oral reading, both successes and errors are studied to reveal the ways in which children learn to read. These developmental-minded researchers do not deny the possibility of planning classroom or remedial teaching based on such testing; but they are questioning the emphasis upon errors rather than upon successes as the meaningful indications of an oral test. They believe that it is more significant to attempt to assess the child's efforts at maintaining sense, or his reaction to the context of the sentence, than to analyze in terms of letter or letter-sound mismatches. They feel that teachers and clinicians should be trying to discover what the child can do and is doing in the reading process, not only what kind of mistakes he makes.

Tabulating errors as a basis for retraining also makes the assumptions that correction of a deficit is the most effective treatment for insuring progress;

and that types of errors reflect specific word recognition or word analysis skills, which all children need in order to read. Both these assumptions must be examined.

ORAL VERSUS SILENT READING

A number of studies have explored the relationship between oral and silent reading abilities. Gilmore's data, for example, show a rapid decrease in the correlations between oral error rate and silent reading comprehension from .918 in the second grade to .631 and .693 in third to six, and so on, to .572 and .561 in seventh and eighth grades (18). Fields (16) and Wells (47) extended this type of research to the college freshman level. They agreed that oral reading errors were not very useful at that level in understanding reading difficulties. In fact, Fields reports a negative correlation between oral and silent comprehension, particularly among poor freshman readers.

While a measure of comprehension should be given as an integral part of an oral reading test to differentiate fluent word-callers from successful readers, many authorities agree that oral reading, unlike silent, is not conducive to comprehension. Oral reading is so demanding per se that a reader has little or no opportunity to process, or react to, the ideas presented. The mechanical and vocal demands of oral reading give almost no time for any depth of thinking as in making judgments, in interpreting interrelationships of ideas, or in reading critically. As a result, in testing comprehension during oral reading only the simplest questions of recall are possible.

Any reader's own study practices—perhaps since the intermediate grades—reflect an implicit recognition that only silent reading produces any depth of comprehension. It becomes the almost universal practice to study by silent reading. Oral reading remains useful for study purposes in memorizing materials such as formulas, poetry, mnemonic devices, and the like but is hardly used in textbook study. Mechanically, too, silent and oral reading differ in that silent requires fewer fixations, shorter pauses, and fewer regressions; for these and for other reasons, it begins to move at a much faster rate than does oral, beginning at about third-grade reading level.

However, there are those who continue to argue that oral reading does reveal silent reading behavior, like Swanson (43). Because his college freshmen tended to make a similar number of errors in oral reading and in reading short phrases tachistoscopically, Swanson believed that he had demonstrated a similarity between oral and silent reading. If these two methods of presentation of reading matter—oral and tachistoscopic reading—were similar processes, why, then, was Swanson unable to show any high correlation between any single type of error in the two situations? Swanson's further correlations of total oral reading errors with silent and oral comprehension were positive but low, thus supporting but not proving his argument. Comprehension of short phrases presented tachistoscopically may or may not reflect the depth of comprehension in silent reading. Nor was Swanson able to show a strong correlation between oral reading errors and comprehension.

There can be little argument regarding the parallelism between silent and oral reading for beginning readers. As Gilmore's and Swalm's and other data show, oral and silent reading are much the same process during the first two primary years (18, 42). In fact, for many children of these ages there is only one kind of reading, namely oral, for they vocalize audibly even when asked to read silently. But from this level onward, we believe that the two processes diverge. We do not read all the words when reading silently, as we must when reading orally. We guess more words, skip more, probably use context clues to a greater degree, receive more ideas, and do the task much faster in silent than in oral. In our opinion, although we intend to continue to use oral reading tests, it remains to be proven that these reveal what the reader does when reading silently above primary grades.

Accuracy of oral reading does not, in our belief, reveal either silent or oral comprehension of the reader at any school level. Even at the college freshman level we still see students who can read beautifully orally at sight, with utterly no comprehension. And fluent word-callers like these are common at earlier ages. Similarly, as Fields (16) and others have shown, poor oral readers of college age may often demonstrate good silent but poor oral comprehension.

If, as we argue, silent and oral reading are not closely similar processes except at very primary levels, what is the justification for using an oral reading test, generalizing its implications to silent reading? What can we learn from an oral reading test that is relevant to the diagnosis of reading difficulties? This leads us, of course, to the questions of what we should try to observe during oral reading, what the meanings of the observations or records are, and how they may be translated into profitable instruction.

ERROR TYPES

As soon as we approach the question of what should be recorded by the examiner during an oral reading test, we discover that there is little agreement in the definitions of errors, or even what an error in oral reading is. The kinds of errors that are tabulated vary from one study to the next and from one standardized oral reading test to another. Seemingly, the categorizations used reflect simply the examiner's a priori concept of what is going on in the oral reading act and whether he wishes to find deficiencies to be corrected or to discover how the child tries to make sense from the context.

To illustrate, in 1932 Marion Monroe (33) used the following system:

MONROE DIAGNOSTIC READING EXAMINATION
ORAL READING ERRORS

Faulty vowel	Substitution of words
Faulty consonants	Repetition of words
Reversals	Addition of words
Addition of sounds	Omission of words
Omission of sounds	Words aided

Monroe's concern with letter sounds is apparent in her system of classification, an emphasis not generally followed, at least in such great detail, by later investigators. In contrast, the errors tabulated by those constructing or using standardized oral reading tests since Monroe's effort have included the following:

1. Omission—of a word, part of a word or group of words (40). Same for Durrell (12), Gates-McKillop (17), Smith and Bradtmueller (39). Gray and Robinson (23), and Silvaroli (38) consider only a whole word or words. Gilmore calls omission of a letter a mispronunciation (18).
2. Addition—of a word or part of a word (40). Same for Durrell (12), Gates-McKillop (17), Smith and Bradtmueller (39). Gilmore (18) classifies insertions of a letter as a mispronunciation and scores only insertion of a whole word or words as an addition. Gray and Robinson (23) concur in this idea. Silvaroli (38) apparently counts only insertions of a whole word.
3. Substitutions or mispronunciations—in or of any word, according to Spache (40), who counts the error on a word only once, even if repeated by the child. This interpretation was chosen to prevent artificial inflation of the error count when a child repeatedly mispronounces the same word, or makes several erroneous attempts at pronunciation. Most other oral tests count every such mispronunciation or substitution, no matter how often repeated, as another error, as in Durrell (12), Gates-McKillop (17), Gilmore (18), Gray (23), Smith and Bradtmueller (39), and Silvaroli (38). Gates-McKillop (17) include use of a contraction or misplaced accent as an error of this type. Gilmore (18) distinguishes between substituting a real or sensible word for one

in the text, while wrong accent, wrong pronunciation of a vowel or consonant, or omission or addition of one or more letters are called mispronunciations.

Gray and Robinson differentiate between substitutions and mispronunciations, as follows:

a. Gross mispronunciation—little resemblance to the given word.
b. Partial mispronunciation
   (1) part of word is given pupil by tester
   (2) wrong sound or sounds of letters
   (3) omission of one or more letter or letters
   (4) insertion of a letter or letters
   (5) wrong syllabication
   (6) wrong accent
   (7) reversal or inversion within a word
c. Substitution—one or several meaningful words used in place of the given text.

Hardin and Ames (24) have criticized this detailed analysis suggested by Gray and Robinson as unnecessarily refined. They would lump all these types together under the rubric of substitution. Rose-Marie Weber (45) agrees with this criticism, also pointing out that the Gray-Robinson categories would consider almost every nonstandard English expression an error.

4. Repetitions—count only when two or more words are repeated. Both Spache (40) and Gates-McKillop (17) do not count single word repetitions as an error, since they may be due to stammering, tension, or even the child's attempt to figure out the word repeated or one near it. In contrast, Gilmore (18) counts every repetition of a word, part of a word, or group of words as an error, while Gray and Robinson (23) Silvaroli (38), and Smith and Bradtmueller (39) count every repetition of one or more words.
5. Words aided—words told to the child after a five-second wait, according to Spache (40), Gates-McKillop (17), Gilmore (18), and Gray and Robinson (23). Some do not indicate how long the tester should wait before assisting the child, as in Durrell (12), Silvaroli (38), and Smith and Bradtmueller (39). Without such instructions, the error count could be greatly inflated by an inexperienced or overanxious examiner, who is too quick to prompt the pupil.
6. Reversals or transpositions—of a word or part of a word or in word order, according to Spache (40). Such reversals are not counted as such by Gates-McKillop, Gilmore, Gray and Robinson, or Silvaroli. They would probably be considered some type of substitution or mispronunciation by these authors. However, Gray and Robinson do recognize inversion of word order, as Smith and Bradtmueller do. Gates-McKillop offer norms for partial and full reversals, even though the examiner is not instructed to record them during the test.
7. Self-corrections—Interestingly enough, the attitude of oral reading test makers to self-corrections by the pupil varies greatly. Durrell (12), Gates

and McKillop (17), Smith and Bradtmueller (39), and Silvaroli (38) ignore the possibility of self-correction. Gray and Robinson (23) and Spache (40) instruct the examiner to score the self-correction of an error as no error, while Gilmore (18) scores all attempts at self-correction as errors of substitution or mispronunciation.

In addition to these common types of oral reading errors—common in that test makers seem to believe that they should be tabulated—a number of other oral reading behaviors should be noted, according to some authors. For example, Durrell (12) and Smith and Bradtmueller (39) ask the examiner to mark the child's phrasing with vertical lines. Durrell, Gates-McKillop, Gilmore, and Smith and Bradtmueller also have the examiner mark any commas or periods apparently ignored by the child. Schummers (37), Durrell (12), and Smith and Bradtmueller (39) also record "hesitations," which Gilmore defines as a "pause of at least two seconds." Apparently pupils are not supposed to stop to breathe during oral reading, no matter how tense they feel, or to pause to figure out a word, according to these authors.*

Duffy and Durrell (11) and Daw (8) studied a number of other oral reading behaviors, which presumably the examiner would note during the oral testing. Among these are ignoring punctuation, poor phrasing, monotone, fumbling and repeating frequently, word-by-word reading, pitch too high or too low, volume too loud or too soft, using finger, tension during reading, and losing one's place. Several of the authors of oral reading tests have incorporated these and similar observations in check lists supplied with their tests, as in the case of Durrell, Gray and Robinson, and Spache.

OTHER SYSTEMS OF CLASSIFICATION

Other approaches to recording oral errors were used by Biemiller (3), who analyzed the mistakes of forty-eight first graders in terms of nonresponse-stopping at or before a word; graphic similarity (first letter of response matched first letter of given word); and error influenced by the context. In a much larger-scale study, Marie Clay (6, 7) tabulated over 10,000 errors of 100 first graders in Wellington over an entire year. Excluding nouns, she noted such errors as substitution of a word of the same or different morpheme class,

---

*A dissertation by Eleanor Ladd, "A Comparison of Two Types of Training with Reference to Developing Skill in Diagnostic Oral Reading Testing," Florida State University, 1961, indicates that after thirty hours of training, teachers still missed 100 percent of the hesitations.

and the graphic similarity of the error and the correct word. Weber (46) emphasized graphic similarity by noting whether the response resembled the given word in the first letter, first two letters, last letter or last two letters, or combinations of these. She also noted where in the word or where in the sentence the error occurred, and whether it was grammatically correct according to the context of the sentence. In addition, Weber noted the difference in proportions of errors for function words (prepositions, conjunctions, and so on) as contrasted with verbs; the similarity between the error and given word in form class, that is, verb for verb, and other characteristic trends in errors we shall note later.

It is apparent that Weber's earlier critical review of the study of oral reading errors (45) led her away from the common types of error classification. We can almost detect a trend toward a new emphasis upon the graphic similarities between stimulus and response words in oral reading in these studies of Biemiller, Clay, and Weber. It is not yet clear just where this stress upon graphic similarity, as opposed to letter sound or whole word analysis, is leading the diagnostician who is trying to discover what to do for a poor oral reader. Perhaps this may be clarified when we contrast opinions as to the meanings of various oral reading errors. In any event, there is a shift here from a phonic-oriented interpretation of oral reading errors toward a linguistic interpretation. The linguist's concern is determining what the child is doing with the grammar of the sentence as well as its semantics—its meaning—not his reactions to letters or their sounds only.

Kenneth S. Goodman, Yetta Goodman, and their coworkers have played a prominent role in this linguistic analysis of oral miscues. They call reading a psycholinguistic guessing game in which errors (they prefer to call them miscues) are largely grammatical substitutions based on the syntactic and semantic information from the context, as well as the redundancy of the language (21). Their study of children's behavior while reading orally has strengthened these beliefs (22) and resulted in the formulation of a very different approach to analyzing children's oral reading responses.

In their research, the Goodman group employed a sophisticated taxonomy of cues and miscues in reading.* For our purposes of contrasting systems of studying and interpreting oral reading responses, we are here simplifying the definitions of the categories of miscues tabulated by Goodman. For fuller understanding of this approach, the taxonomy should be consulted in its original presentation.

---

*Kenneth S. Goodman, "Analysis of Oral Reading Miscues: Applied Psycholinguistics," *Reading Research Quarterly*, 5 (Fall 1969), 9–30.

A Taxonomy of Cues and Miscues in Reading (after Goodman)

1. Words in the miscue—The exact response of the reader is copied by the examiner whether it includes a part of a word, a single word, several words or a sentence. In a series of attempts, the last effort of the reader is recorded.

2. Correction—The proportions of successful and unsuccessful corrections are noted, and the circumstances under which corrections occur.

3. Repeated miscues—When the same miscue occurs repeatedly, only the first is counted in the analysis.

4. Word-phrase identification—Note is taken of the production of a correct response after several miscues on the same word or phrase identification.

5. Observed response in periphery—Goodman believes that a miscue may be due to visual cues in the periphery; he draws an oval around the line on which a miscue occurs, as well as on the line above and below. Another oval is drawn around the two lines above and below the line containing the miscue in the belief that all this area is clearly visible and readable, and that words in this periphery may be influencing the miscue.

6. Habitual association—Two types of habitual associations among words are identified: substitution association, as *pail* for *bucket;* and sequential association, as *happy birthday* for *happy occasion.*

7. Dialect—Although tabulated, dialect miscues are not considered as errors.

8. Graphic proximity—A nine-step scale of graphic similarity between the printed word and the reader's oral response is used. This scale ranges from no similarity through graphic similarities at the beginning, middle, or end, to homographs or words visually identical.

9. Phonemic proximity—A nine-step scale of phonemic similarity ranges from none through initial, medial, and final phonemes, and combinations of these to homophones.

10. Grammatical function—Each miscue is coded according to its grammatical function in the sentence.

11. Function word—Oral responses are coded according to the type of function word involved, as noun or verb marker, verb particle, question, clause or phrase marker, and so on:

12. Grammatical function—The grammatical function of the printed word is compared with that of the oral response.

13. Function word—The printed function words are classified as in 11 above.

The level of the miscue is recorded as follows, noting whether its nature is an omission, insertion, substitution, or reversal.

14. Submorphemic level—as *tacks* for *tracks, tranks* for *tanks, bat* for *bit.*

15. Bound morpheme level—miscues involving inflectional, derivational, and combined form morphemes, as *television* for *televised, unusual* for *usual.*

16. Free morpheme level—as *looked* for *jumped, the young boy ran* for *the boy ran.*

17. Word level—as *the toy was* for *the train was, the little baby cried* for *the baby cried.*

18. Phrase level—The miscue changes the phrase syntactically, as *pick up the sticks* for *pick the sticks up,* or *plants that grew underwater snails* for *plants that grew underwater, snails. . . .*

19. Clause level—The miscue causes a change at the clause level, as *the book you gave me was exciting* for *the book which you gave me was exciting.*

20. Sentence level—The miscue involves such errors as reading a declarative sentence as a question, or reading through terminal punctuation.

21. Allologs—The miscue is the substitution of an alternate form of the printed word, as *can't* for *cannot, will not* for *won't;* and articulation difficulties, as *alunimum* for *aluminum.*

22. Bound or combined morphemes—The miscues coded as in 15 above are subclassified as inflectional suffixes, noninflected word forms, contractional suffixes, derivational suffixes, prefixes, parts of compounds, shifts in suffix types, and base form problems.

23. Syntactic proximity—An eight-step scale is used to code miscues according to the degree that the oral response diverges from the syntax of the printed word.

24. Semantic proximity—A nine-step scale is used to measure the similarity in meaning between the oral response and the printed word.

25. Transformations or grammatical restructuring—Miscues are coded according to whether a grammatical transformation is involved, as *it would be nice to play with one* for *it would be nice to play with a dinosaur.*

26. Intonational miscues—Intonational shifts within words, between words, within a sentence; a shift in terminal intonation, or the substitution of a conjunction for a terminal punctuation.

27. Syntactic acceptability—Syntactic acceptability is judged in terms of the dialect of the reader.

28. Semantic acceptability—Semantic acceptability is judged, without respect to grammar, at the sentence, sentence portion, and passage levels.

Obviously this lengthy and complex system of analyzing oral reading miscues was designed for research purposes in the hands of a linguist. Classroom teachers, school psychologists, and reading diagnosticians would not be apt to use this system, even if they had the necessary background in psycholinguistics. The time involved (which some estimate as about eighteen hours per child) and the difficulty in translating the categories of miscues into appropriate corrective instructional procedures would tend to limit the use of this system. Moreover, these are erroneous concepts of the limits of visual span in a fixation, as in item 5 in the taxonomy, to which some would react negatively.

To facilitate the Goodman concept of oral miscues, however, Yetta Goodman and Carolyn Burke have prepared a simpler version of the system which, presumably, enables others to approach the study of oral reading within the framework of this line of thinking.* Carolyn Burke has also offered detailed suggestions as to the manner in which use of this shorter miscue inventory may be approached.† Since this version is more realistically adapted for those who ordinarily attempt oral reading diagnosis, we shall describe it as we have other systems. For those instructors who wish to introduce this system to their students, the authors have provided a kit of training materials, which, indeed, will be essential for understanding its ramifications. In their materials, teachers are first introduced to an even further abbreviated form of the inventory termed a short form. As described by Carolyn Burke,‡ it is somewhat as follows:

Reading Miscue Inventory—Short Form

Words in Context

The first three questions are to be answered for each substitution, after recording the miscue and the printed word or words in parallel columns. (The author is using the term *substitution* in a very general sense, for it is quite apparent that all miscues would be analyzed in this fashion.)

1. Graphic similarity—How much do the two words look alike?
2. Sound similarity—How much do the two words sound alike?
3. Grammatical function—Is the grammatical function of the reader's oral response the same as that of the printed word? (To answer this question, read the sentence with the reader's miscue in it.)

Structure and Meaning

These questions are answered for each sentence containing miscues. If the sentences of the reading selection are numbered, these numbers can be recorded to enable the analyst to return later to make this evaluation.

4. Syntactic acceptability—Is the sentence containing the miscue syntactically or grammatically correct?
5. Semantic acceptability—Is the sentence containing the miscue semantically (meaning) acceptable?
6. Meaning change—Is there a change in meaning in the sentence as it is read by the child?

---

*Yetta Goodman and Carolyn Burke, *Reading Miscue Inventory* (New York: Macmillan, 1972).

†Carolyn Burke, "Preparing Elementary Teachers to Teach Reading" in *Miscue Analysis,* Kenneth S. Goodman, editor (Urbana: ERIC Clearing House on Reading and Communication Skills, 1973), pp. 15–29.

‡Ibid.

7. Correction and semantic acceptability—Do corrections by the reader of his miscues make the sentence semantically acceptable?

Since each miscue and each sentence involving a miscue is analyzed by this system, it is possible to determine the proportions of *yes* or *no* scorings for each of the seven categories of miscues. With this information, it seems possible to make judgments regarding the extent of the reader's dependence upon phonic strategies (as in questions 1 and 2), on grammatical accuracy (as in questions 3 and 4) or his emphasis upon semantic or meaningful reading (questions 5 and 6), as well as the degree of self-correction exercised by the reader, as in question 7. These various types of analysis are aided by profile or record sheets accompanying the Inventory.

Following the introduction to this Short Form, a slightly longer form is presented, involving nine questions that extend the analysis to include the influence of dialect and intonation upon miscues. The depth and accuracy of the reader's comprehension is sampled in using this approach by having the reader retell as much of the material as he can recall. His recall is to be aided by open-ended questions, such as "Can you tell me any more about this story?"; "What happened after . . . ?"; and other questions that use only the information or clues already supplied by the reader in his recounting of the material.

There are a number of questions to raise regarding the validity and reliability of this approach to studying children's oral reading responses. These will become apparent as we contrast the interpretations given to various oral reading errors, and as we review some of the basic facts known about oral reading. We shall also offer a group of cautions to be observed in testing oral reading that will also aid in the reader's evaluation of the Goodman approach.

Despite these questions about the Miscue Inventory system, it is apparent that the Goodman group has made a significant impact upon practices in analyzing oral reading. In a sense, they have brought together the observations of Weber, Clay, Barr, and others on the graphic and phonemic characteristics of oral reading responses. To these they have added a number of psycholinguistic insights in a system for analyzing oral responses that gives a dramatic new trend to this aspect of diagnosis. Probably no one attempting to offer an oral reading test in the future will be safe in following the previous pattern of exclusive emphasis upon letter sounds and whole word miscues in the device that he offers.

The analysis of oral errors seems to have moved dramatically away from Monroe's emphasis upon letter sounds toward a notation based largely on whole words, as in most current oral reading tests. From this viewpoint, it appears to have moved toward a two-way system of noting graphic similarities and the influence of context. Finally, the Goodman group has given the diagnosis of errors an almost complete emphasis upon the child's apparent dependence upon the syntactic and semantic constraints of the text. Before we can decide which of these diagnostic biases we should follow in analyzing oral miscues, it may be wise to attempt to integrate some of the facts revealed by the various studies. What are the probable meanings of the various kinds of errors? What do these researchers think that their kinds of analysis will tell the diagnostician about a pupil? What kinds of patterns of errors or trends in error tendencies have been revealed? What use are these patterns or trends in interpreting a pupil's needs for instruction?

THE SIGNIFICANCE OF ORAL ERRORS

The meaning of each type of oral reading error that might be tabulated is allied closely, of course, to the examiner's concept of the oral reading process and his convictions about effective corrective steps. If we think that children read by letter sounds, then, like Monroe, we would classify practically every mistake as a phonic error. If, on the other hand, we believe that children also react to word forms, then we would note the graphic similarities among errors and the given text. And, finally, if we think that children err only in the effort to make better sense of the context and that most of these momentary fumbles are spontaneously corrected, then we would be likely to tabulate only the child's failures to recognize the constraints of the context as errors, à la Goodman. To demonstrate this point, let us compare the interpretations given to error types by various authors.

Omissions Omissions of words are often attributed to carelessness, excessive speed, lack of attention, poor sight vocabulary, or poor comprehension, according to many authors. Spache and Spache have pointed out the possibility that omissions may reflect a tendency to use the speed of silent reading in the oral act (41). Omissions of endings are supposed to reflect poor knowledge of inflections reflecting plurals, tense, and so on. Only recently has it been recognized that such inflections may be lacking in the child's dialect and thus, perhaps, are not actually miscues in oral reading (1, 28, 48). Gilmore (18) believes that omissions are so few as to be negligible, while Ilg and Ames (26), Monroe (33), and Madden and Pratt (30) found that this type of error increased with age. On the other hand, Schale (36) reports that this type of error persisted through the second to ninth grades, at about the same proportion, when she used the Gray Oral system of error classification, which tabulated only the omissions of whole words. If omissions of parts of words are included in this tabulation, we may indeed expect them to increase as speed of oral reading grows.

Additions Additions are often attributed to lack of comprehension or to oral language development beyond the pupil's reading level (14). Madden and Pratt (30) report a small increase in this error extending from the third to ninth grade, while Monroe (33) did not detect such a trend in the first six grades. Spache and Spache (41) and Kerfoot (27) suggest that this error may often represent an attempt to elaborate or smooth out the text, in the case of intermediate or older pupils; or it may reflect superficial reading with overdependence upon context clues.

Substitutions Quoting Ekwall, this error is due to inadequate word recognition skills or carelessness, in his opinion. The comparative studies appear to agree that this type of error is greater than all other types, particularly when we include mispronunciations in this category (26, 30, 33, 36). According to Ilg and Ames (26), substitutions gradually shift from those reflecting the visual form of the stimulus word to meaning substitutions by the age of nine. It is probable that substitutions appear in a variety of forms—word form, word part, graphic or phonemic similarity—as well as on the basis of meaning.

Repetitions Repetitions are often attributed to poor word recognition or word analysis skills. However, Goodman (21) felt that his study showed that almost all repetitions were made in an effort to correct a miscue. Among primary children, frequent repetitions may reflect poor directional attack or lack of consistent left-to-right progression, as well as the pupil's attempt to stall while analyzing the word repeated or one near it (41). Madden and Pratt (30) record a small increase in repetitions from primary to junior high school levels, but this trend was not present in Monroe's data.

Words Aided The proportion of words that must be told the reader obviously decreases with development of reading skill, as Monroe's and Madden and Pratt's data show (33, 30). Basically the error reflects poor sight vocabulary or word analysis skills or, perhaps, dependence of the reader, while its absence implies, of course, the opposite.

Reversals Ekwall (14) attributes reversals to lack of right-to-left eye movement, mixed dominance, immaturity, improper instruction, or rapid reading. Monroe's data showed more reversals among poor readers but no relationship to hand-eye preference (33). Malmquist (31) also dismisses the mixed dominance explanation on the basis of his data. Nikas (34) found reversals common throughout the first grade for good and poor readers. In our opinion, they reflect the lack of left-right orientation characteristic of all beginning readers regardless of age; and, as Payne (35) and others have shown, they tend to disappear as reading skill matures.

Graphic Similarity

Substituting a word in oral reading that resembles the given word in the first, or first few, letters but not in meaning* (as *private* for *prairie*) is a common type of error, as a number of the studies cited have shown (3, 6, 7, 46). Since beginning readers have an eye-span of less than a whole word, on the average, and tend to fixate on the beginning and again at the end of the word, there may also be similarity between the stimulus and response in the last few letters, as in *drawn-brown* or *leak-book.*

Sometimes these errors of graphic similarity include a meaningful substitution, as *many* for *most,* or *didn't* for *did not,* or *blue* for *black.* Such an error indicates the pupil's reaction to the context, as well as to word form. In a sense, this is a more advanced or more mature response than that which lacks relevance in meaning.

Graphic similarity errors, then, do indicate a normal reaction to words and should be present if the child is not still blindly guessing at words or drawing substitutes at random from his auditory vocabulary. Graphic similarity plus meaning indicates a further progression toward true reading skill. Clay indicates that about 41 percent of the errors during the first grade were pure graphic similarity, while 79 percent involved both graphic similarity and meaning (6).

Burke and Goodman do not offer rationalizations for each type of miscue they would tabulate. But we shall try to indicate the probable significance of those types for which we can see some usefulness to the examiner who is using an oral test to plan corrective steps for a pupil.

Self-corrections

Ideally the higher the proportion of miscues spontaneously corrected, the greater the pupil's maturity and skill in reading. When meaning is not seriously disturbed, or when the child is so heavily dependent upon word analysis techniques that he is not greatly conscious of meaning, self-corrections decrease markedly, according to Goodman (20).

---

*It is assumed that the child uses the appropriate sounds for these letters.

Response Function Substitutions of words of similar function, as noun for noun, represent a more intelligent approach to reading. Weber (46) and Goodman (22) both found that most of the errors they observed were of this type. Only poor readers offer grammatically incorrect or impossible answers. Burke and Goodman tabulate the percentage of miscues involving each type of word, that is, nouns, verbs, adverbs, adjectives, and the like (4). To us it would seem more practical simply to record the percentage of responses in which word function was correct or incorrect.

Dialect Burke and Goodman note the percent of miscues due to the child's dialect. We shall discuss later typical dialectic errors and their possible interpretation.

Phonemic Noting the differences in the response from the given word in one or several phonemes is tantamount to the graphic similarity category, in most cases. In substituting in this fashion, the stimulus and response words resemble each other graphically and phonemically. Only when the child's knowledge of letter sounds is very poor will there be a phonemic miscue.

Syntax More mature readers tend to preserve the syntax of the sentences that they read aloud. They respond to tense, word function, word order, and other syntactic characteristics even in their miscues, according to Weber (46), Clay (6, 7), and Goodman (21). Only when the child is not achieving comprehension or his dialect interferes does he violate syntax.

Semantics The child who has the concept that reading makes sense or that it resembles normal language substitutes meaningfully by offering responses that are logical, not random or nonsense or merely visually similar.

Intonation Theoretically, intonation in oral reading is indicative of comprehension. But in actual practice many pupils of all ages are observed to supply acceptable intonation even when they are achieving little or no comprehension. Hence observation of intonation is often not very meaningful to the examiner.

OTHER FACTS ABOUT ORAL ERRORS

Influence of Method

A comparison of the oral reading errors of Scottish and American primary pupils by Elder (15) has offered some implications about the effect of reading method upon oral reading. The Scottish pupils began school at five, received much more phonics training, and after three years of schooling excelled American second-grade pupils, that is, pupils of the same age. The Scottish pupils achieved third-grade status on the Gray Oral, as did the third-grade American children who, of course, were a year older. Though the Scottish pupils were significantly higher in errors of mispronunciation, omissions, and repetitions than second-grade American pupils, they made fewer errors in words aided. Although fewer than either group of American pupils, Scottish errors of substitution more often changed the meaning of the sentence than did those of the American pupils. In comparison with third-grade American pupils, the Scottish pupils were significantly slower in rate, fewer in substitutions, and greater in mispronunciations. Reversals and additions showed no differences in either grade.

It appears that the heavier emphasis upon phonics in the Scottish reading program, as we have seen in certain American studies, produced greater independence but less recognition of the contextual meanings. The tendency to use letter sounds as the basic word attack skill also appears to have caused more errors in pronunciation of words as well as a slower reading rate. One might say that the Scottish pupils were better decoders but poorer readers in the sense of attending to the message of the text.

Biemiller (3) tried to show three stages of oral reading among first graders: an early predominant use of contextual information, a nonresponse stage with an increase in graphically constrained errors, followed by a third stage of more graphic and context errors accompanied by fewer nonresponse errors. In criticizing this study, Barr (2) has pointed out that Biemiller failed to recognize the influence of the phonic instruction given during the first year. Under phonics training, Barr found that most errors were nonresponses, nonsense words, or from the child's aural vocabulary, as in Biemiller's second developmental stage. Under sight word instruction, most errors came from other words taught at the same time, with very few substitutions on the basis of letter cues or previously learned words. Sight word instruction led children to attempt word recognition on the basis of their auditory vocabulary and some distinguishing feature such as word length or configuration, not letter cues. Even with phonic instruction, the proportion of nonresponses, nonsense words, and those influenced by auditory vocabulary indicated a loss of sight words and an inability to apply the phonic information being presented, in Barr's opinion. Barr suggests that perhaps an analysis of pupil errors, considered in conjunction with the method being employed, may be used to determine appropriate remedial instruction. In other words, oral errors largely of gross word form substitution, which may or may not be reasonably meaningful, reflect a nonphonic sight word approach. Errors involving graphic similarity, particularly of the beginning letters, many nonresponses, and incorrect letter substitutions producing nonsense or meaningless words reflect a weak phonic skill. Of the present commercial oral reading tests, only the Diagnostic Reading Scales (40) suggest this type of analysis in terms of word form, meaning, and graphic similarity.

List versus Context

Although a number of the commercial oral reading tests offer word lists and suggest that the errors in these lists be combined with those committed in context, there is certainly some question of the validity of this procedure. Payne (35) exposed words tachistoscopically and, as a result, detected trends not present in other studies of oral reading errors. For example, contrary to most other studies, omissions decreased in the fourth–fifth grade, according to Payne, an improbable trend in reading in context in view of the increasing fluency and speed.

To test the value of lists in detecting oral reading error tendencies, Goodman (20) duplicated his lists in the context of stories for primary pupils. He discovered that words in lists were much more difficult than in context, for the average pupil in the first grade corrected two-thirds of his list errors when reading the stories. Second graders corrected three-fourths of their list errors; third graders corrected four-fifths. Since it is almost universally accepted that context influences word choice and miscues in reading, unless the reader is a word caller or overdependent upon letter sounds for word recognition, lists of words cannot reveal the same error tendencies as does contextual reading.

There is, of course, a possible exception to this objection to using word lists in studying oral reading errors in the behavior of beginners. The use of context by primary pupils is probably minimal, and errors in lists, at least in frequency, resemble those in contextual reading. Marie Clay's (7) correlation of .89 between recognition of isolated words and contextual reading; Liberman's correlation of .77 between the number of errors in lists and context (29); and Dykstra's *r*'s of .75 to .81 between word recognition and reading comprehension tests at the end of the second grade (13) indicate the lack of influence of context upon oral reading errors at the primary level, or the fact that these beginning readers tend to show very similar performances in reading word lists or context. The fact that context is not ignored by first graders is shown in Goodman's data, cited above, and in Marie Clay's other report (6) that first graders' error behavior was influenced more by syntactic framework than grapheme-phoneme correspondence.

However, it still remains to be demonstrated that, except perhaps at beginning reading levels, errors in reading lists of words are similar to those committed while reading in context. Moreover, there is the distinct possibility that in reading isolated words the child is forced toward a greater use of letter-sound clues than he is when reading context. Thus lists of words may be a measure of the child's ability to apply his phonic knowledge when no other clues are present, but not a complete measure of his approach when aided by context.

Combining Errors

Another debatable practice in oral reading tests is the combining of errors from easy, moderate, and difficult selections. Is the pattern of errors similar for most children in easy and difficult selections? Is the pattern of errors similar from one type of selection to the next? Using an I.R.I., Christenson (5) found more errors of repetition in easy materials and a greater number of mispronunciations, refusals or words aided, and substitutions in hard materials—trends that seem quite logical. The child is usually given instructional materials at the level at which he was reading reasonably well in the oral reading test. But at the same time corrective instruction is determined by the apparent implications of all his errors collected from several reading levels, above and below, as well as at, his functional level. As a result, remedial instruction may often be directed toward correcting behaviors that may not be strongly present at his instructional or functional level.

As for the similarity of pattern of errors from one oral reading to another, Herlin (10, 25) has demonstrated that the pattern of errors is peculiar to the test, and probably different from that appearing in another test. Using the Monroe materials with present-day pupils, Herlin found that the selections tended to produce the same pattern of errors found by their author more than thirty years before. But, when compared with the Durrell materials, pupils made significantly fewer reversals, additions of sounds, and omissions of words than in the Monroe. On the Durrell, errors of consonant sounds, omissions of sounds, substitutions of words, and words aided were significantly greater. Estimates of reading level differed by six months on the average in the two tests.

In a small study comparing the Gray Oral and an I.R.I., Hardin and Ames (24) showed that the Gray revealed more errors in substitutions and words aided than did the informal test, which yielded more errors in omissions, additions, and repetitions. Estimates of reading level varied by more than a year in over one-third of the twenty-six cases, the Gray rating being higher in two-thirds of these. The percentages of various error types were not significantly different for the entire group in the tests, but some pupils showed marked variations in their patterns of error from one test to the other.

Do We Need Norms?

As Della-Piana (9) has emphasized, the teacher is severely handicapped in planning a valid remedial program for a pupil when she employs the average formal or informal oral test. The data cited indicate that the examiner does not really know which errors are most frequent at the pupil's functional level, or whether the profile of errors is not peculiar to the test used. Moreover, only the old Monroe test and the Gates-McKillop battery offer norms for different types of errors, and, of course, the norms are peculiar to their authors' instruments. While Della-Piana and Herlin have shown that the total number of each type of error tends to rank them as the norms for the Durrell or Monroe would, for many children this is not the case and norms are essential (10).

Good versus Poor Readers

Despite the contrary evidence, many diagnosticians believe that there is a great difference between the oral reading errors of good and poor readers. Reversals, for example, are supposed to be a sign of very poor reading, despite Nikas's (34) evidence that they are common among all types of primary readers, and tend to increase in reading more difficult materials. Two reports from Denmark by Tordrup (44) and Malmquist (31) found no differences in the types of errors of good, average, or poor readers, including reversals. The only difference in Malmquist's large-scale study was in words aided (after fifteen seconds), which were made eight times as often by poor readers as average, and very seldom by good readers, at the first-grade level.

Oral Reading and Dialect

The current studies of the dialects of minority groups make it quite obvious that these differences from standard English affect the pupil's oral reading and thus influence the examiner's estimates of pupil reading ability. Yet only the Diagnostic Reading Scales (40) and Smith and Bradtmueller's Inventory (39) tell the examiner to discount or ignore oral errors due to dialect. Gates and McKillop (17) speak of not penalizing the child for "accent," but it is not clear whether they are referring to dialectal errors or intonation.

Among the black English variations from standard English that are likely to manifest themselves in oral reading are the following (1, 28, 48):

Omissions—of *r* or *l* as in *god-guard, hep-help;* of final consonants and consonant clusters, as *pass-past, row-road,* and others involving *t, d, s, z, g* and *k.*

Substitutions—*i* for *e,* as *pin-pen, pinny-penny,* or *bear-beer;* final *th* becomes *v,* as *breav-breathe;* unvoiced final *th* becomes *f* as *bref-breath;* initial consonant *d* becomes *th;* and certain clusters are changed, as *skream-stream.*

Additions—certain plurals ending in *st* become *stes,* as *testes-tests.*

Syntax—omission of final *s* in third person singular, as *wonder-wonders;* of the *s* in possessives and of prepositions, "He goes (to) the school." Omission of *ed* signifying past tense and of *s* in plurals. Use of a double negative, and substitution for the copula, "He be my dog."

Word order changes—as transposition of the auxiliary verb, "Why she won't come?" and faulty use of the "if" construction, "I asked him did he do it."

With Spanish-English speakers, oral reading will be affected by many vowel confusions and these substitutions (49):

s for *th,* as in *thin*
ch for *j,* as in *judge*
s for *s* as *z,* as in *pleasure, zinc*
p for *b* as in *par*
b for *v* as in *vote*
t for *d* as in *den*
c for *g* as in *goat*
d for *th,* as in *this*
s for *sh,* as in *shoe*
sh for *ch* as in *chew*
j for *y* as in *yellow*
n for final *m* as in *dime*
gw for *w* as in *way*

The differences between Spanish and English sentence structure also appear as the following (49):

Negatives—as "Mary no here," "He no go to school," "No run."

Verb forms—"I go to sing" instead of *am going;* "I see you later," dropping the "will"; "I have twenty years" or "I have thirst"; dropping auxiliaries, as "This man works?" or "Works this man?" Omission of inflections, as "The boy eat."

Word order—"The dress red," "Is Tuesday."

> Other variations—Learning English is difficult because of the presence of sounds and conventions not present in Spanish, such as the *z* sound for *s; ng; wh;* many more vowel sounds; consonant clusters such as *ts, lpt, lkt* in *bats, helped,* and *talked;* and irregular verb forms as *tear-tore, throw-threw.*

As Zintz further points out (49), Indian children (of the Navaho group, for example), have difficulties with the distinction of number, gender, and possessive; definite and indefinite articles; and pronouns, verb inflections, negative questions, and other characteristics of English. Certainly an analysis of a pupil's oral reading that included a count of these dialect variations as oral reading errors can hardly yield an accurate estimate of the pupil's reading ability if we conceive of reading as the ability to understand printed matter.

If we accept the use of oral reading tests as one means of gaining some insight into a pupil's behavior when he is reading aloud—and maybe when he is reading silently—it is apparent that we must attempt to reconcile these various systems for classifying oral errors. Perhaps these systems can be combined into a method of analysis that will yield the maximum amount of diagnostic information to the examiner.

PROBLEMS INHERENT IN ORAL READING TESTING

Validity

Many approaches to the analysis of pupil oral reading habits pay little attention to the validity of the testing, that is, the relevance of the testing material to the pupil's classroom performances. As we have indicated earlier, such common practices as combining errors from selections of varying readability levels and different kinds of content may not yield an accurate picture of the pupil's usual oral reading behaviors. Ideally, his oral reading errors should be tabulated only from selections at the pupil's functional or classroom reading level. We cannot be certain that his errors in difficult material likely to produce a number of miscues (as employed in the Goodman approach) accurately reflect what the pupil will do in the easier material of the classroom reading group. Nor can we be certain that a remedial plan based on a melange of errors from selections ranging above and below his actual reading level will be relevant to his needs.

These facts imply that when an analysis of oral reading is intended, it should be based solely on selections of a known readability level equivalent to the pupil's reading ability. It is true that the content of these samples influences the pattern of oral reading errors. But we do not know exactly what content produces the most valid profile of errors. And, beginning at intermediate grades, we are concerned about his ability to read in a number of content areas. Hence, pragmatically speaking, we should probably employ graded selections from several of these fields to obtain a more complete picture of the pupil's error tendencies. While the profile may be slightly inaccurate in generalizing about the pupil's oral reading in one or two of the content fields sampled, it will be a reasonable general analysis that can be profitably implemented in classroom instructional procedures.

Reliability

The use of short paragraphs, as in many informal and commercial oral reading tests, raises a question about the reliability of the oral reading analysis. There is evidence that the nature of a pupil's errors changes somewhat in selections longer than 250 words from those observed in very brief samples. The Goodmans have recognized this fact in their practice of using an entire story for their testing. More critical, however, to the reliability of the testing, is the number of errors actually analyzed. Almost none of the commercial or informal oral reading inventories recognize that the number of errors analyzed should be about 75–100 for a reliable diagnosis. So large a number of errors is not likely to be found in a single story or perhaps even in a single testing situation. Repeated testing to obtain such a sample may be required to be certain that the remedial plan is formulated on a sound basis.

Comprehension

The ability to read well orally is not strong evidence of the reader's comprehension. For this reason, some oral reading tests include standardized questions and demand at least a minimal performance on these items in estimating the pupil's oral reading level. These questions are analyzed in the course of standardization of the test and their discrimination between good and poor comprehenders determined. Questions too easy or too difficult to discriminate, or those that can be answered on the basis of previous knowledge rather than actual reading of the test sample are thus eliminated. In contrast, the Goodmans and certain other reading test makers are satisfied to sample comprehension simply by asking the pupil to retell the story he has just read. Some encourage the pupil by open-ended or even leading questions that help to elicit more of his memories for the material. Then the spontaneous and prompted recall of the pupil are combined to secure a global impression of the pupil's comprehension. In a sense, this informal approach to sampling pupil comprehension does yield some idea of the pupil's immediate memory for connected material. But, like the literal recall questions commonly asked by teachers, it makes no assessment of judgment, reasoning, interpretation, or the pupil's ability to relate the testing material to his previous learning. Testing simple recall ignores all the facets of comprehension that are considered significant by most reading authorities. Since no criteria of the amount or type of recall that should be expected at various age levels are used, the judgment of pupil comprehension by this approach becomes completely subjective.

Sight Vocabulary

A measure of the primary pupil's sight word vocabulary is often desired in testing oral reading. Moreover, at these early levels there is great similarity between the child's handling of such word lists and his reading in context. Lists of important words for such testing are offered in the Diagnostic Reading Scales, the Durrell Analysis of Reading Difficulty, and other such tests. The Dolch Basic Sight Word List (Champaign, Ill: Garrard Publishing, 1945) is very popular for such testing, although it is too long for testing at one sitting. If such a list is administered as part of the testing of oral reading, errors in it probably should not be combined with those observed in contextual reading. When dealing with isolated words, the pupil is really almost forced to use graphic and phonemic clues, since no other clues are present. Thus a word list enables the examiner to test the limits of the pupil's skill in using graphic or phonemic clues, but may not actually sample his word analysis habits when reading in context. For beginning readers, of course, a list such as the Dolch also indicates which particular words of significance the pupil needs to be taught. Even though it is now old, recent studies of the Dolch List indicate that it is an excellent sample of the most common words needed for beginning reading.

LEARNING PROJECT

Using a graded, standardized oral reading text with which you are familiar, make an analysis of a student's oral reading. If possible, use an oral reading text in which the reading levels of the selections are designated by the author. This will avoid

the meaningless combining of oral miscues from selections significantly above or below the student's functional level. After determining this functional level, as determined by the oral test or other test data, analyze the oral miscues according to the system proposed in this chapter. Base your analysis upon at least 75–100 errors, obtained from the oral test administration and, if necessary, other graded materials at the student's oral reading level.

Group the various categories of errors, as suggested in the proposed system, to determine the student's use of phonic analysis, sight vocabulary, and use of context. Make the comparisons within these categories, and the retesting of words missed in the context of the selections to observe his use of phonic clues, etc. as suggested in the classification system.

In formulating the total diagnosis of the student's oral reading, use your analysis to determine:

1. the relative dependence upon phonic clues in context versus isolated words

2. the student's relative skill in using graphic similarity versus phonic analysis

3. his ability to use phonics in self-corrections

4. the nature of the words on which he most frequently errs, as function words vs. nouns and verbs

5. the apparent effect of the reading method used with him on the nature of his errors in substitutions

6. his dependence upon teacher assistance, as in Words Aided

7. the extent of his use of context clues, as manifest in the comparison of several categories, as suggested in the system of classification.

REFERENCES

1. Ames, Wilbur S., Rosen, Carl L., and Olson, Arthur V., "The Effects of Non-Standard Dialect on the Oral Reading Behavior of Fourth Grade Black Children," in *Language, Reading and the Communication Process,* Carl Braun, editor. Newark, Del.: International Reading Association, 1971, 63–70.
2. Barr, Rebecca C., "The Influence of Instructional Conditions on Word Recognition Errors," *Reading Research Quarterly,* 7 (Spring 1972), 509–29.
3. Biemiller, Andrew, "The Development of the Use of Graphic and Contextual Information as Children Learn to Read," *Reading Research Quarterly,* 6 (Fall 1970), 75–96.
4. Burke, C.L., and Goodman, Kenneth S., "When a Child Reads: A Psycholinguistic Analysis," *Elementary English,* 47 (January 1970), 121–29.
5. Christenson, A., "Oral Reading Errors of Intermediate Grade Children at Their Independent, Instructional and Frustration Reading Levels," in *Reading and Realism,* J. Allen Figurel, editor. International Reading Association Conference Proceedings, 13, 1969, 674–77.

6. Clay, Marie, M., "The Reading Behavior of Five Year Old Children: A Research Project," *New Zealand Journal of Educational Research,* 2 (1967), 11–31.
7. Clay, Marie M., "Reading Errors and Self-Correction Behavior," *British Journal of Educational Psychology,* 39 (1969), 47–56.
8. Daw, Seward Emerson, "The Persistence of Errors in Oral Reading in Grades Four and Five," *Journal of Educational Research,* 32 (October 1938), 81–90.
9. Della-Piana, Gabriel M., "Analysis of Oral Reading Errors: Standardization, Norms and Validity," *Reading Teacher,* 15 (January 1962), 254–57.
10. Della-Piana, Gabriel M., and Herlin, Wayne R., "Are Normative Oral Reading Error Profiles Necessary?" in *Improvement of Reading Through Classroom Practice,* J. Allen Figurel, editor, International Reading Association Conference Proceedings, 9, 1964, 306–09.
11. Duffy, G.B., and Durrell, Donald D., "Third Grade Difficulties in Oral Reading," *Education,* 56 (September 1935), 37–40.
12. Durrell, Donald D., *Durrell Analysis of Reading Difficulty.* New York: Harcourt Brace Jovanovich, 1955.
13. Dykstra, Robert, "Summary of the Second-Grade Phase of the Cooperative Research Program in Primary Reading Instruction," *Reading Research Quarterly,* 4 (Fall 1968), 49–70.
14. Ekwall, Elden E., *Locating and Correcting Reading Difficulties.* Columbus: Charles E. Merrill, 1970.
15. Elder, Richard D., "Oral Reading Achievement of Scottish and American Children," *Elementary School Journal,* 71 (January 1971), 216–30.
16. Fields, Patricia, "Comparisons and Relationships of Oral and Silent Reading Performances of Good and Poor College Freshmen Readers," Master's thesis, Atlanta University, 1960.
17. Gates, Arthur I., and McKillop, Anne S., *Gates-McKillop Reading Diagnostic Tests.* New York: Teachers College Press, 1962.
18. Gilmore, John V., and Gilmore, Eunice C., *Gilmore Oral Reading Test.* New York: Harcourt Brace Jovanovich, 1968.
19. Glass, Gerald G., and Burton, Elizabeth H., *How Do They Decode? Verbalizations and Observed Behaviors of Successful Decoders.* Department of Education, Adelphi University, Garden City, New York.
20. Goodman, Kenneth S., "A Linguistic Study of Cues and Miscues in Reading," *Elementary English,* 42 (October 1965), 639–43.
21. Goodman, Kenneth S., "Reading: A Psycholinguistic Guessing Game," in *Theoretical Models and Processes of Reading,* Harry Singer and Robert B. Ruddell, editors. Newark, Del.: International Reading Association, 1970, 259–72.
22. Goodman, Kenneth S., and Burke, Carolyn L., *Study of Children's Behavior While Reading Orally.* Project No. S425, United States Department of Health, Education and Welfare, 1968.
23. Gray, William S., and Robinson, Helen M., editors, *Gray Oral Reading Tests.* Indianapolis: Bobbs-Merrill, 1967.
24. Hardin, Veralee, and Ames, Wilbur S., "A Comparison of the Results of Two Oral Tests," *Reading Teacher,* 22 (January 1969), 329–34.
25. Herlin, Wayne Richard, "A Comparison of Oral Reading Errors on the Monroe Diagnostic Reading Examination and the Durrell Analysis of Reading Difficulty." Doctoral dissertation, University of Utah, 1963.

26. Ilg, Frances L., and Ames, Louise Bates, "Developmental Trends in Reading Behavior," *Journal of Genetic Psychology,* 76 (1950), 291–312.
27. Kerfoot, James F., "An Instructional View of Reading Diagnosis" in *Reading and Inquiry,* J. Allen Figurel, editor. International Reading Association Conference Proceedings, 10, 1965, 215–19.
28. Labov, William, "Some Sources of Reading Problems for Negro Speakers of Non-Standard English." ERIC Documentary Reproduction Service, No. ED 10688, 1966.
29. Liberman, I.Y., et al., "Letter Confusions and Reversals of Sequence in the Beginning Reader: Implications for Orton's Theory of Developmental Dyslexia," *Cortex* (June 1971), 127–42, as quoted by Barr (2).
30. Madden, Mable, and Pratt, Marjorie, "An Oral Reading Survey as a Teaching Aid," *Elementary English Review,* 18 (April 1941), 122–26, 159.
31. Malmquist, Eve, *Factors Related to Reading Disabilities in the First Grade of the Elementary School.* Stockholm: Almqvist and Wiksell, 1958.
32. Malmquist, Eve, "A Decade of Reading Research in Europe, 1959–69: A Review," *Journal of Educational Research,* 63 (March 1970), 309–29.
33. Monroe, Marion, *Children Who Cannot Read.* Chicago: University of Chicago Press, 1932.
34. Nikas, George B., *Reversal Errors of Children in Oral Reading.* Oswego, N.Y.: State University of New York at Oswego.
35. Payne, Cassie, "The Classification of Errors in Oral Reading," *Elementary School Journal,* 31 (October 1930), 142–46.
36. Schale, Florence C., "Changes in Oral Reading Errors at Elementary and Secondary Levels," *Academic Therapy,* 1 (1966), 225–29.
37. Schummers, J.L., "Word Pronunciation in the Oral Sight-Reading of Third Grade Children," Doctoral dissertation, University of Minnesota, 1956, as quoted by Weber (45).
38. Silvaroli, Nicholas J., *Classroom Reading Inventory.* Dubuque: William C. Brown, 1965.
39. Smith, Edwin H., and Bradtmueller, Weldon G., *Individual Reading Placement Inventory.* Chicago: Follett Publishing, 1969.
40. Spache, George D., *Diagnostic Reading Scales.* Monterey: California Test Bureau, 1972.
41. Spache, George D., and Spache, Evelyn B., *Reading in the Elementary School.* Boston: Allyn and Bacon, 1973.
42. Swalm, James E., *A Comparison of Oral Reading, Silent Reading and Listening Comprehension.* Urban Teacher Education, Livingston College, New Brunswick, N.J.
43. Swanson, D.E., "Common Elements in Silent and Oral Reading," *Psychological Monographs,* 48, 3, 1937.
44. Tordrup, S.A., "Laesendviklungen hos elever med store laesevanskelighder," *Skolepsykologi,* 4, No. 1, Copenhagen, 1967, as quoted by Malmquist (32).
45. Weber, Rose-Marie, "The Study of Oral Reading Errors: A Survey of the Literature," *Reading Research Quarterly,* 4 (Fall 1968), 96–119.
46. Weber, Rose-Marie, "A Linguistic Analysis of First-Grade Reading Errors," *Reading Research Quarterly,* 5 (Spring 1970), 427–51.
47. Wells, Charles A., "The Value of an Oral Reading Test for Diagnosis of the Reading

Difficulties of College Freshmen of Low Academic Performance," *Psychological Monographs,* 64 (1950), 1–35.

48. Welty, Stella L., "Reading and Black English," in *Language, Reading and the Communication Process,* Carl Braun, editor. Newark: International Reading Association, 1971, 71–93.
49. Zintz, Miles V., *The Reading Process.* Dubuque: William C. Brown, 1970.

7 Interpreting Individual Diagnostic Reading Tests

This chapter offers detailed analyses of thirteen diagnostic reading tests that, in the case of some at least, are widely used by teachers and reading clinicians. If at all possible, the various tests reviewed should be available during the reading of the critiques. They are too numerous and too complex to be retained or even comprehended in a single simple reading of the text. Moreover, the reading teacher will want to verify many of the comments made about each test (and particularly those regarding her favorite instruments).

Each review follows a technical outline in examining the structure, rationale, and function of each instrument in such areas as content, construct, and concurrent validity and reliability. These basic concepts of test construction may well be unfamiliar to the average reading teacher, as indeed they are to some of the test authors. To aid in their differentiation, simple definitions of these terms are offered to which the reader should attend closely.

In effect, this chapter is an exercise in critical reading in the evaluation of some common professional tools. Its purpose is not to steer reading teachers toward or away from any particular tests, for, within their limitations, several of these can be very useful for specific areas of diagnosis. Rather, it is our hope that by reading these reviews, reading specialists will be able to answer such questions as these:

1. What types or areas of test evaluation did you learn here that you may use in the future?
2. What are your reactions to the criticisms of one of these instruments that you may have been using?

WE SHALL ATTEMPT TO PRESENT an analytic, critical evaluation of a number of individual diagnostic and oral reading tests. In following this analysis, we suggest that the reader obtain copies of these tests to peruse while reading these comments. Or, at least, the reader should have at hand copies of those instruments that he is using or considering for use, in order to judge the validity and objectivity of our criticisms. For comparative purposes, it would also be useful to consult the reviews of these tests in Buros's *Mental Measurement Yearbooks* and his *Reading Tests and Reviews* (6, 7, 8). With these materials available, the reader will gain not only a more comprehensive and analytic review of these measures but perhaps also some critical skill in test evaluation. (See also our Check List for Test Evaluation in *Investigating the Issues of Reading Disabilities.*)

To the experienced reading clinician, this review may appear to be a collection of odds and ends, for there are great differences among these tests in their approaches, technical qualifications, and the reading behaviors that they sample. But they have one element in common, which is the basis for our selection, namely, they are all administered individually in the course of reading diagnoses.* Several have wide use among reading centers, as the Gates-McKillop, the Durrell, the Diagnostic Reading Scales, and the Gray Oral. Others are very commonly found in the reports of psychologists to schools, as the Wide Range and the Gilmore. A number of others are relatively new, but are obviously intended to capture a portion of the market in reading diagnosis. These include the San Diego, the Classroom Reading Inventory, the Standard, the Slosson, and the Peabody. The Individual Reading Placement Inventory is included because it, too, is intended for individual diagnostic use, albeit with older individuals.

These critiques are not, as some would suppose, the author's seizing of an opportunity to make invidious comparisons between his own Diagnostic Reading Scales and the competing tests. The reader will note that, as in the other reviews, criticisms made by various reviewers of the Diagnostic Scales are acknowledged and its limitations admitted.

To facilitate the reading of these reviews, we have grouped the information under a number of headings. First, a physical description of the parts of each test battery and their apparent purposes are given. *Content validity* is then examined in terms of the similarity of the parts of the test to ordinary

---

*For critiques of group diagnostic tests, see chapters 8 and 9.

reading behaviors and materials, and in terms of the sources of the items used. Does the test sample representative materials and behaviors common to the milieu of the testees? In effect, this is reality testing of the instrument, as Wallace Ramsey (42) might call it. It is not essential that a test approach measurement of a certain reading skill in exactly the way in which that skill functions in the act of reading, as Ramsey seems to believe. For example, there are many ways of sampling meaning vocabulary besides observing whether the student interprets each word in the exact sense that the author intended in a particular reading passage. But, to achieve content validity, the author of a test should show that his approach to measurement of a skill would yield information that is relevant to ordinary instruction in the classroom.

Construct validity is concerned largely with the physical administration and scoring of each test, along with the author's labeling and interpretation of the meanings of his tests and their norms. The making of a test is a laborious process of assembling representative standardization data; item analysis in terms of discrimination between high and low scorers and the difficulty of the items; tests of internal consistency and overlap among subtests; and frequent revision or rewriting of items before publication. The scientific and ethical principles that should guide test construction are easily available (1, 17, 49). Yet the reader will discover that many adverse criticisms are possible in this area in these reviews.

Concurrent validity refers to the data indicating the similarities and differences of a new test from other known instruments. These contrasts usually take the form of correlations between test scores and comparisons of mean scores. These correlations and comparisons are another way of judging whether the author's manner of testing a recognized reading ability yields estimates of pupil performance that are reasonably comparable to existing tests and to classroom performances. The point is crucial because most users of tests tend to employ the results in classroom grouping, placement, and selection of materials for instruction.

Reliability, or the extent to which a test yields consistent scores from one application to another, is a significant aspect of these tests. Authors use different formulas for reliability and report them in different ways. When reporting for a single grade level, the reliability coefficient should be in the .70s or .80s if the test is used to discriminate between individuals. For a several-grade range, reliability should be in the high .80s or above .90 for the same purpose. For a number of these tests, as the Botel, the Gates-McKillop, the Durrell, the San Diego, and the Classroom Inventory, no reliability data are offered by the authors, and we have had to omit this evaluation criterion in our reviews.

Reliability coefficients, however derived, may be artificially inflated if a test is very brief, or if time limits are imposed for each item, or if the test is so sharply scaled that a pupil of any particular grade can do only a small portion of the items. Under such conditions, a pupil would hardly vary his score from one testing to another, and the reliability coefficient that reflects this lack of change would be unrealistically high.

In reporting the reliability of a test, the authors should reveal the standard error of measurement, and explain how to use it in comparing scores on different subtests. No score from a test is an absolute measure, but rather one that would vary in repeated testing. The range of this probable variation, within which the true score may be found, is the standard error of measurement. For example, a standard error of two points on the test means that the pupil's true score is somewhere between plus or minus two points above or below the score obtained. If two individual scores are to be compared, the difference between them should be at least twice the standard error of the test to be a real difference.

We have tried to contrast the strengths and weaknesses of each test reviewed here. But, in the final analysis, the choice of test must be made by the reader with full knowledge of the flaws and inconsistencies present in his selection. As Gabriel Della-Piana has suggested (11), the reading diagnostician must make choices among the diagnostic instruments offered, finally selecting those he can intelligently interpret and apply to remedial plans with confidence. Every one of the tests reviewed here has limitations, and the question becomes one of selecting that test for which the limitations seem minor or readily overcome by additional observation or evaluation of the pupil's reading behaviors.

BOTEL READING INVENTORY (3)

Description The battery consists of four tests: Word Recognition, Word Opposites Reading, Word Opposites Listening, Phonics Mastery Test. The author claims that the tests will reveal the proper instructional level, the free reading (independent) level, and the frustration level of children, as well as an indication of their needs for phonics instruction.

The Word Recognition Test consists of twenty words for each of eight reading levels from preprimer to fourth grade. For the first three grades, the words tested were drawn from five major basal reading series. At the fourth grade, the words were found on every tenth page of the *Teacher's Word Book* of 30,000 words. The test is administered by having the pupil read the lists beginning at a level at which he is likely to secure 100 percent. He continues attempting the words at each level until he falls below 70 percent on two successive levels. The last successful level is interpreted as his instructional level.

The Word Opposites Test requires the pupil to find the opposite of the first word in each line among the four other words on that line. Ten test items are offered for ten levels from first reader to senior high. The test is assumed to be a measure of comprehension in reading. The identical test may then be administered again as a Word Opposites Listening in which the key words and possible opposites are read to the pupils. If there is a difference in the scores

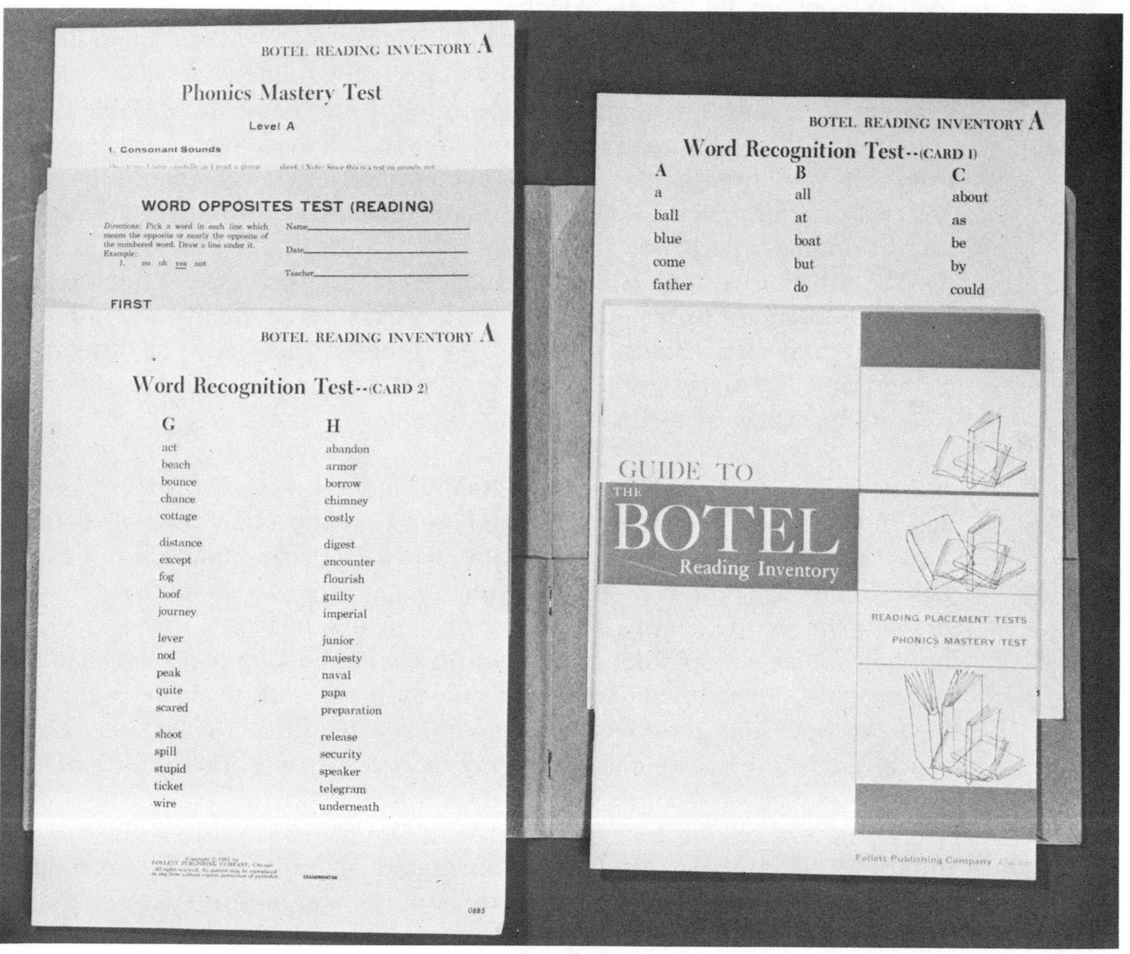

Botel Reading Inventory

on the two administrations of the test, this is interpreted to indicate higher reading potential than reading performance. No explanation is offered for those cases in which a difference is small or completely lacking or reversed, nor are there any data regarding a difference due to the practice effect of taking the same test twice.

The Phonics Mastery Test asks the pupils to listen to groups of words and then to write (1) the initial consonant sound of the word (eighteen items); (2) the consonant blend (nineteen items); (3) the consonant digraph (five items); (4) two or more words that rhyme with each of four given words and have the same group of ending letters. A second part of the test asks the pupils to write short or long according to the nature of the vowel in the words read to them (ten items); and to write the double vowel or "vowel changed by a consonant" (vowel plus *r*) present in the words read to them (nine items). The third part of this test asks the pupil to circle the number of syllables in the words read to him (ten items); and to circle the number of the syllable that is accented in the words read to him (ten items). All these tests are offered for use in the first three grades, and 100 percent mastery is considered the most desirable performance. Any lesser score indicates presumably a need for further phonics instruction.

With fourth graders, testing begins with a Nonsense Words Test in which children are expected to read the words aloud in the manner indicated by the author's hypothetical phonetic respelling with accents as he designates. If the pupil is "successful" on this test (no standards are given), the other phonics tests may be skipped.

Content Validity

If we assume that the reading program is indeed a basal reader, then the selection of items for the Word Recognition Test at primary levels is defensible. Whether the test is valid for any of the programs that are not highly basal-oriented is, of course, questionable. There is also the question of grading the words simply by reason of their use in basals. This is simply pooling subjective opinions of what words should be taught at each level, not proof of the individual difficulty of the words or their validity in discriminating between poor and good word recognition vocabularies of children. For the fourth-grade level, selecting words randomly from a list is not evidence of their difficulty, value for reading, or their discriminative power.

The source of the items in the Word Opposites Test is not given by the author; thus we have no information regarding their value for reading or discriminative power or the manner of grading them in levels.

The content of the Phonics Mastery Test is an abbreviated sampling of the items commonly taught in each area. In none of the subtests of consonant sounds, blends, digraphs, vowel digraphs, and diphthongs is there a complete coverage of the items of the phonics curriculum. Yet the tester is led to assume that if the child is successful with any group of the test items, no further training in that phonic skill is necessary.

Construct Validity

The administration of the Word Recognition Test as a sight word list is commonplace in tests. But the author offers no evidence of the validity of his list as a measure of this skill. Similarly, he offers no support for the interpretation of the Word Opposite Reading Test as a measure of comprehension, nor of the Listening version as a measure of potential. We have no way of judging how accurately a difference will indicate the child's future reading performances. The author's rationale for interpreting this test as a measure of potential is probably based on his realization that opposites tests have long been used as measures of verbal intelligence. Even if we assume his test to function in this fashion, as an estimate of verbal intelligence, this is still no evidence of its value as a predictor of future reading, for such verbal tests are not efficient predictors for many pupils (41).

The Phonics Mastery Test requiring children to write the sounds heard in words is not identical with the analysis of the sounds of visual symbols, as in reading. It may not sample phonic skill in the act of reading as much as in spelling.

Apparently no normative testing or actual standardization of these tests was ever attempted. The performances expected in the Word Recognition and Word Opposites tests of 70–90 percent and 70–80 percent were based on the a priori standards commonly employed in informal inventories, standards that do not truly reflect any observed reading behaviors of pupils (as we point out in *Investigating the Issues of Reading Disabilities).*

Concurrent Validity

The author offers no information in his manual regarding the similarities of performances on his test to other established instruments. However, he does offer some such data in a pair of articles published some eight or nine years later (4, 5). He cites validity coefficients of the Word Opposites Test with an informal test of .78 to .94; and of .74 with the Standard Reading Inventory; and of .73 with the Diagnostic Reading Scales (3). The comparisons are meaningless, for comprehension in the informal test was measured by the child's performance on workbook exercises accompanying the basal selections (which may or may not have been good measures of comprehension); and in the Standard and Diagnostic Reading Scales, oral and silent reading performances were averaged. Thus we have only comparisons between his Word Opposites Test and three meaningless scores derived from the other tests.

In a later article, Botel (5) claims to have established each child's proper instructional level by several teacher-administered informal oral tests. He then compares his combined score from the two word lists with this teacher judgment and three *silent* reading tests. Since the Botel and the informal tests used the same a priori standards for oral reading, they tended to agree, as we might expect, more than with the three silent reading tests. The only significant observation possible from these data was the fact that the correlations between the silent tests and his test or the informal tests dropped markedly from second grade to sixth grade. The implication was present that oral and silent reading tests show increasingly less similarity between the two modes of reading as reading ability develops. The two types of oral testing tended to maintain marked relationship, as would be expected. Hence the comparisons between the oral tests do not support evidence of the validity of the Botel as a measure of anything except oral sight reading (without estimate of comprehension).

Daniel (9), who cites a correlation of .69 between the two word list tests of Botel, questions the value of giving both tests when there is so much overlap. He also cites *r*'s of the Botel total (a rough average of the grade placement on the two word lists) with the Gates Advanced Primary of .81; with an informal test, of .70; and with teacher judgment, of .54.

Reviewers of the Botel Inventory (7) have criticized it for lack of normative data, no information on the derivation of the scoring criteria, and no data on validity or reliability, as we have here. The Inventory may be a measure of some facets of reading, but the author has not yet demonstrated this fact.

DURRELL ANALYSIS OF READING DIFFICULTY (13)

Description This battery of tests was first offered in 1937 and revised in 1955. It now consists of an oral, a silent, and a listening comprehension test; lists for testing word recognition and word analysis; and a number of brief supplementary tests on letters, letter sounds, visual memory, spelling, and handwriting. Check lists of difficulties detected in the major tests are offered, as well as for indicating the probable instructional needs of pupils as revealed by the entire battery. Several of the tests are normed only for the primary grades, while others may be used during the first six grades.

Content Validity The Oral Reading Test comprises eight reading selections presumably graded to represent elementary grade levels. Norms for rate of reading only are presented; they extend only to the sixth grade even on the seventh- and

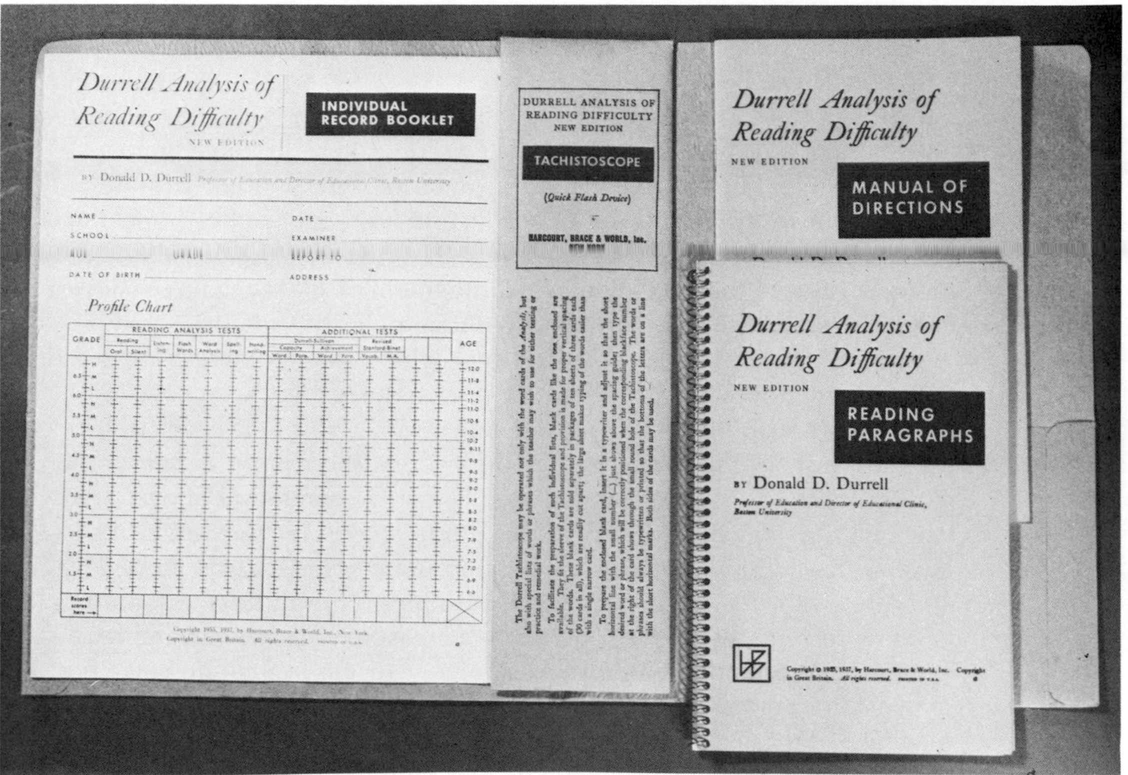

Durrell Analysis of Reading Difficulty

eighth-grade selections. The child is timed while reading each selection, beginning with one at his grade level and continuing until he makes seven oral errors or fails to read the selection in two minutes. The oral errors are recorded and combined from all the selections attempted for later analysis. Narrative reading is sampled in the first four grades and content fields in the succeeding four levels. The use of the same standard of oral reading errors for all selections regardless of length or grade level leads us to suspect that it reflects the author's judgment rather than actual pupil performances. Despite the use of comprehension questions, no judgment is made of the child's performance.

This Oral Reading Test was present in the 1937 edition and was not revised or restandardized in 1955. Hence the standards offered, which are really just rate of reading, are more than thirty years old. When the Spache Readability formula was applied to the first five grade levels of selections, the ratings were I—1.5; II—1.7; III—2.1; IV—2.8; and V—3.1.

The Silent Reading Test is also identical in content and norms in the 1937 and 1955 editions. For its eight grade level selections, norms extending only through the sixth grade are offered. Readability estimate of the first five selections were I—1.5; II—1.8; III—2.2; IV—2.7; and V—3.3, indicating the parallel structure in difficulty of these first two tests and also their unrepresentativeness of common school materials used in these first five grades.

The Silent Reading Test is scored in terms of the amount of spontaneous plus prompted recall efforts of the reader and his reading time. What the child does not recall spontaneously in a tell-back of the selection may be elicited by the questions of the examiner. Final judgment of silent reading ability of the child is based, however, on the rate of reading norms (of 1937) only.

The Listening Comprehension Test, which was an oral reading test in the 1937 edition, now simply bears a new label. The reading selections for the old oral test were in each case moved downward one grade level to form the listening test, in the first seven grade levels. The former eighth-grade oral reading selection is now labeled as a listening sample of "above Grade 6." Readability estimates of the first four grade level selections indicates I—2.1; II—2.4; III—3.0; and IV—4.0, a lack of accurate scaling also criticized by Eller and Attea (15). No evidence is offered to support the author's assumption that this oral reading test could function as a measure of listening comprehension or potential for improvement in reading; or for his scaling downward of the oral test to form the listening measure. The original test was scored in rate of reading and recall memories, but is now scored by comprehension questions. The derivation of the new standards for comprehension are apparently the a priori judgment of the author that pupils should be able to answer all but two of the seven to nine questions appended to each selection, that is, 71 to 77 percent. There is no evidence that this test was ever restandardized as a measure of listening comprehension.

The Word Recognition and Word Analysis lists are new in the 1955 revision, and new norms are offered for them. The lists are placed in a slide case and a small card slid past an opening, presumably at half-second intervals for the first exposure or flash presentation. If the pupil is unsuccessful in naming the word, the slide is opened to permit a second, untimed attempt. The author assumes that the pupil can make only one fixation in the half-second exposure and thus cannot analyze the word during the flash presentation. Since many children above the first-grade level can make several fixations in a half-second, the author's distinction between instantaneous sight recognition and recognition by some form of word analysis is lost. The hand tachistoscope, difficult to manipulate in precise half-second intervals without some sort of timing device, becomes almost unmanageable as the end of the list approaches (22). However, the two exposures and the recording of the pupil's responses do permit the examiner to make some observations of the pupil's habits of word attack, at least in a list.

The first supplementary test is one of letter knowledge sampled by asking the child to name the printed letters (or to point to those named), to match the printed letter with a two–three second exposure in the tachistoscope, and to copy the letters. Twenty-eight capitals and a similar number of lower-case letters are used. Apparently, the practice effect in using the same letters for two or three successive tasks is ignored.

The validity of this test is probably based on the studies of Durrell and others, who have shown that knowledge of letters is highly prognostic of reading success in the beginning stages of reading. However, it has never been established whether this type of test is a reflection of learning aptitude, verbal intelligence, parental ambition, or socioeconomic status. Since the names of letters do not enter into the reading act, the values of the test are questionable.

A test for primary children of the first three grades in Visual Memory of Words is given by short-term exposures of letters and words of gradually increasing length for a total of twenty items. The child must select the letter or word exposed from five or more items offering reversals, whole or part confusions, and the like. The author assumes, reasonably enough, that this is a measure of visual perception of word elements, but he gives no evidence of its relevance to early reading success. The discriminative value of the test in mid-third grade, where the average child is supposed to do 90 percent of the items, is doubtful.

The same test is adapted to the intermediate grades by short exposure of a series of words (fifteen items), which the child is supposed to write from memory. The test is very difficult for fourth graders, who are expected to do only one-third of the items.

Hearing Sounds in Words involves asking the pupil to circle one of three words that resembles a spoken word in initial consonant, or initial digraph or blend, or final consonant, or initial and final sound, for a total of twenty-nine items. In effect, the pupil is to react not to the word as such, but only to the portion that he is to match with the spoken word. The test runs out of ceiling rapidly, for mid-third graders are expected to score 97 percent of the items (twenty-eight out of twenty-nine), although the author recommends it for any children reading at third grade or below. The child's ability to learn sounds is sampled by repeated presentation of a number of words beginning with each of three sounds. Then he is asked to indicate whether one of the three sounds is present at the beginning of some ten words told to him. No norms or interpretation are offered for this test. If thus successful with initial sounds, the same procedure is followed for eight final sounds, again with no norms or interpretation. Presumably these tests assess the pupil's ability to learn to associate sounds and letters, but its validity is not demonstrated by the author.

The child's knowledge of sounds is further sampled by asking him to give the sounds of sixteen consonant blends and digraphs. Children reading on a second-grade level or below are to be given this superficial sample of phonic information. No assessment of vowel sounds of any nature, or of single letter sounds, is attempted.

A test of phonic spelling of words is next offered. The intermediate-grade child is to attempt to spell fifteen polysyllabic, difficult words with some resemblance in his spelling to the sounds of the words. Partial successes or failures are apparently ignored; the word is scored as correct only if all the sounds of the word are represented in some fashion in the child's spelling. Norms for total words spelled phonetically only are given. No instructions for categorizing the types of errors and their possible implications for instruction are given. In fact, only variations in the graphic representation of consonant sounds are recognized in the author's suggestions for scoring.

A Spelling test with two lists of twenty words each for primary and intermediate pupils is included. The norms for this test are identical in the 1937 and 1955 revisions of this battery. Both lists are much harder than common spelling tests, for pupils at the highest grade levels tested with each list are expected to score only 80 or 75 percent correct. No instructions for analyzing spelling errors in terms of apparent phonic skills are offered, nor are there norms for such types of errors.

Handwriting speed is the last of the subtests of the battery. This is sampled by having the child write any word that he can or copy letters (in the first grade) or copy one of the oral reading paragraphs that he read earlier. The norms for the test are perfectly regular in an increment of ten letters per minute per grade, from the second to the sixth, unlike most other handwriting norms, which show irregular increments from grade to grade. Present norms are identical with those in 1937 except that they have been shifted up one step. Apparently today's children are writing precisely as fast as the children of 1937 did who were a year younger!

Construct Validity

Beginning testing at the pupil's grade level in oral (and again later in silent) will often result in an inability to rate a child's performance, if he is a poor reader. Moreover, a rating based on three selections as suggested by Durrell is impossible for a poor third grader, as Spache (46) and Della-Piana (10) have pointed out. A basal paragraph read without error cannot be established by

Durrell's system of beginning to test the child at his grade level, nor can it be guessed at by the tester, as Durrell suggests.

The value of rate norms for sixth graders in reading selections of seventh- and eighth-grade levels, as in both the oral and silent tests, is questionable. Nor can these tests be given in any order, as Durrell suggests, for, as Della-Piana has noted and Kasdon (27, 28) has proved, if poor readers were started with the silent first, they would probably make higher scores on the oral, than if the order was reversed. The author's directions to wait five seconds before telling the child a word—and that this five-second interval is to be determined by counting to five slowly—are conflicting and misleading (10). The suggestions to measure eye-voice span by sliding a card ahead of the child or to observe and count his eye movements while he reads are both useless procedures if intended to reveal these reading behaviors.

The combining of oral errors from all the oral selections attempted would conceal rather than reveal the pupil's error tendencies in reading at his functional level. Moreover, in this test the rate measure, the only criterion of success in oral reading, is depressed by using a selection at grade level and two more above this point, when compared with rate performances on other standardized oral reading tests, as shown by Spache (46). For this reason, we might well expect the Durrell reading test to give lower estimates of ability than do other tests.

The oral reading test actually does not sample or rate comprehension, and that measured in the oral and silent tests is pure recall, as Harris has said (25). Moreover, use of the same levels of paragraphs in both the oral and the silent would fail to sample thoroughly those silent levels that might be feasible for the pupil. Even when some record of comprehension is made, as in the oral test, no use is made of it in judging the child's reading level. A tell-back as a measure of comprehension, as in the silent test, is severely criticized by numerous reviewers of the test (7).

Absolutely no data are offered by the author on the size or nature of the standardization population, if there was one, for the 1937 or 1955 revisions. No data are offered in the Manual on the reliability of any of the measures or their validity in predicting reading behaviors.

Many users have remarked favorably on the Check Lists of Difficulties and the Profile Chart offered by the author. Although both of these suggest some comparisons among the results of the various tests, the manner in which these tests were constructed often makes these comparisons meaningless. For example, how do we evaluate oral and silent reading when the norms for both are over thirty years old? How compare either of these with the listening test constructed in 1955, for which there is no evidence of actual standardization? How can we compare any of these three with word recognition and word analysis scores based on a new population in 1955? When tests are standardized on unlike populations, as is true throughout this battery, direct comparisons even based on grade level scores are of almost no value.

Concurrent Validity

Several reports have appeared in the literature that offer some evidence of the validity of the Durrell battery. Eller and Attea (15) found correlations of .90 to .92 among the Durrell, the Gates-McKillop, and the Diagnostic Reading Scales in oral reading. Among the word lists of the three batteries, the scores correlated from .92 to .96. These authors also compared these three oral reading tests with the Iowa Test of Basic Skills, a silent test, which we do not consider a very meaningful comparison. No other published data of which we are aware support the validity of any of the other Durrell subtests.

According to Herlin's dissertation (28), Durrell's suggestion for combining oral errors from the passages read produces a pattern peculiar to his tests; hence it may not be a sound guide to corrective steps.

GATES-McKILLOP READING DIAGNOSTIC TESTS (20)

Description

Gates, the senior author, first offered a battery of diagnostic tests in 1936. These were revised in 1945 and, for the present version, again in 1962. The battery is undoubtedly the most complete of its type, for it includes seventeen measures of reading skills and two forms of the entire battery. Perhaps the only major facet of reading not sampled is silent reading, for which the senior author offers a number of other tests.

Content Validity

The first test is one of oral reading of seven paragraphs of a continuous story (identical with that in the 1945 edition). The pupil is to read through the first four paragraphs, at least until he commits eleven or more errors on two consecutive paragraphs. The number of errors is translated into raw scores, summed for the paragraphs, and interpreted as a grade level by tables supplied by the authors for the first seven grades. No measure of comprehension is attempted, and no data on the standardization population are offered (for this or for any of the other tests). The selections have been criticized as stilted, artificial, and unrepresentative of normal school reading in the upper levels.

Oral errors are recorded but analyzed only for the first four paragraphs.

Norms are given for various types of errors, for average, good, and poor performances.

A forty-word list is then presented in half-second exposures, followed by a similar eighty-word list under untimed presentation. The purpose of these lists is to permit observation of the pupil's word recognition habits in isolated words and to compare these tendencies with his oral reading errors. A twenty-six-item phrase reading test with timed presentation by the hand tachistoscope is also offered for comparison with the oral and word recognition tests, although its purpose and significance are not clarified.

Knowledge of word parts or word attack skills are sampled in four subtests:

1. Blending common word elements to form artificial words.
2. Giving the letter sounds of all the consonants and two sounds for each vowel.
3. Naming all the capital letters.
4. Naming all the lower-case letters.

Since letter names are not essential to analysis of unknown words, as letter sounds are, the labeling of the letter-naming tests as word attack skills seems questionable.

Recognizing the sounds heard and associating them with visual symbols is sampled in four more subtests:

1. Nonsense words—The child is asked to mark nonsense words as they correspond to those given orally by the tester.
2. Identifying the initial letter corresponding to the beginning sound of a word given by the tester.
3. Same for final letter sounds.
4. Identifying the vowel corresponding to the medial sound in a word given by the tester.

Auditory blending is tested by giving the parts of a word separately and slowly, then asking the pupil to pronounce the total word.

Supplementary tests include the use of the untimed word list as a spelling test; an oral word-meaning vocabulary test; a syllabication test of reading nonsense words composed of common word elements scored only if child can blend the elements, not whether he pronounces them correctly; and, last of all, an auditory discrimination test of listening to and discriminating similar or dissimilar words.

We might quibble with some of the titles given some tests, as the syllabication test, which really measures blending and is thus almost identical with the earlier blending test; and the labeling of letter-naming tests as measures of word attack skill. But it is apparent that the Gates-McKillop battery does sample a wide variety of reading behaviors.

Construct Validity

The battery has been criticized by various reviewers as being too long and laborious; demanding complicated scoring; offering no comparable measure of potential or silent reading; and lacking instructions in how to eliminate certain tests or make a selection and thus shorten testing time (7). The authors suggest comparisons among subtest scores but give little indication of the meanings of these comparisons. No reliability or validity data are offered for any of the tests (7).

We are critical of the highly detailed norms offered for each test, when standard errors of measurement are not offered to enable the examiner to determine the probable significance of differences between subtests. Since many of the subtests have fewer than twenty items, the standard error for these is probably about 2 in raw scores. It would have been a simple matter to clarify this to users of the test by indicating the size of significant differences in raw scores or grade scores between subtests. Assigning a grade score to a zero raw score, as in the Phrase test, is a questionable procedure. Offering a grade score for every single item in many of the subtests, as though children would progress evenly each month in the number of successful items is, again, misleading. There is ample evidence that reading skills do not grow by similar, regular increments in the successive months of the school year. However, it should be noted that all norms for the 1962 versions of the subtests differ from the 1945 norms, implying that the tests were actually restandardized. It is interesting to note that in most tests the reading performances of the normative population of 1945 were superior to the children of 1962.

Certain of the tests may not actually function in the manner that the authors assume. For example, the oral vocabulary, in which the test item is read to the child, is not directly comparable to other measures of vocabulary, as in the Stanford-Binet or WISC. The subject does not define the word meanings, as in these other tests. Rather, he listens to the stem, as "A head is part of a ______," and selects one of four possible answers offered auditorily. It is probably a measure of auditory vocabulary rather than "oral" vocabulary. The Spelling test requires oral responses that are not necessarily a reflection of written spelling or error tendencies in that medium.

The norms for error types in the oral reading test are desirable, even though they may present a pattern of errors peculiar to the test. Unlike other normative studies of oral errors, the Gates-McKillop norms indicate decreasing omissions and increasing mispronunciations as fluency and accuracy increase. But the lack of a measure of comprehension and of a description of the normative population limit the use of the test.

The distinction between flash and untimed word recognition is doubtful when exposure intervals of a half-second are used. Analysis involving several fixations could occur in the flash presentation during this brief exposure. Nor is there good evidence that the word recognition errors in these word lists will be comparable to those in the oral reading in context.

Concurrent Validity

The authors offer no comparisons of their tests with other similar measures. Eller and Attea (15) found correlations for the oral reading grade score of .90 to .92 among the Durrell, Gates-McKillop, and Diagnostic Reading Scales. The three word recognition tests of these batteries were related in the order of .92 to .96. There are no other validity studies of the other tests of the Gates-McKillop battery with which we are familiar.

GILMORE ORAL READING TEST (21)

Description

The Gilmore Oral Reading Test consists of two forms, each of ten reading selections, for individualized testing in grades one through eight. Separate scores are derived for accuracy, comprehension, and rate of oral reading in both grade scores and stanines.

Since the authors believe that silent and oral reading are relatively synonymous, the test is offered as an overall measure of reading ability.

Content Validity

The first seven reading selections are narrative, while the three most difficult selections tend to resemble content field reading. The child begins reading in a selection two grade levels below his grade placement. If he makes only one or two errors, he is then tested on successively more difficult paragraphs until he makes ten or more errors. Five comprehension questions are appended to each selection measuring simple recall, and the child's performance on these, however poor, does not halt the testing procedure. Rate for reading each selection is recorded in seconds.

The gradation of the difficulty of the paragraphs was determined by the total number of words in the selection; consulting a list of basal reader words; gradual increase in polysyllabic words; the average sentence length; and the percentage of complex sentences. While these criteria would probably produce selections of increasing difficulty, the lack of a point of objective

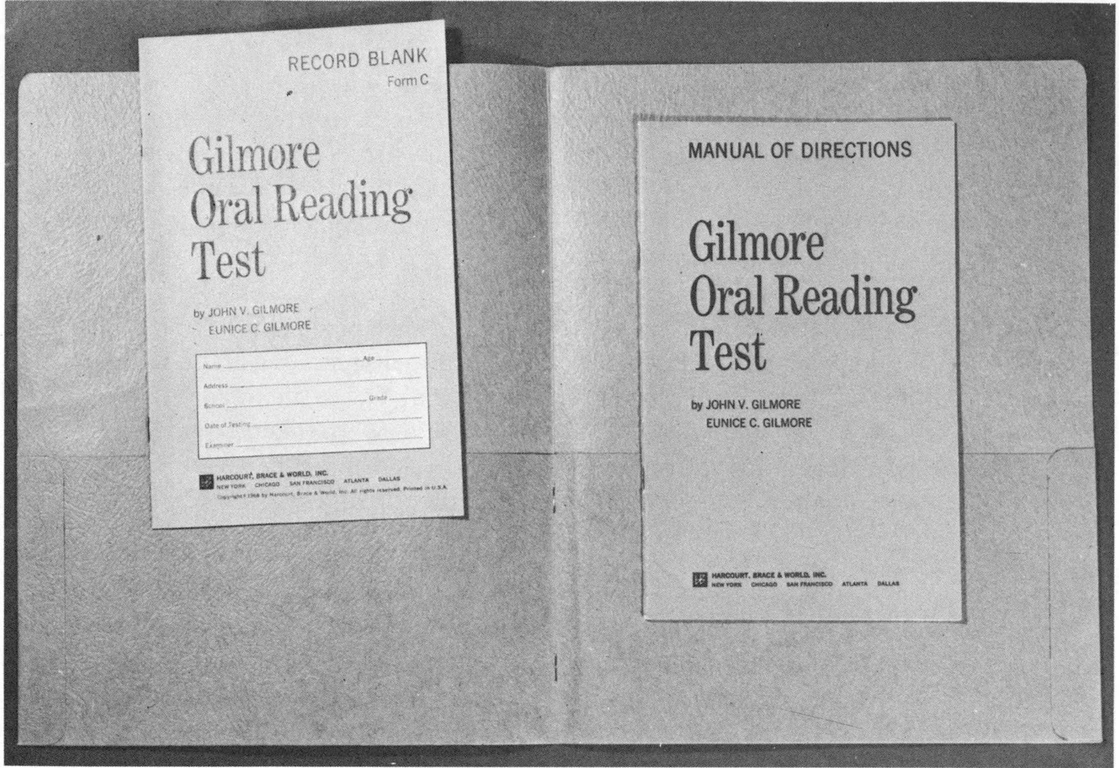

Gilmore Oral Reading Test

reference, such as a readability formula, leaves us with no real information as to the actual reading levels of the selections. In other words, it has not been demonstrated that the Gilmore test will reflect children's performances in normal school materials, for we have no indication that the test materials resemble such materials in their gradation.

Construct Validity

In recording oral reading errors, the authors follow several procedures quite unlike most other oral tests. Omissions or additions of one or more letters, errors on vowels or consonants, and even wrong accent are all subsumed as mispronunciations. Only whole words are considered in counting omissions and additions. Failure to observe punctuation is marked, as are hesitations or pauses of two seconds or more in attempting a word. As some studies show, accuracy in marking hesitations is extremely poor, even after considerable practice, aside from the subjective nature of the judgment involved.

Strangely enough, self-corrections are scored as errors. No real use is made of this error tabulation except for the casual suggestion that combining the error types in all paragraphs scored will indicate pupil needs, a dubious suggestion.

The scoring of the comprehension portion of the test is derived from the sum of all the correct answers given in all the scorable paragraphs. Moreover, the pupil is given additional credits for comprehension in paragraphs above the levels that he had actually attempted to read. Just how such a score should be interpreted in terms of the quality or depth of comprehension that we may expect in the classroom when the child reads in instructional materials is not clear. The comprehension score cannot be interpreted as indicating probable classroom performances in materials appropriate to the child's reading level.

Rate of reading is derived by dividing the sum of all the words read by the total seconds elapsed in all the test paragraphs. Again, this unique way of determining rate in words per minute from a variety of selections ranging from easy to difficult yields data irrelevant to children's performances in classroom instructional materials. It does not indicate the pupil's probable rate of reading in materials of any particular level.

Reliability

The reliability coefficients cited by the author are adequate in accuracy (.84 to .94) but unacceptable in comprehension (.53 to .60) or rate (.54 to .70) for individualized testing (8). Although the authors cite standard errors of measurement for the raw scores derived from the test, they do not instruct the user how to apply these in judging the significance of differences among rate, comprehension, or accuracy, or their meanings in terms of obtained raw scores.

Concurrent Validity

The authors cite correlations between the accuracy score and several silent reading tests used in the First-Grade reading studies ranging from .75 to .85; with the Gates word list of .81 to .90; and the Wide Range Achievement Test (another word list) of .91.

Correlations with two other oral reading tests, the Gray and the Durrell, are also given as .77 to .80 in accuracy; .45 to .50 in rate; and, with the Durrell, of .59 in comprehension. Since these other tests do not yield separate scores in comprehension or rate of reading, it is not clear how these correlations were derived. It may be that the author is comparing his three scores with the single scores yielded by the Gray and the Durrell.

Harris et al. (26) were critical of the inflated grade scores found in the Gilmore in their first-grade slum child population, when comparisons were made with informal or standardized group silent tests or other oral reading tests.

GRAY ORAL READING TESTS (22)

Description Four forms of thirteen brief reading selections are offered for testing from first grade to college levels. The first three selections are for first grade, the next five are for grades two to six, and the last five increase roughly in difficulty by two grade levels each. The test is offered for both diagnostic use and placement in reading groups.

Content Validity The first five selections are narrative, while the remainder sample various content fields. The brevity of the selections, averaging about sixty words each and only three or four sentences at the upper levels, tends to produce marked difficulty of vocabulary in order to insure increase in their levels. With the exception of primary pupils, it is expected that each subject will read at least five passages.

Oral errors are recorded according to the authors' system of distinguishing gross mispronunciation of an entire word from seven subtypes of partial mispronunciations. Only whole word errors are tabulated as omissions, insertions, substitutions, repetitions, or inversions of word order. The proportions of these errors are intended to give insights into needed instruction, although no norms are provided. A brief interpretation of the meanings of the error types is offered. The error count, of course, would be derived from the pupil's reading of all the passages attempted. Hardin and Ames (24) have criticized as unnecessary the fine distinctions among types of mispronunciations and have suggested that all these could be subsumed under the heading of substitutions.

Construct Validity These tests were standardized on 502 children drawn from several states. But their average I.Q. is given as 110, indicating that the group was somewhat better than average in mental ability (and socioeconomic status?). The standardization, however, is labeled as tentative.

The testee's oral reading is recorded in terms of errors, half or full credits for the four literal comprehension questions on each passage, and time in seconds. Time and errors only are combined into a score for each passage, and the sum of these scores is translated into a grade score. Although it is to be noted by the examiner, accuracy in comprehension does not influence the judgment of the pupil's oral reading level and the test is not intended as a measure of comprehension.

Standard errors of the grade scores are given for every score, with their interpretation and meaning illustrated for the user. Separate sex norms for boys and girls, rather than combined norms, are offered for each form of the test. Some users would prefer a combined norm, as most classrooms are mixed. But the authors' norms do indicate a marked difference in performances according to sex, and they would probably argue that, since the results are to be used in individual diagnosis and placement, the differentiation is justified.

Reliability Reliability coefficients among the four forms ranged from .969 to .983, a highly satisfactory level, if we assume that a measure of oral reading independent of comprehension is desirable.

Concurrent Validity As evidence of concurrent validity, the author cites the increments in score from one grade to the next among pupils chosen as representative by the schools cooperating in the standardization. Jerrolds, Callaway, and Gwaltney (30) cite correlations of .7869 with their informal test and .8221 with the Diagnostic Reading Scales. As cited earlier, Gilmore (21) reported ambiguous correlations between his test and the Gray of .77 in accuracy and .45 in rate.

The extension of this oral reading test to grade levels at which oral reading plays a very small part in classroom activities or placement in reading groups raises an interesting question. Do the authors believe that an oral test can still function in placement or diagnosis of instructional needs at post-elementary levels? Will the results of the test be relevant to a classroom program that employs silent reading (of textbooks) almost exclusively?

INDIVIDUAL READING PLACEMENT INVENTORY (45)

Description This inventory is offered for the assessment of reading abilities of youth and adults who are functioning below seventh grade. It purports to measure the instructional, independent, and frustration levels of reading (by Betts's arbitrary standards) and the present potential language level.

Content Validity Testing begins with a Word Recognition wheel in which words are exposed one at a time in a slot for one second each. If the reader responds within the time interval, he is credited with flash recognition; if not, the word is exposed again for his analysis. Word recognition level is determined by the highest

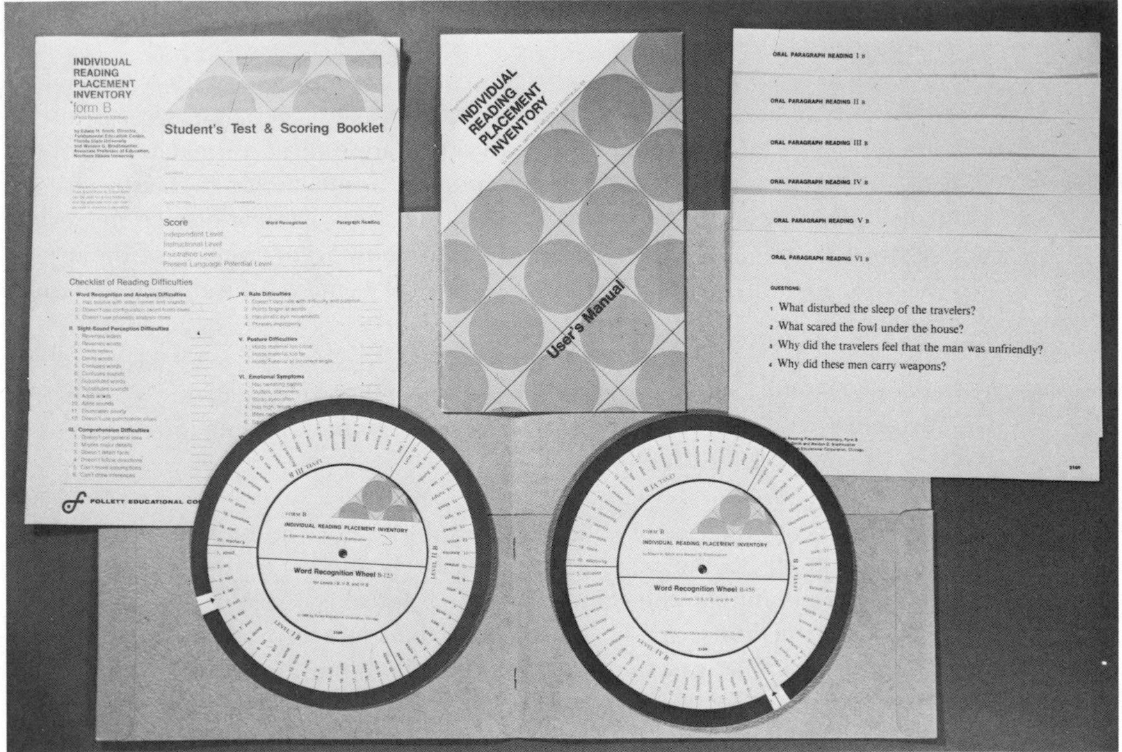

Individual Reading Placement Inventory

level list in which he recognizes 90 percent of the twenty words by flash plus analysis. The last level of adequate performance is considered his instructional level; the one above, as frustration level; the one below, as independent level. Apart from the distinction of performance levels on arbitrary and questionable grounds, the interval of one second for flash viewing would fail to give any distinction between immediate recognition and that obtained by word analysis. Actually the authors make no use of the two possible performances in their scoring, and the complicated testing procedure seems superfluous.

Oral reading begins at one level below the instructional level found on the Word Recognition test, a sensible procedure for establishing rapport. Oral errors of phrasing, hesitation, words aided, omissions, repetitions, and additions of whole words, punctuation marks omitted, reversals, and "phonetic pronunciation" are recorded with a special set of symbols. Scoring is illustrated, but none of the error types is defined in detail. Hesitations are simply defined as a "pause in the flow of oral reading" (or an extra long breath?). No time interval is suggested before offering a word to the reader, which implies that the frequency of this error may well reflect the examiner's anxieties. The reading selections were graded by a readability formula to determine their appropriate levels. Except for one or two on vocations, shopping, and so on, they do not appear to be particularly adapted to adult reading interests.

The reader continues with successive paragraphs until he misses ten or more words or fails 50 percent of the four comprehension questions. Unlike most oral reading tests, the comprehension questions emphasize inferences and conclusions more than literal or recall performance. The failure level represents the frustration level; the last successful level, the instructional; and the level below that, the independent. In determining reading success, the suggested tabulation of errors is modified so that only two to three punctuation marks ignored, words omitted or inserted, or told by the examiner, or reversed are actually counted as single errors. The recording of mispronunciations or repetitions is ignored in determining the final performance. Even the criterion of less than ten oral errors is disparaged by the authors, who recommend basing final estimates only on comprehension. Under these circumstances, it seems pointless to ask the examiner to record these errors that are later ignored.

In later instructions, however, the authors contradict the use of comprehension as the criterion of reading level; they refer the user to the ten-word errors standard. While the trained examiner would probably exercise his own judgment in weighing errors versus comprehension, inexperienced testers might well be confused by these conflicting instructions.

Language potential is next assessed by reading to the testee the selections above the reader's last oral reading level. If the testee has been tested as far as the sixth-grade level, however, there are no selections left for this assessment of potential. No evidence is offered regarding the validity of this testing procedure as a measure of potential for growth in reading.

Supplementary tests of auditory discrimination, phonic skills, and letters are offered in the testing booklet. The ten-item auditory discrimination test asks the testee to repeat one of the four given words that begins with a different sound than the others. Similar five-item tests are used to detect the discrimination of short and long vowel sounds. Others ten-item tests measure the ability to discriminate ending consonant sounds and initial blends and digraphs. All these tests are purely auditory, which raises the question of their relevance to the use of phonic clues in the act of reading. In effect, they are a pretest of auditory readiness for phonic training, not direct measures of the ability to apply phonic clues. Such tests may well be pertinent in youth and adult groups unfamiliar with English letter sounds, but they are not diagnostic of instructional needs in phonics.

Testees scoring below first-grade level in the Word Recognition test are to be given a supplementary measure of knowledge of capital and lower-case letters. Both names and sounds of the letters are to be given by the testee.

No standards are offered for any of these supplementary tests, since they are assumed to sample the testee's "phonic generalizations" and to indicate instructional needs. While this interpretation is possible—if we assume that phonic skills are actually sampled—some indication of strengths and weaknesses would be helpful to guide the teacher. Perfect performance in all these supplementary tests, as the author expects, is not the usual finding or a necessity for reasonably successful reading. There is no evidence that all successful readers possess or employ all phonic techniques to the nth degree in order to read comprehendingly.

Concurrent Validity

Wunderlich and Bradtmueller (50) compared teacher estimates of instructional levels with those found by the Individual Reading Placement Inventory. The correlations ranged from .34 to .49, which led the investigators to criticize the teachers for overestimating low students and underestimating high testing students of the sixth-grade level.

Reviewers of this test (7) have criticized it for lack of information on the standardization group, as well as for the paucity of reliability and validity data. For what they are worth, correlations are cited of .78 to .89 with three silent reading tests in migrant adult and junior-senior high school groups. The mean scores in the four tests are not cited; thus the meaning of the comparisons is limited.

Reliability

Reliability data offered by the authors on the correlations between forms in seven small groups of junior-senior high school retarded readers and adult basic education students range from .91 to .98, satisfactory levels for individualized testing. These data probably refer only to the instructional level as determined by the oral reading subtest.

SAN DIEGO QUICK ASSESSMENT TESTS (34)

Description

The San Diego Quick Assessment Tests are a good example of the current trend toward the use of highly informal testing devices. The group of tests consists of a graded word list, graded word opposites, and an oral reading inventory. A pattern of learning test is also offered by the same source.

Content Validity

The graded word list is composed of thirteen groups of ten words each, presumably representing reading levels from preprimer to the eleventh grade. The source of the words is not given, nor are any data on the validity of the test.* Pupils are to attempt to read aloud each group of words, and their reading levels are indicated by the hardest list on which the pupil misses two or more words. This scoring instruction is, of course, misleading. What the author probably intended to say is that the child's reading level is that point at which he reads all or all but one of the words correctly, for this is the level to be recorded on the test protocol, and is called the independent reading level in an article coauthored by LaPray (33).

The graded word opposites is offered as appropriate for testing pupils poor in comprehension. When the teacher reads a word, the pupil reads and circles its opposite among three alternates. Eight pairs of opposites are offered for each grade level from first to fifth. The child's grade level is determined by that point at which he misses two or more of the opposites (or rather by the level below the point of failure). The source of these words is not given.

The Quick Oral Inventory is composed of brief oral reading selections ranging from preprimer to fourth grade level. Each selection is from twenty to twenty-two words in length, with four questions each to be used if, in retelling the story, the pupil cannot retell at least three of the four-to-six recall items expected. All selections are narrative and quite simple. Success in oral reading is indicated by no more than three oral errors in a selection (85–86 percent accuracy) and the recall of at least three facts (50–75 percent recall) spontaneously or with the aid of the questions.

The Pattern Learning Test involves teaching three words in each of three sessions—one with a picture clue, one with meaning (contextual) clues, and one with sound (phonic) clues. After an interval of fifteen minutes, the three words presented in the preceding session are tested; then three new words are taught and reviewed. The order of presentation—picture, meaning, and sound—is rotated among the three lessons; and total learning of the nine words is tested in the order in which they were presented in the fourth session, all in one morning. Teaching in this fashion is suggested for a Friday, with the follow-up test for the following Monday morning, although the instructions do not indicate that this procedure is essential.

*An earlier article by LaPray and Ross (33) attributes the list to basal glossaries and the Thorndike list.

Testing of the pupils' learning may be done individually with the flash cards used in the lessons, or by a group test in which children circle each of four examples of the given word among ten alternates. The delayed recall shown by the pupils' performances on the Monday testing, using the same short group tests employed in the three testing situations the previous Friday, is considered the best measure of the child's learning pattern. The final test is scored for each type of presentation separately in terms of the total percentage of correct matchings for each type of item on the group test. The author suggests that a comparison of the child's scores on the three types of presentation may then be made and an appropriate teaching approach chosen. She indicates that, in her opinion, the picture clue approach represents the basal method; the sound approach indicates readiness for a creative writing method (language-experience?); and success in both sound and meaning approach indicates the need for a self-selection (individualized) program. If the pupil scores well on all three modes of presentation, a combination of the language-experience and phonic analysis approaches is indicated, according to the author.

Concurrent Validity

Although the author refers frequently to other commercial oral reading tests (such as the Wide Range Achievement and the Gilmore) as though they could be used interchangeably with her instruments, she gives no comparative data to support this implication. The only claim to validity offered for these tests is contained in an article on the word lists (33). The claim is made that in all except four cases in more than 100 testings, the test results agreed with teacher judgments of pupils' instructional levels.

Construct Validity

The resemblance of the San Diego Quick Assessment tests to other informal measures and to the Botel Inventory is obvious. With such examples to imitate, the author apparently does not feel any pressure to demonstrate that the tests she has selected measure what they claim to assess. The graded word lists and the so-called test of comprehension, the word opposites, are of unknown sources, of unknown value in learning to read, and of dubious discriminative power. In fact, the author suggests that her readers who wish to do so can construct similar tests simply by selecting at random from the basal word lists in a set of readers not familiar to the pupils. If followed, this suggestion would indeed produce measuring instruments just about as dependable as those the author offers. It would seem that any group of words drawn at random from any set of basal readers is as learnable, discriminative, and significant for learning to read as any other set, or so the author assumes.

The oral inventory appears to have been composed by the author, for it certainly is not similar in its selections to basal readers. When assessed by the Spache formula, the very brief reading selections measure out as follows: the preprimer 1.5; the second reader, second half, 3.1; the third- and fourth-grade selections both at 3.9+. Rescoring these last two by the Dale-Chall formula indicates readability estimates of 4.5 for the third-grade selection and 4.98 for fourth-grade. In addition to the faulty scaling of these selections, their length of twenty–twenty-two words each raises some doubt of the adequacy of the sampling of pupil oral reading ability.

The scoring of oral reading errors is alluded to in the oral inventory, but the system of scoring is actually offered only as part of the word lists. Errors are to be tabulated as to their position in each word—initial, medial, or final—and according to the miscues on phonemes, prefixes, suffixes, or root words only. No distinction is made among omissions, additions, or substitutions, and so on, or any other of the usual types recorded except reversals; nor are any error types defined for the examiner. A few examples of scoring indicate that the author expects the examiner to record only the exact phoneme miscalled; errors due to word form, context, or other factors are not distinguished (substitution of *quickly* for *quietly* is considered an error in root word; *street* for *straight,* an error in a long vowel).

The Pattern Learning Test can be questioned on a number of grounds. For example, there is no evidence that the words presented by different modes are equally learnable in terms of their associated meanings or concreteness. To illustrate, the three words taught by picture clues are all concrete—*can, bride, match;* two of those taught by meaning association are abstract—*wait, long, jar;* while two of the sound association items are concrete—*splash, pin, rope.* The only attempt to control the variability among words is in terms of their phonemes: each method offers one word of the CVC pattern, one word with a long vowel sound and one word ending in a digraph. It appears that LaPray conceives of word recognition as being exclusively a sound-symbol relationship, rather than one in which context, word form, associated meanings, and experiential background play a part.

It is also doubtful, to this writer, that an attempt to determine the preferred learning modality of a pupil can be reliably assessed by teaching sessions or tests involving comparisons among only three words (even assuming that the steps outlined sample each modality). The small number of items fails to recognize the greater learning capacities of bright children, for, as Mills found with his Learning Methods Test, even ten words per lesson failed to identify the dominant modality among bright children (38). Yet the author specifically recommends her own Pattern Learning Test in preference to the Mills instrument.

An entire appendix to the LaPray text is devoted to other informal tests of letter and word reading, word meanings, a modified cloze, a silent reading inventory, and so on. However, no instructions for administering or interpreting any of these is offered; hence it seems pointless to evaluate them.

An article by Victor Froese (18) provides some relevant data on these San Diego Quick Assessment Tests. Froese compared the three word lists offered by LaPray, the Standard Reading Inventory of McCracken, and that contained in an unpublished Informal Reading Inventory. Children at the second-, fourth- and sixth-grade levels were tested by all three lists. The grade level predictions of the three lists were significantly different; moreover, when compared in terms of the total words correctly read, the LaPray evidenced a significant relationship to performances on the other two tests only at the second grade. The words used in the LaPray list were distinctly different from those in the other two lists and yielded very different estimates of pupil reading levels. Froese naturally questioned the equivalence of the three lists and their validity in predicting pupils' classroom reading levels.

STANDARD READING INVENTORY (36)

Description The Standard Reading Inventory is offered for individualized testing from preprimer to seventh-grade reading levels. It consists of eleven selections for oral reading, eight selections for silent reading, and eleven word lists. The battery is intended to yield measures of recognition vocabulary in isolation and in context, oral reading errors, comprehension in silent and oral reading, and oral and silent speed of reading.

Content Validity The oral reading selections and word lists were based on the vocabulary and content present in three widely known basal reader series. The Spache and the Dale-Chall readability formulas were employed to analyze and rank the oral reading selections. As additional evidence of content validity, the author cites the opinions of reading experts in ranking the oral selections, along with two applications of these selections in school situations. There was marked similarity between expert rankings and the author's arrangement of the reading selections, and the selections did seem to reflect higher scores at each grade level tested. A study of the subtest scores for a group of thirty-five third graders indicated that there was a hierarchy of difficulty in their items, except for one subtest of interpretation. Actually these studies are not evidence of the validity of the content of the tests, but rather are indications of its construct validity in that the tests seem to discriminate among pupils of different grades.

The question of content validity, that is, whether a test based on the vocabulary and content of three basal series can be used as a general test for any and all pupils, remains unanswered.

Construct Validity

Each of the subtest scores is compared with a scoring sheet offering standards at each grade level for the frustration level, the instructional level (questionable and definite), and the independent reading level. A composite judgment is made from the child's performances at various grade levels in determining these levels of performances. In keeping with the viewpoint found in many informal inventories, McCracken expects higher performances in all subtests at the independent level than for the instructional or the frustration level. In fact, the author tells us that a pupil must score at the higher standards of the independent level in all the subtests at a given level before he would be permitted to read a book of that level independently. In other words, even though a child's reading interests and his degree of silent comprehension might indicate adequate performance in silent reading of a book of a certain level, he may not be permitted such books. Like the authors of many informal inventories, McCracken offers no evidence supporting this attitude of limiting pupils' breadth of reading experiences.

The word lists, or Isolated Recognition Vocabulary as the author terms them, are administered by sliding the cards past a hole in a cardboard holder, a hand tachistoscope. The examiner is instructed to expose the words as rapidly as possible, provided the child is responding instantly. However, the instructions indicate that a maximum of ten seconds will be allowed if the child needs it to study a word. This implies that the child will be given two presentations of a word: a flash presentation and a longer exposure if he needs it. No distinction is made in scoring the two types of responses, for all correct answers are simply summed to obtain the score on a list. In view of this manner of scoring and the lack of a time limit on the flash exposures, the use of the tachistoscope seems pointless in several respects. Telling examiners to expose as "rapidly as possible" leaves the actual exposure time entirely to the vagaries of the examiner. Moreover, Froese's comparison of word lists (18) indicated that the flash exposure used by McCracken did not yield different pupil scores than did untimed responses. Like the present author, Froese questions the need of any flash device, at least in the manner suggested by McCracken.

In addition to the estimation of sight vocabulary attempted by these word lists, McCracken suggests that they be used to guide the examiner in the selection of the opening oral reading test. He recommends that oral testing begin two grade levels below the highest level in which the child recognizes immediately twenty-three of the twenty-five word items. Since word recognition and oral reading performances are often similar at primary grade levels, and since it is desirable to begin testing at a level that is probably easy for the child, this use of the word lists is defensible.

The testing of oral reading presents a number of unusual or even unique features that some examiners may find confusing. The reading selections for both Forms A and B are printed in the Manual. The same booklet containing the reading selections also contains all the directions for the examiner for all tests. Unless the examiner has memorized all instructions and scoring procedures, this Manual has to be shuttled back and forth between child and examiner, which seems an unnecessary bother. This point is particularly pertinent because McCracken's system of recording oral reading errors differs markedly from the systems of other common tests. And yet the complex instructions for this recording (which, of course, is done while the child is reading) are at that time in the booklet from which the child is reading and therefore inaccessible to the examiner.

McCracken's system of recording oral errors is unnecessarily detailistic and complicated (8). For example, if the examiner pronounces a word for the child, after a wait of five seconds, he is to write a *P* above the word. If the examiner must pronounce the word twice, two *P*'s are written. If several adjacent words are pronounced for the child, these must be enclosed by a bracket and again labeled *P*. Since any of the three errors count only as a single error, different markings for each seems superfluous. Again, in scoring repetitions four different markings or symbols are apparently necessary.

Similarly, in scoring mispronunciations, the word is to be written phonetically above the correct word as the child mispronounces it, and circled if he does not correct his mispronunciation. If time does not permit writing the child's mispronunciation, a wavy line is inscribed above the word. Again, we fail to see the justification for three types of marking to indicate a single type of error, particularly when the circled words (which were not repronounced correctly by the child) do not affect the scoring of oral errors.

Other peculiarities in McCracken's scoring of oral errors are treating a substitution as though it always included an omission; scoring reversals as a type of substitution; scoring words aided (pronunciation), mispronunciations, omissions, substitutions, and additions only as word recognition errors; and totaling these separately. A separate score in total oral errors is then computed by adding to the sum of word recognition errors other mistakes involving repetitions and punctuation, as well as all self-corrected word recognition errors (such as those in which the child repeats the correct pronunciation of a word after having been prompted by the examiner). The standards for total oral errors at the definite instructional level demand oral accuracy of 92 percent to 95 percent from the preprimer to seventh-grade levels. These are obviously arbitrary standards set by the author, for as Powell has shown (39), no large-scale studies of oral errors indicate that pupils actually read with these degrees of accuracy, especially at primary grades.

Beginning with the primer level, some selections are designated for silent reading; the child, in effect, alternates reading silently and orally. Each selection is accompanied by ten recall questions that are recorded separately as oral or silent recall. The expected performance in comprehension (recall) in all these selections at all levels is 60 percent from both oral and silent reading for the questionable instructional level, and 70–80 percent for the definite instructional level. These are obviously a priori standards set by the author rather than reflections of the actual performances of pupils, which would probably be much greater.

The use of the 60 percent level of comprehension for the questionable instructional level may, of course, be intended as a minimum standard rather than the usual performance in classroom materials. But designating 50 percent comprehension as representing frustration is not supported in a recent study. Ekwall, Solis, and Solis (14) found that in using a polygraph to measure the frustration level in reading, children were not frustrated at the 50 percent comprehension level. In fact, the polygraph did not indicate increasing reaction by the children until comprehension fell to an average of 42 percent. Good readers, in contrast, sometimes evidenced frustration at higher comprehension levels.

The author uses a unique system of scoring these comprehension questions. He credits those answered spontaneously during a tell-back of the story as unaided responses; then he has the examiner ask the remaining questions and those previously answered incorrectly. But both types are summed to score the pupil's performance.

In addition to the comprehension questions measuring recall after silent or oral reading, three to five questions labeled Total Interpretation are offered from the primer on. Two or three of these questions can readily be recognized as reflecting inferences that might be drawn from the content of the reading selection. Because they are inferential, such questions will evoke variable or even contradictory answers from children in terms of their own interpretations of similar life situations. But the author offers no typical or modal answers to guide the examiner, simply instructing us to score any reasonable (?) answer as correct. This, of course, leaves the scoring dependent upon the vagaries of the examiner's interpretations.

Beginning at the second-grade level, a word or two contained in the selection is substituted for the so-called interpretation questions. The child is asked to find the word in the selection, to read the sentence containing it aloud, and then to give the meaning of the word as used in that sentence. Thus the Total Interpretation score is a mixture of inferential questions and of deriving word meanings from context. Incidentally, acceptable answers to the word meaning questions are not given by the author but are left to the examiner's judgment. Exactly what this subtest (which varies in its nature from one level to the next, and for which the author avoids giving any reliability data) is measuring is a moot question.

The oral reading selections are also used to sample Vocabulary in Context from the preprimer to third-grade levels. Ten words are underlined in each story above the preprimer level, and twenty-four words so marked in the preprimer selection. According to the author, these test recognition of vocabulary in context, as contrasted to the word lists, which are considered measures of vocabulary in isolation. A comparison of pupil skill in deriving word meanings from context versus isolated word naming would be desirable, but this test fails to accomplish this purpose. The two vocabulary tests are not parallel in their items to any appreciable degree, nor are the words in context necessarily identifiable by contextual clues. In fact, most of the Vocabulary in Context items are not supported by contextual or structural leads and would have to be recognized at sight. In effect, the author has simply constructed another sampling of sight vocabulary of the basal series from which he drew his items, under a different label. No rationale for the two methods of sampling the same skill is offered.

During the oral and silent reading by the pupil, the examiner is asked to record the elapsed time in seconds for each selection; standards are given for each performance. Like the present writer, Guszak (23) translated McCracken's standards for the definite instructional level to words per minute, the usual form in which speed of reading is expressed. He claimed that the standards for the sixth and seventh grades for oral reading were 150 wpm, while those for silent for the same grades were 245 and 300 respectively. There was an error in Guszak's computations, however, for the correct figures, according to McCracken's standards for the sixth and seventh grades are oral 130 wpm, in sixth and seventh, silent 204 in sixth, and 240 in seventh. In our opinion, not only are the silent reading standards too high, as Guszak complained, but so also are the oral reading standards. We consider oral reading at the rate of 130 words per minute as extremely fluent, not an average performance, as McCracken implies. As for the silent reading, comparison of a large number of silent reading tests indicates an average rate of 176 words per minute in sixth grade and 216 wpm in seventh as expected performances.

It is quite possible that the exceptionally high rate of reading standards suggested by McCracken—at least for the sixth and seventh grades—reflect the nature of his reading selections, for it is well known that reading rate will vary with the type of material being read. McCracken's selections are drawn from nature study and social science beginning at the fourth grade. But, almost seminarrative in style, they are relatively easy reading. Applying the Dale-Chall formula to the entire oral and silent reading selections, in the revised form suggested by Powers et al. (40) yields an estimate of 4.9 for the sixth grade oral selection and a 5.0 for the silent reading selection. This implies that the sixth-grade selections are respectively fourth- and fifth–sixth-grade levels. The seventh-grade selections, as evaluated by the same formula, are 5.4 for the oral and 5.6 for the silent; in other words, both are of fifth–sixth grade readability level. Thus the faulty scaling of these sixth- and seventh-grade reading selections may account for the unusually high rate of reading standards offered by McCracken.

Since the exact rate of reading is not a significant matter during primary grades, in our opinion, we question the values of standards for the first and second grades.

Concurrent Validity

In his Manual, McCracken quotes correlations of his instructional level with the California Reading Test for seventy-nine second-grade children of .87. Comparing his instructional level with the comprehension section of the Stanford Reading Test for seventy-seven third-grade children gave .77, while his word lists correlated .88 at this level with the vocabulary section of the Stanford. These data imply a reasonable degree of similarity to other reading tests, at least at the second- and third-grade levels.

In a 1970 article (37) McCracken offers additional concurrent validity data in a comparison of his test with the Botel Inventory. In a very bright population from a demonstration school, mean reading levels for grades one to six in the Botel and Standard Reading Inventory were not consistently different at the definite instructional level. At the questionable instructional level, the McCracken gave consistently lower mean reading scores, two to fourteen months different from the Botel. In the same population, McCracken's definite instructional level was consistently lower than the paragraph meaning section of the Stanford Reading Test by two to seventeen months in mean reading levels. Since McCracken interprets the independent level as being lower than the instructional, it is apparent that his measure of silent reading ability would yield scores much lower than the Stanford. Correlations between the instructional levels of the Botel and the Standard ranged from .79 and .78 to .95, in the same select population in grades one to six. If we ignore the tendency to lower estimates of reading ability, these are reasonable validity correlations.

In this same article, McCracken interprets the correlations between the Botel and his instrument as supporting the concept of the instructional level (since that term is used by both authors) and proving that this level can be measured reliably. The data prove nothing of the sort, of course, since they simply indicate some similarity between two commercial tests (no matter how labels are applied), and they do not bear upon the question of reliability of their measurements of the instructional level. Very wisely, McCracken retreats from his untenable position in a later paragraph, admitting that these data do not affirm the validity of the concept of instructional level or the standards employed by either test. He also acknowledges that there is no evidence that pupils instructed at their "instructional" level will necessarily learn to read better, or worse, or more easily than if taught with materials of other levels.

We have already referred to Froese's pertinent study (18), which found that there were great differences in the grade levels obtained from the word lists used by McCracken, those of the San Diego Quick Assessment battery, and those of an Informal Inventory.

Reliability

McCracken reports in his Manual test-retest correlations between Forms A and B for small groups extending over a range of six grades. Correlations for the frustration, definite, and questionable instructional and independent levels range from .86 to .91 for this sample of six grades. Other test-retest correlations for eight of the nine subtests (that on interpretation is omitted) in grades one to six range from .68 for word recognition errors to .99 for vocabulary in isolation.* Since in actual use of the test, the final evaluations of instructional, independent, and frustration levels are a global judgment based on results in all of the subtests, these reliability correlations are certainly reasonable. The low reliability of the word recognition errors subscore may reflect the author's complicated scoring system, as much as the instability of children in making such errors in his reading selections. Moreover, perhaps wisely, the author makes no attempt to suggest an interpretation of the meanings of word recognition errors or their role in remedial instruction. Nor does he attempt to relate any other subtest scores to corrective instructional steps that might be used in the classroom.

The author offers no intercorrelations among the subtests, for he recognizes that they are probably highly intercorrelated. Yet he offers check lists of probable reading difficulties and a chart of comparative strengths based on the results of these same subtests. If, as we have pointed out, there is

*This must be a series of correlations for different populations, for some subtests for grades one through three and in other cases for all six grades, since not all subtests are applicable over the six-grade range, but this is not made clear by the author.

considerable overlap among certain of the tests, then these intertest comparisons can only be misleading.

At the very end of the Manual, McCracken offers a group of stories and questions for measuring listening comprehension. The questions for each story are a melange of types: recall, interpretation, inference, and defining words. The pupil's answers are recorded in the same indirect fashion as in the oral and silent selections, with spontaneous answers to any questions that occur during a tell-back of the story being counted separately from answers given to direct questioning. Again, however, both types of responses are added together to obscure the significance of the categorizing. In these listening comprehension selections, however, more rigid standards are imposed, for to evidence comprehension the pupil must (1) answer four or more questions correctly during the tell-back; (2) answer several more questions correctly in answer to direct questioning; (3) achieve a total of seven or more correct answers; and (4) give answers during the tell-back that are complete sentences. Why?

The author does not justify his more exacting standards for listening comprehension than for comprehension in oral or silent reading; or the point in scoring spontaneous and elicited responses separately and then adding them together for the scoring; or the reasons for numbering the sequence of the child's answers of both types, as he gives them. McCracken offers no guide as to the expected difference in terms of the child's verbal mental ability, bilingualism, or language experiences. Apparently the examiner is to assume that if listening comprehension is higher, the child is an underachiever. No explanation is proffered for those cases in which there will be no differences or in which listening will be inferior to instructional level.

CLASSROOM READING INVENTORY (43)

Description The author, Nicholas J. Silvaroli, offers this instrument as a substitute for the informal inventories that require much of a teacher's time and for group reading tests, which, he feels, do not yield sufficient information about pupil needs. The Inventory is composed of three sections: words in isolation, oral reading paragraphs, and a graded spelling survey, for grades two through eight. A second set of paragraphs is included for use in oral, silent, or hearing capacity level testing, if the teacher chooses to use them.

Content Validity The Graded Word Lists contain twenty words each for preprimer, primer, and first to sixth grade. Each pupil is to begin with the preprimer list, pronouncing each word as the teacher records until he reaches a level at which he fails on five or more words. The Graded Oral Paragraphs are then begun at the level corresponding to the highest word list in which the pupil recognized all the words. Silvaroli's recording of oral errors is quite simple, involving only repetitions—*R* and a line over; insertions—indicated by a caret and the insertion; substitution—line through word, substitute written above; omission—circle word omitted; and words aided—put P above word pronounced for child when it is apparent that he does not know. Perhaps only this last type can be criticized for vagueness, for the teachers could vary considerably in the speed with which they react to a child's hesitation over a word. Some teachers would probably prompt more quickly and hence score more such errors than would others. Some time limit to be observed before prompting would help control this variability.

The oral reading paragraphs extend from preprimer to sixth-grade level only. Just how this test could also function in assessing the reading of seventh and eighth graders, as the author claims it will, is not very clear, unless used only with retarded readers of those levels. The paragraphs are drawn from fiction, nature study, science, and social science. The selections, relatively brief, range from 24 words at the preprimer level to 128 at the fifth-grade level in Form A, and from 24 to 174 words at the sixth grade in Form B. The paragraphs were graded by the Spache, Dale-Chall, and Flesch formulas and are intended to resemble elementary reading materials.

The Spelling Survey offers fifteen words for each level from preprimer to seventh grade. As is true for the other materials in the Inventory, no specific source is revealed for this section.

Construct Validity

Rather than translating scores on the word list into grade scores, each level is treated as an entity; and the estimate of word recognition ability is that group in which the child scores more than 75 percent correct. The use of this level as a guide to beginning oral reading testing is certainly desirable, particularly at primary levels where oral reading and word recognition performances are very similar. But the arbitrary standards of more than 75 percent correct may or may not represent normal performances of ordinary children. The author offers no data that his choice of words for each list is characteristic of the reading vocabulary of that grade level; nor that most children reading successfully at that grade level recognize more than 75 percent of his word list. Hence the word list may or may not function as a guide to oral reading testing.

Five questions are offered for each oral reading selection and are categorized as belonging to three types: fact, inference, and vocabulary. In scoring the child's answers to these questions, the teacher is supposed to note consistent errors in any one type of question. There are, however, only four questions of the vocabulary type in the entire eight selections in Form A or Form B. Since the pupil is not likely to be asked to read more than three or four paragraphs (which might thus include only one or two questions of this type), how does the teacher detect "consistent errors" in this measure of defining words in context? What is the meaning of "consistent errors"?

Some of the inference questions cannot be deduced from the reading material, but rather depend on the pupil's informational background, as in Q.5 at grade one; Q.2 at grade four in Form A; Q.3 at grade four in Form B. Some questions labeled inference, as Q.1 and Q.5 at grade three, Form B, require facts given in the story, not inferences. It is apparent that these comprehension items have never been analyzed for differentiation or validity; thus, recording them in terms of "comprehension errors" would be pointless, in our opinion.

In scoring the total of word recognition errors in the oral reading paragraphs, the author designates zero to two errors as indicating the pupil's independent level (98 to 100 percent accuracy); one to six errors as the instructional level (92 to 96 percent up to first grade; 94 to 95 percent in second to sixth in oral accuracy). In comprehension, pupils are expected to achieve 75–100 percent at the independent level, and at the instructional level, 50 to 63.5 percent. Again, it is obvious that these standards were set by the author—as is the common practice in informal inventories—and do not represent true pupil performances. Hence they may or may not be relevant to pupil classroom performances.

No data regarding the standardization of this inventory, its validity, or reliability are offered by the author. The author has simply created an abbreviated informal inventory with all the usual questionable assumptions about actual pupil reading performances.

DIAGNOSTIC READING SCALES (47)

Description The battery is intended for individualized testing of normal and retarded readers at elementary levels and of retarded readers at junior and senior high levels. It was first published in 1963 and revised in 1972. The revision consisted of only minor changes in the testing materials and a considerable expansion of the Manual. Two new tests of auditory abilities were added in the revision.

The Scales consist of three word recognition lists of fifty, forty, and forty words each for use with pupils of the first six grades. The lists are intended to function simply as a pretest to indicate the best level for testing oral reading, not as a formal measure of any major reading skill. Two reading selections are offered for eleven reading levels extending from primer to eighth grade. The parallel selections at each level are separated in the record booklet, since it is intended that only one selection be used in initial testing at each reading level. Eight supplementary tests of phonic knowledge, blending, initial consonant substitution, and auditory discrimination are also offered.

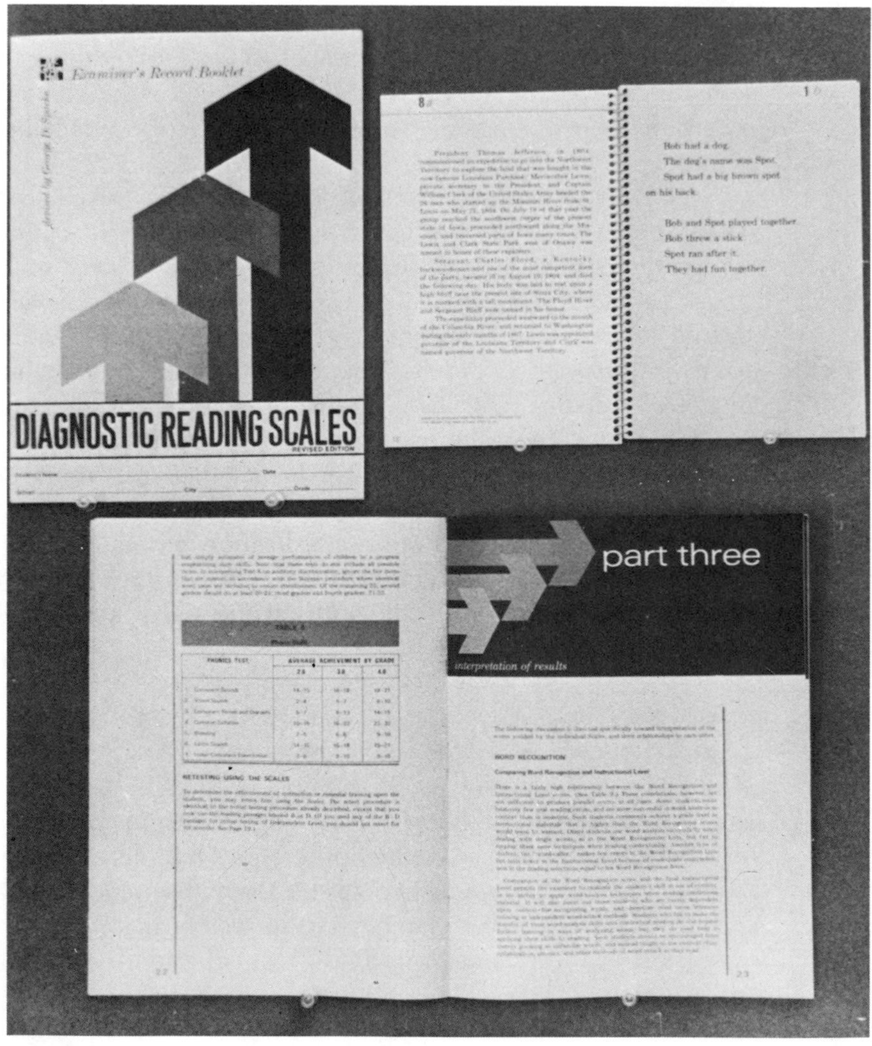

Diagnostic Reading Scales

Content Validity

The word lists were drawn from standard studies of primary reading, speaking, and writing vocabularies. Their order of difficulty was determined by trials with pupils, and their order of presentation was thus determined.

The twenty-two reading passages simulate the range and content of materials commonly used in schools. They are narrative in the first four grades; and they sample the fields of social science, science, and nature study in the fourth- to eighth-grade levels. The Phonics Tests sample the areas of consonant sounds, vowel sounds, consonant blends and digraphs, and common phonograms, as well as the pupil's performances in blending sounds, in substituting initial consonants, and in auditory discrimination of pairs of words. The order of presentation of the items of these phonics tests was determined by item analysis of their difficulty.

The reading passages were graded by the Spache and Dale-Chall readability formulas and in terms of pupils' performances during the early trials in oral reading errors and comprehension. Direct comparisons were made between each pair of parallel selections and also with a third passage drawn from an established contemporary oral reading test in grading and equating the reading selections. Teacher judgment of pupil reading abilities was also used as a criterion for the appropriateness of difficulty of the selections and for a comparison with test estimates of pupil reading levels.

In standardizing the Scales, 2081 pupils were used in establishing the oral reading error norms; 1939 of these entered into the oral comprehension norms, and 1269 provided the silent reading comprehension norms. The pupils were drawn from both rural and urban schools in four states.

Construct Validity

After the word lists have been administered, the child is asked to read a selection at a level just below his word recognition score. After he reads the selection orally, his comprehension is checked by seven or eight questions, largely of the recall type. Oral reading errors are recorded by the examiner as the child reads by a simple system: omissions are circled; additions, indicated by a caret, are written in; substitutions, by crossing out the printed word and writing in the pupil's pronunciation; reversals, by a curved line; words aided (after five seconds), by crossing out the printed word. Repetitions of two words or more only are counted and marked by an arrow from right to left under the words repeated. Hesitations and self-corrections are not counted as errors. Regional or dialectal mispronunciations are also not counted as errors. In most respects, this error recording deliberately resembles the systems of other well-known oral reading tests to facilitate its use by the examiner.

Norms are given for the maximum number of oral reading errors and for the minimum correct answers to the comprehension questions. The oral errors represent the mean number of errors plus one standard deviation of the pupils in the standardization population in reading each passage. Thus, a pupil who reads a selection with fewer errors than the standard has read it as well as the great bulk of pupils of that grade level. The standard for comprehension is 60 percent correct, a minimum as we have noted, for in the actual standardization pupils usually read with greater comprehension than this level. This minimal standard of acceptable comprehension was established by repeated analyses of the standardization data in comparing mental ages and reading scores. Higher standards for comprehension were found to yield underestimates of reading ability as related to mental ages or teacher judgments of pupil performances.

To perform successfully in the oral passages, the pupil must show minimal or better comprehension and must make fewer oral errors than the norm. If so, he is then tested on the next most difficult level. The oral testing continues until he fails in either oral errors or comprehension. The final successful level of oral reading is considered to represent the proper instructional level of the pupil.

After the oral testing, the pupil is permitted to read the next most difficult passage silently, and his performance is judged solely on achieving the minimal comprehension standard. This procedure is based on the assumption that many pupils can read silently with adequate comprehension some materials that are harder than those used in instruction. The author offers data on small groups from first to sixth grade, indicating that both the mean and median independent (silent reading) level was higher than the instructional by following this procedure. The proportion of children achieving a higher level in silent than in oral reading gradually increased from slightly less than 50 percent in the first grade to 55 percent in the second. Eller and Attea (15) criticized this testing procedure, yet their own data for third graders showed that 53 percent scored higher in silent than in oral.

Harris (25), also criticizing the standards for comprehension and oral errors, suggests that, since they differ from the hypothetical standards often used in informal inventories, the examiner can use his own standards. (We do not agree that hypothetical standards are preferable to actual standardization data or that pupils' performances in this test could be accurately judged if such arbitrary standards were applied.)

Other reviewers of the test have been disturbed by the fact that the author has rejected the hypothetical informal inventory standards and procedures. We believe that we have presented sufficient evidence in our discussion of such inventories in our *Investigating the Issues of Reading Disabilities* to justify rejecting their standards and assumptions. When the pupil fails to achieve the minimal standard in silent reading, the last level of successful performance is designated as the independent level. The assumption is that the pupil can read some materials of interest or value to him silently at that level with adequate comprehension. When silent reading testing is completed, the examiner begins to read the next harder selection to the pupil to estimate his potential level. This continues until the pupil falls below the minimum standard for comprehension. In support of this procedure, the author offers a number of studies. One primary-grade study offers correlations ranging from .35 to .83 for predicting pupil performance on the California Reading Test, and *r*'s of .40 to .81 in predicting the instructional level on the Scales. In both these sets of data, there is a comparison between the measured potential level at the beginning of the school year with reading test performance at the end of the year. Another study of retarded readers cited yielded a correlation of .66 of potential level with true gain after remedial work. A second study cites an *r* of .73 of potential level with true gain in independent level and of .62 with true gain in a word list for a group of retarded readers after remedial training.

In these same two studies, even the independent level predicted true gain in instructional level in terms of correlations of .83 and .32 and of .89 with true gain in independent level after tutoring. To our knowledge, these are the only data supporting the use of auditory comprehension as a measure of potential for gain, in any standardized test we have reviewed here.

Ramsey criticizes the phonics tests as failing his criterion of reality in that they do not test the skills in the same manner as that ability is used in the act of reading (42). He is referring, of course, to the tests of consonant, vowel, consonant blends, and digraphs, some of which do deal with the sounds of isolated letters or clusters. His criticism is not applicable to the tests of blending, common phonograms, or the new tests of initial consonant substitution or auditory discrimination, for these do simulate reading behaviors as they normally occur. The four tests of the sounds of phonemes are artificial, in a sense, in that they ask for the reproduction of the sound of a single letter or cluster, an act that may or may not occur frequently in the act of reading, unless the pupil is taught by a synthetic method. But, regardless of the teaching method used, the pupil must master these sounds for successful phonic analysis, and the tests do provide a simple way of sampling this knowledge. Tests do not have to parallel exactly some aspect of the act of reading, as in the case of tests of sight vocabulary, meaning vocabulary, and comprehension, in order to give some insights into the pupil's needs for training. If we accepted Ramsey's definition of reality in testing reading, the only acceptable type of test would be one of oral or silent reading of passages, with a consequent loss of much diagnostic information that might be obtained if other types of sampling were used.

In his review of the test, Dale Bryant (5) argued for separate norms for timed and untimed responses in the Word Recognition tests. We disagree on several counts: First, without some type of automatic timing device, this differentiation would be lost at the hands of the ordinary examiner. We have already pointed this out in criticizing the faulty operation of the cardboard tachistoscope as used by Durrell and McCracken. Second, Froese (18) found no real difference in scores for timed and untimed responses. Third, the purpose of observing the pupil's word recognition habits in isolated words, which is a subordinate goal of the word lists, is not necessarily improved by using timed and untimed responses. We are likely to learn more by recording an untimed, repetitive effort by the child than by observing timed responses.

Ramsey's criticism of our use of recall type questions instead of a variety of types is based on the assumption that various types of questions can be reliably identified and shown to measure different aspects of comprehension (42). As a matter of fact, no factor analysis of reading tests has yet shown that different types of thinking are really assessed by these various types of questions. The components of the reading act appear to be vocabulary difficulty, relationships among ideas, and inductive and deductive reasoning, not the types of ideas identified by labeling questions such as main ideas, details, conclusions, inferences, and the like. In the actual construction of the comprehension questions, we did try to include some that demanded more than recall, such as Q7, 2C; Q3, 3A; Q8, 3C; Q6, 7A; and others. But many of these questions did not prove discriminative between good and poor comprehenders; they were consequently eliminated. It may seem desirable to sample comprehension with a variety of questions that appear to sample different types of thinking. But no test maker has yet demonstrated that this approach does in fact sample the kinds of facts or thinking that he believes he is testing.

Concurrent Validity

The validity of using the Word Recognition lists as a pretest to oral reading is supported by the author's correlations of .78, .65, and .69 with the instructional level, for the three lists respectively. As we have remarked before, these support the relationship between word recognition and oral reading ability and justify our use of the word lists as a pretest. They do not prove the validity of the lists as an overall measure of word recognition ability or any other major reading skill, nor were they intended to. The decreasing relationship between word recognition and general reading ability is evidenced in a series of correlations in the Manual. The correlations between our word recognition lists and the California Reading Test decrease from the first to sixth grade from .87 and .92 in first and second grades to .63 and .71 in fifth and sixth.

Eller and Attea cite validity coefficients between our word lists and those of Durrell and Gates-McKillop of .93 and .92; and in oral reading of .92 and .90 (15). Oral reading mean scores were .5 lower on the Durrell and .3 lower on the Gates than in our tests in Eller and Attea's third-grade population. Eller and Attea's criticism of the fact that our word list gives a mean score .8 higher than Gates and .5 more than Durrell is irrelevant, for the purpose of our test is not to offer a measure of sight vocabulary but to function only as a pretest. Unlike Gates and Durrell, we do not offer the word list as a formal measure of sight vocabulary.

Jerrolds, Callaway, and Gwaltney (30) compared our oral test, the Gray-Robinson, and an informal inventory. Correlations between the Gray-Robinson and the Scales were .8221; between the Scales and the informal inventory, .948. Mean oral reading scores on the Scales were approximately seven months higher than the Gray and six months higher than the informal test. The only explanation that we can offer for the higher estimates of oral reading when using the Scales than for the Gray, Durrell, Gates, or informal test is our unique procedure of using actual pupil performances in oral errors (mean plus one standard deviation) as contrasted with the arbitrary standards used by some of the other authors. Since our norms are based on pupil performances rather than the very demanding arbitrary standards of most of these other tests, we can expect our estimates of reading ability to be higher.

Other criticisms of insufficient normative data—made by Della-Piana (11) and Bryant (5)—are answered in the revised Manual. The occasional need of a second paragraph in testing at a particular grade level is also recognized in the Manual. However, examiners are warned against using the parallel paragraphs frequently in initial testing, for they would then lack fresh test passages for a retest. Testing with single passages for each grade is adequate for reliability, as we shall point out. It is, of course, insufficient for broad generalizations about pupil ability in reading each type of material.

Several other validity studies are reported in the Manual. These involve a comparison among teacher judgment, the oral section of the Scales, and the Metropolitan Reading Test at the first grade; and comparisons of the oral and silent reading scales with the California Reading Test. At the first grade, the Scales agreed with teacher judgment within three months in 55 percent of the cases, while the Metropolitan showed the same degree of agreement in none of the cases. The correlations for oral reading and the California ranged from .67 to .87; for silent reading and the California, from .64 to .79 in samples from second to sixth grade.

Reliability

Several types of reliability data are offered in the Manual for the Scales. Correlations of instructional, independent and potential levels obtained from the eleven passages labeled A-C used for initial testing, with the corresponding B-D passages were .99, .98, and .99 respectively. It would appear that estimates of reading ability based on single passages from the A-C part of the test are markedly similar to estimates from the parallel passages. These correlations were based on a six-grade range of pupils and, of course, would be lower in a single-grade, homogeneous group. But the correlations are certainly sufficient to justify the assumption that the two sets of reading passages measure in similar fashion.

Reliability coefficients for the instructional and independent level for a ten-week interval were .84 and .88 respectively. These correlations were probably reduced by the fact that daily remedial tutoring was given these pupils during the interval and the gains varied from pupil to pupil. Reliability coefficients for primary classes in potential level for a five-month interval were .94 in first grade, .67 in second, and .90 in third. Kuder-Richardson 21 coefficients of internal consistency (or reliability) were .91 for List One, .87 for List Two, and .91 for List Three.

None of these data, of course, prove that an instructional level is necessarily the optimum level for classroom materials. But the constant use of teacher judgment in constructing and validating the Scales does argue that the instructional levels found will distinctly resemble the grade levels of the materials chosen by the average teacher to be used in classroom instruction. To our knowledge, no other instrument available has made this attempt to validate its use of the term. As for our unique way of testing for independent level, we believe that the results show it to be much more realistic than the common system of limiting independent reading to materials easier than the instructional level. Our system results in broadening greatly the variety and number of materials that can be made available to children for independent reading in a great many of the cases tested. Among those tests employing the concept of testing auditory comprehension to determine potential for growth, only the Scales have attempted to produce data to support such predictions.

A final criticism offered by some reviewers of the Scales is the lack of interpretation of the meanings of types of oral reading errors (8). We have deliberately avoided attempting to assign specific causes to each type of oral error, for the multiplicity of possible causes would make such statements misleading. Moreover, we do not believe that combining and categorizing the oral errors from several levels of reading will reflect the child's error tendencies in instructional materials. We believe that error patterns vary from very easy to very difficult materials and cannot be combined to plan corrective steps.

Rather, we suggest that the examiner review all the oral and word list errors with the child to permit an intensive analysis of his word recognition skills. To contrast word recognition in isolation with that in context, we suggest that the examiner have the child reread those sentences in which errors occurred to see whether he can make use of the context in a less threatening situation. We offer check lists of error types and word analysis behaviors to enable the examiner to contrast the pupil's use of word form, word function, or graphic clues to word recognition, as well as his phonic and structural analysis skills. Another check list for each area tested is also offered in generalized, descriptive terms to aid the examiner in planning for future instruction.

WIDE RANGE ACHIEVEMENT TEST (29)

Description The WRAT was designed as a tool for the study of reading (word recognition), written spelling, and arithmetic computation. It was first standardized in 1936, and a revision begun in 1957 was completed in 1965. The reading test begins with asking the child to write his name, name thirteen capitals, or match ten capitals. With individuals of eight years of age, testing begins with the seventy-five-item word recognition list.

The authors do not clarify the reasons for the 1965 edition nor describe what changes, if any, were made in the tests other than separating the items into two levels: for ages five to eleven and for twelve and over. In personal correspondence with the reviewer (8), the authors report that the new form differs in content only in minor ways. In other words, the 1965 version offers the 1936 test with new normative data. This impression is strengthened by the fact that, in citing various studies of the test, the authors seldom distinguish between those referring to the 1936 or the 1965 version.

Content Validity The reading test is administered by having the subject read aloud the words of Level I if he is under twelve and Level II if older. If Level I is used, the child is first asked to write his name and name at least two of the letters in it, to name thirteen capitals or, if unsuccessful in this, to match ten capitals on the page. These opening items provide scores equivalent to a status below first grade, which may be intriguing but has no practical meaning. The corresponding grade norms given for items correct then extend upward to the end of college, grade 16.2.

The source of these word items is not given by the author, but it is apparent that they are graded in difficulty. Correctness of response is judged solely by the pronunciation of the words, for which the author supplies a key. No corrections are offered, but the child must progress through the items at ten-second intervals. Mispronunciations due to colloquialisms, foreign accent, or defective articulation are accepted. Dialectal pronunciations are not mentioned and presumably would be considered incorrect. Testing stops when the child has twelve consecutive failures.

It is not quite clear what reading skill is really being measured here, other than standard pronunciation of a group of difficult words. The fact that a child may know the meaning of a word even though his pronunciation is not perfect, or that he might be able to derive the meaning from context are ignored. The known fact that word recognition skill, if that is what is being measured, has a significant relationship to comprehension in reading only at primary grades, and that this relationship diminishes through later grades, is ignored. Even the authors seem a bit confused as to the nature of this test, for, although they insist that there is a dichotomy between intelligence and achievement, their data from some sort of a factor analysis indicate that 28 percent of the variance on the test is accounted for by a general factor, probably intelligence, and 30 percent more is accounted for a verbal factor (vocabulary). Moreover, they constantly refer to the fact that scores in their tests consistently vary with intelligence test results in a number of places in the Manual. They also used the I.Q.'s obtained from their standardization data to develop their reading norms so that these would reflect the achievement of mentally average groups. The numbers of cases tested seems adequate, but no description of the population is offered. It is not clear just what types of cases these norms apply to (8). Since the source of the test items is unknown, so is its relevance to classroom reading performances. Nor is this sort of a measure of pronunciation suitable for other uses claimed by its authors such as "diagnosis . . . disabilities in persons of all ages"; "determination of instructional levels in school children"; "assignment of children to instructional groups . . ."; "checking of school achievement of adults referred for vocational rehabilitation and job placement"; "selection of students for specialized technical and professional schools"; and so on.

Concurrent Validity

The authors' concepts of validity in terms of comparison with similar instruments is quite unique. They claim that such validity is established best by comparisons with *unlike tests* and by the internal consistency of the instrument. The only relevant study reported by the authors on the present edition of the test that is offered in support of validity are the comparisons of the mean scores of groups of adults varying in education and a group of private-school children of unknown ages. Because the mean scores did tend to vary among the adults in keeping with their educational and mental levels, the authors consider this proof of the "high sensitivity of the WRAT to educational and environmental conditions." No explanation is offered as to exactly what reading ability is being measured, however. And to some readers of these data they would better prove that the WRAT is, in effect, a concealed measure of intelligence as much as of school achievement. All other studies cited by the authors are comparisons of the 1946 version of the WRAT with contemporary tests. In these, correlations with the New Stanford Paragraph Reading test for 389 children were .81; and, with the New Stanford Word Reading, .84 in a group of unknown size in the seventh and eighth grades. Without knowledge of the size of the upper elementary group, or the range of grades in the larger (?) group of school children, these correlations cannot be meaningfully interpreted. The mean scores should also have been reported in these studies to enable us to judge whether there are consistent differences between these tests. A study reported by Garlock et al. (19), probably of the 1965 edition, reports correlations of .914 in accuracy and .685 in comprehension between these scores on the Gilmore Oral Reading Test and the WRAT. Gilmore cites a correlation of .91 between his accuracy score and the WRAT (21). These data again support the impression that the WRAT measures word recognition as determined by tabulating oral reading errors, a skill that is highly relevant to ordinary reading performances only at primary levels.

Other data offered by the authors in support of validity include several tables of intertest correlations among the reading-spelling-arithmetic sections, and a number of correlations with quotients and subtests from individual intelligence testing. These latter are, of course, evidence of the influence of intelligence upon the reading test results, which may account for the great overlap between the reading and spelling subtests (correlations from .799 to .938 in Level I and .858 to .928 in Level II). They are not evidence, as the authors claim, of the validity of their tests as measures of what are commonly called reading or spelling.

Reliability

A number of reliability coefficients are offered by the authors for each age level from five to twenty-up. These are extraordinarily high, ranging from .981 to .993. They are inflated by the fact that subjects do not complete the test and that a ten-second time limit is imposed on responses. No information is given in support of these unusual reliability coefficients regarding the practice effect, the time interval between tests, or whether retesting was done by the same examiners, all of which would have affected the data.

An interesting aspect of the discriminative ability of the WRAT is found in inspecting the grade norms. Despite the fact that the word list is seventy-five words, only a small portion of it functions in testing in the lower elementary grades. Twenty-one items—the writing, naming, and matching of letters—function below the beginning of the first grade. Sixteen items are relevant to first-grade reading, thirteen to second-grade, six to third-grade, six to fourth-grade, and five to sixth-grade. In other words, progress in reading equivalent to a year's growth is being measured, according to the authors, in five to sixteen items of word recognition in these grades. This sampling of reading ability drops successively to about three items per grade level in the test's upper levels. In effect, we are asked to believe that a test requiring recognition of an average of four words per grade (75 words ÷ 16 grades) is a significant measure of overall reading ability. Perhaps this sharply accelerated scaling of the test is a partial explanation of the extremely high reliabilities reported by the authors.

SLOSSON ORAL READING TEST (44)

Description The Slosson Oral Reading Test is a two-page piece containing both the test and the scoring instructions. It consists of ten lists of twenty words each, ranging from the primer level through the eight grades, plus one additional list for use in the high school. The examiner is to start the pupil on a list in which he hopes the pupil can pronounce all twenty words. If any mistakes are made on the starting list, the instructions are to drop back to an easier level, at which all items can be pronounced correctly. Testing continues until the pupil cannot read all the words of a list. All the correct responses are then added, as are all the words on easier levels below the perfect starting list. This sum is then translated into a grade equivalent, called the Reading Level of the pupil. The entire procedure of testing and scoring is supposed to take about three minutes, according to the author.

Content Validity The source of the word lists is standardized school readers, according to the author, although it is apparent that they are, in a sense, graded in difficulty. Correctness of response is judged by pronunciation of the words only. The pupils are to be paced through the items at five-second intervals, by the examiner calling out the number of each item or uncovering words with a card. If more than one response is offered by a pupil, the item is considered incorrect, even though one response may have been correct. In other words, the test is, in effect, a measure of sight word vocabulary only, not the ability to analyze words or the pupil's familiarity with their meanings, or his comprehension of these words as they might be used in context.

The author gives no key to the correct pronunciations that he expects, assuming perhaps that the pronunciation is obvious. This procedure, of course, ignores regional pronunciations and leaves the judgment of the correctness of response open to the subjective opinion of the examiner (who may or may not accept regional variations). Dialectal pronunciations (which, for example, may involve the dropping of endings) are specifically mentioned as errors by the author. This rigidity (and variability) of scoring, of course, makes the test culturally biased and inappropriate for testing any children other than those using perfectly standard English, or those whose regional pronunciations agree with that of the examiner. Thus the validity of the test for general use is extremely limited.

As in the WRAT, recognition vocabulary is considered equivalent to the complete act of reading. While this relationship is marked at primary reading levels, it sharply diminishes in later grades as correlations between sight vocabulary and other facets of reading such as comprehension and meaning vocabulary drop in significance. There is certainly some question of the meaningfulness of a score in word calling in judging pupil reading ability above the primary grades.

Concurrent Validity

The only comparison with other oral reading tests offered by the author is that of a group of 108 children from first grade through high school. There was apparently no difference in the means of tests. This comparison was probably done with the first edition (1955) of the Gray Oral Reading Tests, since it is reported in the 1963 Slosson manual. The correlation for this multiple-grade sample is given as .96. Since the Gray tests never did employ any measure of comprehension, this is a comparison, in effect, between two word-naming tests. It certainly is no proof that either test is a thorough measure of reading ability.

Construct Validity

There is the question whether this test is not a concealed measure of intelligence. Its similarity to the WRAT, in which such a relationship was consistently present, supports this criticism. It is quite possible that the high correlation with the Gray Oral over a ten–twelve grade range may reflect the influence of mental age, as much as any parallelism in measuring reading.

The imposition of a five-second time limit for the pupil's recognition of each word is certainly sufficient both for instantaneous recognition and even analysis to arrive at the pronunciation. But if the pupil does attempt analysis aloud, he is not credited with the item, even if one of his attempts is correct. This scoring procedure, which differs greatly from the normal reading process, penalizes a child for attempting to use phonic or structural clues. Thus the testing procedure becomes highly artificial and can hardly reveal the level of materials that the pupil can deal with comprehendingly while employing his various word attack skills.

The selection of test words from "standardized school readers" is a meaningful source only at primary and, perhaps, elementary levels. Such readers are not available as a source of test items above these levels. How, then, was the list for high school derived? Or did the author simply establish a scaled list of words arranged in order of difficulty and, we hope, discriminability to make his test? Even if basal readers were the sources of words, the sampling is a very narrow one, which might well be inappropriate in nonbasal reader programs such as the linguistic, language experience, ultraphonic systems, and individualized reading approaches. At best, the source is a biased selection favoring only one type of reading program. The author gives no information regarding the size or nature of the population on which the test was standardized, if indeed any standardization was attempted.

Reliability

As evidence of the reliability of his test, the author offers a single coefficient of .99 derived by a test-retest interval of one week. In his opinion, this reliability suggests that the test can be used at frequent intervals to measure progress. The lack of data regarding the size, nature, or range of grades in the group tested makes this reliability coefficient almost meaningless. Without these additional facts, we could not possibly know whether the test is reliable enough for comparisons between successive testings of the same individual.

In all probability the reliability claimed by the author is inflated by the speed factor (five seconds per item; three minutes for the entire test); by the obvious brevity of testing in twenty words per grade level with testing stopped at the first list containing an error; and by the sharp scaling of the items. The average child tested will be assessed under speeded conditions and with a relatively small number of words. Under these procedures, it is quite unlikely that his score could vary greatly from testing at one-week intervals; hence we have what appears to be a very high reliability coefficient.

Interestingly, the author's table for converting raw scores to grade equivalents proceeds by exactly equal intervals throughout its entire range. Somehow or other, the number of words correct is always twice the grade equivalent. While such a parallelism could conceivably happen if the differences in difficulty between successive words were precisely the same throughout, it is most unlikely if we compare with similar tables in other word-naming tests. The table was probably based on the regression equation between some reading grade score and items correct on the test, rather than reflecting the actual mean raw scores of pupils at various grade levels. Thus another artificiality is added to the interpretation of the test.

PEABODY INDIVIDUAL ACHIEVEMENT TEST (12)

Description

The battery includes five subtests to be administered individually, including the two in reading—Reading Recognition and Reading Comprehension—with which we shall be concerned. The test was standardized, however, in a particular order: Mathematics, followed by the two reading tests, one in Spelling, and a final test of General Information. The order of the reading tests is to be followed, according to the authors, even when the other subtests are omitted. Total time for the five tests is estimated at thirty to forty minutes.

The Reading Recognition test contains eighty-four items ranging from matching nine letters of the alphabet in a multiple-choice group of four, and nine individual letters to be named by the subject, through a scaled series of individual words to be read aloud. This test is considered a measure of oral reading or word attack skill by its authors, although most observers would term it a sight vocabulary or word-naming measure. The authors recognize that it may not function above fourth grade as a measure of word attack skills, since readers may not be able to pronounce the word even when they have sophisticated word attack skills because the word is not present in their hearing or speaking vocabulary. We suggest that the test may not actually involve word attack skills below the fourth grade because many of the words will be present in the sight word vocabularies of such children, if the list is a true sample of common basic words.

The Reading Comprehension subtest contains sixty-six items each of single sentences, which the subject reads silently. Like all tests in the battery, the reading selections are presented on plates propped up in easel fashion before the child. After having read each sentence, the next plate is exposed and the child asked to indicate which of four pictures best represents the meaning of the test sentence. This method of response was chosen because the authors considered it less difficult and more objective than having the subject write answers or answer orally or read multiple-choice alternatives.

Content Validity

The Reading Recognition test started with basal vocabulary lists. The authors attempted to sample readers of what they call the analytic "look and say" type as well as the "synthetic or phonic" approach. To some observers, such terminology represents several misconceptions of current reading instruction. It proposes a false dichotomy between the basal reader method and the phonics approach in failing to recognize that both systems train children in phonic skills and that the difference between these systems is simply a matter of the degree of emphasis given these skills. The terminology of the authors also indicates that they are unaware of the competing analytic and synthetic phonic methods, either of which may be integral parts of what these authors call a "look and say" series.

Moreover, basal word lists are almost nonexistent—or at best almost meaningless—above the intermediate grades, for here the introduction of a wide variety of intensive content field reading extends the potential reading vocabulary far beyond any core or basic word list that would be common to many reading series. It is true that Harris and Jacobson (27) identified what they called core word lists for the intermediate as well as the primary grades, but they did not attempt to establish basic lists above this point. Rather, they offered lists of the technical vocabularies of four content fields, as these authors probably did.

It is quite possible to establish the discriminative and difficulty values of a list of words that can challenge the word recognition abilities of students of all ages. But what significant reading ability does this sample? It is not a measure of meaning vocabulary or the verbal intelligence factor, as in the lists of the WISC or Stanford-Binet. It is not necessarily a measure of word analysis skills at any level, for the words may be completely familiar as wholes or too unfamiliar and complex to permit pronunciation even with good analysis skills. It is not simply a measure of sight vocabulary, for the time allowed for recognition (fifteen seconds) would permit considerable analysis, if that were necessary. It is not a true measure of oral reading, for it ignores such facets of that process as expression, fluency, and intonation. How then will this test of word naming relate to instructional grouping, to selection of instructional or supplementary reading materials, to oral reading performances in the classroom, or to the silent reading that is the chief mode in levels above the primary grades?

The Reading Comprehension test is presented in a unique fashion of single sentences presented on successive plates and answers indicated by pointing to an illustration that reflects the central meaning of each sentence. This format probably reflects the senior author's experiences in constructing the Peabody Picture Vocabulary Test. Whether reading single sentences of increasing difficulty and choosing a picture that indicates each central meaning actually samples sustained silent reading in longer selections (and thus reflects or predicts classroom performances) is, of course, debatable.

Sentence reading tests do tend to yield reasonably valid samples of general reading at primary levels at which the child's task is basically one of word recognition. But, beyond this point, there is much more to reading than simply pointing to illustrations that indicate the ideas of single sentences. It is, of course, possible to construct a measure composed of single sentences that increase in difficulty by lengthening the items, by introducing more difficult vocabulary, and by increasing the complexity of the sentence structure, as these authors have done. But such an approach tends to sample largely the vocabulary component of the reading process, making little demands upon the other basic elements of reading, as recognizing relationships of cause and effect among ideas, or deductive or inductive reasoning in a group of ideas. As in the case of the Reading Recognition test, it remains to be demonstrated that this test is relevant to its probable uses by classroom teachers or to any significant classroom reading performances. As we shall note later, the authors have offered no information that bears upon this question for either of their reading tests.

Construct Validity

In the Reading Recognition test the correct response is based on a dictionary pronunciation with regional variations recognized as acceptable in the scoring guide. These pronunciations are listed on the reverse side of the plates to be immediately available to the examiner. No mention is made of dialectal pronunciation as black or Spanish-American pupils might enunciate the test words. Presumably, then, if only a dictionary pronunciation or a regional variant of this is acceptable, dialectal responses will be scored as incorrect. Such scoring would reflect a cultural bias in this test, for there is now ample evidence that reading standard English with dialectal intonation or pronunciation does not reflect poor reading. It would appear that the Reading Recognition test may not be suitable for testing children of varying linguistic and cultural backgrounds.

A time interval of fifteen seconds for a child's response is suggested in the Manual. How this interval is to be timed is left to the examiner's discretion, which we believe is an uncontrolled variable. Counting or guessing at seconds elapsed is certainly an undependable procedure, while stop watches are usually not available to classroom teachers. If this timing is to be observed, the directions for controlling should be more precise. In any event, the interval is far longer than the quarter-second to half-second periods necessary for single word recognition; thus word analysis skills as well as sight vocabulary skills have ample time to operate.

Starting point for the reading tests is suggested as the level of the raw score in the initial mathematics test or the preceding reading test. In other words, it is assumed that the child will function at or above the same level in any two consecutive tests. Particularly with older students, for whom variability rather than similarity between academic skills is the rule, this assumption of equivalence from one test to the next may make for fumbling in establishing the basal success level, as the testing procedure requires. In fact the norms for PIAT increase in variability consistently from ages 5–0 to about 15–0 thus confirming our observation.

This basal level is to be established at the lowest point at which the subject makes five consecutive correct responses. Testing then continues until there are five errors in any seven consecutive responses. All items below the basal level are considered correct even though, in trying to find the basal level, *some were incorrect.* All items above the ceiling level accepted as final are considered wrong, again even though some had been answered correctly. A more realistic measure to our mind would be to credit correct answers as correct and wrong answers as incorrect. Even though the items are arranged in order of difficulty, this is group data that may not be true for individuals. A child could conceivably miss two items in a series of seven and yet be able to answer a number of items supposed to be more difficult. There is, of course, the need to establish a cut-off point in testing with a list of this type; the authors' criterion of five errors in the last seven items tested seems reasonable. But when testing is initiated at too high a level, two or more ceilings may be established. Only the lowest one is used in scoring, and all answers above this point are considered incorrect, a procedure that we feel may result in underestimations in some cases.

A very desirable feature of the tests is a three-minute set of demonstration and training exercises, as they are termed, that precedes each test. In view of the rather unusual way in which the tests are administered, as in the case of the Reading Comprehension, pretesting trials may well be essential.

The standardization population was about 200 subjects at each grade level from twenty-seven school systems in nine geographical areas of the country, excluding Alaska and Hawaii. An urban, a suburban, and a rural school district was sampled in each of the nine areas, for a total of 2889 cases. The population was carefully selected to represent a reasonable cross-section of public school children according to sex, race, and parental occupation. Norms extend from the kindergarten to the twelfth grade. The authors are to be commended for the effort involved in this standardization and, unlike so many authors, for making all the pertinent data available in the Manual.

The PIAT raw scores can be translated into four types of derived scores: grade equivalents, age equivalents, percentile ranks, and standard scores. The Profile sheets permit the examiner to record and graph the individual's scores in any of these four ways. In each, a comparison with the M.A. or I.Q.

ability level of the child is suggested, although the authors emphasize strongly the limitations in grade and age equivalents, as well as those inherent in interpreting percentile ranks. However, standard errors of measurement are given only for raw scores and for differences between subtest raw scores at six grade levels. In view of the authors' advice to use standard scores for comparative purposes, it is not clear why the standard errors of measurement were not given for such scores. In illustrating the use of these raw score standard errors of differences between subtest scores, the authors supply two hypothetical profiles in which the graph and the differences in grade equivalents seem to indicate large differences when they are really largely insignificant. For example, the hypothetical score of 3.8 in general information, which is at least eight months greater than any other area and is much higher on the graph of scores, is not significantly greater than the next-best score of 3.0 in spelling. For unsophisticated users of these profiles, which includes most classroom teachers, such illustrations, as well as the statistical interpretations required, will be just too much. If standard scores are the best for comparative purposes, why not simplify the situation by recording only these in the profile sheet and supplying the standard errors of measurement for these scores?

Concurrent Validity

Information regarding the validity of the subtests of the PIAT is conspicuous by its lack in the current Manual. Correlations of each subtest with the Peabody Picture Vocabulary Test are given for six single grades but the meaning and significance of these is obscure.

These data bring us back to the authors' suggestion that the child's scores should be compared with his M.A. or I.Q., probably to determine whether he is achieving at a point equal to his potential. Yet the correlations between the PPVT and Reading Recognition average .545; those with Reading Comprehension, .66. Do such data imply that pupils tend to function academically at their mental ability levels?

Only one comparative study of a small group of educable mentally retarded adolescents achieving at the third-grade level is cited. This report cites correlations of .95 between the PIAT Reading Recognition and the WRAT Reading Test. In effect, this is a correlation between two word-naming tests and probably proves only that both scales are similar in the order of difficulty of their items. It gives no real indication of what reading skill is being measured in either test but simply supports the accuracy of scaling of items in both tests. The studies necessary to demonstrate the concurrent validity of this battery will probably be conducted by other research workers, the authors hope.

Reliability In the Reading Comprehension subtest, test-retest reliability coefficients cited by the authors range from .61 to .78 for single grade ranges. They tend to decrease markedly as grade levels increase. The similar reliability coefficients for the Reading Recognition test range from .81 in the kindergarten to .94 in the third grade. These correlations tend to reflect the nature of the reading task, word naming vs. recognizing pictorial representation of the meaning of a sentence, as well as the difference in the inherent difficulty in scaling a group of words vs. that in scaling central ideas of sentences. The reliability coefficients are high enough, if replicated in other studies, to support comparisons among groups and individuals, at least in the case of the Reading Recognition test, provided the users of the Profile sheet can understand the unnecessarily complex explanation of the significance of difference between subtest scores.

LEARNING PROJECT

1. An obvious application of the ideas presented in this critical review of individual diagnostic tests would be the analysis of an instrument not treated here, in the same style. A group test intended for diagnostic purposes or an informal inventory might be so analyzed.

2. Another exercise in understanding test construction and evaluation might take the form of attempting to point out how the limitations of a favored test might be compensated for or lessened by varying the administration and interpretation, or supplementing the test by other diagnostic instruments. This constructive reevaluation of a test should be related to the adverse criticisms offered here and in other sources such as Buros's *Mental Measurement Yearbooks* and his *Reading Tests and Reviews.*

3. Not all the criticisms cited here will necessarily be accepted by those using some particular test. They may be given the opportunity to defend their chosen instrument before the group and attempt to justify its continued use. The presentation may take the form of a debate with opposing views of the pros and cons of the instrument offered by various members of the class.

REFERENCES

1. American Psychological Association, *Ethical Standards of Psychologists.* Washington, D.C.: The American Psychological Association, 1963.

2. Barrett, Thomas C., editor, *The Evaluation of Children's Reading Achievement.* Perspectives in Reading, No. 8. Newark, Del.: International Reading Association, 1967.
3. Botel, Morton, *Botel Reading Inventory.* Chicago: Follett Publishing, 1962.
4. Botel, Morton, "A Comparative Study of the Validity of the Botel Reading Inventory and Selected Standardized Tests," in *Reading and Realism,* J. Allen Figurel, editor. International Reading Association Conference Proceedings, 13, 1969, 721–27.
5. Botel, Morton; Bradley, John; and Kashuba, Michael, "The Validity of Informal Reading Testing," in *Reading Difficulties: Diagnosis, Correction and Remediation,* William K. Durr, editor. Newark, Del.: International Reading Association, 1970, 85–103.
6. Buros, Oscar K., *The Sixth Mental Measurements Yearbook.* Highland Park, N.J.: Gryphon Press, 1965.
7. Buros, Oscar K., *Reading Tests and Reviews.* Highland Park, N.J.: Gryphon Press, 1968.
8. Buros, Oscar K., *The Seventh Mental Measurements Yearbook.* Highland Park,: Gryphon Press, 1972.
9. Daniel, John E., "The Effectiveness of Various Procedures in Reading Level Placement," *Elementary English,* 39 (October 1962), 590–600.
10. Della-Piana, Gabriel M., "Analysis of Oral Reading Errors: Standardization, Norms and Validity," *Reading Teacher,* 15 (February 1962), 254–57.
11. Della-Piana, Gabriel M., *Reading Diagnosis and Prescription.* New York: Holt, 1968.
12. Dunn, Lloyd M., and Markwardt, Frederick C., *Peabody Individual Achievement Test.* Circle Pines, Minn.: American Guidance Services, 1970.
13. Durrell, Donald D., *Durrell Analysis of Reading Difficulty.* New York: Harcourt Brace Jovanovich, 1955.
14. Ekwall, Eldon E., Solis, Judy K. English, and Solis, Enrique, Jr., "Investigating Informal Reading Inventory Scoring Criteria," *Elementary English,* 50 (February 1973), 271–274, 323.
15. Eller, Wm., and Attea, Mary, "Three Diagnostic Reading Tests: Some Comparisons," in *Vistas in Reading,* J. Allen Figurel, editor. International Reading Association Conference Proceedings, 11, Part 2, 1966, 562–66.
16. Farr, Roger, *Measurement and Evaluation of Reading.* New York: Harcourt, Brace, Jovanovich, 1970.
17. Farr, Roger, *Reading: What Can Be Measured?* Newark, Del.: International Reading Association, 1969.
18. Froese, Victor, "Word Recognition Tests: Are They Useful Beyond Grade Three?" *Reading Teacher,* 24 (February 1971), 432–38.
19. Garlock, Jerry, Dollarhide, Robert S., and Hopkins, Kenneth D., "Comparability of Scores on the Wide Range and the Gilmore Oral Reading Tests," *California Journal of Educational Research,* 16 (March 1965), 54–57.
20. Gates, Arthur I., and McKillop, Anne S., *Gates-McKillop Reading Diagnostic Tests.* New York: Teachers College Press, 1962.
21. Gilmore, John V., and Gilmore, Eunice C., *Gilmore Oral Reading Test.* New York: Harcourt Brace Jovanovich, 1965.
22. Gray, Wm. S., and Robinson, Helen M., editors, *Gray Oral Reading Test.* Indianapolis: Bobbs-Merrill, 1967.

23. Guszak, Frank J., "Dilemmas in Informal Reading Assessments," *Elementary English,* 47 (May 1970), 666–70.
24. Hardin, Veralee, and Ames, Wilbur S., "A Comparison of the Results of Two Oral Tests," *Reading Teacher,* 22 (January 1969), 329–24.
25. Harris, Albert J., *How to Increase Reading Ability.* New York: David McKay, 1970.
26. Harris, Albert J., Coleman, J.C., Serwer, Blanche L. and Gold, L., *A Continuation of the Craft Project.* New York: Associated Educational Services, 1968.
27. Harris, Albert J., and Jacobson, Milton D., *Basic Elementary Reading Vocabularies.* New York: Macmillan, 1972.
28. Herlin, Wayne Richard, "A Comparison of Oral Reading Errors on the Monroe Diagnostic Reading Examination and the Durrell Analysis of Reading Difficulty," Doctoral dissertation, University of Utah, 1963.
29. Jastak, J.F., and Jastak, S.R., *Wide Range Achievement Test.* Wilmington: Guidance Associates, 1965.
30. Jerrolds, Bob W., Callaway, Byron, and Gwaltney, Wayne, "A Comparative Study of Three Tests of Intellectual Potential, Three Tests of Reading Achievement and the Discrepancy Scores Between Potential and Achievement," *Journal of Educational Research,* 65 (December 1971), 168–72.
31. Kasdon, Lawrence M., "Oral versus Silent-Oral Diagnosis," in *Reading Diagnosis and Evaluation,* Dorothy L. DeBoer, editor. International Reading Association Conference Proceedings, 13, No. 4, 1970, 86–92.
32. Kasdon, Lawrence M., "Silent Reading Before Oral Reading? *Ohio Reading Teacher,* 2 (1967), 6–8.
33. La Pray, Margaret, and Ross, Ramon, "The Graded Word List: Quick Gauge of Reading Ability," *Journal of Reading,* 12 (January 1969), 305–7.
34. La Pray, Margaret, *Teaching Children to Become Independent Readers.* New York: Center for Applied Research in Education, 1972.
35. McCracken, Robert A., "The Development and Validation of the Standard Reading Inventory for the Individual Appraisal of Reading Performance in Grades One Through Six," in *Improvement of Reading Through Classroom Practice,* J. Allen Figurel, editor. International Reading Association Conference Proceedings, 9, 1964, 310–13.
36. McCracken, Robert A., *Standard Reading Inventory.* Klamath Falls, Oreg.: Klamath Printing, 1966.
37. McCracken, Robert A., and Mullen, Neill D., "The Validity of Certain Measures in an I.R.I.," in *Reading Difficulties: Diagnosis, Correction and Remediation,* William K. Durr, editor. Newark, Del.: International Reading Association, 1970, 104–10.
38. Mills, Robert E., *Learning Methods Tests.* Fort Lauderdale, Fla.: The Mills Center, 1970.
39. Powell, William R., and Dunkeld, Colin G., "Validity of the I.R.I. Reading Levels," *Elementary English,* 48 (October 1971), 637–42.
40. Powers, R.D., Sumner, W.A., and Kearl, B.E., "A Recalculation of Four Adult Readability Formulas," *Journal of Educational Psychology,* 48 (1958), 99–105.
41. Preston, Ralph C., "The Reading Status of Children Classified by Teachers as Retarded Readers," *Elementary English,* 30 (April 1953), 225–27.
42. Ramsey, Wallace, "The Values and Limitations of Diagnostic Reading Tests for Evaluation in the Classroom," in *The Evaluation of Children's Reading Achieve-*

ment, Thomas C. Barrett, editor. Perspectives in Reading, No. 8, Newark, Del.: International Reading Association, 1967, 65–78.

43. Silvaroli, Nicholas J., *Classroom Reading Inventory.* Dubuque: William C. Brown, 1965.
44. Slosson, Richard L., *Slosson Oral Reading Test.* East Aurora, N.Y.: Slosson Educational Publications, 1963.
45. Smith, Edwin H., and Bradtmueller, Weldon G., *Individual Reading Placement Inventory.* Chicago, Follett, 1969.
46. Spache, George D., "A Comparison of Certain Oral Reading Tests," *Journal of Educational Research,* 43 (February 1950), 441–52.
47. Spache, George D., *Diagnostic Reading Scales.* Monterey: California Test Bureau, 1972.
48. Winkley, Carol K., "What Do Diagnostic Tests Really Diagnose?" in *Diagnostic Viewpoints in Reading,* Robert E. Leibert, editor. Newark, Del.: International Reading Association, 1971, 64–80.
49. Wood, Dorothy Adkins, *Test Construction.* Columbus: Charles E. Merrill, 1961.
50. Wunderlich, Elaine, and Bradtmueller, Mary, "Teacher Estimates of Reading Levels Compared with I.R.P.I. Instructional Level Scores," *Journal of Reading,* 14 (February 1971), 303–8.

8
Analyzing and Teaching Analysis Skills

Certain assumptions frequently appear in the reading clinician's attempts to assess the word analysis skills of a poor reader. Among these assumptions are the beliefs that there is a definite hierarchy of learning of certain skills and that these skills are interlinked, the earlier skills forming the foundation for later skill development. It is also usually assumed in most reading programs that these skill steps should be learned in some certain sequence to insure successful reading. And despite the known individual differences among children, particularly in intelligence and auditory abilities, it is generally assumed that children will learn this continuum in its entirety; for if any skill step is not learned, it will be the cause of reading failure.

By reviewing what scanty evidence there is regarding the actual degree of learning and use of all the word analysis skills in the act of reading, this chapter challenges some of these assumptions. Evidence is presented to show that some early skills rapidly fall into disuse or, at least, make little contribution to comprehension by intermediate grades. Many successful readers are found to lack some of the skills commonly thought essential and to substitute other approaches to word recognition. These observations are offered to raise some doubts about the usual testing procedure of expecting relatively equal development in all word analysis skills.

A critical review of the content and methods of the phonics, structural analysis, contextual analysis, and syllabication programs is offered to contrast current research and opinion. Following this, several common word analysis tests are discussed in detail. Finally, the author offers an approach to the evaluation of word analysis skills by a diagnostic spelling test. The entire test—directions for administering, scoring, and interpreting—are presented, together with a summary of the research studies upon which it is based. These Spelling Errors Tests are offered as a supplementary tool in studying the word analysis habits of pupils.

As you read this chapter, consider the following questions:

1. What is the author suggesting regarding the interpretation of a pupil's performances in a number of phonic skills?

2. How does the author suggest that the profile of a pupil in a variety of subtests in word analysis should be reviewed?

3. What are some of the alternatives to direct remediation of apparent weaknesses in phonics or syllabication?

BEFORE ATTEMPTING TO DISCUSS ways and means of analyzing a reader's word analysis skills, it is essential to review the development of such skills as well as their influence upon success in reading and spelling. Is there a hierarchy of skills that build upon each other and thus tend to insure better reading and spelling? Do most good readers learn and apply these skills of word analysis while reading as a result of the sequential training emphasized in most reading programs? In other words, can we justify the common practice of observing and testing a pupil at each step of the hierarchy that we assume—and then keying our remedial instruction to the areas of deficiency?

THE DEVELOPMENT OF WORD ANALYSIS SKILLS

Several spontaneous ways of recognizing words appear in the early stages of learning to read. Among these clues are word length and probably shape, as in *grandmother, elephant, Christmas, Halloween,* and similar words. Once such words have been introduced in meaningful settings, they tend to be recognized readily, probably because of their distinctive length, their shapes, and the familiarity of their meanings. Similarly, words that have a number of ascending or tall letters tend to be retained more easily. In contrast, short words, those without distinctive profiles or familiar clusters of letters, and those lacking familiar meanings, such as *for, to, more, they, then,* are much more difficult to recognize in isolation or context.

Beginning readers have difficulty in distinguishing among a letter, a word, or a sound of a letter, and in recognizing that a letter or a word is being used in incorrect order, according to Marie Clay (10) and others. Even though children do apparently use the first letter of a word as an aid in word recognition, this is really a trained response that often takes almost a year to develop (10, 24). Associating sounds with letters or letter clusters does not often appear as a spontaneous clue but rather reflects the nature of instruction.

The sounds of the consonants are often taught as the first phonic skill, and even first graders gradually learn to use these associations and the context in their word recognition attempts, even before they have learned any vowel sounds. Beginning phonic instruction with consonant sounds is realistic because many consonants are ascending or descending letters, and they have relatively few variations in the letter-sound associations that must be learned. Yet these are not simple skills, for they make demands upon verbal intelligence, auditory discrimination, and memory and sequencing, as well as upon the child's ability to understand such abstractions as letter, sound, word, consonant, and so forth.

Several research studies have attempted to chart the development of word attack skills that are learned as a result of direct instruction. Boyd (6) tested pupils in fifteen phonic skills in the second to sixth grades. The most rapid growth of these appeared in the second and third grades, while further development in the intermediate grades was much slower. In fact, Boyd's results indicated that many of the skills had not been mastered by average readers, even by the sixth grade. A similar study in grades three to six by Plattor and Woestehoff (28) employed a commercial test with a number of subtests of word analysis techniques. In a sample of over 1000 children, they charted progressive growth in measures of locating elements (small words within a word), syllabication, and locating root words. Such skills as phonic elements in a word, beginning sounds, rhyming sounds, and letter sounds appeared to get worse with advancing grade level, as determined by the percentage of pupils achieving their grade level norm. Yet overall reading ability, as measured by a general survey test, was good among these pupils, for 89 percent of those in the third grade and 80–81 percent in the fourth to sixth achieved at expectancy level.

If we compare these results with the sequence of skills usually taught, it would appear that those first taught (letter sounds, rhyming, beginning sounds) in the primary grades either deteriorate or fall into disuse by pupils as they advance in grade level. Is this trend present because the skills are insufficiently learned for permanence? Or is it possible that these primary phonic skills drop out of pupil's practices because they fail to aid comprehension in the more difficult materials read in intermediate grades? We are inclined to subscribe to the explanation that the primary phonic skills lose their efficacy as reading materials advance in difficulty.

Although it is not recognized by many, the phonic skills are taught under the assumption that in translating the letters into sounds and thus pronouncing the word, the pupil will recognize it. But this assumption is true only when the sound and meaning of the word are familiar to the child. If he has not heard the word frequently in meaningful settings, he has no auditory associations stored in his memory bank, as it may be called. Thus, even though he may decode the word correctly, he cannot react comprehendingly. And, as the vocabularies of the content areas he attempts to read expand, the reader is frustrated in word recognition through primary phonic skills with constantly increasing frequency, for a large proportion of the terms used are not common to everyday conversation.

There is supporting evidence for this explanation of the deterioration in the average pupil's use of beginning phonic skills. Good readers—or, shall we say, the bright pupils—do tend to score higher in most phonic skills at least as far as the fourth grade (4, 5, 19). But these same studies show a decreasing influence upon comprehension for the letter-sound learnings, while more advanced skills such as words in context, syllabication, and root words assume greater significance.

Beyond the primary grades there are other arguments against the emphasis upon phonics as the basic word recognition tool. For example, Smith and Holmes (34) have pointed out that word recognition by letters (or letter sounds) soon disappears as reading ability increases. Word identification is too fast to believe that it occurs by letter-to-letter analysis; words cannot be identified readily if their constituent letters are presented singly and consecutively; the reaction time for a whole word is scarcely longer than that for a single letter; and, finally, it has been shown that words can be identified under conditions in which the component letters are not individually discriminable (34). Research of the last century further demonstrated that four–five words in a meaningful sequence can be identified in the same time that it takes to recognize four–five unconnected letters or two unconnected words.

It seems logical to include other word analysis skills besides phonics and the intermediate-grade skills of syllabication, root words, and the like in this brief overview of the development of word attack skills. But we shall defer discussion of all the skills to later in this chapter in order to be able to give each full consideration. We feel that the background material on the relationships of these abilities to spelling and reading comprehension should be presented before offering an outline of the instructional content for each area.

WORD ANALYSIS SKILLS, SPELLING, AND COMPREHENSION

There is ample evidence of the importance of certain word analysis skills for success in spelling. Russell (33) found his poor spellers to be significantly inferior in giving letters for letter sounds, in blending letters to form syllables and words, and in spelling one- and two-syllable nonsense words. Similarly, Spache (39) showed that poor spellers commit more errors of nonphonetic substitutions for letters, and omissions of sounded letters and syllables.

Compared with good spellers, they made fewer errors in phonetic additions and substitutions, thus manifesting their unfamiliarity with the alternative ways of representing the sounds of English. By the very nature of its task of translating auditory stimuli into written symbols, spelling probably makes more demands upon phonic skills than reading does. It is true that reading involves the reverse process of decoding written symbols into spoken words; but many other clues aid the word recognition process, making the role of letter-sound associations less important in the reading process than they probably are in spelling.

The question of how essential word analysis skills are for successful reading comprehension can be debated quite vehemently. Our common classroom and clinic practices imply that most teachers believe that learning these skills is absolutely necessary for practically all children. And for the past half-century at least, every basal reading system in America has emphasized these abilities as though they were basic to learning to read. Yet the evidence in studies that have attempted to measure this relationship is not entirely supportive of these practices.

Benz and Rosemier (5), for example, correlated six word analysis skills with reading comprehension in the fourth grade. No single skill showed more than a moderate relationship, .555 for words in context being the largest correlation. Four of the skill tests combined accounted for only slightly more than 30 percent of the variance in reading comprehension. And all six tests accounted for 33 percent of the variance. In converse terms, 66 to 70 percent of comprehension was independent of these analysis abilities. A second report by the same authors (4) reports a higher relationship, with 57 percent of the variance in comprehension being accounted for by the group of six skills tests when intelligence was added. But the point remains that some skills seem to have very little effect upon comprehension at the fourth-grade level, and even all six combined have only a moderate effect.

Using other tests of analytic skills and comprehension, Hackney (19) found relationships much like the other studies. His good readers also were better in word analysis skills than were average readers, who, in turn, were superior to poor readers. But Hackney discovered that variability in performance on the skills tests increased as reading ability decreased; this implies that good readers tend to score better in all the word analysis skills, while average and poor readers may do well in some and poorly in others. The study appears to justify the common diagnostic practice of testing retarded readers in all the word analysis skills and basing remedial work on these results. But Hackney did not try to discover which analysis skills were most significantly related to reading comprehension at this intermediate grade level (19). The superiority of good readers in all the skills tested is not necessarily proof of the essentiality of all of them for reading, for these results may have reflected the influence of the variations in intelligence of the good, average, and poor readers. Since, at this grade level, intelligence plays a significant role in reading comprehension, it may well be that there were distinct differences in this aspect among the three levels of reading ability identified. Children who score higher in comprehension, perhaps because of superior reasoning abilities, may well be expected to excel in analytic skills for the same reason. In contrast, the Benz and Rosemier correlations show that, at the fourth-grade level, there is great variability in the effect of each analysis skill upon reading comprehension rather than that all skills are significantly related to good comprehension. These *r*'s varied from .098 for beginning sounds to .555 for words in context.

We interpret these studies to indicate that (1) good comprehenders seem to be effective in most word analysis skills, although some of this apparent superiority may be due to greater intelligence; (2) all readers tend to vary in ability from one skill to another; (3) the various skills are not of equal importance in achieving comprehension, for some primary skills tend to make little contribution in intermediate-grade reading.

Unfortunately, none of these studies reported the individual scores of the readers of varying ability, which would have enabled us to determine whether (as some might assume) all good readers were better than all average and poor readers in all the skills tests. Rather, in all probability, we would have discovered that some average, and perhaps even some poor, readers excelled or equaled some of the good readers in certain skill areas. This would be the expected finding, for human beings do not tend to develop equally in any large number of skills, but rather to develop individual patterns of strengths and weaknesses. To put this another way, all good comprehenders would not show the same profile of a high level of performance in all word analysis skills. Although such results are often expected by teachers and seem to be implied in the norms for subtests, they are not justifiable expectations. Individual pupils exercise various skills to different degrees to achieve the same end result of comprehension.

This manifestation of normal variability in a group of related skills raises again the question of the proper approach to remediation of a pupil's reading difficulties. Are low scores in the profile of analytic skills really indications of handicaps, or may they be due to normal variability in development? When he shows weaknesses in some areas of diagnosis, can we assume that these must be retaught before he can achieve greater comprehension? Should we automatically correct apparent deficiencies, or should we reinforce his strengths? If we immediately proceed to repair each low performance in a word analysis skill, we are assuming that all the skills are essential for all pupils; and that all are equally supportive of comprehension regardless of the reading level of the pupil and the nature of the materials that he is attempting to read. We would be ignoring the diagnostic information inherent in his profile, which may tell us how he achieves comprehension. If, as we have implied, the word analysis skills differ at various reading levels in their significance for comprehension, and pupils achieving similar success employ various analysis skills in varying degrees, how can we justify a stereotyped correction of deficiencies approach?

Some may argue that all analysis skills are necessary because they form an interrelated hierarchy with each skill built upon the previously learned level. For example, they may insist that a pupil could not deal with phonograms or syllables without first learning individual letter sounds and being able to distinguish short and long vowel sounds. Yet Wylie and Durrell (43) found that first graders learned whole phonograms more easily than they learned short vowel sounds. And both Groff (17, 18) and Glass and Burton (16) show that pupils do not use individual letter sounds or the relevant rules for sounds or syllables in word analysis but rather tend to deal with familiar letter clusters. Most students develop the habit of analyzing words by dividing them into easily pronounceable units called graphophonemes or vocalic center groups usually composed of a vowel or vowel digraph and the adjoining consonants, as *toas-ter* or *butt-er.* This type of segmentation may appear after instruction in individual letter sounds, or it may be promoted by beginning instruction with an emphasis upon phonograms of high frequency in the reading vocabulary. If normal readers can so achieve without continuing to use many of the primary analytic skills and their rules that we emphasize in the sequence, how can we persist in justifying all that instruction?

Richard T. White (41) has reviewed intensively the research upon a hierarchy of interlocking skills such as those in word analysis. He finds that the scanty research trying to support the idea of a hierarchy is very poor and inconclusive. None of the research was very conclusive in proving that such hierarchies exist, are essential sequences, or result in learning for all pupils. There are some obvious interrelationships among the word analysis skills, of course; but, as the studies we have just cited imply, it would be possible to abbreviate the sequence or to drop some of the emphases upon various segments. Besides, although there are many sequences offered by various reading systems, there is almost no definitive research clarifying how the sequence of skill development should be arranged nor exactly which skills are definitely prerequisite to later skills. Any suggestions we shall offer later regarding the order or interdependence of various word analysis skills are, like those from any other source, based on logic not proven facts.

Let us recapitulate the ideas as we have proffered thus far. Although we now commonly offer considerable training in phonic skills in the first grade, the child progresses relatively slowly in learning to use these at first because of the cognitive demands, as John Downing, of the University of British Columbia, would say. In the second and third grades, these primary skills show marked development and probably make a distinct contribution to word recognition and consequently to comprehension. Then these skills seem to deteriorate or fall into disuse beginning at about the fourth grade, at about the same developmental period in which a marked acceleration in rate of silent reading tends to appear. We are not positive of the reasons for this deterioration but assume that it is probably due to such factors as the pupil's tendency to use fewer letter or letter-sound clues to word recognition, a normal concomitant of increasing rate; and perhaps to the diminishing efficacy of letter sounds in contributing to auditory recognition of the vocabulary words being read. Good readers tend to retain knowledge of the primary analytic skills, but whether they actually use them frequently to achieve word recognition is questionable. Most readers seem to gravitate toward a pattern of word analysis based upon common pronounceable units (which often violate the basic phonic and syllabication rules). Moreover, by the fourth grade it is apparent that many of the phonic skills make little contribution to comprehension, and dependence upon them may diminish for this reason also.

We are not implying that there is no value in teaching beginners common letter-sound associations, for there is ample evidence that they do help evoke the auditory memories of the very familiar words in which beginning reading materials are usually phrased. Rather we are strongly implying that these early skills soon lose their potency and probably should be replaced by more mature, more relevant word analysis skills. There are also present in these studies two obvious implications for diagnosis and remediation. When dealing with pupils, regardless of age, who can read intermediate-grade materials with reasonable comprehension, it is pointless to attempt to assess their primary phonic skills. Letter-sound associations just do not help unlock the pronunciation or the meaning of the terms of the content fields. Similarly, emphasizing these skills in remediation simply because they are weak, without reference to the pupil's present reading level, is not justified. In contrast, we recommend testing those word analysis skills commonly taught at and above the pupil's grade level of performance. The extent of the pupil's ability to decode letter-sound associations would be explored only when the more mature skills were badly defective and silent comprehension was weak. Then, if both intermediate and primary word analysis skills were very poor, we would then attempt to determine, first, whether the pupil had the basic auditory abilities to learn any of these skills, and second, whether he would respond positively to an auditory approach to learning to read better.

It is also possible that the pupil may be helped by strengthening and sharpening his use of those few mature word analysis skills for which he shows even rudimentary ability. It is quite conceivable that his comprehension and facility in word recognition may be improved by working with those word analysis practices that he already uses crudely, without dropping back to the primary letter-sound associations. And, as we shall point out later, an emphasis upon a more intelligent use of context clues will facilitate better comprehension, even when letter-sound associations are almost completely lacking. The cloze procedure research indicates that, when entire words are omitted at regular intervals of every ten words, the average pupil can supply the exact word in at least two out of every five omissions in materials at his reading level. When this native ability to use context is strengthened by special training, the pupil's need for phonic clues to word recognition diminishes markedly.

TEACHING PHONIC SKILLS

Phonic Skills

The phonics program in the leading basal readers of this decade follows this outline:

Readiness Level

Auditory awareness of common sounds, their intensity, pitch, duration, sequence, and quality.

Auditory perception of rhythm, rhyme, and alliteration.

Auditory memory for tones, patterns, directions, and spoken material.

Auditory discrimination among sounds; noises; letter sequences; initial consonants; rhyming words; initial, medial, and final sounds in words.

Readiness-Preprimer

Fourteen or so initial consonant sounds, three or so final consonant sounds. Some systems offer a few consonant digraphs and a number of phonograms as rhyming elements.

Primer

Seven or eight more initial consonants, five or six final consonants, several consonant digraphs, blends, a few short vowel sounds, vowel diphthongs and digraphs, and a varying number of phonograms.

First Reader Short vowel sounds are completed and long vowel sounds introduced; three or four of the difficult initial consonants, ten or more consonant blends, several more final consonants, and digraphs, three or four vowel diphthongs and digraphs, vowels with *r,* and a number of phonograms.

Second Reader The remaining initial consonants, a few more consonant digraphs, ten to fifteen more consonant blends, four or more vowel diphthongs and digraphs, and another group of phonograms.

Third Reader Two to five consonant digraphs, the remaining blends, a few more vowel diphthongs and digraphs, and another group of phonograms.

The actual content of phonics instruction as offered in the five leading basal series is as shown in the table "Phonics in the Basal Reading Program."

The commonly accepted sequence in the phonics program progresses from easy initial consonants first to final consonants (and some in the medial position) to consonant blends and short vowel sounds. Then it offers long vowel sounds, vowel diphthongs and digraphs and vowels with *r.* Harder consonant sounds, blends and digraphs, as well as vowel digraphs and diphthongs, are gradually introduced over the three-year span. The teaching of phonograms varies from one series to another from ten to sixty-six per year and from none at all to one series that presents 240 such units during the primary period. The program often includes training in consonant substitution (changing the initial consonant to form a new word, as *look–book*) and in blending letter sounds into larger units and words, as well as silent letters.

The sequence varies from this general pattern in a few series, which offer long vowel sounds before any others, or omit all types of vowel combinations entirely, or teach vowel sounds as though joined with the consonant *(ca-t),* or combine the use of the context and the initial consonant sound as a basic clue. Current systems contrast learning letter sounds in isolation versus their recognition in known words, or they emphasize analysis letter by letter *(kuh-a-tuh)* versus analysis by larger units such as the phonograms. Phonics sequences vary from one author to the next; and, although they are often fiercely defended, they usually represent strong beliefs more than research results.

What Does the Research Say?

The research on phonics instruction and its outcomes is voluminous and often contradictory and inconclusive. But we shall attempt a précis of those facts that we believe are clearly established.

PHONICS IN THE BASAL READING PROGRAM*

	CONSONANTS				VOWELS				
	INITIAL	FINAL	DIGRAPHS	BLENDS	LONG	SHORT	DIPHTHONGS AND DIGRAPHS	WITH R	PHONOGRAMS
Readiness-Preprimer	b, c, d, f, g, h, l, m, n, p, r, s, t, w, y	p, t, k	ch, sh, wh, th						
Primer	j, v, x, k	b, t, d, n, l	ck, ll, ss, ng	pl, st, bl, tr	i	i, y as i	ay, ow, ea	ar	ill, ide, ite, ine, all, and, ipe, etc.
First Reader	q, z, c (s)	s (z) k, m	kn, st gh, gn	fr, gr, gl, sl, sm, br, cl, fl, dr	e, i, a, o, u	a, e, o, u	ea, ee, ai, oo	er	id, im, eel, ed, ill, eat, ame, etc.
Second Reader	g (j) c (k, s)	y (e)	tch, kw qu	nt, cr, sn, sk, pr, ng, str, spr, sc, nk			ou, oa, oi, oy, ew	or, ir, ur	ook, alk, ang, ing, ink, unk, ail, etc.
Third Reader	f (ph)	f (gh)	ch (s) ck (k) wr	sp, sw, scr, squ, ft, lt			op, ei, ui, ey, ay		igh, ight, ump, oy, ought, ear, tion, eigh, etc.

*This synopsis is derived from data offered in George D. Spache and Evelyn B. Spache, *Reading in the Elementary School,* 3rd edition (Boston: Allyn and Bacon, 1973), pp. 456–60.

1. No system produces overall superiority when several reading behaviors are considered. A heavy dose of phonics or of those systems emphasizing isolated letter sounds tends to produce stronger ability to decode or name words, as this is commonly measured in word recognition tests. But such systems tend to deemphasize meaning and to produce poorer scores in tests of word meaning, comprehension, and even spelling, particularly among pupils of lesser mental ability. In fact, there are strong negative correlations between the time spent in phonics instruction and achievement in word meaning or comprehension, in one study (21).

2. Despite the variations in the teaching sequences, one system seems to produce reading success or failure in about the same proportions as another. No system succeeds in promoting fluent reading among all its pupils. And any great amount of emphasis upon phonics may be contraindicated among lower mental ability pupils, and those with language or auditory deficiencies.

3. Probably any phonics training should be preceded by an evaluation of the pupil's auditory abilities and, if so indicated, by a period of training intended to improve these discriminations. Then the nature and amount of subsequent phonics instruction must be modified by the degree of success of the preparatory training.

4. Skill in letter sounds or other phonic elements is not an absolute necessity for all pupils, for it is obviously possible to teach reading to pupils who exhibit a variety of auditory handicaps, as deafness, poor acuity, inaccurate discrimination, weak auditory memory, and the like. We also teach reading—again with difficulty, of course—to pupils whose mother tongue or dialect lacks sounds common to English. Some of these handicapped individuals never learn to produce precisely some of the letter-sound associations of standard English, yet many learn to read well enough for their educational and life needs.

5. Phonics is only one of the fundamental clues to word recognition and should not be overemphasized to the exclusion of other techniques such as use of the context, structural analysis, and visual analysis. Moreover, phonics is most effective in the primary vocabulary and must be supplemented or supplanted by other techniques of analysis as reading demands grow beyond the beginning levels.

6. Letter-sound associations are an aid to beginning reading, not a method of learning to read. Although reading does involve translating printed symbols into auditory memories of spoken words, this is only the primary step in the entire act of processing, interpreting, reacting to, and assimilating what is being read.

7. The values of phonic rules are highly debatable. Pupils of lesser

mental ability learn the principles only with difficulty, and, moreover, some observers doubt that many pupils apply the generalizations as an aid to word analysis while reading (16, 22, 23, 30). In fact, two studies by Hillerich (22, 23) appear to indicate that first or second graders taught vowel rules showed no superiority in word recognition and were inferior in reading comprehension to pupils who had learned only to discriminate short and long vowel sounds. The vowel rules seemed to function for the pupils only in a measure of reading nonsense words but not in a variety of other reading behaviors.

Critical evaluations of the utility of phonic generalizations have been made by several authors (3, 7, 11, 12) in reading materials of the first six grades. Of the mass of 121 different rules found in the literature, less than ten meet the criteria of being applicable at least 75 percent of the time in a significant number of words. The rules meeting these criteria are the following:

> Vowels—When *y* is the final letter in a word, it usually has a vowel sound. When there is one *e* in a word that ends in a consonant, the *e* usually has a short sound.
>
> Vowel digraphs—In these double vowel combinations, the first vowel is usually long and the second silent: *oa, ay, ai,* and *ee.*
>
> Vowel with *r*—The *r* gives the preceding vowel a sound that is neither long nor short. (True also for vowel with *l* or *w.*)
>
> Consonants—When *c* and *h* are next to each other, they form only one sound. *Ch* is usually pronounced as in *kitchen, catch,* and *chair,* not as *sh.* When the letter *c* is followed by *o* or *a,* the sound of *k* is likely to be heard. When *c* is followed by *e* or *i,* the sound of *s* is likely to be heard. When two of the same consonants are side by side, only one is heard.

Burmeister (7) suggests several additional principles that seem reasonably functional. We might phrase them in this fashion:

> *G* followed by *e, i,* or *y* has the sound of *j;* otherwise it has the hard sound of *g* as in *gate.* These double vowels usually form a diphthong (two vowel sounds): *au, aw, ou, oi, oy.*

Carol K. Winkley (42) and several authors of basal readers add an emphasis upon accent generalizations. Based on her finding that intermediate-grade children trained in accents scored higher in ability to attack new words, in vocabulary, and in comprehension, Winkley recommends these principles:

> A. When there is no other clue in a two-syllable word, the accent is usually on the first syllable.

B. Primary accent is on the root word in inflected or derived forms of words, as those ending in *ed, ing, tion,* and so on.

C. Primary accent is on the root word when prefixes as *in, re, de, ex* are present.

D. If there are two vowel letters together in the last syllable, that syllable is accented.

E. When two like consonants adjoin, the preceding syllable is usually accented.

F. Primary accent is on the syllable preceding *ate* in a three-syllable word.

G. In words of three or more syllables, one of the first two syllables is usually accented.

These rules depend upon prior training in syllabication, about which we will have more to say later. Data on their frequency and stability are also lacking except for the first and third, which are supported by the studies of Clymer, Emans, and Bailey (11, 12, 3).

There is strong evidence that the learning of these rules is most effective (and their application in the act of reading more probable) if they are approached inductively, that is to say, by leading children to recognize and to verbalize the patterns rather than by teaching them directly. Practice in trying to see and describe a relationship in a group of examples, urging pupils to explain what they did and their reasons for it when analyzing an unknown word (as contrasted with telling them the word), will help promote understanding and application of these principles. Asking pupils to collect words that illustrate a phonic generalization already familiar to them, and questioning them on the means that they employ to recognize unfamiliar words while they are reading orally or silently are also helpful. For successful reading, we must try to establish the habits of making some sort of effort to get at each unknown word when reading, even if by a logical guess, for every bit of reading matter is supposed to make sense. The spontaneous associative reasoning that pupils mentally evolve as they perceive the rules inductively makes a significant contribution to their retention and application.

8. In approaching each phonic element, deal only with words as units, not sounds isolated from words. If possible, employ words already in the reading vocabulary of pupils as examples of the letter-sound association in teaching each element.

9. The number of phonograms or large units that might be taught is several hundred. But many of these are relatively infrequent or have many alternative pronunciations. Our study (36) of their frequency and stability in a number of word lists and other sources indicates that the most functional are the following:

ail, ain, all, and, ate, ay, con, eep, ell, en, ent, er, est, ick, ight, ill, in, ing, ock, ter, tion, and possibly, *ake, ide, ile, ine, it, ite, le, re, ble.*

10. After consonant, short vowel, and long vowel sounds have been learned, pupils may be guided into a systematic approach to word recognition by phonic analysis. There is certainly greater chance of successful recognition if the task is approached by a systematic exploration of the possible alternatives. These exploratory steps would take the following sequence:

A. What is the sound of the first letter (or letters)?
B. What word beginning with this sound would make sense here?
C. How many vowels are there? Where are they?
   (1) If there is one vowel in the beginning or middle, try the short sound of the vowel.
   (2) If there is one vowel and an *e* at the end, try the long sound of the vowel.
   (3) If there is one vowel at the end, try the long sound.
   (4) If there are two vowels next to each other or at the end, try the long sound of the first vowel (except in *oi, oy, ou, ew, oo, au, aw*).
D. Now say the word. Do you know it? If not, try the other vowel sound.
E. Does the word seem to make sense? If not, write it down, and get help later from your teacher or your dictionary. Go on with your reading.

Once training in contextual analysis is begun this fifth step is modified to include such additional analytical steps, as described later.

11. Phonic skills operate in reading and writing and, as we have shown, are significant for spelling success. Hence the training must promote their translation from one medium to the other. This implies that pupils should learn such associations as the name and common sound of a printed letter and the graphic representation of each common sound. In other words, phonics practice should involve giving sounds for printed letter combinations; writing letters for given sounds; writing words and nonsense words at dictation; enunciating the sounds as one is writing words or tracing them; and giving sounds for letters or combinations named.

ALTERNATIVES TO PHONICS

It is possible to learn to read without having much phonic skill, although word recognition and the acquisition of reading vocabulary are, of course, considerably hampered. We have known students who graduated from the secondary school despite an almost utter lack of phonic knowledge. One pupil we recall could not match a single phonic combination in a test of fourth-grade level.

Her sole methods of word recognition were context and the dictionary, and her score in an appropriate reading vocabulary test was, of course, extremely low.

Diagnosis in these cases must first establish whether there are any real auditory deficits in acuity that prevent discrimination among the pitches distinguishing speech sounds. If acuity is normal, other auditory skills that presumably are trainable would be assessed—as auditory discrimination, memory, and sequencing—and the obvious training steps begun. Another essential diagnostic step would be the evaluation of the pupil's ability to form auditory associations with printed symbols, as by the Mills Learning Methods Test (26). This comparative measure of the pupil's ability to learn through auditory channels probably should be repeated several times during the auditory skills training to monitor its effects. If improvement in the use of auditory clues to word recognition appears, continuation of the auditory training seems indicated.

When the auditory training does not appear fruitful or when irreparable hearing losses make such instruction almost pointless, alternative techniques of word recognition are important. Intensive practice in word recognition, perhaps by the cloze procedure and other types of contextual analysis, is one such alternative. Another is the emphasis upon learning to recognize words through kinesthesia—tracing and writing words while saying them. This approach is reinforced by the use of the language-experience approach to learning to read. Or this system of using the pupil's own vocabulary as the medium of learning may prove to be the preferred emphasis if the kinesthetic training proves ineffectual. Any of these alternatives to phonic analysis will be strengthened by intensive practice in classifying words to build a depth of meaningful associations (8). Thus the use of contextual clues to word meanings is reinforced, and the usual ill effects of poor phonic skills upon acquisition of reading vocabulary are lessened.

TEACHING STRUCTURAL ANALYSIS

The purpose of training in structural analysis is to facilitate word recognition by inflectional endings, possessives, compound words, prefixes, suffixes, contractions, and roots or stems. Among the common elements at primary levels are these:

Prefixes—*un, re, ex, be, de, dis, in*
Inflections—*s, es, ed, ing, 's, d, e-ing, y-ed, y-ies, ly, f* to *v*

Suffixes—*er, est, en, ful, less, ness,* various forms of *ion,* and *ous, ment, ish*

Contractions—*aren't, can't, couldn't, didn't, don't, haven't, i'd, i'll, i'm, i've, isn't, it's, o'clock, one's, he'd, he'll, he's, that's, they'll, wasn't, you're, you've*

The functional values of prefixes, suffixes, and roots in terms of their frequency, consistency of pronunciation, and meaning, as well as their spelling variations, raise several very pertinent questions. Can we effectively teach such units as *in,* which has at least three or four meanings *(in, into, not)* and a variety of spellings *(in, im, il, ir, em, en)?* How much of this can we expect the average pupil to absorb and use in word analysis? How many of the hundreds of Greek and Latin stems can children really learn and apply? Should we eliminate all such word parts with multiple meanings and spellings, as some recommend?

We have evolved a list of these structural units of relatively high frequency in reading matter with single meanings for each. In the intermediate-grade levels particularly, these may be presented as meaningful units. Other word parts that are unacceptable on the single meaning criterion but are frequent in reading and children's writing may be taught as visual units or easily pronounceable letter clusters without emphasis upon their multiple meanings. (See table on page 224.)

We have some doubts about the possibility of average, and less than average, ability pupils' learning and using even this abbreviated list of structural elements, particularly those that are taught with meanings. There is only very weak supporting research indicating that many pupils make much eventual use of their exposure to this instruction. Moreover, when we scan a recent basic reading vocabulary list based on basal readers and content textbooks for the first six grades, the frequency of words with these meaningful units is discouraging (20). For the seventeen combining forms and prefixes we find only one prefix, *in,* which occurs in more than ten of the words in this 7613-word count. The others are present in a range of one to nine different words. It is true that some of these words, as *telegraph, microphone, automobile,* and *automatic,* appear hundreds of times in the basals and content books sampled. But is it efficient to burden the child's memory with structural units that occur in a small number of words in which word recognition is aided by length, shape, and probably a multiplicity of associations? Might it not be more efficient to teach practically all these structural units simply as visual, easily pronounceable units and have them function in this manner in word recognition?

STRUCTURAL ANALYSIS

MEANINGFUL UNITS	VISUAL UNITS
Combining Forms	
auto—self	*aqua*
micro—small	*audio*
phono—sound	*bene*
poly—many	*cred*
tele—far off	*junc*
	mit
	pon, pos
	scrib, scrip
	vert, vers
	vide, vis
Prefixes	
circum—around	*a, ab*
extra—beyond, outside	*ad*
in—in, into	*ante*
intra, intro—inside	*anti*
mis—wrong	*con, com, col*
non—not, the reverse	*contr*
out—more than, beyond	*de*
over—too much	*dis, di*
self	*e, ex*
syn—together	*inter*
under—below	*per*
up—up, above	*peri*
	post
	pre
	pro
	re
	sub
	super
	trans
Suffixes	
self	Noun—*ance, ence, tion, cion, sion,*
wise—manner	*ism, ment, al, ic, meter, scope, fer,*
	ity, gram, graph
	Agent (one who)—*eer, ess, ier, ster,*
	ist, stress, trix
	Adjectival—*est, fic, fold,*
	from, wards, less, able, ible, ble,
	most, like, ous, ious, eous, ose,
	ful, way, ways

TEACHING CONTEXTUAL ANALYSIS

Teachers' manuals and other such sources tend to pay lip service to the teaching of contextual analysis without being very specific as to the exact nature of these clues to word recognition; hence they deal rather vaguely with ways of stimulating their development. The fact that even children seem to recognize spontaneously the functions of words in ordinary sentences is shown by their tendency to substitute words of appropriate form, tense, number, and the like. Some studies seem to find that when oral reading errors are analyzed for their grammatical consistency, the great majority are quite logical and grammatically defensible. Thus it is obvious that contextual clues to word recognition play a very significant role in reading. But, until recently, we had no idea of precisely what the process involved, other than the pupil's imitation of normal sentence structure and word function.

Ames (1) attempted to formulate a classified list of contextual clues by having graduate students describe the introspection that they engaged in to complete the blanks in cloze selections. Fourteen clues to word recognition were thus identified by these mature students, but whether these function among younger individuals remains in doubt. Several other studies have approached the identification of the context clues used by elementary pupils by constructing modified cloze tests offering a variety of contextual, configuration, beginning, and ending letters, as well as Ames's clues (13, 31, 32). Their results are indicated in the chart of contextual clues on page 226.

These results are not very clear-cut, for two of the three studies explored clues by configuration and graphic elements rather than the reasoning processes used by intermediate-grade pupils to identify words with the aid of the context. Although pupils were assumed to be using some sort of contextual aids in these two experiments, we know no more about the nature of this effort than we did before. Rankin and Overholser, on the other hand, constructed their cloze materials so that each blank space could conceivably be completed by the use of a specific grammatical or other clue in the adjacent textual matter. In accepting their results, we have to assume that the pupils actually used the clue offered in most cases. We can add to these implied contextual clues the influence of the form class of the words identified. As shown among secondary students by Quealy (29), the form class most often responded to correctly are in order of easiest to hardest: nouns, adjectives, verbs, and adverbs.

Aulls (2) has criticized this research into contextual analysis as based on a priori judgments, as Ames's graduate students' introspection, for example,

CONTEXTUAL CLUES IN THE ORDER OF EFFECTIVENESS IN WORD RECOGNITION

AFTER EMANS AND FISHER (13)	AFTER ROBINSON (32)	AFTER RANKIN AND OVERHOLSER (31)
Only vowels omitted	Blank space	Words in series
Multiple-choice answers given	Shape of word given	Modifying phrase or clause
Beginning and ending letters	Shape plus beginning letter	Familiar expressions
Word represented by line of same length as word	Shape plus beginning and ending letters	Cause-effect
Beginning letter only		Association
Words represented by lines all of same length		Referral clues
		Synonyms
		Definitions
		Prepositions
		Question and answer
		Comparison and contrast
		Main idea plus details
		Nonrestrictive clause or appositive phrases

being applied to the efforts of elementary pupils. He argues that there is equally strong psycholinguistic evidence that the significant elements in word recognition or identification are position of a word in a sentence, bilateral distribution of the text (meaning clues on both sides of the omitted word), grammatical class form, word frequency, and syntax. At this point in our knowledge of exactly what helps the reader to identify an unfamiliar word, we probably should include in our training both viewpoints of useful contextual aids.

To promote greater skill in contextual analysis we might include these training steps:

1. If the systematic approach to phonic analysis outlined earlier has been taught, add additional steps to the system, such as this:
(As Step 5.) "If you still don't recognize the word, read the rest of the sentence (or paragraph in technical materials). Now do you have any idea what the word means? If not, read the entire sentence again. If you still don't recognize the word, write the word down and get help from your teacher or the dictionary later. Go on reading."

2. Prepare a number of cloze selections of the various types, deleting, for example, every fifth noun or every fifth verb or adjective or adverb. Clarify the function of the omitted words for each selection, for example, "The words left out in this selection name something." Discuss the answers offered and the pupils' reasons for their choices.

3. Expand the use of cloze exercises to the deletion of any fifth or tenth word, thus giving practice in deducing mixed form classes of words. Discuss pupils' answers.

4. Cloze exercises requiring less preparation time may be constructed by dittoing series of unrelated sentences in each of which a word is omitted. The position and form of the omitted word should be varied, with the nature of the exercise being diversified by sometimes inserting initial letters or blends; by omitting only the vowels of the test word; by using familiar rhymes, jingles, or stories; by placing a nonsense word repeatedly in the place of the omitted words; or by supplying the initial pronounceable letter cluster or syllable or the basic phonogram of the word in each blank space. (See *Reading Activities for Child Involvement,* by Evelyn B. Spache (35), for a wide variety of such exercises.)

6. Cloze exercises of any length can be prepared to practice each type of reasoning in contextual analysis. One set may give a clue by using words in series, another by defining the omitted word, another by offering a synonym. Thus, if desired, each kind of contextual clue (plus others offered spontaneously by the pupils) may be practiced, discussed, and added to the experiential background of the pupils. Avoid the use of formal terminology in discussing these types of contextual clues. Spontaneous explanation of their own reasoning processes by the pupils lays a foundation for their future use. Terminology does not.

7. The essential habit of using such clues to word recognition may be fostered by frequently questioning pupils on the means that they employed to derive the meanings of any difficult words in something just read orally or silently. Questions leading the child to verbalize his word analysis attempts reinforce this behavior in the act of reading. We feel that such questions should be an integral part of every check of pupil comprehension.

TEACHING SYLLABICATION

The pragmatism of teaching syllabication as currently offered is strongly challenged by a number of competent researchers. Patrick Groff (17, 18), for example, points out that the syllable is diversely defined by the scientists of various fields, that correct word pronunciation often does not correspond to the formal syllables, and that our instruction in syllabication is relevant only to spelling and printing conventions, not to word pronunciation or word analysis. Glass (15), like Groff, questions the utility of most syllabication principles because of their rapidly decreasing value; as reading vocabulary expands, an increasing number of exceptions occurs. He also points out that, as they mature, pupils make almost no use of the rules nor do they practice accurate syllabication in attempting word analysis. Speaking as a linguist, Wardhaugh (40) repeats these criticisms, pointing out the contradictions among phonological, morphological, visual, and typographic segmentation of words. Syllabication has no "truth" value, he declares, although dividing words into pronounceable units is a practical way of helping students to learn to read and spell.

These facts make formal instruction in the usual conventions of syllabication indefensible. The principles are not true, nor do they function for most individuals (except for printers who must divide words at the end of a line). But since readers do tend to attack words part by part, we should aid them by providing a few basic concepts. They should try to say the word part by part, using the following guides:

1. Each single vowel or combination, except for an *e* at the end of a word, indicates a basic part (syllable).
2. When the part is a VC or CVC unit, try the short sound of the vowel (closed syllable).
3. When the vowel seems to fall at the end of the part or the word except for a final *e,* try the long sound of the vowel (open syllable).
4. If you do not recognize the word at the first trial, try the other vowel sound.

To support this type of analysis of a word, part by part, emphasize practice with the list of phonograms given in paragraph 9 of the earlier discussion of phonics and the Visual Units listed in the table on structural analysis. All the critics of syllabication mentioned above recommend this emphasis upon such units as a reinforcement for the tendency of readers to segment words in attempting analysis.

ANALYZING PUPIL WORD ANALYSIS SKILLS

Diagnostic testing of word analysis skills by commercial tests is still in a state of great confusion. Of the twelve or thirteen skills that conceivably should be tested, no available test includes all of them. Those skills included are only sampled, not covered thoroughly. The same skill is measured in any of a half-dozen ways. And no current test attempts to sample the pupil's skill in types of contextual analysis. To illustrate, because of their frequency in instructional programs, we would certainly expect some measure of the child's knowledge and use of consonant sounds; yet this sample ranges from none at all in one test, ten or so in several others, to a third that samples all twenty-one consonants. One test asks the child to listen to and identify the isolated letter sound and also to look at the letter and give its common sound. Other ways of presumably sampling the same ability include choosing one of three rhyming words beginning with a given sound; matching words in a series that have the same beginning or ending consonant sound; spelling words at dictation; and selecting a word that begins with the same sound as a pictured object. Some tests sample consonant sounds only as beginning letters, others sample them again as final letters, while others sample only consonant blends and digraphs. Apparently there is little agreement among the authors of word analysis tests regarding the content of each area of phonics or the manner in which that knowledge is supposed to function in the act of reading. Only two of the instruments we shall examine have attempted to show that their particular method of sampling each skill is significantly related to early reading. The others are satisfied to show that the score derived from the sum of all their subtests has some relationship to reading. One or two authors apparently believe that their tests must have validity because they sample each facet of phonics thoroughly, a fairly reasonable assumption in view of the current almost universal practice of treating phonics instruction as an essential part of the reading program.

The reader will recall that a number of the diagnostic batteries that we critique in chapter 7 include subtests of word analysis skills. It may be desirable to review the criticisms offered there while reading about these instruments solely devoted to word analysis skills in order to compare the respective testing practices.

California Phonics Survey

This test, by Grace M. Brown and Alice B. Cottrell (Monterey: California Test Bureau, 1963), is for grades seven–thirteen. A seventy-five-item, forty-five-minute test, it offers separate scores on long vowels, short vowels, and other vowels; consonant blends and digraphs; consonant-vowel reversals; use of configuration; word endings; negatives; opposites; sight words and rigidity. The profile is assumed to indicate the areas of needed remediation, but the number of items in each subtest is often so few that the reliabilities for separate skill diagnosis are, in our opinion, doubtful. As we suggested in our discussion of the development of word analysis skills, the significance of some of the primary phonic skills tested here is questionable at the secondary and college reading levels, except perhaps in certain extreme cases.

Doren Diagnostic Reading Test of Word Recognition Skills

This test, by Margaret Doren (Minneapolis: American Guidance Service, 1973), samples twelve skills in second and third grades, although norms are offered for the first four grades in terms of total score. Despite its title, the lack of any grade level standards for the subtests precludes obtaining any diagnostic information. Reliability for the subtests ranges from .53 to .88, which indicates that some might be used for diagnostic purposes if the author had supplied norms. The author claims a validity of .90 of the total score with a silent reading test in grades one to four. This unusually high relationship with reading certainly implies that the test samples skills of significance at these grade levels. But these data were derived from the original standardization in 1956. Despite many changes in items, or their order, or in the length of subtests, no new data based on the present edition of the test are offered. And the lack of subtest norms raises strong doubts about the values in using the test to assess the various phonic skills.

Perhaps the author assumes that any subtest score less than perfect indicates an area for remediation and therefore that separate norms for the subtests are not essential. But if we compare the content of her test with the common instructional program, it is obvious that nearly perfect scores could not be expected until perhaps the end of the third grade. How, then, do we judge the progress of ordinary first and second graders who are only gradually learning this content? Apparently only by their total score.

Some of the subtests employ rather unusual testing techniques, as, for example, the measure of beginning sounds that asks the child to circle one of three rhyming words to complete a given sentence. In our opinion, this approach samples consonant substitution and contextual clues as well as the possible use of beginning sounds, and its title is consequently misleading. Sight word vocabulary is supposed to be measured by a task of matching one of three real or nonsense words representing the phonetic spelling of a given word. Certainly much more than simple sight word recognition, which normally occurs without much analysis at all, is being sampled here.

Another pertinent question arises in attempting to utilize the norms from a test standardized in 1956. Since 1966–67 there has been an increasing emphasis upon phonics training, in the first and second grades particularly, with much of the former three-year program being concentrated in these early grades. How accurately, then, can Doren's norms reflect current reading programs?

As for its concurrent validity, the Doren total test score does show high relationship with certain other word analysis tests and with teacher rankings of pupil reading ability (25). It is regrettable that this test with such favorable potential remains impotent in achieving its diagnostic role.

Diagnostic Reading Test, Word Attack Skills

This instrument (Mountain Home, N.C.: Committee on Diagnostic Reading Tests, 1963) is offered and normed for grades four to thirteen. Two subtests sample the matching of sounds in given words and the ability to indicate the number of syllables in a group of fifty relatively difficult words. We question whether testing the matching of sounds in words is really relevant to the word analysis habits of secondary and college students in view of the evidence that these skills begin to deteriorate by intermediate grade. The other subtest of syllabication may be more relevant at these levels, however. We may note parenthetically that we have compared the results on this syllabication test with knowledge of rules at the college freshman level and found very little relationship ($r = .15$). In view of this observation, the meaning of this test of syllabication becomes simply a comparison of the resemblance of the students' spontaneous habits of word segmentation to the actual syllables as defined by convention. If the similarity is slight, does it necessarily follow that the student cannot succeed in reading when using his own concepts of word division?

For a gross sample of the general phonetic knowledge of pupils, as in a screening test, this instrument will be serviceable. But it needs to be supplemented by detailed testing of specific word analysis skills if diagnostic information is desired. In their present form, neither of the subtests nor the total score provides any clues to remediation.

McCullough Word-Analysis Tests, Experimental Edition

These tests, by Constance M. McCullough (Boston: Ginn, 1963), sample eight phonic and other word analysis skills in grades four to six, with subtests of seven to thirty items each. The skills tested include initial blends and digraphs; phonetic discrimination; matching letters to vowel sounds; sounding whole words; interpreting phonetic symbols; dividing words into syllables; and root words and affixes. The author offers her device as a classroom tool rather than as a diagnostic instrument. For this reason the test was not widely standardized but simply tried out on a small population. This group was well above average in mental ability (average I.Q. 108.5), and their scores tended to cluster at the upper end of the score range. These limitations need not preclude use of the measure for assessment in a classroom if the local performances are used as standards.

Reliability for the total test was .94 and from .68 to .97 for the subtests in a single grade sample from the normative population. If this degree of reliability is found in other groups, some of the subtests can be used for individual comparisons and diagnosis. A comparison with two other group tests—the Doren and the Silent Reading Diagnostic—revealed concurrent validity coefficients for total scores around .80 and good relationships to teacher rankings.

The test can be praised for its breadth of sampling of mature word analysis skills in contrast to competing tests that tend to overemphasize primary phonic skills. The relevance of the original norms to current reading programs can also be answered by using local standards as found among today's pupils.

Phonovisual Diagnostic Test

This test, by Lucille D. Schoolfield and Josephine B. Timberlake (Washington, D.C.: Phonovisual Products), was formerly a spelling test. It is now offered "to discover the child's phonetic weaknesses." The interpretation suggested is that the child's spelling errors and violations of spelling rules indicate his needs for phonic training. The test is intended for use from the second grade onward but is actually composed of words of fourth-grade difficulty. No data on reliability, validity, or norms are presented by the authors.

It is true that the spelling performances of pupils do, in a sense, reflect their phonic knowledge, for poor spellers make more errors involving letter-sound associations than normal pupils do. But a spelling sample does not reflect precisely the process of decoding. One cannot generalize from spelling errors to specific phonic skills in reading. Finally, we fail to see how any significant diagnostic information can be obtained about the behavior of primary pupils when using a test of intermediate-grade difficulty.

Roswell-Chall Auditory Blending Test

This device, by Florence G. Roswell and Jeanne S. Chall (New York: Essay Press, 1963), is administered individually to pupils of the first four grades. It consists of three subtests of ten items each in which the phonic elements of words are pronounced separately for the subject, who is expected to blend them into whole words. One group consists of a consonant plus a vowel or vowel digraph or diphthong; another, of an initial consonant or digraph plus the rest of the word; and the third, of words composed of three separate phonic elements.

The test was tried out on a group of sixty-two black urban pupils and twenty-five disabled readers. Reliability data, apparently based on this normative population, offer split-half correlations of .86 to .93 over a four-grade range, and one of .94 for the disabled readers. Validity coefficients with oral and silent reading tests are quoted from .26 to .66, and one of .70 with an oral test for a small group of disabled readers in the third to fifth grades. Use of this instrument has not been widespread; hence it is not possible to determine whether the reliability or validity data would hold up in other populations. Moreover, it is very doubtful that the authors' figures for such atypical groups would apply in more normal populations.

The authors believe that ability to blend given sounds into words, as they measure it, is highly significant for reading. Our confidence in this hypothesis would have increased if the authors had explored various methods of testing the blending skill and demonstrated the superior validity of their approach. The research on blending is often contradictory and inconclusive, and the data supplied for this instrument do nothing to help clarify this area.

Roswell-Chall Diagnostic Test of Word Analysis Skills

This five-part instrument, by Florence G. Roswell and Jeanne S. Chall (New York: Essay Press, 1959), is offered for grades two to six. The subtests assay sounds of consonants and consonant diagraphs (ten items); short vowel sounds in monosyllables within sentences; five pairs of words on the final *e* rule *(fin–fine);* twelve one-syllable words containing vowel combinations; and eight polysyllabic words for the child to pronounce. The words used to measure the child's knowledge of phonic elements, as in the short vowels, final *e,* and vowel combinations subtests, are common sight words that many pupils easily recognize without analysis. Only when the words were unknown to the testees could the examiner assume that they had used phonic analysis (or some other technique) to read the words.

No normative, reliability, or validity data are offered in the manual for the test. Nor does the evidence that fifth graders score higher than second graders, that a group of disabled readers scored poorly, and that scores on the test increased with levels of reading ability, prove anything about the nature of the test other than that it measures something or other related to reading (sight word vocabulary?). Nor do the moderate correlations with silent and oral reading tests cited in this article clarify exactly what the test is measuring, for an adequate test of sight word vocabulary would yield similar correlations (9).

In a comparative study of word analysis tests by McCall and McCall (25), this instrument was the poorest of four similar tests in validity for predicting reading.

Silent Reading Diagnostic Test

This widely used ninety-minute battery of tests (Chicago: Lyons and Carnahan, 1955) yields twenty scores. Six reflect word recognition patterns, four sample error tendencies, nine test word recognition techniques, and one involves word synthesis. Several of the subtests are questionable, as those of Locating Elements and Root Words, which asks the pupil to find a small word within a larger, and the Word Synthesis test, which assays blending ability of words divided at the end of a line. The divisions do not follow normal syllabication, though.

Norms are based on a "typically midwestern community," but the size of the population is not given. Reliability in a group of forty-nine third graders is quoted for the subtests as ranging from .46 to .97. Fortunately for its use, these inadequate data are supplemented by several research articles. Benz and Rosemier (5) found the apparent validity of the subtests of words in context, syllabication, and root words much greater than the measures of word elements, beginning sounds, and rhyming sounds in a fourth-grade population. However, as reported in another article, the validity coefficients for these six subtests ranged from .09 to .55, with all six accounting for only slightly more than 33 percent of the variance in reading (4). McCall and McCall (25) report validity coefficients for this test around .80 in a comparative study of word analysis tests. In contrast, Murray and Karlsen (27) found the subtest scores in the Silent Reading Diagnostic consistently higher than parallel tests from the Gates Diagnostic. There were significant differences between the means and the standard deviations in ten of eleven subtest comparisons in this study.

At this point, we might make the observation that group tests of word analysis skills (Silent, Doren, McCullough) seem to agree with each other fairly well (average intercorrelations around .80), but they tend to differ distinctly in their results from those obtained from individual tests (Gates Diagnostic, Roswell-Chall Diagnostic). The group tests also show better relationships to teacher rankings and other group reading tests than do the individual tests (25). But these relationships are based on the total scores of the various group tests, which may simply mean that one gross estimate of reading ability tends to resemble another (while specific skill testing naturally yields different estimates). This implies, it seems to us, that if the reading teacher wants an overall estimate of the pupil's word analysis skills, one of the better group tests will give this information about as well as another. But if she wants diagnostic information on specific analysis skills, she will have to look for some instrument other than most of those we have reviewed here.

Stanford Diagnostic Reading Test

Two levels of this instrument, by Bjorn Karlsen, Richard Madden, and Eric F. Gardner (New York: Harcourt Brace Jovanovich, 1968), are offered from mid-second to mid-fourth and mid-fourth to mid-eighth grades. Level 1 measures comprehension, vocabulary, auditory discrimination, syllabication, beginning and ending sounds, blending, and sound discrimination. Level 2 omits the beginning and ending sounds and the auditory discrimination and adds a test of reading rate.

Reliability coefficients are given as above .90 for auditory discrimination, blending, and sound discrimination; .87–.92 for beginning and ending sounds; and .73–.79 for syllabication. Validity coefficients for the same tests range from .51 to .71. It would appear that, with the possible exception of the blending test, differences among subtest scores will be meaningful, particularly if we use the authors' suggestion of considering a two stanine difference as significant. The blending test correlates with several of the other subtests as high as .76 to .85. This overlap is so great as to raise the question of the identity of blending as an independent subskill, the same point made earlier with respect to the Roswell-Chall Auditory Blending Test.

If the situation demands a complete diagnosis of word analysis skills, it appears that none of these group or individual tests includes all the skills or even all of the content of each skill area. Even the McCullough Word Analysis, which duplicates all the areas covered in the Stanford except auditory discrimination, and samples three additional areas of phonic discrimination, phonetic symbols, and roots and affixes, would provide an incomplete assessment. It may serve as the initial group test to isolate undeveloped skills or pupils who may need attention. But it would have to be supplemented by measures of consonant substitution, phonograms, short versus long vowels, and vowels with *r, l,* and *w.* These areas could, of course, be sampled by teacher-made tests or, better still, by selecting subtests from some of the individual diagnostic batteries we reviewed in chapter 7. The Spache Diagnostic Scales, for example, offer relatively complete tests in all these latter areas except the vowels with *r, l,* and *w.*

SPELLING ERRORS TESTS

Another informal approach to the diagnosis of phonic skills that we have used is the Spelling Errors Tests. We devised these tests to provide a rapid method of collecting samples of a pupil's tendencies to spelling errors. Obviously they permit a much more rapid and effective method than scanning the pupil's writings in search of misspelled words. We have found them useful in cases of reading or spelling disability when another view of the pupil's word analysis skills is desirable.

Construction of the Tests

We began construction of the Spelling Errors Tests by reviewing a score or more of the published attempts to devise a classification system of spelling errors (37). These systems were critically analyzed for objectivity, clarity of definition, and ease of application; and a new system was evolved. The validity and reliability of the proposed classification were examined in a group of intermediate-grade pupils, and the system was further refined (38). A series of modified list spelling tests for grades two–four, five–six, and seven–eight was formulated that would offer a controlled number of opportunities for each type of error in the new classification system.

The spelling test words were chosen from Gates's list (14) by three criteria: their frequency in common spelling lists and curricula; their grade placement; and their common misspellings. The only words selected for the tests were those in which a single type of error was common in more than 50 percent of pupils. Ten words exemplify each one of the twelve error types identified in the classification system, for a total of 120 words in each test. For convenience in scoring, the twelve expected errors are repeated in the same order in each successive group of words. Incomplete words or those with more than three errors are included in a thirteenth category—unrecognizable or incomplete. Pupils may, of course, not misspell a test word in the expected fashion. If so, any error up to a maximum of three in a word is tabulated according to its type.

Gates's study of spelling errors was completed in 1937, and there may be some question of its applicability to today's pupils. But it is a very comprehensive collation of error tendencies and, to our knowledge, is the only body of data of this type. Moreover, changes in the spelling habits of pupils and spelling curricula do not appear to have been significant in the period since its publication.

Administering the Tests

The Spelling Errors Tests are administered like most spelling tests of the type called "modified list." After putting an appropriate heading of name, date, and grade on their papers and numbering the lines on the page for 120 items, the pupils should be given the following instructions (insofar as they are appropriate):

"I am going to give you a spelling test on this paper. It is a rather long test but you won't find it very hard. There may be a few words you haven't studied before, but I want you to try to spell these new words the best you can.

This is not one of your regular spelling tests. What you do on this test will not affect your spelling marks. Let's start now and see how well we can do.

"I will read the word, then use it in a sentence, and then say the word again. Wait until I say the word the last time after the sentence before you begin to write."

With young or immature children, the test should be given in two or three sittings on successive days to prevent undue fatigue.

Scoring the Tests

From our studies of various methods of classifying spelling errors (37), we have evolved the following principles or rules that we follow in scoring the Spelling Errors Tests. As we have suggested before, this system of classification could be further refined to include other types of spelling errors. But such refinement serves no useful purpose, according to our experiences in understanding the pupil's error tendencies. Therefore, we classify all the mistakes that the pupil makes under these types.

Rules for the classification of misspelled words are as follows:

General

1. A maximum of three errors in a single word will be tabulated.
2. No specific error will be entered more than once.

Omissions

An omission is one in which a letter or letters of the test word are omitted in the child's attempt at spelling, without any attempt at substitution.

1. silent letter—the omission of a consonant or vowel that is silent in the ordinary pronunciation of the word. This includes silent final *e* and the silent or subordinate vowel of a diphthong. As *wether–weather, reman–remain, fin–fine.* The omission of the silent letter in a digraph (as *w* in *wr*) is included here.
2. sounded letter—the omission of a letter that is sounded in the ordinary pronunciation of the word. This includes the omission of the major or sounded vowel of a diphthong. As *requst–request, plasure–pleasure, personl–personal, juge–judge.*
3. double letter—the omission of one of a pair of successive, identical letters, as *suden–sudden, adress–address, sed–seed.*

Additions and Repetitions

An addition is one in which a letter or letters are added. The correct letters of the test word are present in the portion of the word in which the error of addition occurs. A repetition of a letter or letters of the test word is considered an addition.

4. doubling—the repetition of a single letter. As *untill–until, frriend–friend, deegree–degree, allmost–almost.*

5. nondoubling—the addition of a single letter not repeating the preceding letter.

Transpositions or Partial Reversals

6. A transposition or partial reversal is one in which the correct sequence of the letters of the test word is disturbed. It usually takes the form of reversing the sequence of two letters. It may also take the form of interchanging the letters on either side of a central letter, as *was–saw.* Includes the transposition of syllables.

Phonetic Substitutions

A phonetic substitution is one in which a letter or letters similar in sound to those of the test word are substituted. The letters of the test word for which the substitution is offered are, of course, omitted.

7. vowel sound—substitution of a vowel or vowel and consonant for a vowel of the test word. As *prisin–prison, calender–calendar, wimmin–women.*

8. consonant sound—substitution of a consonant that is an alternative sound for a consonant of the test word. As *cecond–second, vakation–vacation, jentle–gentle.*

9. syllable—substitution of a similarly sounding syllable for a syllable of the test word. As *purchest–purchased, financhel–financial.* Includes also the substitution of a single letter for a syllable. As *naborhood–neighborhood, stopt–stopped, ameless–aimless.*

10. word—the substitution of an actual word grossly similar in sound. As *weary–very, colonial–colonel.*

Nonphonetic Substitutions

A nonphonetic substitution is one in which a letter or letters dissimilar in sound are substituted in the test word. The letter of the test word for which the substitute is offered is, of course, omitted.

11. vowel—substitution of a vowel or vowel and consonant for the vowel of the test word. As *stition–station, strick–struck.*

12. consonant—substitution of a consonant or vowel and consonant for consonant of the test word. As *watching–washing, inportance–importance.*

Unrecognizable or Incomplete

13. These are words that contain more than three errors; are combinations of letters not forming a real or misspelled word, being unrecognizable as the test word; or are words entirely omitted or only partly completed. As *cano–cotton, libt–liberty, di–decided.*

Interpreting the Tests

Norms for the various types of errors are given on the Record Sheet. These were derived from the author's study of fifty elementary school children (39). We have compared our norms with the results of twenty-two earlier studies of spelling errors (38) among students ranging from the elementary through college level. The similarity between our data and those of the earlier studies shows that the tendencies to misspell in certain ways are similar at all levels. Our norms may be used at any educational level for judging the error tendencies of a pupil.

The norm on the Record Sheet indicates the range of errors of average pupils. For example, 9 to 17 percent of the errors of the average pupil may be expected to be Type 1—omission of a silent letter. If the pupil makes fewer than 9 percent of such errors, he has made significantly fewer than the average pupil. Conversely, if he has made more than 17 percent, he is making this type of error to an excessive degree, much more often than the average pupil. The figures for the other types of errors are interpreted in the same fashion.

A pupil who makes a greater proportion of errors of a certain type than the norm is in the worst 16 percent of the population in making this type of error. Making fewer than the lower limit of the norm indicates that the pupil is superior to all except the top 16 percent of the population with respect to this type of error.

We have compared the performances of pupils who were good spellers and those who were poor spellers in an earlier study (39). We found that—despite the fact that they were good spellers—when we made a study of their errors, these pupils tended to show distinct error tendencies. These tendencies, which might be considered characteristic of good spellers, were as follows:

1. More errors of Type 5—addition of a single letter.
2. More errors of Type 9—phonetic substitution for a syllable.

Thus good spellers tend to make such errors as *ck* for hard *c, shead* for *shed, pleashure* for *pleasure,* and *naborhood* for *neighborhood, stopt* for *stopped.* These better spellers tend to make errors of phonetic substitution of vowels, consonants, and syllables as using *s* for soft *c, ea* for long *e, are* for *air* as in *repair,* and so on. These errors show the awareness of the sound characteristics of words and letters, the greater skill in phonics, and better auditory discrimination found in good spellers.

Poor spellers, on the other hand, make more errors as follows:

1. Type 2—omission of a sounded letter.
2. Type 11—nonphonetic substitution for a vowel.
3. Type 12—nonphonetic substitution for a consonant.
4. Type 13—unrecognizable or incomplete.

Such errors as omitting a letter clearly heard in the pronunciation of a word, using vowels and consonants that could not possibly represent the sounds of a word, and misspelling so badly or incompletely that the word cannot be recognized are characteristic of pupils really lacking in knowledge of phonics and sounds, as well as in poor auditory discrimination. These deficiencies are very often found among those with poor word analysis or spelling skills.

For a reliable estimate of error tendencies, a minimum of 100 misspelled words must be analyzed. Thus it may be necessary to utilize a second more difficult test or to collect misspellings from the pupil's spontaneous writings to supplement the number obtained by the initial test.

SPELLING ERRORS TEST, GRADES TWO TO FOUR

1. bite–bit
2. and–an
3. arrow–arow
4. almost–allmost
5. dark–darck
6. ankle–ankel
7. bead–beed
8. bush–buch
9. flies–flys
10. bare–bear
11. bags–bogs
12. bottom–botton
13. boxes–boxs
14. bridge–brige
15. asleep–aslep
16. also–allso
17. negro–negrow
18. ate–aet
19. creep–creap
20. buzz–buss
21. bull–bool
22. four–for
23. pail–pale
24. bump–bunp
25. fasten–fasen
26. farther–father
27. bigger–biger
28. later–latter
29. plank–planck
30. born–bron
31. cotton–cotten
32. cave–kave
33. gain–gane
34. here–hear
35. did–ded
36. him–hin

SPELLING ERRORS TEST, GRADES TWO TO FOUR (Continued)

37. breast–brest
38. hatch–hach
39. cutting–cuting
40. lose–loose
41. rent–reant
42. giant–gaint
43. caught–cought
44. fishing–fiching
45. laughing–lafing
46. buy–by
47. flew–flow
48. am–an
49. comes–coms
50. bound–bond
51. broom–brom
52. melon–mellon
53. so–sow
54. drum–durm
55. dollars–dollers
56. lace–lase
57. looked–lookt
58. deer–dear
59. he–hi
60. jumping–junping
61. cookies–cookes
62. march–mach
63. dropped–droped
64. until–untill
65. books–bookes
66. girl–gril
67. hall–holl
68. mice–mise
69. paw–por
70. eight–ate
71. her–har
72. rich–rick
73. match–mach
74. crack–crak
75. glass–glas
76. welcome–wellcome
77. coming–comeing
78. field–feild
79. ton–tun
80. often–offen
81. though–thow
82. bake–back
83. hoe–how
84. lamp–lanp
85. alone–alon
86. starve–stave
87. hammer–hamer
88. lily–lilly
89. hop–hope
90. nickel–nickle
91. obey–obay
92. pony–pone
93. babies–babys
94. meat–meet
95. hot–hat
96. room–roon
97. awhile–awile
98. street–steet
99. begged–beged
100. hoped–hopped
101. an–and
102. patch–pacth
103. cellar–celler
104. recite–resite
105. parties–partys
106. rake–rack
107. let–lat
108. seem–seen
109. cracker–craker
110. studying–studing
111. bonnet–bonet
112. already–allready
113. grab–grabe
114. piece–peice
115. heap–heep
116. slice–slise
117. aim–ame
118. pear–pair
119. red–rad
120. bedroom–bedroon

SPELLING ERRORS TEST GRADES FIVE AND SIX

1. basement–basment
2. barley–barly
3. address–addres, adress
4. already–allready
5. fever–feaver
6. angel–angle
7. creek–creak
8. advice–advise
9. accept–except
10. birth–berth
11. hoe–how
12. bedroom–bedroon
13. beast–best
14. capture–capure
15. arrest–arest
16. chose–choose
17. fled–flead
18. chief–cheif
19. beef–beaf
20. base–bace
21. compare–compair
22. deer–dear
23. reward–reword
24. improved–enproved
25. cleaning–clening
26. governor–govenor
27. account–acount
28. chosen–choosen
29. chest–cheast
30. candle–candel
31. celebrate–celabrate
32. advice–advise
33. mere–mear
34. eight–ate
35. stump–stomp
36. kindergarten–kindargarden
37. wrist–rist
38. carrying–carring
39. appear–apear
40. handful–handfull
41. export–exsport
42. freight–frieght
43. harbor–harber
44. crash–crach
45. parties–partys
46. fare–fair
47. flew–flow
48. themselves–themselfs
49. earnest–ernest
50. forward–foward
51. approve–aprove
52. helpful–helpfull
53. forty–fourty
54. giant–gaint
55. beggar–begger
56. decided–desided
57. aid–ade
58. fought–fort
59. tip–tep
60. thinking–thinging
61. hope–hop
62. government–goverment
63. allow–alow
64. hoped–hopped
65. tar–tare
66. deceive–decieve
67. destroy–distroy
68. blaze–blase
69. claim–clame
70. due–dew
71. cost–cast
72. jumping–junping
73. knitting–nitting
74. dodge–doge
75. canned–caned
76. proper–propper
77. using–useing
78. hose–hoes
79. honor–honer
80. deuce–deuse
81. aim–ame
82. groan–grown
83. pump–pomp
84. import–inport
85. bruise–bruse
86. pumpkin–punkin
87. beginning–begining
88. dining–dinning

SPELLING ERRORS TEST GRADES FIVE AND SIX (Continued)

89. closing–closeing
90. niece–neice
91. conductor–conducter
92. practice–practise
93. babies–babys
94. herd–heard
95. slip–slep
96. gross–grose
97. buying–bying
98. quarter–quater
99. finally–finaly
100. fearful–fearfull
101. ninth–nineth
102. puzzle–puzzel
103. earliest–earlyest
104. prize–prise
105. underwear–underware
106. loan–lone
107. stir–ster
108. attack–attach
109. failed–faled
110. stitch–stich
111. bluff–bluf
112. lining–linning
113. giving–giveing
114. shield–sheild
115. fragrant–fragrent
116. reduce–reduse
117. phone–fone
118. loss–lose
119. step–stap
120. lamp–lanp

SPELLING ERRORS TEST, GRADES SEVEN AND EIGHT

1. completely–completely
2. adjust–ajust
3. accommodate–accomodate
4. administration–addministration
5. construction–construcktion
6. angle–angel
7. ballot–ballet
8. response–responce
9. accepted–excepted
10. pause–paws
11. stump–stomp
12. congratulate–congradulate
13. condemn–condem
14. boundary–boundry
15. afford–aford
16. amendment–ammendment
17. complexion–complextion
18. chapel–chaple
19. accordance–accordence
20. selected–celected
21. companies–companys
22. principle–principal
23. reward–reword
24. gratitude–graditude
25. acquire–acuire
26. breadth–breath
27. addressed–adressed
28. control–controll
29. completed–compleated
30. Christian–Christain
31. basis–bases
32. type–tipe
33. grateful–greatful
34. choir–quire
35. cost–cast
36. attack–attach
37. affectionately–affectionatly
38. badge–bage
39. affair–afair
40. compel–compell
41. exist–exsist
42. guardian–guardain

SPELLING ERRORS TEST, GRADES SEVEN AND EIGHT (Continued)

43. compliment–complement
44. absence–absense
45. hereafter–hearafter
46. clause–claws
47. flew–flow
48. gross–grose
49. approach–approch
50. delicious–delicous
51. affection–afection
52. arise–arrise
53. regret–regreat
54. label–lable
55. affect–effect
56. anticipate–antisipate
57. duties–dutys
58. coarse–course
59. Sabbath–Sabboth
60. import–inport
61. autumn–autum
62. official–offical
63. connect–conect
64. arouse–arrouse
65. owing–oweing
66. receiving–recieving
67. celebration–celabration
68. underwear–underware
69. concern–consern
70. council–counsel
71. stir–ster
72. improved–inproved
73. arrangement–arrangment
74. substitute–subsitute
75. correct–corect
76. limited–limitted
77. pleasing–pleaseing
78. ruffle–ruffel
79. benefit–benifit
80. concert–consert
81. compare–compair
82. capitol–capital
83. pump–pomp
84. thinking–thinging
85. clothe–cloth
86. quantity–quanity
87. commission–commision
88. occasion–occassion
89. refer–refere
90. seize–sieze
91. calendar–calender
92. hence–hense
93. niece–neice
94. border–boarder
95. slip–slep
96. themselves–themselfs
97. cocoa–coco
98. temptation–temtation
99. communicate–comunicate
100. rebel–rebell
101. regard–reguard
102. siege–seige
103. applied–applyed
104. extension–extention
105. claim–clame
106. desert–dessert
107. fell–fill
108. kindergarten–kindergarden
109. courtesy–curtesy
110. appropriate–appropiate
111. disappoint–disapoint
112. remit–remitt
113. remembrance–rememberance
114. villain–villian
115. approval–approvel
116. discussed–discusted
117. phone–fone
118. formerly–formally
119. hoe–how
120. line–lime

There are a number of other spelling tests available that claim to serve a diagnostic function as ours does. Their universal flaw is that the test words

SPELLING ERRORS TEST—RECORD SHEET

NAME ______________________ DATE ____________ GRADE __________
SPELLING ERRORS TEST FOR GRADE _____

TYPES OF ERRORS	NO.	PERCENT	NORM
1. Omission of a silent letter	____	______	9–17
2. Omission of a sounded letter	____	______	5–17
3. Omission of a doubled letter	____	______	3–10
4. Addition by doubling	____	______	1–5
5. Addition of a single letter	____	______	7–19
6. Transposition or reversals	____	______	2–7
7. Phonetic substitution for a vowel	____	______	11–25
8. Phonetic substitution for a consonant	____	______	5–14
9. Phonetic substitution for a syllable	____	______	2–8
10. Phonetic substitution for a word	____	______	0–5
11. Nonphonetic substitution for a vowel	____	______	1–4
12. Nonphonetic substitution for a consonant	____	______	2–5
13. Unrecognizable or incomplete	____	______	0–13

selected to measure the child's knowledge of a phonic element or a spelling or phonic convention are not always true examples of error in this element or convention. The test words do exemplify a certain phonic element or a rule; but, according to Gates's study, pupils do not usually misspell each word at the expected point. Moreover, no alternative ways of interpreting the pupil's misspelling if it does not follow the author's expectations are given in these diagnostic spelling tests. These limitations are not present in the Spelling Errors Tests offered here.

To make this contrast stronger, we may compare the Kottmeyer Diagnostic Spelling Test for Primary Levels (Manchester, Mo.: Webster Publishing) with the data on common misspellings given in the Gates study (14). The test is composed of seventy-five words, in sixty-seven of which the tester is to look for the child's misspelling of a particular phonic element or principle. The testing of the child's spelling of each element is tested by one to five words. In all, forty-two different phonic elements, phonic rules, and spelling conventions are sampled in sixty-seven words. The last eight items test only the gross spelling of a mixture of homonyms, along with a few difficult words.

Each test item was compared with Gates's data to determine whether the pupils were likely to misspell the phonic element or convention that the author suggests as significant in each word. This comparison answers the question whether this test will yield diagnostic information about the pupils' knowledge of phonics in spelling. In the sixty-seven test items intended to provide an opportunity to observe a pupil's misspelling of a phonic element or convention, thirty-eight were found to be likely to work in this fashion. Sixteen words are not commonly misspelled in the fashion that Kottmeyer expects and would not be likely to yield the information desired. For example, the word *doll* is supposed to test the child's spelling of the final *ll*. Gates indicates that 79 percent of the misspellings of this word involve not the *ll* but the *o*. Again, in the word *reading*, the examiner is to note whether the child used the *ing* suffix. But 89 percent of the usual misspellings of this word involve the *ea* vowel combination, not the *ing*.

In nine other words, Gates's tabulation of pupils' misspellings indicates doubt in a majority of cases that the error would involve the phonic element intended to be tested. For four of the test words no comparative data were available in the Gates study. It appears that only thirty-eight of the sixty-seven items (56 percent) in the Kottmeyer Diagnostic Spelling Test for Primary Levels would be likely to function in the expected fashion and thus reveal the pupil's phonic skills in spelling. This author would also question the reliability of a diagnosis based upon one to five samples of the pupil's ability to represent a particular phonic element.

LEARNING PROJECT

1. Administer the appropriate Spelling Errors Test to one or several children and analyze their errors. Examine the errors for indications of phonic knowledge and use of syllabication. What were their most frequent errors and the probable meanings of these? In what errors were they in excess of the norms? Which errors showed some intelligent use of phonic or syllabication information? Which did not?

2. Make a chart contrasting the content of the various tests in the area of phonics, structural analysis, and contextual analysis. Does any test assess pupil performance in all of the skills of any of these skill areas? If you were to use one of these tests in your diagnosis, how would you have to supplement it?

3. Administer a battery of phonics tests to several average or good readers (as judged by their ability to read with adequate comprehension in materials at or above their grade placement). Use a test, preferably, which gives separate norms for each subtest. Compare their performances in the various phonic subskills to determine whether they are equally strong in all subskills. Interview the pupils and also have them read orally to discover what word analysis techniques they seem to use most frequently in order to obtain the pronunciation and meanings of difficult

words. Discuss your findings with the class in an attempt to interpret their implications.

REFERENCES

1. Ames, Wilbur S., "The Development of a Classification Scheme of Contextual Aids," *Reading Research Quarterly,* 2 (Fall 1966), 57–82.
2. Aulls, Mark W., "Toward a Systematic Approach to How the Reader Uses Context to Determine Meaning," in *Reading: The Right to Participate,* 20th Yearbook, National Reading Conference, 1971, 312–19.
3. Bailey, Mildred Hart, "The Utility of Phonic Generalizations in Grades One Through Six," *Reading Teacher,* 20 (February 1967), 413–18.
4. Benz, Donald A., and Rosemier, Robert A., "Concurrent Validity of the Gates Level of Comprehension Test and the Bond-Clymer-Hoyt Reading Diagnostic Tests," *Educational and Psychological Measurement,* 26 (1966), 1057–62.
5. Benz, Donald A., and Rosemier, Robert A., "Word Analysis and Comprehension," *Reading Teacher,* 21 (March 1968), 558–63.
6. Boyd, R. D., "Growth of Phonic Skills in Reading," in *Clinical Studies in Reading III,* Helen M. Robinson, editor. Supplementary Educational Monographs, No. 97, 1969, 68–87.
7. Burmeister, Lou E., "Usefulness of Phonic Generalizations," *Reading Teacher,* 21 (January 1968), 349–56, 360.
8. Catterson, Jane, "Inductive vs. Deductive Methods in Teaching Word Attack Skills," in *Challenge and Experiment in Reading,* Proceedings International Reading Association, 7, 1962, 121–23.
9. Chall, Jeanne S., "The Roswell-Chall Diagnostic Reading Test of Word Analysis Skills: Evidence of Reliability and Validity," *Reading Teacher,* 11 (December 1958), 178–83.
10. Clay, Marie M., "Emergent Reading Behavior," Doctoral dissertation, University of Auckland, Auckland, New Zealand, 1966.
11. Clymer, Theodore, "The Utility of Phonic Generalizations in the Primary Grades," *Reading Teacher,* 16 (January 1963), 252–58.
12. Emans, Robert, "The Usefulness of Phonic Generalizations above the Primary Grades," *Reading Teacher,* 20 (February 1967), 419–25.
13. Emans, Robert, and Fisher, Gladys M., "Teaching the Use of Context Clues," *Elementary English,* 44 (March 1967), 243–46.
14. Gates, Arthur I., *A List of Spelling Difficulties in 3878 Words.* New York: Teachers College Press, 1937.
15. Glass, Gerald G., "The Strange World of Syllabication," *Elementary School Journal,* 67 (May 1967), 403–05.
16. Glass, Gerald G., and Burton, Elizabeth H., *How Do They Decode? Verbalizations and Observed Behaviors of Successful Decoders.* Department of Education, Adelphi University, Garden City, New York.
17. Groff, Patrick, *The Syllable: Its Nature and Pedagogical Usefulness.* Portland: Northwest Regional Educational Laboratory, 1971.

18. Groff, Patrick, "Dictionary Syllabication—How Useful?" *Elementary School Journal,* 72 (December 1971), 107–17.
19. Hackney, Ben H., Jr., "Reading Achievement and Word Recognition Skills," *Reading Teacher,* 21 (March 1968), 515–18.
20. Harris, Albert J., and Jacobson, Milton D., *Basic Elementary Reading Vocabularies.* New York: Macmillan, 1972.
21. Harris, Albert J., Serwer, Blanche L. and Gold, Lawrence, "Comparing Approaches in First Grade Teaching with Disadvantaged Children Extended into Second Grade," *Reading Teacher,* 20 (May 1967), 698–703.
22. Hillerich, R. L., "Vowel Generalizations and First Grade Reading Achievement," *Elementary School Journal,* 67 (1967), 246–50.
23. Hillerich, R. L., "Teaching about Vowels in Second Grade," *Illinois School Research,* 7 (1970), 35–38.
24. Marchbanks, Gabrielle, and Levin, Harry, "Cues by Which Children Recognize Words," *Journal of Educational Psychology,* 56 (April 1965), 57–61.
25. McCall, Rozanne A., and McCall, Robert B., "Comparative Validity of Five Reading Diagnostic Tests," *Journal of Educational Research,* 62 (March 1969), 329–33.
26. Mills, Robert E., *The Learning Methods Test Kit.* Fort Lauderdale, Fla.: The Mills Center.
27. Murray, Carol-Faith, and Karlsen, Bjorn, "A Concurrent Validity Study of the Silent Reading Tests and the Gates Reading Diagnostic Tests," *Reading Teacher,* 13 (April 1960), 293–94, 296.
28. Plattor, Emma E., and Woestehoff, Ellsworth S., "Specific Reading Disabilities of Disadvantaged Children," in *Reading Difficulties: Diagnosis, Correction and Remediation,* William K. Durr, editor. Newark, Del.: International Reading Association, 1970, 55–60.
29. Quealy, Roger J., "Senior High Schools Students Use of Contextual Aids in Reading," *Reading Research Quarterly,* 4 (Summer 1969), 512–33.
30. Railsback, Charles E., "Consonant Substitution in Word Attack," *Reading Teacher,* 23 (February 1970), 432–35.
31. Rankin, Earl F., and Overholser, Betsy M., "Reaction of Intermediate Grade Children to Contextual Clues," *Journal of Reading Behavior,* 1 (Summer 1969), 50–73.
32. Robinson, H. Alan, "A Study of the Techniques of Word Identification," *Reading Teacher,* 16 (January 1963), 238–41.
33. Russell, David H., *Characteristics of Good and Poor Spellers: A Diagnostic Study.* Contributions to Education, No. 727. Teachers College, Columbia University, 1937.
34. Smith, Frank, and Holmes, Deborah Lott, "The Independence of Letter, Word and Meaning Identification in Reading," *Reading Research Quarterly,* 6 (Spring 1971), 394–415.
35. Spache, Evelyn B., *Reading Activities for Child Involvement.* Boston: Allyn and Bacon, 1976.
36. Spache, George D., "A Phonics Manual for Primary and Remedial Teachers," *Elementary English Review,* 16 (April–May 1939), 147–50, 191–98.
37. Spache, George D., "A Critical Analysis of Various Methods of Classifying Spelling Errors I," *Journal of Educational Psychology,* 31 (February 1940), 111–34.

38. Spache, George D., "Validity and Reliability of the Proposed Classification of Spelling Errors II," *Journal of Educational Psychology,* 31 (March 1940), 204–14.
39. Spache, George D., "Characteristic Errors of Good and Poor Spellers," *Journal of Educational Research,* 34 (November 1940), 182–89.
40. Wardhaugh, Ronald, "Syl-lab-i-ca-tion," *Elementary English,* 43 (November 1966), 785–88.
41. White, Richard T., "Research into Learning Hierarchies," *Review of Educational Research,* 43 (Summer 1973), 361–75.
42. Winkley, Carol K., "Which Accent Generalizations Are Worth Teaching?" *Reading Teacher,* 20 (December 1966), 219–24.
43. Wylie, Richard E., and Durrell, Donald D., "Teaching Vowels Through Phonograms," *Elementary English,* 47 (October 1970), 787–91.

9 Analyzing and Improving Silent Reading Skills

The heart of silent reading ability is, of course, comprehension. But, despite a myriad of test labels and dozens of theories and models, we have no general agreement upon the nature of comprehension or its cognitive components. Hence a number of arguments are presented against using what appear to be the obvious results of group tests of silent reading ability.

Yet a number of insights into silent reading behavior can be obtained by a study of the major results of a group test. Patterns of high rate–low comprehension and low rate–high comprehension can be identified and their causes explored. The possible effects of subvocalization, although often overemphasized, may be detected and corrected. The various reasons for a low score in vocabulary, as rate of reading, lack of reading experience, poor word analysis skills, overdependence upon inappropriate analysis techniques, and other causes may be revealed. Detailed suggestions are offered for these diagnostic steps used to follow up a group reading test.

Diagnosis of silent reading ability among disadvantaged pupils presents a number of unique problems. A number of these problems inherent in using and interpreting common group reading tests are discussed, and some solutions and alternative procedures are suggested.

On the positive side, it is noted that diagnosis of comprehension ability can be sampled and its development promoted by teachers' questioning practices. Prereading and postreading questions of the open-ended or reasoning and factual types are contrasted. Several other studies of teacher questioning strategies are reviewed, and their implications for pupil comprehension are pointed out.

In reading this presentation of a different approach to diagnosis and development of comprehension, consider these questions.

1. Do you agree with the author's citation of the limitations of group silent reading tests? If not, can you support your disagreement?

2. What other insights into silent reading behavior, in addition to those suggested here, have you found it possible to gain from group tests (other than the supposed implications of subtest scores)?

3. Have you previously considered the impact of teachers' questioning practices upon the development of pupil comprehension? What is your reaction to this concept?

TO BEGIN THIS CHAPTER with negative criticisms of the use of group silent reading tests as diagnostic tools seems somewhat inappropriate. It resembles the writer's trick of setting up a straw man, which he then demolishes and replaces with his pet panaceas. Yet in this area a direct attack upon the almost universal practice of using group reading tests is really essential. No true diagnosis of silent reading skills except for a few minor details is possible with group instruments. This fact the reader must acknowledge if he is to recognize that the suggested diagnostic approaches are more than alternative to the group tests.

WHY NOT GROUP TESTS?

As we have cited most of these objections to group reading tests elsewhere in detail, a quick review will suffice for the present.

Skills Measured

The list of comprehension skills that group reading tests claim to measure is almost endless. Some writers enumerate at least fifty to sixty, and a review of current group tests indicates that they claim to measure at least twenty to twenty-five of these. But factor analyses of groups of tests to identify common components have seldom succeeded in finding these discrete skills. All that group tests appear to measure—no matter what the titles claim—are the three elements of a word meaning factor, a relationships-among-ideas factor, and a reasoning factor. In other words, the overlap among the subskills supposed to be measured by the test is so great that there is usually little or no justification for using the results. Diagnostic profiles based on comprehension subskill performances are often relatively meaningless.

The futility of using group tests for diagnosis of silent reading abilities is not confined solely to the area of comprehension. The variations in content and in the manner of measurement affect rate of reading estimates as well as comprehension scores. Some instruments attempt to sample a number of comprehension skills in such brief subtests that they become simply measures of rate in various contexts. Some tests sample comprehension and rate in bits and pieces of reading matter, while others employ much longer examples of continuous reading. Obviously these different approaches to measurement of the same skill area cannot yield comparable results.

Emans, Urbas, and Dummet (6) recount their frustration experienced in trying to reconcile the results of two group reading tests used to evaluate a new developmental program. According to both group tests, the two groups of students using contrasting materials made significant gains in rate and total score, but not in vocabulary or comprehension. In one test the differences in gains of the student groups were insignificant in all areas; in the other test, one group was significantly superior in rate gain. According to one group test, one training program was no better than the other, while the other test indicated that one program produced superior progress in rate of reading. Which results should the experimenters believe? How should they evaluate the contrasting training programs? In this case, the authors chose to accept the superior rate scores on the test that sampled continuous reading. They rejected the results of the other test (Gates Survey) because it sampled the rate of secondary pupils in very brief, low reading level paragraphs and confounded its results by including the time to answer questions in its rate of reading score. As Farr and Anastasiow (7) and other reviewers of group tests demonstrate, the lack of comparability of such tests is a common problem in assessing instructional outcomes and in attempting diagnosis.

Informational Background

We might also question the meaningfulness of group tests of comprehension because of their implicit demands upon the reading background of the pupils tested. Measures of comprehension often do not actually determine the pupil's retention of various types of facts in a particular selection. Unless the content is entirely novel, some students have always read more widely in this subject than others. This experiential background enables them to recognize word meanings and to perceive relationships among ideas better than can some of their peers (who may be more widely read in other areas). Reading experiences not only contribute to development because of the practice element, but they also provide a storehouse of words and facts that promote better comprehension. These two elements of the reading process become so interlinked that it is sometimes almost impossible to determine whether reasoning with the facts presented in a selection or background memories are the basis of a comprehension performance.

Theoretically this influence of the familiarity of the subject upon the reader's comprehension can be minimized by careful test construction. But Applebee's (2) study indicates that such care is not always exercised by test authors. He gave his subjects only the first noun in each reading selection and the usual multiple-choice questions for each item in two standardized reading tests for intermediate grades. Even fourth graders and poor sixth-grade readers were able to answer significantly more questions than chance would have permitted. What, then, could we say that these tests actually measure—comprehension of certain reading passages, or the ability of pupils to make choices among answers, or their skill in relating previously learned materials to the questions provided?

In one of his articles on this subject, J. Jaap Tuinman* emphasizes the importance of insuring "reading dependency" in the comprehension questions used with a reading selection. Defined briefly, reading dependency is the degree of certainty that an item testing comprehension cannot be answered without reading the selection. Ideally, attempts to answer an item without reading should not exceed chance expectation. But Tuinman cites a number of analyses of common reading comprehension tests in which many of the items could be answered without reading, sometimes almost as many as were answered correctly after a reading.

Such observations as these, and that of Applebee given above, raise serious questions regarding the validity of many group tests as actual measures of reading comprehension. The test maker could eliminate this flaw (and a few do) by testing the ability of an appropriate population to answer items without reading, and then revising or deleting the invalid items. Many so-called reading comprehension tests (both group and individual) measure instead the sophistication and informational background of the reader.

Norms

Most reading test authors try to assemble scores from a widely diversified population scattered throughout a large geographical area. The collection of scores becomes known as a national norm but, because of its breadth and diversity, actually does not resemble any particular group of students to whom the test is subsequently administered. When rural, urban, and suburban pupil scores, for example, are combined, to which of these constituent groups do the standards really apply? Our school surveys indicate that there are normally significant differences among the academic performances of these

---

*J. Jaap Tuinman, "Asking Reading-Dependent Questions," *Journal of Reading,* 14 (February 1971), 289–92, 336.

three groups of students, between boys and girls, between schools of different sizes, and so on. Most test norms represent a conglomeration of scores from all these types of populations. Hence each class or each pupil is often being compared with a standard derived from pupils quite unlike themselves.

Norms are commonly manipulated to yield standards for each school month as well as for grade levels above or below those tested in the standardization. These extrapolated scores between the grade levels at which the test was actually administered or above and below these levels are mathematical probabilities, not actual pupil scores. Studies of repeated testing with the same instrument do not indicate a regular progression of increasing scores month after month (18), as most test norms imply. Nor can extrapolated scores always predict accurately how the pupils above or below the appropriate levels of the test would perform.

Tests and Teacher Rankings

Some group tests are defended by their authors because in a general sense they tend to agree with the teachers' overall rankings of pupil reading ability. But teacher judgments are a fallible criterion, for they represent a gross, global evaluation that tends to ignore real pupil differences in skill areas. A recent study exposes this halo effect that overlays teacher judgments of pupil abilities (20). A group of teachers was given descriptive check lists of reading behaviors in comprehension, vocabulary, and word analysis to use in rating their individual pupils. The detailed check lists were assumed to be an aid in distinguishing the strengths and weaknesses of the pupils. But no discrimination was present in the results, for the ratings for the three skill areas overlapped greatly for each pupil. Total scores on group tests agree with teacher rankings because both represent a relatively meaningless overall impression of significantly differing performances in a number of skill areas.

Despite these difficulties in interpreting group tests, we know that most diagnostic efforts will begin with such tests. Assuming, then, that there has been a very careful selection of a group test, we can now suggest how its results may be an initial diagnostic step.

ANALYZING GROUP TEST RESULTS

Interested teachers sometimes try to obtain more information from group measures than just the test scores (14). They may examine the pupil's responses to various types of items for identifying what they believe are strengths and weaknesses. But this item analysis assumes that there is a sufficient number of each type to give a reliable estimate of pupil ability. It also assumes that each type of item also identifies a discrete reading skill, as main ideas versus details and the like. However, both the assumptions are seldom true in the average group reading test. Even if we assume that the subskill identified is discrete (which, as we pointed out above, is seldom true), few group tests offer sufficient items of any particular type for reliable judgments. When there is a sizeable number of similar items, they are often designated as belonging to the same subskill; a separate score is usually obtained, in which case, of course, item analysis by the teacher is unnecessary. But despite these common fallacies in the interpretation of group reading tests, let us try to offer some positive suggestions.

As patterns of performance in the various skill areas may be observed in many group tests, let us review some of these common patterns or symptoms and illustrate possible diagnostic follow-up steps. We consider the group test results as simply the initial step in exploring the etiology of a pupil's reading problems.

Rate and Comprehension

Rate of reading scores are relatively meaningless without a related comprehension measure, for rate should vary from one reading situation to the next according to the reader's purposes, attitudes, and reading background; the nature of the content; and the difficulty of the content. The problem to be solved by the teacher is not whether the pupil's rate of reading is too slow or too fast, but rather how the speed he employs in each task aids or hinders him in accomplishing the true purposes of the situation.

A pattern of high rate–low comprehension is often taken at face value as indicating a need for comprehension training. It is also quite possible that the pattern may be due to overconfidence resulting in superficial comprehension, or to the illusion that rapid reading is the best approach to almost any material. This impression has been fostered by a meretricious overemphasis upon "speed reading" in many commercial courses and even some reading centers. It is true that increasing rate does help improve comprehension in simple materials as the rate approaches the speed of association possible for the reader; while extremely slow rate impedes reading as a true thinking act and thus reduces comprehension. But increasing rate in difficult materials (to the point where the reader is visually contacting only a small proportion of the printed words) always results in decreased comprehension. In such a performance, the reader is not really processing the ideas presented and hence cannot retain them. Unfortunately, many students have been deluded into thinking that high rate is synonymous with effective reading. At the secondary and college level, the number of students who seek help from reading services with the sole intention of increasing their speed of reading and thus solving all their academic problems is disturbingly great.

In some cases, the high rate–low comprehension pattern may reflect the student's attempt to beat the test by covering as many items as possible. Because test taking is equated with grades in the student's world, he logically tries to obtain as high a score as possible by employing what, for him, may be an inefficient speed. The point may be unearthed by an interview with the student regarding his attitude toward the test and an exploration of whether his performance was typical of his reading, as he views it in comparison with that of other students. Rather than comprehension drill, he may profit from counseling regarding the true nature of the reading act for a student, the relationships between rate and comprehension, and the difference in the purposes of recreational and study-type reading. A retest with a parallel form, with instructions intended to produce his usual performance, may help to clarify the diagnosis.

Another possible explanation of a high rate–low comprehension pattern may lie in the word analysis practices of the reader. Through lack of interest or aptitude for deriving word meanings from context or other analytic techniques, some students simply ignore unknown words and blithely read on. Typically, these students tend to score low in the vocabulary section of the group test. Interviews may also reveal a lack of organizing habits as note-taking, underlining, and summarizing, which might have helped comprehension. Many students suffer from the illusion that one quick reading of study-type materials suffices for ordinary academic demands.

We have found that many of these high rate–low comprehension students benefit from instruction and practice in acquiring study skills. Few present-day students receive adequate help in organizing their personal regimen, in exploring systems of note-taking, in reviewing, and in scheduling their study and related study habits. They are unaware of the accumulated information and guidelines in the psychology of learning. Their personal system of studying or organizing materials—or, in other words, their comprehension—has evolved haphazardly and often ineffectually. This area can be explored by standardized tests of study skills (although these may reflect information more than practice), informal measures of study practices, and interviews. We frequently ask the student to describe in detail precisely what he does in studying a textbook. In this fashion, as faulty or omitted practices are revealed, relevant instructional materials and practice are prescribed. In some instances, we ask a student to keep a record of his daily activities on an hourly basis for at least a week. This personal regimen is then reviewed critically with the student and alternative time arrangements suggested. Having reviewed the contents of all the leading how-to-study books appropriate to the student's age, we prescribe and provide him with relevant portions to read. His reactions to these and his experiences in adapting their suggestions over a week or two are discussed in later interviews.

It is apparent that our concept of ways to improve comprehension ignores the usual skill-drill approach of providing practice materials in what are supposed to be comprehension subskills. In contrast, we strongly believe that, given sufficient basic verbal intelligence, comprehension is based on mechanical and personal organization. Sometime in the future when we understand cognitive abilities more clearly and when training materials in ways of reasoning become available, we shall add this facet to efforts to improve comprehension. Meanwhile, we reject the assumption that comprehension is improved by repetitive practice in answering what is usually a stereotyped pattern of questions (that may not be relevant in the next body of study material faced by the student). It is our experience that the drill of this type produces only a superficial gain in the precise pattern of questions repeated in the material, without transfer to other reading situations. There is ample evidence that training in answering a limited variety of questions narrows the reader's retention toward finding the answers to the expected questions, thus actually reducing breadth and depth of his comprehension. In comparison, supervised practice in analyzing one's own study techniques, exploring alternative procedures, and adapting those that appear to aid, promotes permanent changes in student efficiency in meeting academic demands.

The pattern of high rate–low comprehension may be related to test anxiety or pressing personal problems. Neville, Pfost, and Dobbs (19) have shown that even elementary pupils with very high test anxiety showed a distinct loss in comprehension after a six-week's reading improvement program. Fear of tests or disorganization because of severe emotional problems may have a dramatic effect upon comprehension for some students. This possibility can be revealed only by interviews with a sympathetic instructor.

In this manner, it may be revealed that what the student really needs is not training in comprehension but rather professional guidance in solving his personal problems. If and when these are relieved with the assistance of appropriate social work or administrative personnel, he may return to functioning at his normally adequate level in comprehension.

Patterns of test scores involving very low rate of reading pose another series of diagnostic problems. Low rate–high comprehension may imply perfectionism in reading in that the reader conscientiously tries to retain almost everything contained in the reading selection. Some of these cases honestly believe that the goal of any reading is complete retention. They may read very cautiously, frequently rereading portions, doggedly trying to memorize rather than to interpret. Some transfer their extremely slow rate to almost all types of materials, often complaining about not having time to do any recreational reading (which they would handle at the same low rate anyway). Training in exercising flexibility in rate, in fitting rate to the purpose for the reading and to its difficulty, and in practicing reading under time pressure or with reading machines is indicated here.

Sometimes the low rate–high comprehension profile is accompanied by a weak vocabulary score. This may imply that the reader's slow working rate is influencing the latter score. One may assume that, since vocabulary is a significant element in reading comprehension and the pupil is a high comprehender, the low vocabulary score does not indicate a real vocabulary deficiency. An exception to this logic may be present in the case of an overachiever of less than average intelligence. A parallel form of the same test, with a comparison of the scores under timed and untimed conditions can help clarify this pattern. This can be readily arranged by having the pupil circle the number of the vocabulary item that he is working on when the time limit expires. Then he is permitted to attempt the remainder of the test without a time limit. The usual scaling of vocabulary tests in sharply ascending difficulty tends to prevent the untimed measure from giving a very exaggerated estimate of vocabulary knowledge. Rather this untimed testing, if significantly higher than in the timed testing, enables the teacher to judge the pupil's breadth of vocabulary without the depressing effect of his slow working rate being present. This dual kind of testing would, of course, be most meaningful when used only with those pupils who complete a less than average number of items in the timed administration. When the two administrations of the vocabulary test do not yield significantly different results, exploration of the pupil's word analysis skills is indicated.

Many sources would attribute very low rate of reading to such factors as word-by-word reading, narrow recognition span, many regressions, and other faulty eye-movement behaviors. The fact that these causes cannot be detected except by use of the eye-movement camera (which is not available in most cases) does not seem to affect the frequency of these diagnoses. Training in flash card or machine reading of phrases is commonly mistakenly prescribed. As we have pointed out elsewhere, no one really reads in phrases or large word groups, mechanically speaking. Eye-movement camera standards indicate that the normal recognition span only becomes as great as one whole word per fixation at about the tenth grade. Interpreting phrases is completely a mental act, part of the processing of reading matter dependent upon the reader's familiarity with English sentence structure. Extreme myopia does tend to force reading by very small units, perhaps almost letter by letter, with corresponding low rate in most cases. But when the eye-movement record indicates a less than normal recognition span and myopia is not present, the explanation usually lies in the reader's skill or the nature of the material. Selections that are too difficult in vocabulary or concept load, very unfamiliar in content, or phrased in the reader's second language are more often than not the cause. Excessive dependence upon letter phonics, which induces the child to process words in very small units, will contribute to this condition. Or, in some instances, the reader has an ingrained habit of slow reading and has never been taught how to vary his rate. These contributing factors are readily corrected.

Subvocalization has often falsely been identified as the basis of slow reading in older subjects (by those who have a training program in rapid reading to offer). But, as Edfeldt has demonstrated (5), subvocalization is an integral part of silent reading. Because reading is so closely allied to speaking, low-level movements of the tongue never entirely disappear while reading silently. It is true that beginning readers of any age who are attempting to make the transition from oral to silent reading often subvocalize even audibly. And, because they are literally saying the words to themselves, their rate of silent reading is limited to their speed of speech. But this condition is characteristic only of readers who have not progressed beyond perhaps a first- or second-grade reading level, or who are just learning to read in a second language. They can be readily helped to make the transition to silent reading by teaching them to compress their lips, to monitor lip action by hand pressure, to diminish tongue movement by eating or sucking candy while reading, or by placing a pencil crosswise in the mouth. Slowly accelerating reading in very simple materials by time pressure, pacing devices, or controlled reading of continuous matter, while monitoring oneself for lip movements, will help these individuals, if direct treatment seems necessary. However, as we observe in most classrooms, pupils eventually make the shift to true silent reading with a consequent marked acceleration in rate at about the third-grade level, with a minimum of attention to their tendency to subvocalize.

Very poor rate in oral reading or what amounts to naming words one by one is a common phenomenon among primary or poor readers. It reflects, of course, the problem of the paucity of the reader's sight vocabulary. Since most of the words that the child is attempting to read are only imperfectly known, he tends to fumble in recognition of almost every other word. Flash card or machine drill in reading phrases is again pointless. The child just cannot recognize quickly enough of the words in a phrase to read it smoothly, and he certainly cannot process words by phrases. Drill in memorizing sight words in isolation or lists is also unsound. Aside from their physical characteristics, words are learned and retained because of their meaningful associations. This fact seems to support the child's reading largely in sentences of his own composition—the language experience approach. Only in such materials can we be certain that the words are familiar and the sentences meaningful. Reading very simple plays, rhymes, and familiar jingles helps the beginner move toward the fluency in reading for which the teacher is aiming.

Vocabulary

A low vocabulary score may have three or four possible explanations. One we have already mentioned is the effect of very slow rate in depressing performance in this area. Another possibility is, of course, that the apparently poor vocabulary reflects lack of development in word meanings. This hypothesis can be accepted only if the comprehension score is also below average, for then it is apparent that lack of breadth in word meanings is probably affecting both test results. Occasionally we find a pupil who obtains average or better comprehension but whose knowledge of word meanings is actually poor. Usually this pupil does not read widely (or his vocabulary probably would not be so limited), and he makes superlative use of the context while reading. Thus he obtains reasonable comprehension despite a basically limited vocabulary. A cloze test is probably the best measure of contextual analysis that we have. The administration of a selection with every tenth word omitted for a total of about fifty such items is easily arranged for the analysis of these few exceptional cases. In materials of appropriate difficulty, the pupil with average contextual analysis skill identifies 40–45 percent of the deleted words. In those cases with low vocabulary and relatively poor comprehension, which are more common, the task becomes one of further exploring the probable causes.

Poor vocabulary development may be due to inadequate word analysis skills or overdependence upon a technique that is not effective at the pupil's reading level. Phonic analysis skills, as we have emphasized in another chapter, fail to function very effectively as reading materials broaden in vocabulary usage. Phonics cannot produce recognizable words when these terms are not already auditorily familiar. Thus pupils who persist in attempting only phonic analysis in intermediate grades and above are handicapped in obtaining word recognition or word meanings. Clues to the pupil's methods of word analysis in silent reading may be obtained by questioning him on the steps he actually used in ascertaining the meanings of a number of words in a selection that he has just read. Or a similar approach may be used after he has completed a cloze test. Some pupils cannot readily introspect or verbalize their analytic attempts. An additional oral reading test or trials with several lists of isolated, difficult words may help to clarify the pupil's procedures. There is some risk in assuming that his analytic habits are identical in oral or silent reading or lists. But a series of these observations in all three reading tasks will provide some answers regarding the pupil's analytic habits, whether they are varied or solitary, whether they are appropriate to the difficulty of the material, and what additional training in this area seems indicated.

At least two other factors may be responsible for a low vocabulary performance: reading experience and the nature of the content of the vocabulary test. These factors are interlinked, since reading experiences do tend to promote vocabulary development, particularly in the areas of the reader's interests. Hence he tends to develop a broader vocabulary in those areas in which he reads most widely. Vocabulary tests in general are a very crude way of sampling the development of an adequate stock of word meanings. They are minute samples from the corpus of thousands of words that pupils may know. Hence it is quite possible that the items of a particular test may not sample the areas of vocabulary strength of an individual pupil. We need to sample the several vocabularies (in the event of a low score on a general test) as a diagnostic follow-up step, perhaps in addition to the exploration of his word analysis skills.

Several standardized tests, as the Diagnostic Vocabulary Test (Committee on Diagnostic Reading Tests) and the earlier editions of the California Reading Test (California Test Bureau) permit the comparative study of content field vocabularies. These will be useful in clarifying whether there are areas of strength as well as weakness or whether the vocabulary deficiency is general.

Sometimes poor vocabulary performance is simply a matter of less than average verbal intelligence. Vocabulary development has been recognized as closely predictive of intellectual ability and school success since the beginnings of intelligence testing. Occasionally an individual of low intelligence, sometimes called an "idiot savant," demonstrates remarkable vocabulary ability. But more often vocabulary and intelligence are closely similar. A comparison of the mental age of a pupil, derived preferably from an individual test, with the age level of his vocabulary score may aid in making this diagnostic decision. It is possible that, when mental age markedly exceeds the vocabulary level, remedial effort in this area may be justified. When mental age is equal to, or distinctly lower than, the vocabulary, remediation may be contraindicated. We can aid this latter type of pupil in continued vocabulary development, however, by trying to increase his word analysis skills to a maximum level of efficiency, and by attempting to stimulate the breadth of his reading.

This comparison of mental age and age level achieved in some part of a reading test, although a common practice, should be made with some reservations. There are no real data to show that standards derived from testing of average pupils really apply to the mentally handicapped even when they are equated in mental age (4). Furthermore, there is no good reason to expect similar performances, each equivalent to mental age, in various school skills. Rather we know that variability among skills, even for the same individual, increases with age. Subtests of reading batteries do seem to discriminate good from poor readers among the mentally retarded. But precisely how do ordinary norms apply to this segment of the population? We do not know which is the best basis of comparison—mental age versus norm, actual age versus norm, grade placement versus norm, or some weighted combination of mental and chronological age versus norm. There have been many attempts to devise weighted formulas combining these factors into a prediction of expected performances. But, as we point out in discussing these in chapter 6 of *Investigating the Issues of Reading Disabilities,* these formulas are based on a priori judgments of what is normal growth in any and all skills for each combination of mental and chronological ages. Unfortunately (or fortunately), human beings do not develop equally in various skills; moreover, the formulas ignore other significant variables such as language, environment, and instructional factors. In other words, when both intelligence and vocabulary are low, the decision to initiate remediation must include consideration of such subjective factors as the language and socioeconomic background, the educational levels (and aspirations) of the parents, and the learning capacities of the pupil. Of course, a comparison can be made among the various skill areas tested, with strengths as well as weaknesses of the mentally handicapped child being identified. Then the teacher must decide whether improving the strengths or correcting the weaknesses will be more effective treatment and the greatest benefit for this particular pupil, in view of what she knows about him.

DIAGNOSIS AMONG DISADVANTAGED PUPILS

Diagnosis among those pupils that we term disadvantaged presents a number of problems peculiar to this group. Their limitations in language, experiential background, and educational aspirations raise questions regarding the applicability of our common testing devices. Also, because of these handicaps, these pupils present symptoms of a nature quite different from those commonly met in the majority of middle-class subjects with reading difficulties. As in the case of the mentally handicapped, we really do not know what levels of skill performances to expect or what standards to apply to pupil performances among disadvantaged students.

The reliability and validity of many of the formal and informal tests commonly used in schools are questionable when used with disadvantaged pupils. The spread of scores is less than normal; the motivation of pupils is weaker; and the disadvantaged pupil is more fearful of tests, less competitive, and less conforming. All these factors tend to reduce the reliability of the test results (9, 29). The content of most reading and readiness tests is culturally biased toward middle-class mores. One study determined by item analysis that only one-third of the items in a widely used readiness test and one-fifth of those in a common reading test met acceptable levels of validity and difficulty when used in an economically deprived urban sample (10). Not all studies report low reliability coefficients for the total scores on such tests, but rather the inappropriateness for this population may be manifest only in certain subtests (1, 10, 17, 25). Tests of auditory vocabulary, auditory discrimination, and word meaning, for example, seem among the most inefficient for this population (12, 17, 24).

Other factors that influence test results with disadvantaged pupils are the use of time limits, the pupils' lack of test sophistication, the racial difference between the examiner and the pupils, and the inappropriateness of the directions, scoring, and norms. Long-range predictions are extremely tenuous because of the declines in pupil aspirations and achievement, and parent aspirations (3, 9).

As a result of all these negative factors, school surveys of urban children both in England and America (27) uniformly indicate that the proportion of poor readers is directly related to socioeconomic status, often reflecting race or ethnic origin of the pupils. Poorer performances by these groups are also present in other tests frequently used by reading diagnosticians, as verbal intelligence, visual perception, auditory discrimination, sight vocabulary, auditory vocabulary, and oral language usage.

The significance of the pupil's language, or its lack, and his use of dialect upon reading performances is a subject of warm debate. Some authors react very negatively to the claim that there is a language deficiency among these pupils. They insist that there is a system of grammar and syntax present in the pupils' dialect, and that this recognizable language does suffice for most of the pupils' life needs, except perhaps in the school (8). When studies of oral language usage among black children, for example, seem to indicate a lack of many words common to beginning reading, it is argued that this is no proof that the children do not understand these words or that they cannot read them. A recent study of Seminole Indian children appears to support this argument. When the vocabularies of the pupils' language-experience stories were compared with the Dolch List, 60–67 percent of such words, plus 150–200 others, were present in the stories (13). Furthermore, when tested in reading the entire Dolch list, these children misread only about 14 percent of the function words and one-third of the nouns. For beginning readers, as these children were, these performances would be considered very acceptable.

The effect of dialect upon performances in reading is similarly argued pro and con. All recognize that estimates of oral reading ability are usually depressed among dialect-speaking pupils when they are reading to a standard English-speaking teacher. But many argue that dialect does not interfere with the comprehension of standard English (8, 15). They insist that dialect users do learn to read and to listen to other dialects although keeping to their own speech. An experiment in rewriting a reading test in black dialect, for example, did not alter comprehension scores for either black or white pupils (11), although the more complex questions did seem easier for black pupils when phrased in their dialect. Related studies in correcting dialect in the hope of improving reading have tended to prove fruitless. Yet a sizeable number of experts insist that some sort of a program in oral English must be used with bilingual or dialectal children before they can really be expected to progress in reading. Rosen and Ortega's extensive review of programs (26) for these pupils implies that because the problems of timing, content, methodology, and goals are not yet defined, results are consequently largely equivocal. But the controversy tends to persist.

Some argue that intensive training in English sentence structure and idioms is essential for many of the minority linguistic groups. It is true that the differences in word order and the meanings of idiomatic expressions among

Spanish, the Indian languages, and English are a source of reading difficulty for bilingual children. But again this is not a crucial handicap, for intensive training programs in sentence structure do not tend to result in improved comprehension.

The questions plaguing the diagnostician are not whether disadvantaged pupils have a language deficiency or a language deviation, or whether they are handicapped in reading performances by their use of dialect. Rather the diagnostician's quandary is how to evaluate the reading of such pupils and to determine their needs—with tools that are admittedly somewhat inappropriate. Some would answer this situation by abandoning the use of any standardized tests of intelligence or achievement. They argue that all such measuring instruments are unfair, inaccurate, and discriminative in their construction and standards. But schools do have the capability of establishing local norms on the entire school population if it is relatively homogeneous, or even local racial or ethnic norms if it is a mixed population. The differences among these subtypes of local norms are apt to prove very small; if so, they should be combined into the single local norm.

It would be most unwise to publicize these local norms, for there would be immediate and justifiable repercussions from the community. The knowledge of their existence and their use should be limited to those administrative personnel concerned with instructional practices, along with the reading teachers, school psychologists, and counselors. Their sole purpose would be to permit the comparison of individuals and groups with an identical population, as in assessing the outcomes of ordinary or special instructional programs, remedial work, certain instructional materials, and the like. Local norms do not make our tests more appropriate for disadvantaged pupils, but they do diminish the effect of the cultural bias in national norms.

Alternative suggestions to this problem of evaluating the reading of disadvantaged pupils include the rewriting of our tests in dialect or the mother tongue, reading tests to pupils, and substituting cloze tests for other measures of comprehension. But the studies of reading tests in black dialect (11) or of Spanish versions of readiness and reading tests (1, 22) do not show that the predictive validity or reliability of the instruments is significantly improved or that pupil scores are increased materially. Disadvantaged pupils do score higher when achievement tests are read to them (21), but the only value of such a procedure in diagnosing reading ability would be as a measure of auditory comprehension. It is certainly a practical approach for classroom use in assessing content learning of pupils handicapped in reading but has limited application in reading diagnosis. In contrast, substituting cloze tests for other measures of comprehension does have a number of advantages. The cultural bias usually present in the directions, the scoring, or the norms of standardized tests is obviated in the cloze procedure.

Rankin and Culhane (23) have shown that completion of 40–45 percent of the items in a cloze test is equivalent to 75 percent comprehension, and 60–65 percent cloze to a 90 percent performance. There is some evidence that different types of deletions sample varying facets of comprehension. For example, structural deletions (every fifth or tenth deletion of words excepting nouns) tend to measure detailed comprehension. Lexical deletions (every fifth or tenth noun) tend to measure understanding of main ideas. The nature of the deletion may also be varied to sample various word analysis techniques of the reader, as we mention in chapter 8. Thus it would appear that, if it is essential to eliminate cultural bias in reading tests, the cloze procedure is a flexible and viable alternative with multiple uses.

Another alternative to standardized tests in working with disadvantaged pupils is the use of work sample measures (28). Utilizing only the instructional materials of the classroom, we can evaluate a wide variety of reading and study skills. By structuring a problem-solving task in classroom materials, we can sample such behaviors as reading of charts, graphs, maps, and diagrams; use of the various parts of a book; skill in dictionary use; rate and comprehension in various content fields; speed and accuracy in scanning tables; and flexibility in rate and comprehension in keeping with specific directions that vary the purpose for reading. As McDonald has emphasized (16), this sampling of versatility and efficiency in task-oriented ways enables evaluation of a much broader spectrum of reading behaviors than do common tests of rate, vocabulary, and comprehension. With care in framing directions and using groups of the child's own peers as appropriate standards, we also avoid much of the cultural bias present in formal tests.

A SUBJECTIVE APPROACH TO DIAGNOSIS OF COMPREHENSION

We have criticized the objective measurement of thinking skills in reading and, in a sense, left our readers without any resource for sampling the child's reasoning processes. Yet, undoubtedly, various ways of thinking are present in the silent reading act, as inductive and deductive reasoning and the recognition of the interrelationships of ideas. And many reading teachers will want to observe and understand the kinds of thinking that a pupil seems to be able to do while reading.

This concern is certainly justified, for we see students of all ages who seem to be able to show nothing but sheer memorization of facts after reading.

Generalization, interpretations, or translations of the content of a passage seem beyond their capabilities. Other students in need of help can generalize or interpret, but these are superficial or impressionistic behaviors for which the student cannot recall the supporting facts. Still others seem to be able to read only in a literal sense; they cannot recognize implications or cause and effect or other relationships. Since these inadequacies handicap pupils as they advance academically, diagnosis and treatment are amply justified. If, as we have claimed, clues to the reader's command of cognitive processes while reading cannot be determined with great validity by the usual reading tests, how, then, can the diagnostician approach this problem?

A possible answer may be found in the use of structured questions that purport to sample the various cognitive processes and end-results of reading. For example, in his book *Classroom Questions: What Kinds?* Sanders* has categorized types of questions that sample the thinking processes in reading. His scheme includes the following:

1. Memory—recognizing or recalling information given in the passage.
   a. for facts—as, Who, What, When, Where.
   b. for definitions—as What does ______ mean? Define ______. Explain what is meant by ______.
   c. for generalizations—as, What events led to ______? How did ______ and ______ cause ______?
   d. value judgments—as, What is said about ______? Do you agree? What kind of person was ______?
2. Translations—expressing ideas in different form as, Tell me in your own words about ______. How could you illustrate ______? How could we restate ______?
3. Interpretation—seeing relationships among facts, generalizations, or values
   a. comparative—as, How is ______ like ______? Is ______ the same as ______? Why not?
   b. implications—as, What will ______ and ______ lead to? What would happen if ______?
   c. inductive thinking—as, What facts support the idea that ______? What is the author trying to tell you about ______?
   d. quantitative—as, How many times did ______? How many causes of ______ can you name?
   e. cause and effect—as, Why did ______ happen? Why did ______ do ______? How did ______ and ______ affect ______?
4. Application—solving a problem that requires the use of facts, generalizations, and the like, as How can we prove ______? What plans

*Norris M. Sanders, *Classroom Questions: What Kinds?* (New York: Harper and Row, 1966).

would we make to ________? How could you use this information to ________?

5. Analysis—recognizing and applying logic to a problem; analyzing an example of reasoning, as, Some people believe ________. Is this correct? Why not? Why do you suppose the boy ________?
6. Synthesis—using original, creative thinking to solve a problem, as, What other titles could you think of for ________? What other ending ________? How would you like to change this story?
7. Evaluation—making judgments, as, Did you enjoy this? Why? What do you think of ________ in this story? The author said ________. Is this a fact or his opinion?

In many details, this is not a clear-cut differentiation of the mental processes in reading. But it can be a starting point to understanding what a reader gains from his efforts. Providing the student with appropriately scaled materials and using one or two of the seven types of questions repeatedly will help clarify the reader's command of each of these cognitive processes. Students of average or better intelligence can be expected to be able to employ any of these ways of thinking. When they apparently cannot, there is ample evidence that this inadequacy may well be due to the lack of teacher emphasis upon the process in earlier instruction. Guszak's study* of teacher questioning has demonstrated quite dramatically that overemphasis upon simple memory or recall has tended to handicap versatility in comprehension among elementary pupils.

When the reading teacher has determined by repeated observations that the student apparently does not use a certain type of essential thinking, the remedial course is quite obvious. She may repeatedly ask the student to attempt to answer questions that appear to sample the missing cognitive process. Occasionally she will find a piece of commercial material that emphasizes this type of thinking. For example, Thelma Thurstone's *Reading for Understanding* (Science Research Associates) offers practice in interpretive thinking at many reading levels. Beginning with simple levels of this material, the student will gradually learn to react in this fashion. Maintenance of this cognitive skill requires frequent use of this type of question in the reading teacher's recurring probing of the reader's comprehension, in addition to those demanding other types of thinking. There are very few published training materials that lend themselves to this approach, unfortunately, for the development of cognitive skill developmental materials has been very slow. Most of the drill books in comprehension offered for this purpose tend to

---

*Frank J. Guszak, "Teacher Questioning and Reading," *Reading Teacher,* 21 (December 1967), 227–34.

present a stereotyped pattern of questions repeatedly, when, in our opinion, the student really needs to acquire versatility in answering questions that vary constantly in accordance with the nature and purpose of the reading. Until such materials become available, it is apparent that teachers will have to prepare their own training programs.

Furthermore, there is a danger in using materials stressing a certain process too long or too slavishly. There is strong evidence that repeated use of a type or pattern of questions tends to channel the reader's thinking toward finding certain types of answers only. Thus comprehension, in the overall sense, becomes limited rather than improved.* In other words, if the reading teacher uses her own or some commercial material intended to stimulate a type or pattern of thinking, once the reader has apparently learned this process, further training should demand a variety of processes, including that type recently acquired.

The use of prereading questions or advanced organizers, as they are called, will make a contribution to comprehension improvement. For effectiveness, these questions should stress related pupil experiences; suggest how to recognize the relationships present or how to organize the material; give hints to generalizations or to principles that may be drawn. Obviously, the American research indicates that they should not be very specific or detailed.

Postreading questions should be used at relatively short intervals, as after several paragraphs or a short section, rather than being administered at the very end of the passage, Frase and his fellow workers in this field tell us. Use in this fashion, with particular emphasis upon the last half of the material, promotes breadth and depth of comprehension of both literal and interpretive types.

David B. Doake, of Christchurch Teachers College of New Zealand, has recently completed a very detailed study of the relative merits of pre- and postreading questions in improving student comprehension.† He contrasted the effects of both factual and reasoning questions offered before or after reading upon immediate or long-term retention of facts and key ideas and their supporting information. Among his results were the following:

> Postreading reasoning questions facilitate the long-term retention of key ideas but not necessarily the facts supporting these ideas. Moreover, such

---

*Lawrence T. Frase, "Boundary Conditions for Mathemagenic Behaviors," *Review of Educational Research,* 40 (June 1970), 337–48.

†David B. Doake, "An Investigation into the Facilitative Effects of Two Kinds of Adjunct Questions on the Learning and Remembering of Teachers College Students During the Reading of Textual Materials with an Associated Study of Student Reading Improvement Incorporating a Survey of Their Textbook Reading Habits, Attitudes and Problems," Master's thesis, University of Canterbury, 1972.

questions cause the reader to take significantly longer for his study than any other type of procedure tested.

Prereading reasoning questions were the best for long-term retention of key ideas and their supporting facts, but not for immediate postreading recall of the relevant facts. Reading or study time was not materially increased by this procedure.

Postreading factual questions helped the reader's long-term retention of key ideas and their explanations, but this value was counterbalanced by the additional reading time demanded. Just as much learning may be stimulated by prereading factual questions or simply directing the student to "read carefully."

Prereading factual questions resulted in relatively poor immediate recall of relevant facts, and also increased the student's reading time more than any other procedure.

When adjunct questions were given to students to be used with a reading assignment, they favored the practice, tended to use the questions as prereading directions, and preferred to be required to write out the answers. Moreover, students interpret this directed reading procedure as facilitating their required reading, making it more efficient, and helping to improve their reading ability. These last two impressions of the students were confirmed by comparisons with control groups not exposed to directed reading.

Doake's study adds a number of dimensions to our knowledge of how to use questions to improve our students' textual reading. The superior values of prereading reasoning questions, as indicated in much of the American research, is confirmed; and other values for improved reading efficiency and reading skills are added. Moreover, his study indicates that, unless New Zealand college students differ greatly from their American counterparts, guiding or directing their textbook reading is appreciated greatly by the great majority of such students. In his quotations of the personal comments of the students receiving these treatments, there are many strongly negative comparisons with the practices of those instructors who simply assign chapter readings, who give pop quizzes without warning, or who, in other ways, fail to give guidance to their students' study. We see no reason why the implications of this research on directing student reading are not significant for teachers of any content subject from perhaps intermediate grades onward.

Teachers' questioning strategies or question sequences during reading or content field lessons also strongly influence pupil comprehension. Guszak has shown that the most common pattern, unfortunately, is simply a question and a congruent response, Q = Rt. Another pattern involves a Question-Response episode in which the teacher offers a purpose-setting question or a guiding or rhetorical remark; then, without waiting for student reactions, immediately asks a second direct question. Teachers frequently repeat a question, without clarification or rephrasing, when the response is unacceptable (assuming that they recognize that the response is incongruent, which is not always the case). In seeking to improve these questioning practices, Hilda Taba* has explored extensively the nature of teacher-pupil interaction She has attempted to distinguish three levels of postreading discussion: concept formation (differentiating, grouping, categorizing); generalizations and inferences; explanation or prediction. The best results are obtained, Taba found, when teachers gradually move through these successive levels of thinking. Beginning at the more complex levels or moving toward them early tends to abbreviate the discussion or to cause it to deteriorate to low levels.

The critical reader may raise the pertinent question of how our use of types of questions differs from the questions in standardized tests. Are not both testing the pupils' ability in comprehension subskills? We do not believe, however, that these approaches are equivalent. Tests tend to label the pupils' answers according to the types of facts that he can report after reading, such as main ideas, details, conclusions, inferences, implications, and the like. These types of facts are then identified as independent subskills to be developed by training. However, factor analyses of reading tests do not find these to be discrete skills, but rather elements of larger reasoning processes such as inductive and deductive reasoning and recognizing relationships among ideas. Our question scheme, in contrast, tries to identify the broader relationships among ideas and the mental processes. For example, we would not emphasize the four types of memory or the five types of interpretation as independent processes and attempt to train a pupil in each subtype, as reading tests imply that we should. We would be concerned with the student's memory process, not the precise kinds of facts, generalizations, judgments, or whatever he can recall after reading. Memory is not a unitary trait and in distinguishing kinds of memory, we may use some of the same labels we find in reading tests. But our goal is not improving each subtype of memory that can be identified. It is to improve the pupil's recall of what he has read and to stimulate this recall by a variety of questions that sample this process.

Zahorik† has contributed a very pertinent study of teachers' questioning and feedback and pupils' perceptions of these question-answer practices. Among the teacher patterns that he identified as most frequent were simple

---

*Hilda Taba, "The Teaching of Thinking," *Elementary English,* 42 (May 1965), 534–42.

†John A. Zahorik, "Pupils' Perceptions of Teachers' Verbal Feedback," *Elementary School Journal,* 71 (November 1970), 105–14.

positive remarks—"good," "all right"; response development—"Why is . . . ?" or simply adding to or repeating the pupil's response; development of a lesson—asking for additional answers after one pupil responds or going on to different questions after a correct pupil response. Zahorik decries the fact that these teacher comments are seldom negative, nor do they elaborate or give clues or explanations to the pupils. Given the transcripts of the questions-answers-teacher feedback remarks, the pupils were asked to react to these patterns. They were queried as to whether the teacher's feedback made them feel anything; told them the right answer or whether they were wrong or told them nothing; led them to improve their answer or to correct their wrong answers or neither of these. The pupils, in general, responded that these teacher patterns did give some feeling and information on their correctness. But the common patterns of feedback did not, in the pupils' minds, give any explanation, direction, or clue to improving their responses.

Zahorik strongly suggests that teachers employ more elaboration or explanations clarifying why an answer is or is not correct; more help for the student in modifying his initial response; more praise or confirmation and less neutral feedback to correct answers. As in Guszak's study of teachers' questions and Taba's hierarchy of questioning, we see the need for more efficient communication from teachers to pupils to aid their thinking (and feeling) processes in responding to questions.

Feedback from the teacher should certainly do more than indicate whether the pupil's answer is correct. It should include (1) further questioning to help the student clarify his thinking or his answer; (2) questions that ask the pupil to offer supporting proof for his answer; (3) questions that ask him what the implications of his answer are, as "If . . . is true, what about . . . ? or "Why is . . . true?"; (4) permitting other members of the class to raise questions about a pupil's answer, to which he will respond in defense or clarification of his point; (5) asking leading questions based on the pupil's response to enable him to elaborate. In these and other ways, teachers' questioning can support and stimulate pupils' thinking in reading and reporting or interpreting.

Since informational background affects comprehension, as we have pointed out, efforts to aid pupils in this respect are most desirable. These may take the form of (1) introducing him to materials of gradually increasing difficulty in areas of content in which he is weak; (2) broadening his background by interesting the pupil in areas of reading other than those of his current interests; (3) helping him to find resource materials in the current areas of his study; (4) helping him to improve his skills in word analysis and thus to increase his reading vocabulary; and (5) aiding him in devising some systematic ways of retaining the technical vocabularies that he is encountering, such as a private list, word cards, a useful dictionary, techniques of vocabulary review, and the like.

LEARNING PROJECT

1. Debate the probable effects upon pupil comprehension of drill in repeatedly answering the same pattern of questions, as we find it in many published materials. Argue the pros and cons of this approach in contrast with practice in answering varied questions with differing degrees of feedback.

2. Select a piece of reading matter appropriate to the reading abilities of several pupils who differ decidedly in their comprehension ability. Prepare a series of questions on the selection including factual, cause-effect, chronology, implications, and synthesis, at least. Include also evaluation questions that demand the personal reactions, judgments, and associative thinking of the reader. Ask a very good and a poor comprehender to read the selection and to answer the questions. What comparisons can you make in terms of overall comprehension, and involvement of the reader with the material?

REFERENCES

1. Arnold, Richard D., "Reliability of Test Scores for the Young 'Bilingual' Disadvantaged," *Reading Teacher,* 22 (January 1969), 341–45.
2. Applebee, Arthur N., "Silent Reading Tests: What Do They Measure?" *School Review,* 80 (November 1971), 86–93.
3. Bordie, John G., "Language Tests and Linguistically Different Learners: The Sad State of the Art," *Elementary English,* 47 (October 1970), 814–28.
4. Cawley, J.F., "Reading Performances Among the Mentally Handicapped: A Problem in Assessment," *Training School Bulletin,* 63 (1966), 11–16.
5. Edfeldt, Ake W., *Silent Speech and Silent Reading.* Chicago: University of Chicago Press, 1960.
6. Emans, R., Urbas, R., and Dummet, M., "The Meaning of Reading," *Journal of Reading,* 9 (May 1966), 406–9.
7. Farr, Roger, and Anastasiow, Nicholas, *Tests of Reading Readiness and Achievement: A Review and Evaluation.* Reading Aids Series. Newark, Del.: International Reading Association, 1969.
8. Goodman, Kenneth S., with Buck, Catherine, "Dialect Barriers to Reading Comprehension Revisited," *Reading Teacher,* 27 (October 1973), 6–12.

9. "Guidelines for Testing Minority Group Children," *Journal of Social Issues,* supplement, 20 (April 1964), 127–45.
10. Hammill, D., and Wiederholt, J.L., "Appropriateness of the Metropolitan Tests in an Economically Deprived, Urban Neighborhood," *Psychology in the Schools,* 8 (1971), 49–56.
11. Hockman, Carol H., "Black Dialect Reading Tests in the Urban Elementary School," *Reading Teacher,* 26 (March 1973), 581–83.
12. Hutchinson, J.O., "Reading Tests and Nonstandard Language," *Reading Teacher,* 25 (February 1972), 430–34.
13. Kersey, Harry, and Fadjo, Rebecca, "A Comparison of Seminole Reading Vocabulary and the Dolch Word Lists," *Journal of American Indian Education,* 11 (October 1971), 16–18.
14. Ladd, Eleanor M., "More than Scores from Tests," *Reading Teacher,* 24 (January 1971), 305–11.
15. Laffey, James L., and Shuy, Roger, *Language Differences: Do They Interfere?* Newark, Del.: International Reading Association, 1973.
16. McDonald, Arthur S., "Reading Versatility Twelve Years Later," in *Reading: The Right to Participate,* 20th Yearbook, National Reading Conference, 1971, 168–73.
17. Mishra, Shitala P., and Hurt, M., Jr., "The Use of Metropolitan Readiness Tests with Mexican-American Children," *California Journal of Educational Research,* 21 (1970), 182–87.
18. Netley, C., Rachman, S., and Turner, R.K., "The Effect of Practice on Performance in a Reading Attainment Test," *British Journal of Educational Psychology,* 35 (February 1965), 1–8.
19. Neville, Donald, Pfost, Philip and Dobbs, Virginia, "The Relationship Between Test Anxiety and Silent Reading Gains," *American Educational Research Journal,* 4 (January 1967), 45–50.
20. Olshavsky, Jill, Andrews, Nancy, and Farr, Roger, "Convergent and Discriminant Validity of Informal Assessment of Reading Skills," in 23rd Yearbook, National Reading Conference, in press.
21. Otto, Wayne, Canman, Mary Jane, and Jensen, Delores, "Factors Related to Poor Readers' Achievement Test Performances," *Journal of Reading Behavior,* 3 (Fall 1970–71), 1–5.
22. Personke, Carl R., and Davis, O.L., Jr., "Predictive Validity of English and Spanish Versions of a Readiness Test," *Elementary English Journal,* 70 (November 1969), 79–85.
23. Rankin, Earl F., and Culhane, Joseph W., "Comparable Cloze and Multiple-Choice Comprehension Test Scores," *Journal of Reading,* 13 (December 1969), 193–98.
24. Robinson, H. Alan, "Reliability of Measures Related to Reading Success of Average, Disadvantaged and Advantaged Kindergarten Children," *Reading Teacher,* 20 (December 1966), 203–8.
25. Robinson, H. Alan, and Hanson, E., "Reliability of Measures of Reading Achievement," *Reading Teacher,* 21 (January 1968), 307–13, 323.
26. Rosen, Carl L., and Ortega, Philip D., "Language and Reading Problems of Spanish-Speaking Children in the Southwest," *Journal of Reading Behavior,* 1 (Winter 1969), 51–72.

27. Russell, Jennifer, "Reading Surveys," *Reading,* 4 (December 1970), 13–18.
28. Spache, George D., "Classroom Techniques of Identifying and Diagnosing the Needs of Retarded Readers in High School and College," in *Better Readers for Our Times,* International Reading Association Proceedings, 1, 1956, 128–32.
29. Williams, Robert L., "Abuses and Misuses in Testing Black Children," *The Counseling Psychologist,* 2 (1971), 62–72.

part four

REMEDIATION

10 Strategies of Remedial Reading

Although seldom formally stated, there are many models or theories of remediation. Here we examine only nine such theories, but there are probably several others that could be identified. All practitioners in the field of remedial reading follow, perhaps intuitively, at least one of these models, although they may borrow techniques from other models upon occasion. This trend may not be as naive as it seems, for reading practitioners are often limited in following courses of treatment they would like to employ because of lack of funds, staff, and the like.

We have tried to recognize the rationale of each of the treatment theories and to differentiate among their individual techniques. Like everyone else, we have our own preferences for certain models, but this review was not written to indoctrinate readers in our beliefs. There is no one best approach to remediation, and even among these approaches there is very little evidence of any hierarchy of effectiveness. But since we are dealing with human beings who constantly vary in their needs and responsiveness to different courses of treatment, it is absolutely essential to be familiar with a variety of approaches. Even if the treatments we can offer are limited by our personal skills and training or by the available facilities, the recognition of alternative approaches should motivate us toward flexibility and, eventually, diversification.

In considering these strategies of remedial reading, try to answer these questions as objectively as you can:

1. Which of these theories of remediation agrees with your concept of remediation?
2. Have you recognized clearly the limitations of this model? What are they?
3. Which concepts and techniques could you add to your present practices or your theory of remediation that might result in greater effectiveness in some cases?

THERE ARE SEVERAL ASPECTS of this review of strategies of remedial reading that are affecting its author and may have a similar effect upon the reader. We have already treated both diagnosis and related remediation techniques in most of the significant areas. This chapter, in treating the rationale behind each system of remedial approach, will, in a sense, offer a very condensed summary of what has already been presented. To avoid this boring, repetitive quality, perhaps this chapter should be read before most of the others, but that is a matter of personal choice. We shall refer frequently to the chapters that are relevant to each strategy of remediation to enable the reader to move back and forth from this chapter to the fuller treatments, if he so chooses.

But this parallelism or repetition is essential, we believe, to make this contrast of concepts of what remedial training really is and what it is supposed to do. There is no best way to do remedial reading, for it appears that all these strategies seem to work almost equally well. Hence our purpose here is to lead the reader, who probably has a particular rationale, to realize that it may be narrow and that other approaches may be more effective.

Finally, we may disappoint some readers who expect us to draw some definite conclusions about the comparative effectiveness of these strategies. Although many comparisons are available in the literature, final conclusions regarding the best of these approaches is impossible, in our opinion. The results of varying strategies are dependent upon so many factors (that probably were not controlled or equated in most of the comparative studies) that definitive statements about the merits of this or that system are purely opinionated. Each strategy works well for some therapists with certain personal attributes and training, but none could or should be used alone by most reading teachers. If this is recognized, then the improvement of our effectiveness as remedial therapists depends upon our ability to match our personal abilities to techniques in relating to pupils, or to improve these by specific training with the goal of increasing our efficiency. This chapter is intended to help in these decisions regarding the thoroughness of our present approach and the possibilities of broadening and deepening it.

PSYCHOLOGICAL OR COUNSELING APPROACH

Rationale The basic concept of those who approach remediation through psychological or counseling techniques is that retardation in reading is only one manifestation of the individual's social and emotional adjustment to life's demands. It follows on this belief that treatment emphasizes helping the retarded reader to overcome, or to learn to deal with, his maladjustment so that it does not interfere with academic success (42). Psychological or counseling treatments may be the only techniques applied to the individual, or they may be combined with common forms of remedial work. It is not really considered significant to reading success whether the personal maladjustment preceded or followed the reading failure, or appeared simultaneously. This does not mean that the person's personal history is insignificant in the diagnosis, for the duration of his problems, their possible origins (if they can be established), the role of the family and siblings, and the severity of his maladjustment will certainly be studied and will affect the treatment plan. Basically, the rationale of this strategy is that the individual must be aided to function more effectively as a member of society. Progress is measured in terms of his development of more effective ways of coping with life, not solely in terms of his improvement in reading. Reading may spontaneously improve with adjustment; but, if it does not and its lack is significant to the individual, more direct treatment of the disability may then be indicated.

In viewing other strategies, the counselor or psychologist buttresses his stand by pointing out that the success of almost any approach depends upon the interpersonal relationship established between pupil and teacher, not on methods, materials, or teaching techniques. In other words, successful remediation is based on a counseling relationship that supports the pupil in coping with the problem of reading. He does not insist that, therefore, only he, the counselor, can be successful in remediation, but rather that a treatment, no matter what its form, cannot be effective if the counseling element is lacking. To some, this may sound like an arrogant, prejudiced viewpoint, but only if they are quite unfamiliar with the implications of the comparative research.

Techniques

Among the techniques that have been used in treating retarded readers in the framework of the psychological or counseling strategy are the following:

Nondirective Counseling The relationship with the therapist is characterized by permissiveness, empathetic reflection verbally of the subject's expressed feelings, and acceptance and respect for him as an individual. The primary tool—conversation between the therapist and subject—may center around the reading problem or any other topic desired by the subject. The treatment is intended to aid the subject in realizing and capitalizing on his own resources for solving his problem.

Directive Counseling

The relationship is between one who is basically an authoritarian or guiding figure and an unsuccessful learner. Basic tools are helping the student to achieve personal organization through planning, scheduling, or self-discipline, perhaps suggesting relaxation techniques to relieve physical or emotional tensions; giving guidance in study habits; arranging for direct instruction in reading; and utilizing other clinical resources to assist the pupil in specific problem areas, as marital or sex problems, physical therapy, speech, hearing or vision difficulties, and vocational guidance.

These two varieties of counseling may be accomplished in individual or group sessions or in programs that involve both. Directive group therapy is most common in schools and colleges, partly because a greater number of persons trained in that approach is available among school personnel, and partly because it is more economical of time in view of the number of students to be served.

Examples

The number of reports on nondirective therapy for poor readers has probably lessened in past decades from the peak period of the 1950s, when its application was a matter of wide interest. Among those reporting currently, Abrams and Belmont (1) compared individual versus group psychotherapy versus special reading instruction versus combined group and individual therapy. The group of pupils receiving special reading instruction scored significantly higher in the posttreatment reading test. In contrast, many of the earlier reports found nondirective group or individual therapy more productive of reading gains than the usual reading instruction or an approach combining both techniques. Some researchers also report that this approach, while effective in improving reading, was more significant in its effects upon personality adjustment. Still other writers found dramatic results in grades and persistence in school, without apparent marked changes in personality or reading ability. Results of nondirective therapy may be expected to vary with the nature of the emotional problems of the pupils, for there are indications that for certain types, such as those characterized by personal disorganization and a high level of anxiety, it is not so effective as a directive, structured group or individual approach.

Directive therapy reports continue to appear with great frequency, reflecting perhaps its wide use in education. Muller and Madsen (34), for example, showed that relaxation by tensing then relaxing muscles, followed by reading aloud and listening to the teacher read, reduced the anxiety of a number of seventh-grade pupils in a ten-week program. Reading achievement was apparently not affected at the end of the training period. Winkler, Tiegland, Munger, and Kranzler (55) were unsuccessful in producing any changes in grade point averages or personality as measured by a group test by fourteen half-hour counseling sessions. One of the questions unanswered by this sort of research is whether dramatic results can be obtained in such short periods of time. Lawrence's British study (28) was more positive in finding greater gains in the standard word recognition test used as a measure of reading for groups given counseling than for those offered remedial instruction alone or combined with counseling. It is relevant here to note that pupils used as tutors for other pupils are much more effective if given some training in principles of counseling, according to Niedermeyer (35, 37).

Play Therapy As in the case of nondirective psychotherapy, of which it is a variant, play therapy has evoked much less interest in work with retarded readers than was true in the early 1950s. Briefly, play therapy retains the qualities of permissiveness, reflection of feelings, acceptance, and respect of its subject. The difference lies in the fact that the medium of communication between therapist and subject is through reaction to the child's feelings as expressed in play. Water, balloons, clay, dolls, and other playthings are available for the child's choice. During use of these, the therapist observes the child's behavior and tries to evoke and reflect back any accompanying feelings. By expressing his feelings—recognizing them verbally without guilt feelings because of the acceptance by the therapist—the child is relieved of expressing them overtly or covertly in threatening situations; thus his adjustment improves.

Examples We have not found any recent reports on play therapy for retarded readers, although it is undoubtedly being employed in some schools and clinics. We can refer, however, to the original reports of Virginia Mae Axline (3) and Robert E. Bills (6, 7). Axline's experiences probably initiated wide interest in this treatment technique. Bills's two experiments seemed to demonstrate that well-rounded academic gains in reading and other areas were stimulated among poorly adjusted poor readers. Well-adjusted readers, who would normally not need such treatment, did not show such gains, as we would expect. Among other children, also under ten to twelve years of age, the combination of remedial instruction with play therapy has proved valuable for those who are resistant, negative, or anxious. Such treatment seems equally efficacious if the play therapy precedes or accompanies remedial instruction for these types of children. As we suggested in chapter 5 on diagnosis in personality, parallel treatment techniques are puppetry, role-playing, and dramatization if conducted in similar manner.

Counseling with Parents

Although parents have long been recognized as a vital element in pupil adjustment and school success (and treatment programs involving parent counseling have been common in psychotherapy and private counseling), comparative studies of the effects of combined treatment of parent and child are relatively recent. Among those reporting that counseling for parents of retarded readers, plus remedial instruction or counseling for their children, tends to result in improved reading are Peck and Rabban (38), Spieth (47), and Thayer (51). The pupils involved ranged from second to eighth grade in these groups. A similar study of the effect of parental counseling with mothers of first graders (10) and some older pupils (48) produced expected gains in readiness or reading for the children, who apparently received no special reading instruction. The extent of the changes in maternal attitudes appeared to be directly related to pupil attitudinal changes and gains in reading in this latter report. The obvious value of counseling for parents has led to the formulation of specific training programs for mothers in communication skills (2, 50), in child management (2), and in teaching reading at home (11, 19, 36).

McKinley's doctoral dissertation gives some clue to some of the reasons why this parental counseling is necessary and effective (32). Three groups of mothers—those of retarded readers, those of pupils referred to the clinic but found normal in reading, and those of normal nonclinic cases—were compared by the Parental Attitude Research Inventory in their attitudes on child rearing and mother-child relationships. All three groups appeared similar in this instrument and in a measure of their own personality adjustment. But, when asked to project their child's responses to the same personality test, the Rosenzweig Picture Frustration Study, there were significant differences between the groups of mothers. Mothers of retarded readers and the suspected retarded underestimated their children's defensiveness and resistance to the adult figure. They also overestimated their children's ability to handle conflict with others in a constructive or peace-making manner. The poorest predictions were made by those mothers whose own patterns of adjustment were abnormal. As a total group, parents of retarded readers may not appear very different in personality or the tone of their child-rearing practices from the general population, but there are often subtle flaws in their parent-child relationships.

Bibliotherapy

There are several ways of using books to aid in the adjustment of the poor reader. One would be to ascertain the personal traits found in the characters of stories, matching them with children in the hope that they would be inspired to emulate these traits (27). Another approach recognizes that the effect of books upon readers is more subtle and complex. The reader must first identify with the book character, a recognition that may have to be pointed out in prereading or postreading discussion with the teacher and perhaps other pupils. If the child blocks in identifying, because it would increase his anxieties or bring his own unresolved conflicts up to the verbal level, we must try again with another story. If identification occurs, the child must also be able to, or be led to, empathize with the feelings exhibited by the book character, to recognize in them, as it were, his own feelings. The ability to empathize and to experience vicariously the emotions of the character can be stimulated by role-playing and, again, pupil-teacher discussion.

The third stage of bibliotherapy is that of insight into the character's solutions of its conflicts and the recognition by the reader that by analogy or imitation, he, too, may find solutions. This is a crucial stage that, like the others, does not necessarily develop spontaneously from the reading. The success of the entire process, in fact, depends upon skillful counseling by the teacher. Some would say that this is too complex a task for ordinary teachers, but there is ample evidence to the contrary (30). Teachers are by training perhaps better equipped to initiate and to follow up this process by helping the child implement his insights in constructive action than are most adults with whom children come into contact.

One of the advantages of bibliotherapy is that it is a logical relationship between a teacher and a retarded reader. It may be conducted as an adjunct to almost any other treatment approach with subjects of any age. It may make a contribution to the rapport between teacher and pupil, for it appears to have a basis in common interests. When successful, the values obtained are dramatic returns for the relative investment of that precious commodity, time for counseling. For those desiring fuller treatments of bibiliotherapy and source lists of books suitable for various ages, there are several available resources (30, 45, 57) and also a recent list by Schultheis.*

OPERANT CONDITIONING

Rationale Stated briefly, the basic concept of operant conditioning is that behavior, skill development, or learning is most effective when scheduled in small steps in a planned sequence leading to a specific goal. The learning schedule is planned

*Sister Miriam Schultheis, *A Guidebook for Bibliotherapy* (New York: Psychotechnics, 1973).

and tested to insure successful progression of all learners, and reinforcement of each step is arranged by self-knowledge through providing a continuous answer key. This concept first appeared in education in the form of teaching machines, which fed the steps to the pupil and provided the answer reinforcement in a controlled fashion to prevent copying or cheating. Programs were the materials inserted in the teaching machine and were soon available as separate workbooks. These concepts are probably familiar to most teachers, for programmed workbooks are now in wide use.

Programmed Learning

Programming learning of pigeons and other animals has been successful in many laboratory experiments since the original work by Pavlov, a Russian scientist, who perhaps first demonstrated the technique. Programming learning of children, as in the area of reading, has apparently been successful in many reports, but some questions of its overall validity persist. As Summers (49) and Levine (29) have pointed out, there are serious questions about the applicability of programming in many areas of reading, and about its suitability for group use without any attempt to relate the program to the child's needs, wants, interests, or learning style. Programming often provides well-planned materials, permits children to progress at their own rate, provides records for analysis of errors, and even helps teachers to learn more about the intricacies of development in certain skill areas. But a skill development package assumes that the act of comprehension can be broken into tiny bits, practiced, and then, magically as it were, recombined into the flow of comprehension, a questionable and unproved assumption. On the other hand, most critics see its relevance in some of the more or less mechanical skills related to reading, as dictionary and library use, phonics, word recognition, study skills, structural and contextual analysis, and the like. Personally, this writer would question just when programmed materials, even for these skills, are really appropriate. We do not see them as desirable for initial teaching, but rather as supplementary practice material to be used after the basic insights into the process and its values to the reader have been recognized by the learner, and then to be used later for development of speed and accuracy only. Used in their proffered sense, programmed materials and their use resemble the skill development strategy, for which we offer a critique below.

Performance Contracting

The apparent ease with which children's skills can be manipulated by programming, plus material reinforcements or rewards, has led to a spate of trials in programs guaranteed to produce the desired results at the hands of publishers or even industrial contractors. Performance contracting, as it is called, has been introduced to many school systems in which the reading success of the pupils has not been acceptable to the administration. In a tongue-in-cheek article, Roger Farr, J. Jaap Tuinman, and B. Elgit Blanton (18) have pointed out how simple it would be to realize a large profit in performance contracting. Using the results of a controlled experiment as the basis for their argument (53), these critics showed that by use of material rewards for improved test performance, without any reading instruction, dramatic gains in apparent reading ability were obtained. Significant gains in vocabulary and comprehension and the number of test items of each attempted were stimulated by the promised rewards of radios, sweatshirts, and candy bars.

These are not isolated criticisms of the fallacy of using test results as measures of the effectiveness of operant conditioning techniques in developing reading abilities. Many such attacks have been published in general media as well as in professional literature. Our point is that the exact role of programmed instruction in the field of reading has still not been established.

Behavior Modification

Another outgrowth of the theory of operant conditioning has been its application in behavior modification, a recent and spreading phenomenon. This approach resembles the ancient system of rewards and punishments known to most parents and teachers. In application, when a specific behavior of the subject to be modified is identified, a system of constant rewards or punishments to reduce this behavior or induce a substitute action is instituted (22, 24). As we shall see, the rewards and punishments may take a variety of forms, each calculated to motivate the subject to change his behavior. Reports of successful behavior modification programs for mentally retarded, delinquent, hospitalized mental patients, and many others are available. But we shall concern ourselves only with the results in terms of reading development.

Examples

Using electric shock as punishment when certain letters were exposed tachistoscopically, Bloomer (9) was able to show more errors—particularly among those who felt that the shock was strong—even when students did not know what letter was associated with shock. Drawing the analogy with the threat of the teacher in oral reading, Bloomer reasons that stress or punishment tends to produce poorer reading.

To massive verbal rewards, a group of ten–thirteen-year-olds responded with greater reading performance than that achieved in a control group given conventional remedial treatment (13).

High-anxious intermediate-grade boys showed no effects from money rewards, while low-anxious tended to reduce errors in successive oral reading tests (15). Punishment by fines for poorer performances had no effects.

Pikulski (39) used social reinforcement or verbal praise in contrast to material reinforcement by candy M & M's or a buzzer in a word-picture association task. Middle-class children were affected positively by the social type of reinforcement, but for the lower class only girls were similarly affected. The author questions the general assumption that material reinforcers are more effective for most lower-class children.

Ellson et al. (16) have devised a program for tutors to use with children of primary ages. When this was added to regular instruction twice a day, there was significant reading growth, particularly for poor readers. These authors claim that their program is more effective than direct tutoring because more time is spent in reading instruction rather than in the many supportive activities commonly used by tutors, although no proof of this conjecture was offered. In their material, the pupil-teacher interaction is reduced to reading a script.

Hardyck and Petrinovich (23) claimed to have eliminated subvocalization during silent reading, especially among the higher I.Q. high school and college students. They fastened an electronic buzzer to the throat to alert the pupil to his subvocalization. One hour of such training seemed to suffice to eradicate the subvocalization, at least temporarily. The effects of such training on word analysis and comprehension were not noted.

Among other apparently successful behavior modifications were the use of tokens exchangeable for various objects as awarded for improvement in reading (24); tokens exchangeable for grades and letters of recommendation that were awarded for punctuality, attendance, not creating a disturbance, completing assignments, and similar behaviors among high school remedial pupils (31). Thomson (52) contrasted material reinforcements of pencils, erasers, candy, and social reinforcement by praise for improvement in a weekly spelling test. In later three-month intervals, material reinforcements were made intermittent, while social reinforcement remained constant. The best results were obtained from continuous material reinforcement, plus the social. But the intermittent material reinforcement in the second trial period did not cause losses, although low scorers did not begin to respond until this second period of training. As in several other studies, this experiment raises questions about the essentiality of constant reinforcement.

As we have remarked, the spread of behavior modification has been great, both in this country and in Britain (56). As apparent in the few examples of its application given above, all the facts about the relative values of various types of reinforcement for both sexes, for different social classes, for children of varying mental ability, and for those differing in personality have not yet been found. But basic guides for teachers who wish to try behavior modification are readily available (17, 20, 41).

THE PERCEPTUAL DEFICIT THEORY

Rationale A growing group of practitioners in remedial reading seems to believe that the basic cause of much of the retardation in reading is due to a specific perceptual deficit in the visual, auditory, or visual-motor areas. Their diagnoses emphasize pinpointing this deficit by a variety of tests in elements of visual or auditory perception and correcting the reading disability by treatment to overcome this suspected deficit. We have reviewed these diagnostic procedures in detail, evaluating the outcomes of the programs, especially in visual perception, in chapters 1 and 16 of *Investigating the Issues of Reading Disabilities.* Here, instead of repeating that mass of material, we shall examine the logic of those who endorse this strategy of remedial work.

The first of the basic questions raised by those critical of this concept of reading disability is whether it is possible to establish the problem as a specific deficit in a visual or an auditory subskill. They point out that the subskills in each area have not been shown to be independent. In the case of the auditory channel, there is probably considerable overlap among auditory discrimination, span, and synthesis, as well as acuity, discrimination of pitch, loudness, timbre, or rhythm. Second, the significance of any one subskill for success in reading is very small, almost negligible, except perhaps in a small number of extreme cases. For example, any of the designated components of visual perception usually tested under this approach, as figure ground, spatial relations, hand-eye coordination, visual span, or form discrimination show very limited influence upon reading.

Third, there is the question of the interrelatedness of the visual and auditory channels. Some claim that they are independent and that training should be given via only one channel in reading instruction (26). Others, who are equally self-assured, insist that reading is a multimodal act in which visual and auditory stimuli are being processed simultaneously. These would insist on a teaching method involving successive visual, auditory, kinesthetic, and tactile (VAKT) presentations. One group (8) insists that the visual input is actually a hindrance to learning and would teach words by writing them on the child's back with a forefinger, while the child hears and writes the word! One western reading center insists on using the kinesthetic method of tracing and writing words as the basic remedial approach. Another midwestern clinic apparently gives fundamental visual training in binocular coordination to all clients. All claim cures of reading retardation because of their own peculiar technique, and undoubtedly they have case records to prove it.

It is true that various visual and auditory materials have certain merits and effects upon the child, as in pictures versus films, records versus filmstrips, and so on (43). But the question of the actual integration—if there is such in the act of reading—and the relative role of the various sensory stimuli in learning words, for example, is still unanswered. Even if this information existed, we still need to discover how individual learners vary in use of the different inputs, for they do. Then we need to establish the validity of various methods and their relative dependence upon different channels and the interaction among learner, channels, and method, an interaction only suggested by preliminary research.

We are not attempting to say that no pupils fail in reading because of problems in the visual and auditory channels. But it is only perhaps in the area of visual defects where the interaction of subskills is known and prescriptive treatment is possible. Most of the other visual and auditory subskills are of unknown or little significance and are probably interrelated in ways as yet not well understood in the act of reading.

These logical defects in the perceptual deficit approach will probably not deter remedial teachers from trying to determine in what areas the child seems weak or undeveloped, and then offering the related training procedures, such as we outlined earlier in chapters 2 and 3 on these learning channels. Since the treatment does appear to help pupils' progress in reading—although we do not know why it seems to work—this practice will continue. If the treatment produces permanent improvement, a point we shall examine later in looking at follow-up results, the practice is perhaps justifiable until that time when the research clarifies what our procedures should be. Personally, we are not quite sure of this conclusion, however, for the quest for panaceas to cure reading disability in this particular framework of thinking is disturbing.

ORGANIZATIONAL APPROACHES

Rationale While others seek cures for reading disability in manipulating sensory channels or behavior modification or counseling, or whatever, there are a great many, especially administrators, who find their answers in new organizational patterns. Teachers are often obsessed with the image of the *three:* three reading groups, three levels of reading materials. Others favor interclass grouping, homogeneous or heterogeneous grouping, or, in the extreme, complete individualization. Interest groups, "join us when you want to" groups, pupil teams, committees, and so on, are the suggestions of others. Activity centers or self-diagnostic reading centers, where children try out books by counting the number of unknown words on the fingers of one hand (54), are still other organizational attempts to cure the reading problem.

Some of these arrangements do lend themselves to greater pupil development in responsibility for self-improvement, pupil mobility, and activity in learning, and, as we have seen, probably promote more desirable pupil-teacher relationships. But, unfortunately, the research indicating that any of these greatly affects reading development is very weak. Of all the organizational changes that are supposed to be helpful, only those advocating using pupil teams or pupil tutors seem currently to be achieving an impact upon pupil growth in reading. Whether these results reflect the Hawthorne effect or the impetus of the individual attention given the pupils (and whether the effects persist) remains to be demonstrated.

Concerning pupil tutors and aides, we have, however, learned these facts:

> Both pupils and tutors gain in their reading abilities, and tutors show improvement in school attendance, school behavior, and other traits. The age of the tutor may be the same as the pupil being helped or older. In any case, some training for the tutor in personal relations is desirable and profitable in producing greater gains for his pupil.
>
> Tutored pupils seem to make more progress than those in ordinary classrooms, even when instruction time and curricula are held constant (4).
>
> Peer tutoring, in some instances, appears even more effective than that by adults.
>
> In tutoring arrangements, there seem no differences between the effectiveness of individual or small-group work.
>
> When peers correct pupil work, there is greater motivation, besides more efficient and quicker work, than when assignments are brought to the teacher for correction. There is also less threat to the retarded pupil and consequently less anxiety in peer correction. Gains in reading ability were also greater in this arrangement (21).
>
> Four hours per week of tutoring is much more effective than two hours, which seems to produce little improvement. Tutoring in addition to the regular program is possibly more effective than the latter alone.
>
> The number of adults used as tutoring aides beyond one does not increase results. Aides, like pupil tutors, are more effective when given training.
>
> The use of aides has been shown to improve the attention span of

younger pupils and to make other contributions in personalizing the instruction.

In the emphasis upon the values of training in counseling relationships and in this use of pupils and aides for tutoring purposes, we see another recognition of the significance of this pupil-teacher psychological interaction.

THE SKILL DEFICIT APPROACH

Rationale Probably the oldest and most widely observed strategy of remedial reading is that based on skill deficit analysis. Following the pattern of Marion Monroe in the 1930s, oral reading errors of the subject are carefully noted, categorized, and used as *the* basis of remediation. The errors in each type of phoneme as vowels and consonants are tabulated; and the exact nature of the error (as omissions, substitutions, additions, and so on) are also counted. This approach is so widespread that its description is really unnecessary. To complete the picture, though, we might point out that the remedial procedures usually following this diagnostic approach tend to emphasize improvement of phonic skills and word recognition, even with junior and senior high school retarded readers, and sometimes even with college students. We are aware, of course, of the use in some quarters of measures of other reading skills, with the types of training then employed; but this discussion will come later. Our purpose of this quick review is to establish a basis for examining the assumptions regarding learning to read or the correction of retardation inherent in this detailed analysis of oral reading errors.

Assumptions in the Skill Deficit Strategy

As in the perceptual deficit theory of remediation, the purpose of skill deficit analysis seems to be to identify that type of minor reading performance in which the subject is not highly skilled. As we view it, this strategy makes the following assumptions (to which we shall add our comments):

Reading is a matter of skill development achieved largely by practice on each identifiable ability. Yet no one has been able to discover the proper sequence of training in specific areas, or even the best sequence within each skill area. Even the existence of the separate skills stressed, as in the area of comprehension, is doubtful.

Reading is basically an oral act, a word recognition task. The language experiences that undoubtedly affect reading performances are ignored in this definition.

> Reading orally reflects what goes on in silent reading; hence analysis of oral reading errors, in the manner cited above, will reveal the silent process. This belief is true probably only in part, for it ignores the influences of the child's mediation and associative thinking while reading silently. Only perhaps in some mechanical details may what is observed in analysis of oral reading errors be true for silent. And even this similarity is weak because of the possible modification of word analysis habits observed in the oral act by the child's mediating processes while reading silently.
>
> Reading is basically a decoding act, a translation of graphemes into phonemes; the basic and perhaps only significant word recognition technique is decoding. In contrast, there is irrefutable evidence that reading is more than decoding, perhaps even in the very first complete sentence read by the child. When oral errors are tabulated somewhat differently, as illustrated in our chapter 6 on the analysis of oral reading, it is quite obvious that, from their beginnings, readers employ other word recognition clues such as familiarity with common sentence patterns, word function, graphic clues in letter clusters, context clues based upon probabilities, and so forth.
>
> The tabulation of oral reading errors in the Monroe style reveals the decoding skills of the pupil, hence indicating his needs for training in this area. This belief is a corollary of the definition of reading as a decoding act, a logical extension of that fallacious concept of the act of reading. While these needs may truly exist, as among primary pupils, their primary emphasis in remediation reflects the narrowest concept of the reading act.

By this time, the reader who is familiar with this author's other publications, as the Spache Diagnostic Reading Scales, may begin to question his sincerity. How can he justify offering a diagnostic reading instrument like the Scales and at the same time find all manner of fault with its apparent rationale? Our answer is that we tried to prepare a better instrument than those available, which would permit diagnosticians to function more effectively with their present skills. The instrument is intended simply as an initial tool to organize the diagnosis of a pupil's reading performances only. If examined carefully, it is apparent that more than just oral reading error analysis will be obtained, for there are also measures of silent and oral comprehension, auditory comprehension, phonic skills, and certain auditory abilities. Furthermore, the analysis of oral reading errors includes observation of the child's use of graphic, word form, and word function clues, as well as the usual phonemic analysis. As recognition of the limitations of the phonemic analysis approach spreads among reading teachers, we intend to continue to modify our Scales to match and to support their broadening concepts of diagnosis. While awaiting this millennium, we shall continue to make efforts such as those offered here to stimulate reading teachers' thinking in this direction.

We are certainly not alone in our criticism of the skills deficit approach to remediation. Diane J. Sawyer* has recently reiterated many of these points. As she points out, the overemphasis upon the repair of deficient skills results often in repeated reteaching the same skills in each period of remediation, a practice that follow-ups indicate does not cure the reading problem, for it tends to persist or recur. Matching of the prescription formed by testing a number of subskills to remediation, while logical, is not a panacea. Finally, this writer reemphasizes that a true hierarchy of skills, as implied in many diagnostic tests, systems approaches, and programmed materials, has not been shown to be a real or even significant guide to remediation.

Like the present author, Sawyer emphasizes the importance of the pupil's self-concept as a person, as a reader, and in relation to others. She recommends attention to the degree of autonomy, or independence of constant teacher direction, shown by the pupil. Apparently she leans toward the belief that remediation is not entirely something that the teacher does to the pupil by intensive instruction in his missing skills, but is rather a process involving training in more efficient thinking, in improvement of self-concept, and a sense of reality about one's own needs and abilities, supported greatly by the pupil's own efforts as his self-insights grow.

THE LANGUAGE DEFICIT STRATEGY

Rationale

There is an approach to solving our failures to produce adequate reading ability for a large proportion of school pupils offered in the language deficit strategy. The concept is that the lack of language development is responsible, especially with socioeconomically deprived or racial or ethnic minority pupils. If their language growth and facility could be stimulated, beginning even in the preschool years or, in any event, prior to their introduction to reading instruction, the extent of reading retardation in these groups would be greatly diminished.

Techniques and Examples

Among the steps employed with this rationale are preschool and early school language stimulation through the Head Start, Follow Through and similar Federally sponsored programs; special prereading, linguistically oriented training such as those intended to correct dialect and to provide familiarity with English sentence patterns and the like; and many types of programs, such as those in Title I and Compensatory Education, in which language develop-

*Diane J. Sawyer, "The Diagnostic Mystique—A Point of View," *Reading Teacher,* 27 (March 1974), 555–61.

ment was only one of the goals. Some programs take the form of training parents of these language-deprived children in communication skills, in child-rearing practices, in stimulation of language and cognitive growth, and in education for tutoring their children in readiness or early reading skills and others. In direct work with young children, approaches include giving them books written in their own dialect or language, teaching them to speak standard English using the patterns of instruction created for adults in the Teaching English as a Second Language materials, intensive oral language practice (using the linguistic reading materials as especially suitable to these groups), and so on.

While agreeing that language development is significant to reading, many critics reject the basic tenets of the language deficit theory. They say that it is absurd to claim that these pupils do not have a language, for they do communicate adequately in their culture. What they do not have is middle-class English, nor do they need it. Attempts to change dialect, even when successful, appear to have little or no impact upon reading success, nor do the programs in syntax, structural linguistics, sentence patterns, or Teaching English as a Second Language. The critics point out that these children do learn to read in standard English materials, and even to use such a dialect in dealing with their middle-class teachers (only). There is no evidence that the cognitive capacities of pupils who speak a dialect is therefore retarded, for any language or dialect provides for, and permits, any cognitive process.

Rosen and Ortega (40) have offered a comprehensive summary of the research pertinent to the language deficit strategy. They do not find the intensive, early introduction to English, the TESL programs, and the linguistics programs as satisfactory or successful solutions to the reading problems of language-handicapped children. Not only have these programs failed to accomplish their goal of insuring reading success, but, as Rosen and Ortega point out, they are also ignoring the child's ego identification with his language and his culture, the child's needs not for another dialect but for growth in communication. In summary, we must assume that simply teaching the child to speak standard English will overcome any handicaps in his background of poverty, racial discrimination, instability of the family unit, unemployment, and lack of educational opportunities—a most unlikely assumption.

THE MECHANICAL STRATEGY

Rationale Stimulated by the persuasiveness of salesmen and the creativity of manufacturers of "reading training" devices, many reading teachers have sought solutions for their problem children through mechanical types of training. The purveyors of these instruments promise to increase the eye-span of poor readers, thus to increase their rate of reading, to improve comprehension, to produce speed and accuracy in word recognition, and to teach phonic skills as well as almost any other skill area. They offer to eliminate regressions, to reduce the duration of fixations and the number of fixations, to reduce vocalization, to reinforce attention, and to break slow-reading, word-by-word patterns. Obviously this strategy is based on an utterly mechanistic concept of the act of reading, that is, one determined by the nature of the reader's eye movements and one in which increases in rate of reading tend to overcome most or all types of reading difficulties.

Techniques and Examples

We shall review this area in detail in chapter 11 on mechanical methods of improving reading. Rather than repeating all this material, we are here briefly summarizing the indications of the related research.

The studies of machines in improving word recognition are quite inconclusive. While word recognition can and probably should be accomplished rapidly, training with this goal is pointless until a host of associated meanings are created and the words stressed are entirely familiar.

Training to change eye-movement patterns in the hope of improving reading is dealing with one of the end processes of learning to read, rather than one of the foundations of the act. Eye movements reflect reading ability, not cause it to be good or poor.

Eliminating regressions might well destroy the basic habits of word analysis and tend to stultify the mental processes of judgment and interpretation in reading.

Increasing eye-span in a fixation is literally impossible, in any really significant degree. The size of the span does not discriminate between good and poor readers, is not a constant behavior but one determined by the difficulty of the material and other factors, is not amenable to training, and is significantly different in far-point training from that present in reading a book.

The number of fixations is not consistent per group of words, even among good readers. Like span, it reflects the mediating and word analysis processes demanded by the material, as well as the purpose of the reader.

Duration of fixations reflects the comprehension process of the reader. While it may be reduced as material permits greater speed of reading, this result is as readily achieved by maturation in reading and ordinary classroom training as by most mechanical devices.

Subvocalization to a marked degree will, of course, reduce silent reading rate to the reader's speech rate. But its complete elimination, as contrasted to its reduction, is probably impossible, for silent reading is a language (vocal) act at least in part. Besides, in making the transition from oral to silent reading, most pupils learn to function with a minimum of subvocalization, with simple suggestion and training in the ordinary classroom.

The actual contributions of mechanical training such as that in rate of reading are in promoting a set for faster reading, greater use of contextual clues, better visual discrimination, and probably more acute attention. If the training is broad enough, greater flexibility of rate may appear, and facility in skimming and scanning may be promoted. These contributions are not necessarily present in group use of the devices unless the material is relatively simple; the trainees are handpicked to eliminate those with comprehension, vocabulary, or word analysis skill lacks; the training matter is true reading material; the exposure of the reading matter permits the reader to use his own pattern of span; and the design of the device resembles distinctly the usual act of near-point reading, that is, continuous material, with normal return sweeps to the next lines and with controlled readability of the material.

If we contrast these results of the use of many of the mechanical devices with the claims of their producers, it is apparent that their role is not so much in remedial training but in developmental work with normal or good readers. Only when the reading difficulty of the subject is inflexibility of rate or habitual slow rate in all materials—at a speed far below the verbal facility and associative thinking speed of the individual—does the mechanical strategy seem relevant.

THE COGNITIVE OR LEARNING STYLE STRATEGY

Rationale During the past two decades, there has slowly developed a body of information about the cognitive or learning style of students and its relation to method, as in teaching word recognition. Various tests have been devised to distinguish habits of thinking or processing information and thus to permit categorizing individuals. There is little doubt that pupils solve problems or learn new material while apparently using different mental patterns. For example, Beller (5) distinguished children of a descriptive style of learning as contrasted to a relational style. If we comprehend his terms, we may assume that in recognition tasks some employed description to aid retention, while others saw relationships among the words that aided them. In a very large scale study, Metfessel and Seng (33) identified the learning style of low-achieving ethnic minority children as more response to visual and kinesthetic stimuli than to oral or written; poor attention span for many types of situations; longer perseveration in a simple single task; and better learning by inductive than deductive approaches. Chilman (12) calls the learning style of such children: concrete, pragmatic, personal, and physical, perhaps the learning style of the nonverbal or cognitively immature person.

Sawyer* would contrast such cognitive styles as these:

> constricted—unable to exercise selective attention and to ignore pictures, noises, and individual letters within words. May need to subvocalize or even read aloud to self in order to concentrate.
>
> flexible—able to choose easily what is significant in word recognition, in the ideas and relationships among ideas.
>
> field dependent—unable to relate textual information to other experiences, or to restructure it in new insights or meanings; cannot move from facts to their broad implications; cannot see relationships among ideas and their ultimate applications.
>
> impulsive—too quick to respond in word recognition, and hence more prone to errors than are slower, reflective children.

Other types of contrasting learning styles are analytic-synthetic, subjective-objective, field dependent–field independent, and the like. The meanings of these terms are fairly obvious, but their frequency implies that the exploration of learning style is based on contrasting concepts, tests, and interpretations, as Coop and Sigel have pointed out (14).

In many instances, the experiments in relating the child's learning style to the method of presentation have taken the form of paired associate learning tasks. Groups of words and pictures, words and symbols, or lists of words are presented for paired learning. The child's performances are judged in terms of the time and number of trials or repeated presentations that he requires for learning all the pairs. There are significant clues to the teaching of word recognition in either developmental or remedial instruction found in these paired associate learning experiments. We listed a dozen or more of these implications for learning letters and words in chapter 2 on diagnosis in vision and visual perception, and contrasted the practices found workable in these experiments with common teacher practices. In effect, these are important studies in relating the child's thinking processes to teaching presentation, a significant application of the cognitive or learning style strategy.

The values of this particular concept of the learning process in reading are still limited largely to the teaching of word recognition, visual discrimination, and vocabulary, although some applications have been extended to other

---

*Diane J. Sawyer, op. cit.

fields such as math. At present, we have gained specific suggestions, however, that can and should be applied in these areas of reading instruction and when dealing with ethnic minority children. Eventually we hope that these cognitive strategists will explore more fully the other major areas of comprehension and rate of reading and will offer helpful suggestions. We are heartened by the current explorations of influences upon comprehension already completed by these writers (which we reviewed in chapter 9 on silent reading abilities) and look forward to future studies of these types.

THE DYSLEXIA OR SPECIFIC LEARNING DISABILITY STRATEGY

We have devoted an entire chapter to this particular concept of diagnosis and treatment of reading disabilities, in our *Investigating the Issues of Reading Disabilities.* Among the characteristics of this school of thought that we noted were the following:

> The variability in definitions of what reading disability (or dyslexia, as it is called) is supposed to be is confusing, to say the least. The signs and symptoms of dyslexia are as diverse and confusing as the definitions. The surprising fact that, despite the diversity of opinion regarding the roles of brain damage, heredity, laterality disturbances, and mixed cerebral dominance, the few common treatments parallel the procedures followed by many reading centers that claim only to treat reading disability. The presence of brain damage or suspected brain damage as a basic component of dyslexia is both anatomically, neurologically, and hereditarily untenable.
>
> The signs and symptoms of brain damage as determined by psychometric testing have not been shown to be related to brain pathology. Nor are supposed behavioral signs, EEG testing, finger localization, and right-left discrimination or even birth history infallible indications.
>
> The treatment of brain-damaged poor readers has employed many of the same remedial procedures, as training in visual perception, form discrimination, structural linguistics, and so on, that are used in many reading centers, plus a number of esoteric special programs (44). Most of these treatments have yielded the same equivocal results in the treatment of children actually handicapped by brain damage—or simply suspected of having this difficulty—as they have in ordinary reading clinics.
>
> Chemotherapy for dyslexic pupils or children presumably showing signs of brain damage is becoming widespread in pediatric and clinical practice. The results, although often apparently favorable, are often reported in such poor scientific designs as to be almost meaningless. Perhaps some final evaluation of the specific values of chemotherapy will be possible when the diagnostic and treatment procedures are more carefully controlled.
>
> Cerebral dominance, laterality, and reading relationships are, for the

most part, based on presumptions that are anatomically erroneous. Despite a mass of contradictory evidence, this confused thinking about brain function, hemispheric, eye, and hand dominance persists.

Of the nine strategies of remedial reading reviewed, this last, in our opinion, has the fewest constructive ideas to contribute. In contrast, each of the others has certain merits in treatment practices, even if not in soundness of theory, that the eclectic reading teacher may well adopt in specific cases. To us, the ultimate goal in efficient remediation is the broadening and refining of the diagnostic base sufficiently to permit matching the remedial schedule to the best diagnosis that can be made. We can see no justification for a static diagnostic approach (or even a broad one) that always seems to result in the same treatments, a phenomenon common in observations of remedial teachers and centers. Even if this chapter does no more than challenge or disturb adherents of any one strategy, it will have accomplished its purpose.

LEARNING PROJECT

Arrange to visit and observe a reading teacher or a reading center at work. By observation and, perhaps by interviewing some of the staff, make these evaluations of the service.

1. What basic strategy of remediation seems to guide the work? What treatment techniques are most common?

2. What techniques that may exemplify other strategies of remediation are often used?

3. Ask to read some of the case histories, if you are permitted. Note whether the interpretation of probable causes of reading difficulty seems to differ from case to case.

4. How does the staff try to fit treatment to these probable causes? Or do most cases appear to receive the same basic treatment?

5. What possible improvements in the diversification of treatments and in better integration of diagnosis with remediation can you suggest?

REFERENCES

1. Abrams, Jules C., and Belmont, H.S., "Different Approaches to the Remediation of Severe Reading Disability in Children," *Journal of Learning Disabilities,* 2 (1969), 136–41.

2. Allen, J.E., Della-Piana, G., and Stahmann, R.E., "The Effect of a Parent Training Program upon Reading Achievement of Children," in *Forging Ahead in Reading,* J. Allen Figurel, editor, Proceedings International Reading Association, 12, 1968, 523–32.
3. Axline, Virginia Mae, "Play Therapy—A Way of Understanding and Helping Reading Problems," *Childhood Education,* 26 (December 1949), 151–61.
4. Bausell, R., Barker, Moody, William B., and Waltzl, F. Neil, "A Factorial Study of Tutoring vs. Classroom Instruction," *American Educational Research Journal,* 9 (Fall 1972), 591–98.
5. Beller, E.K., "Cognitive Styles and Methods of Language Training," Paper presented at American Educational Research Association, New York, February 1967.
6. Bills, Robert E., "Non-Directive Play Therapy with Retarded Readers," *Journal of Consulting Psychology,* 14 (April 1950), 140–49.
7. Bills, Robert E., "Play Therapy with Well-Adjusted Retarded Readers," *Journal of Consulting Psychology,* 14 (August 1950), 246–49.
8. Blau, Harold, Schwalb, Eugene, Zanger, Eugene, and Blau, Harriet, "Developmental Dyslexia and Its Treatment," *Reading Teacher,* 22 (April 1969), 649–53.
9. Bloomer, Richard H., "Punishment and Perception," *Elementary School Journal,* 69 (November 1968), 100–5.
10. Brazziel, William F., and Terrell, Mary, "An Experiment in the Development of Readiness in a Culturally Disadvantaged Group of First-Grade Children," *Journal of Negro Education,* 31 (Winter 1962), 4–7.
11. Brzeinski, Joseph E., "Beginning Reading in Denver," *Reading Teacher,* 18 (October 1964), 16–21.
12. Chilman, Catherine S., "Child Rearing and Family Relationship Patterns of the Very Poor," *Welfare in Review,* 3 (January 1965), 9–19.
13. Clark, C.A., and Walberg, H.J., "The Influence of Massive Rewards on Reading Achievement in Potential Urban School Dropouts," *American Educational Research Journal,* 5 (1968), 305–10.
14. Coop, Richard H., and Sigel, Irving E., "Cognitive Style: Implications for Learning and Instruction," *Psychology in the Schools,* 8 (1971), 152–61.
15. Cotler, S., "The Effects of Positive and Negative Reinforcement and Test Anxiety on the Reading Performance of Male Elementary School Children," *Genetic Psychology Monographs,* 80 (1969), 29–50.
16. Ellson, D.G., Harris, Phillip, and Barber, Larry, "A Field Test of Programed and Directed Tutoring," *Reading Research Quarterly,* 3 (Spring 1968), 307–68.
17. Eysenck, Hans J., editor, *Experiments in Behaviour Therapy.* New York: Pergamon Press, 1967.
18. Farr, Roger, Tuinman, J. Jaap, and Blanton, B. Elgit, "How to Make a Pile in Performance Contracting," *Phi Delta Kappan* (February 1972), 367–69.
19. Freshour, Frank W., "Parent Education and Reading Readiness and Achievement," *Reading Teacher,* 24 (May 1971), 763, 769.
20. Graziano, Anthony M., editor, *Behavior Therapy with Children.* New York: Basic Books, 1971.
21. Grice, Joan S., and Wolfe, Lee R., "Peer vs. Teacher Correction of Classwork and Selected Reading Criteria," in *Investigations Relating to Mature Reading,* Frank P. Green, editor, 21st Yearbook National Reading Conference, 1972, 218–27.

22. Hanley, Edward M., "Review of Research Involving Applied Behavior in the Classroom," *Review of Educational Research,* 40 (December 1970), 597–626.
23. Hardyck, C.D., and Petrinovich, L.F., "Treatment of Sub-vocal Speech during Reading," *Journal of Reading,* 12 (1969), 361–68, 419–22.
24. Heitzman, A.J., "Effects of a Token Reinforcement System on the Reading and Arithmetic Skills Learning of Migrant Primary School Pupils," *Journal of Educational Research,* 63 (1970), 455–58.
25. Hively, W., "A Framework for the Analysis of Elementary Reading Behavior," *American Educational Research Journal,* 3 (1966), 89–103.
26. Johnson, Doris J., "Treatment Approaches to Dyslexia," in *Reading Disability and Perception,* George D. Spache, editor, Proceedings International Reading Association, 13, No. 3, 1969, 95–102.
27. Kircher, Clara J., *Behavior Patterns in Children's Books.* Washington: Catholic University Press, 1966.
28. Lawrence, D., "The Effects of Counseling on Retarded Readers," *Educational Research,* 13 (1971), 119–24.
29. Levine, Jane, "Let's Debate Programmed Reading Instruction," *Reading Teacher,* 16 (March 1963), 337–41.
30. Lindeman, Barbara, and Kling, Martin, "Bibliotherapy: Definitions, Uses and Studies," *Journal of School Psychology,* 7 (1968–69), 36–41.
31. Martin, Marian, Schwyhart, K., and Wetzel, R., "Teaching Motivation in a High School Reading Program," *Journal of Reading,* 11 (1967), 111–21.
32. McKinley, Douglas P., "A Study of Certain Relationships of Maternal Personality and Child-Rearing Attitudes to Children's Reading Performances," Doctoral dissertation, University of Florida, 1958.
33. Metfessel, Newton S., and Seng, Mark W., "Correlates with the School Success and Failure of Economically Disadvantaged Children," in *Reading for the Disadvantaged,* Thomas D. Horn, editor. Newark, Del.: International Reading Association and Harcourt Brace Jovanovich, 1970, 75–98.
34. Muller, Sarah D., and Madsen, C.H., Jr., "Group Desensitization for 'Anxious' Children with Reading Problems," *Psychology in the Schools,* 11 (1970), 184–89.
35. Niedermeyer, F.C., "Effects of Training on the Instructional Behaviors of Student Tutors," *Journal of Educational Research,* 64 (1970), 119–23.
36. Niedermeyer, F.C., *Parent-Assisted Learning.* Inglewood, Calif.: Southwest Regional Laboratory, 1970.
37. Niedermeyer, F.C., and Ellis, Patricia, "Remedial Reading Instruction by Trained Pupil Tutors," *Elementary School Journal,* 71 (April 1971), 400–5.
38. Peck, H.B., and Rabban, M., "An Approach to the Correction of Reading Disability through Parent and Teacher Groups," *American Journal of Orthopsychiatry,* 36 (1966), 427–33.
39. Pikulski, John, "Effects of Reinforcement on Word Recognition," *Reading Teacher,* 23 (March 1970), 516–22, 555.
40. Rosen, Carl L., and Ortega, Phillip D., *Issues in Language and Reading Instruction of Spanish Speaking Children: An Annotated Bibliography.* Newark: International Reading Association, 1969.
41. Sattler, Howard E., and Swoope, Karen S., "Token Systems: A Procedural Guide," *Psychology in the Schools,* 7 (1970), 383–86.

42. Spache, George D., "Reading Improvement as a Counseling Procedure," in *Eighth Yearbook National Reading Conference,* 1959, 125–30.
43. Spache, George D., "Auditory and Visual Materials in Reading Instruction," in *Development In and Through Reading,* Sixtieth Yearbook National Society for the Study of Education, 209–25. Chicago: University of Chicago Press, 1961.
44. Spache, George D., "Diagnosis and Remediation in 1980," in *Reading Disability and Perception,* George D. Spache, editor, Proceedings International Reading Association, 13, No. 3, 1969.
45. Spache, George D., *Good Reading for Poor Readers.* Champaign: Garrard Publishing, 1974.
46. Spache, George D., Standlee, Lloyd, and Neville, Donald, "Results of Three College Level Remedial Reading Procedures," *Journal of Developmental Reading,* 4 (Autumn 1960), 12–16.
47. Spieth, P., "Rise III: A Second Continued Experimental Summer Program in Remedial Reading," *Minnesota Reading Quarterly,* 13 (1969), 98–104, 134.
48. Studholme, Janice MacDonald, "Group Guidance with Mothers of Retarded Readers," *Reading Teacher,* 17 (April 1964), 528–30.
49. Summers, Edward G., "Programmed Learning and Reading Instruction," *Conference on Reading, University of Pittsburgh,* 20 (1964), 67–76.
50. Swift, Marshall S., "Training Poverty Mothers in Communication Skills," *Reading Teacher,* 23 (January 1970), 360–68.
51. Thayer, J.A., "Johnny Could Read—What Happened?" *Journal of Reading,* 13 (1970), 501–6.
52. Thomson, Eric W., and Galloway, Charles G., "Material Reinforcement and Success in Spelling," *Elementary School Journal,* 70 (April 1970), 395–98.
53. Tuinman, J. Jaap, Farr, Roger, and Blanton, B. Elgit, "Increases in Test Scores as a Function of Material Rewards," *Journal of Educational Measurement,* 9 (Fall 1972), 215–23.
54. Williamson, Leon E., "Self-Diagnostic Center in the Elementary Classroom," paper presented at the National Reading Conference, New Orleans, December 1973.
55. Winkler, R.C., Tiegland, J.J., Munger, P.F., and Kranzler, G.D., "The Effects of Selected Counseling and Remedial Techniques on Underachieving Elementary School Students," *Journal of Consulting Psychology,* 12 (1965), 384–87.
56. Yates, Aubrey J., *Behavior Therapy.* New York: Wiley, 1970.
57. Zaccaria, Joseph S., and Moses, Harold A., *Facilitating Human Development Through Reading: The Use of Bibliotherapy in Teaching and Counseling.* Champaign, Ill.: Stipes Publishing, 1968.

11 Mechanical Methods of Improving Reading

In the 1950s, the subject of the values of mechanical devices for reading improvement was a matter of sharp debate among reading practitioners. Opinions varied from the stance that machines would solve practically all reading difficulties to the view that such devices had nothing to offer the reading teacher. Despite the furor and a good deal of negative research evidence that we review here, the use of reading training instruments has persisted and even increased. Currently we are seeing, with a very slight research basis, a great expansion of machine use in the form of multisensory presentations of materials.

Research interest in these reading training machines and in the outcomes of their use has diminished greatly. Researchers as well as reading teachers seem to have formed their opinions, either pro or con, and are no longer interested in proving their viewpoints. In fact, most present-day users of these devices seem utterly unaware of the mass of evidence of two decades ago, or even of any of the basic facts about machine training. They accept without question the claims of today's hucksters of machines for permanent improvement of rate, elimination of subvocalization and regressions, increase in perceptual span, and so on.

Mechanical methods of improving rate of reading do have a place in remedial treatment. Some types of machines can be effective for certain types of pupils, with particular difficulties with rate and flexibility of rate. Transfer of the reading speed achieved on the machine to book reading is not usually equivalent, nor are the gains after training permanently maintained. But some pupils do learn to vary their rate with purpose and difficulty of the material and consequently learn to read more efficiently.

In reviewing these studies of machine training for rate improvement, seek answers to these questions:

1. What does it seem that machines can and cannot do for students?

2. Which rate training devices seem to be most defensible in that they simulate the normal act of reading?

3. For what types of pupils and for what purposes might you employ some of the training devices reviewed here?

IT IS APPARENT from even a cursory review of the reports of users of mechanical devices to improve rate of reading that such instruments seem to have certain values. Among the major claims are gains in speed of reading and the improvement of eye-movement characteristics as the elimination of regressions, reduction of the duration of fixations, increase in perceptual span, and reduction of the number of fixations. More recently, such claims have shifted from the emphasis upon eye movements to stress on possible motivational values. Finally, certain miscellaneous advantages are claimed, as reduction of vocalization, a mind-set for breaking away from slow reading habits, and attention reinforcement.

In 1943 and 1946 respectively, Traxler (46) and Tinker (44) reviewed intensively the values of reading training by mechanical devices. Their conclusions were largely negative in that they saw no justification for devices intended to train eye movements, and little contribution of mechanical methods to the broad act of reading. We have attempted here to review the literature reporting the results of controlled reading reported in studies subsequent to the two earlier reviews. It will be necessary to refer to some of those cited by Tinker and Traxler because they bear significantly upon the validity of a number of the claims offered. However, wherever possible, we shall attempt to interpret and evaluate current claims on the basis of current research.

MECHANICAL TRAINING AND RATE OF READING

The primary purpose of most reading training devices is improvement of rate. Many studies are reported to support this aim and to prove its accomplishment, but, as we shall see, they leave many questions unanswered. We do not know, conclusively, how permanent any rate gain resulting from mechanical training is. We cannot be certain how this approach compares in efficiency of effort or time with other methods. We do not know its comparative values alone or in conjunction with other approaches. We are not sure of its specific values for word recognition, comprehension, or other discrete reading skills.

---

*This chapter is adapted from George D. Spache, "A Rationale for Mechanical Methods of Improving Reading," in *7th Annual Yearbook of the Southwest Reading Conference,* 1958, Oscar S. Causey, editor, by permission of the copyright owner, the National Reading Conference.

Many of the current research studies of the results of mechanical training are poorly constructed, inadequately controlled, or statistically evaluated; hence, they are pointless or at best inconclusive. Studies by Allen (1), the Air Force (34), Anderson (3), Barbe (4), Bellows (7), Causey (10), Fiehler (15), Jones (20), Reach and Dotson (35), Smith and Tate (41), Staton and Maize (42), and several studies by Witty (54, 55) used mixed programs involving several other training approaches in addition to the mechanical. All showed gains in rate of reading, but the contribution of the mechanical device, if any, cannot be evaluated. Typical of the equivocal results obtained in some of these studies is the report by Allen. In his study the tachistoscope was considered least valuable by the participating officers. When a drastic cut in the use of this device was made in a subsequent class, this group showed even greater gains in rate and comprehension than earlier groups did. Just what these results prove is difficult to evaluate. Thus all of these studies fail to answer conclusively any of the basic questions concerning the values of mechanical training other than that it apparently contributes to increase of rate.

Comparative evidence that the gain resulting from use of mechanical aids is greater than that obtained by other methods is also lacking. Six studies that bear upon this question have been found: Sutherland (43) was unable to prove that tachistoscopic training for increased perceptual span results in increased rate. Weber (48) obtained similar gains in tachistoscopic and workbook training groups in rate and comprehension. Wedeen (49) found that a rate controller produced rate gains superior to those found in a group trained by workbook and lecture methods or those in an untrained control group. The superior rate gains for the rate controller group were present in a test using the machine but not in common reading tests. Thus Wedeen's results may truly indicate that practice on the rate controller results in ability to read faster when using this aid, not that the mechanical training transfers its effects in toto to ordinary reading. Westover (50) found equal gains from mechanically controlled reading and motivated practice in workbook-type exercises. Wilson and Leavell (53) found increases in rate of narrative reading for groups trained by the Reading Rate Accelerator or by accelerator plus tachistoscope. Groups trained by tachistoscope alone, by a reading skills program, by guided free reading, or by a study skills program gained less.

Other comparative studies are available but tend to yield somewhat contradictory results. Barry and Smith (5) found no significant differences among seven groups employing slightly different materials and methods. All showed appreciable improvement on reading tests. The group using the Iowa films showed gains similar to that in a control group in which "no special treatment" was used. If we may understand that the control group was given no actual reading training, then in this experiment the use of Iowa films appeared to produce no more gain than normal maturation. In a very carefully controlled study, Freeburne (16) contrasted rate gains resulting from perceptual span training, perceptual speed practice, and no formal training. The experimental groups did not show any more gain than the control group did when tested by several reading tests or by a test using the tachistoscope. Another study by Glock (18) contrasted two different types of film presentation with a control group given motivated practice. Like Freeburne, Glock found that teacher variances were more significant than method variances. No one method was best in the hands of all teachers. Lewis (23) compared eye-movement training with lectures and motivated reading. The latter group showed significantly greater gains in rate. Manolakes (25) found superior rate gains in groups trained by rate controller than by this device plus a tachistoscope. Measurements of eye movement characteristics failed to show that the combined training contributed more than the rate controller alone. Thompson (45) found significantly greater gains in rate from a rather stereotyped book-centered course than from a rate controller or even no reading training, with no changes or differences in comprehension among his groups. Surprisingly, losses in flexibility in adapting rate to the difficulty of material was greatest in the book-centered group.

Colvin's (11) recent study contrasted combinations of films, lectures, and programmed text but found no difference in reading or grade point average after twelve weeks among college students. Wooster (56) found no contribution to rate or comprehension in a rate controller as a supplementary part of a course in reading and study skills. Both experimental groups, with or without controller, and the control group given no training, showed significant gains in rate but losses in comprehension. There appears to be little evidence in these various studies that use of any of several mechanical devices consistently produces greater improvement in rate (in brief training programs) than do other approaches. While the devices do seem to contribute to rate increases in longer, more carefully controlled experiments, this is often a reflection of teacher variance and, perhaps, of motivation, as much as a result of the method.

MECHANICAL TRAINING AND WORD RECOGNITION

One final group of studies is available bearing on the values of the tachistoscope in improving accuracy of word recognition. Unfortunately for our purposes, all three studies are so poorly planned that their results are inconclusive. Anderson's (3) results indicate that 95 percent of the seventh graders learned the words offered in a twelve-week period of training. The lack of a control group, however, leaves no indication of the relative efficiency of this learning. Davis (13) conducted digit training with a tachistoscope in a first-grade class. In a posttraining word recognition test, the class median was then compared with previous class medians on a second, different reading test, not given to the experimental group. The confused planning of this experiment leaves us with no real means of evaluating the results. Renshaw's (36) training of word recognition by tachistoscope among first graders is similarly inconclusive. Thus these three studies of the possible values of mechanical training for word recognition yield no usable facts.

MECHANICAL TRAINING AND EYE MOVEMENTS

A subordinate goal often offered for mechanical programs is the training of eye movements. We shall consider in detail the validity of such training for eye movement characteristics such as regression, fixation duration, perceptual span, and number of fixations. Inherent in the goal, though, is the assumption that regular eye movements determine good reading or, as a corollary, that regular eye movements are characteristic of efficient readers. This basic assumption and its corollary are both suspect. Sisson (39) and Walker (47) have shown that there is little evidence of habit or pattern of rhythmical eye movements (same number of fixations per line) in either easy or difficult material or in long or short lines. Ledbetter (22) found significant differences in eye movements for reading in various content fields. Siebert (38) found practically no relationship between "good eye movements" and "good" comprehension in varied subject matter fields. Anderson's (2) comparison of good and poor readers concluded that two important determinants of regularity in eye movements were difficulty of the material read and the purpose of the reading. Fixation frequency, regression frequency, and pause duration increase for both good and poor readers when handling difficult material, although good readers show greater flexibility in adjusting to this material. Tinker (44) cited a half-dozen older studies indicating, in his words, "that oculomotor reactions are exceedingly flexible and quickly reflect any variation in the central processes of perception, apprehension and assimilation." These studies are confirmed by Gilbert's study (17) in which eye movement records showed relationships to intelligence and reading test scores in meaningful material.

These indications might be summarized simply as showing that, first, eye movements reflect the difficulties of the reader in sight word recognition, word analysis, and comprehension. There is little reason to believe that irregular eye movements cause poor reading. Secondly, irregularities are present in the eye movement patterns of both good and poor readers, particularly when they are attempting to read difficult or unfamiliar material. Gilbert again stresses the fact that eye movement records do not accurately predict reading test performances (17). They do not discriminate adequately between good and poor readers. Perfect, rhythmical eye movement patterns exist only theoretically, or possibly when one is reading fluently in extremely simple material. Therefore, the concept that eye movements should be subjected to training in the hope of improving reading is extremely tenuous.

Regressions

Eye movements in the opposite direction to that necessary for the nature of the language being read are often considered indicative of faulty reading and as worthy of correction. Contrary to this common interpretation, Bayle (6) shows that regressions are not always a reflection of lack of word recognition or of word-by-word reading. She distinguishes six types of regressions: (1) after first fixation in the line; (2) within the line, when the span of vision is overreached; (3) for verification; (4) during word analysis; (5) for phrase analysis; and (6) for reexamination of a whole line. She considers many of these types essential to accurate word recognition and thorough comprehension. In another study of the eye movements of good and poor readers during oral reading by Fairbanks (14), it was found that regressions apparently do not cause errors in reading, but rather reflect errors that are central (intellectual) in origin. Fairbanks's observations support the essentiality of such types of regressions as the last three noted by Bayle above. Other experimenters indicate that the number of regressions is indicative of the demands made by the material (style, content, vocabulary, and the like) as well as of the reactions and attributes of the reader such as intelligence, purpose for reading, readiness for ideas or vocabulary, fatigue, and interest.

If these observations are accepted, the complete elimination of regressions by mechanical training might well result in more superficial reading with actual increase in dependence upon context for word meanings, and decrease in detailed as well as general comprehension, a result that has been observed in several studies of the outcomes of such training. The reduction of those types of regressions that do not contribute to more accurate reading, cannot, in our opinion, be attempted successfully without also influencing more essential types.

Duration of Fixation

The average fixation time is another eye movement characteristic that has been extensively studied. In his large-scale study, Gilbert (17) found that the small relationships between average duration of fixation and reading test scores were highest in the primary grades, diminishing markedly thereafter. Buswell (9) suggested that this trait is possibly physiologically determined, since it decreases with age without training and is fairly constant at a given age for a given individual. Perry and Whitlock (31) consider the duration of fixation dependent upon vocabulary level, familiarity with the content of the reading matter, and other elements of comprehension.

It is probably true that the average duration of fixations is slightly reduced as rate of reading increases. This speeding up occurs quite as readily, however, as a result of maturation or ordinary classroom instruction as it does as a result of mechanical training. Extended practice in perceptual speed or reading constant amounts of digits or prose at increasing speeds does not appear to be highly economical of time and expense.

Perceptual Span

Probably the most frequently mentioned goal of mechanical training is increase in perceptual span. Aside from the previously cited studies (Freeburne, Glock, Sutherland, Westover, Weber), which obtained negative results in rate of reading from perceptual span training, a number of writers have questioned the relationships of the trait to good reading. Luckiesh and Moss (24) claim that perceptual span has never been shown to be related to good reading. Span, as measured by the tachistoscope, predicts eye movements in the act of reading very inadequately, according to Robinson (37). The studies of good and poor readers by Anderson (2), Fairbanks (14), Sisson (39), Sommerfield (40), Sutherland (43), Walker (47), and others cited by Tinker (44) indicate that size of perceptual span does not discriminate accurately between degrees of reading ability. Perry and Whitlock (32) point out that size of span is not a constant characteristic. Spans overlap in the act of reading, and—as they discovered in attempting to create reading films—even slow readers appear to use phrases of greater than minimum size.

The terminology used by many writers in this area is somewhat confused. Perceptual span, recognition span, and visual span are used interchangeably, even though they are not synonymous. Visual span refers to the four to eight characters perceived sharply in the area of foveal vision.

Recognition, comprehension, or perceptual span refers to the twenty-four to twenty-five letters of 10-point type which, although they are perceived by less sensitive areas of the retina, are more or less successfully recognized. In connected reading, perceptual span is usually about eight letters for normal readers.

In effect, perceptual span training attempts to increase the accuracy (and often the speed) with which the student recognizes characters seen vaguely in the periphery of the fovea. As Perry and Whitlock point out, this training is frequently highly artificial. The four to eight letters forming the normal perceptual span do not correspond to the conventional division of phrases at a point between words, or in "natural," logical, or thought groups determined grammatically. Thus it appears that much perceptual span training includes more matter than the reader usually recognizes in reading connected material. Devices that pressure the student to recognize ever-increasing spans of digits, words, or phrases are unrealistic about the span actually present in continuous reading or the physiological limits of the visual span or the perceptual span.

A recent experiment by Olsen and Amble (29) introduced several currently popular procedures, in addition to a film presentation, to influence what they term perceptual span. They employed a commercial Phrase Reading Development Program that exposes phrases on film. The theoretical justification for the device is that such training will increase rate of reading and induce reading by phrases. They divided their 232 fourth-grade pupils into four experimental and one control group. One group was exposed to the films appropriate for intermediate pupils with no reinforcement by the teacher. A second group was stimulated to greater attention by requiring them to press a switch for each phrase exposed on the film. A third group, called the contingency group, received maximum social recognition from their peers, from the teacher, and from charts of their progress. A fourth group was submitted to a dual treatment involving the attention-promoting and contingency procedures. There were no significant differences among the four groups on the Phrase Reading Test supplied by the manufacturer. The attention group, however, made substantial gains in both an immediate and a delayed posttest of paragraph comprehension. The group given only the film presentation, as would be the procedure in most situations, showed a decrement in reading comprehension of 1.6 grades at the conclusion of the commercial program when compared with a control group.

Controlled fixation training as used in the Controlled Reader, the Harvard Films (32), or the Perceptoscope filmstrips (30) are examples of perceptual span training that is realistically oriented to the normal reader's usual span of perception. The words exposed in each controlled "fixation" overlap from one exposure to the next. Thus the student is not forced into attempting to use a perceptual span that is unnaturally artificial or too great. In our opinion, this approach is more defensible than the use of constantly increasing spans or fixed "fixations" that are constantly greater than the reader would normally use.

There is evidence in these studies to clarify some of the contradictory or confused results of many experimental attempts to increase span. The lack of marked relationship between perceptual span measured tachistoscopically and reading rate may well be due to the lack of correspondence between perceptual spans used in training and those present in continuous reading. The failure of many experiments in increasing perceptual span to produce significant gains in rate of reading (16, 18, and so on) may be similarly explained.

In summary, it appears from this discussion of perceptual span, that training as now most commonly used, may be psychologically and visually faulty. We shall attempt later to interpret why some of these training programs appear to affect reading rate even though they do not effect a transfer from tachistoscopic perceptual span to reading perceptual span.

Number of Fixations

A fourth subordinate goal of eye movement training devices is often the reduction of the number of fixations. Tinker (44) considers this trait to be highly related to reading speed, but the evidence of Gilbert (17), Anderson (2), and a number of other studies does not confirm this opinion. Needham (28) and Sisson (39), for example, found little consistency in this aspect among good readers. Anderson (2) found no reliable difference in fixation frequency for good and poor readers in difficult material. Morse et al. (26) also found no consistent variation with the difficulty of the material read but recognized the importance of individual or genetic factors. They pointed out that lack of adjustment to varying aspects of the reading material is more characteristic of immature or poor readers. Developmental, individual, or maturational factors apparently far outweigh the factor of difficulty of material. Morse interprets his results to cast grave doubt on the advisability of pacing devices. He believes that training all children in a fixed pattern of eye movements would operate in opposition to the reading process as we find it functioning in children. In working with good readers of college freshman age, Walker (47) found significant differences in fixation frequency between passages varying from easy to difficult, and in reading motivated by different purposes.

Anderson's poor college readers (2) did not vary in fixation frequency according to purpose as much as Walker's group did. But fixation frequency did vary more with purpose than with changes in difficulty.

It appears that fixation frequency is not highly related to reading speed. Differences between good and poor readers are not consistently large or significant. While some individuals, particularly good readers, tend to be consistent or tend to show a habitual fixation pattern, fixation frequency is markedly influenced by the purposes of the reader and a number of his individual characteristics. Difficulty of the material, familiarity with the content, and even format also influence the pattern of fixations. If these elements of the reading situation and the reader modify fixation frequency to a significant degree, training intended to produce a fixed pattern seems unrealistic.

OTHER VALUES OF MECHANICAL TRAINING

There are a number of minor claims made for the use of mechanical devices in reading improvement programs. To our knowledge, none of these has been subjected to scientific scrutiny. Some devices are acclaimed because they provide the opportunity and physical setting for more concentration on the act of reading by providing a point of mental and visual focus, and by eliminating extraneous stimuli such as light and noise. Many clinicians have observed the rapt attention with which their students follow the operations of almost any reading training device.

Certain devices are said to reduce vocalization or lip and tongue movements, since the rapidity of the presentation of the reading matter permits little opportunity for the voco-motor speech processes to appear. Some clinicians believe that rapid reading cannot be achieved without the almost complete extirpation of speech movements. It is undoubtedly true that if gross speech movements accompany silent reading, rate of reading is depressed almost to the level of speaking rates. As every primary teacher knows, elimination of gross speech movements tends to produce true silent reading and to increase silent reading rate. However, there is a belief in some sources that subvocal speech movements cannot, or perhaps should not, be entirely eliminated. To employ mechanical training devices with this latter aim in mind is questionable in their opinion.

Pilant (33) mentions another goal of mechanical training that is becoming increasingly recognized. He says:

> This awe of the machine does help create a proper mind-set for breaking with old habits and putting on new virtues. But it also tends to mislead the mediocre into believing that the machine will do what the mind cannot or the will is too lazy to attempt.

In this same strain, Wilking (51) has noted that many college students do not read rapidly because they are afraid that if they attempt to speed up, they will lose comprehension. But when training devices compel them to progress at reasonable rates, they soon discover that they are still able to comprehend. He also notes the values of intrinsic motivation, attention-getting novelty, and the blandishments of the scientific approach. Other clinicians have noted that mechanical devices can provide supportive therapy for the insecure slow reader; they give reassurance of successful comprehension at higher rates for the perfectionistic slow reader; and they help produce rather dramatic and sudden gains for the habitual slow reader of high academic potential and good language facility.

Perry (31) also stresses the students' confidence in improvement in the skills trained by the device. He says:

> We believe that this aspect of confidence in improvement may explain why devices which give evidence of improvement of "visual span" (to students whose visual span is already larger than they need for the best of reading) produce the results they do produce in the hands of teachers who are themselves persuaded and persuasive.

MECHANICAL TRAINING AND PERMANENT GAINS IN RATE

Several studies give evidence that the rate gains achieved by mechanical training have some degree of permanency (34, 8, 12, 27, 48). The retention of improvement in rate (long-range improvement divided by initial improvement) varies from 51 percent to 84 percent six to twelve months after training. Comprehension scores remained fairly constant in these same studies. If these results are fairly typical of training courses using mechanical devices, they offer a partial answer to the question of the permanent values of such training.

In reviewing the literature on the use of mechanical devices for reading improvement, we have found little evidence that various mechanical devices produce greater improvement in rate of reading than other approaches. Training intended to modify eye movement characteristics such as regression, duration of fixation, perceptual span, or number of fixations is highly questionable. These eye movement characteristics may not be amenable to training since they, like reading success, are significantly determined by the nature of the reading material and attributes of the reader. Other goals of mechanical training—such as motivation and reinforcement of attention or concentration—are as yet unsubstantiated by research evidence, although they are supported by clinical evidence and the opinions of skilled observers.

WHAT DOES MECHANICAL TRAINING ACCOMPLISH?

Since mechanical training programs do apparently contribute to relatively permanent growth of rate of reading, it is not appropriate to dismiss their use as insignificant. Given this value, it is possible that, as Perry and Whitlock have suggested, the devices may be modified to produce even more significant results. If the training does not directly modify eye movements, what, then, does it do? How does it produce changes in reading speed? Could these changes be accelerated by modification of the mechanical approaches now in common use?

We should like to offer several hypotheses regarding the training materials and the emphases of the common mechanical training program. The review of the literature has shown that much of the training material (digits, phrases, words) is arbitrarily chosen. It is offered in gradually increasing spans and at increasing speeds of recognition. These arbitrary training groups, which are often too great for true apprehension, are considerably larger than the perceptual spans commonly used by normal readers. Yet this practice, with widening phrases at increasing speeds, does appear to contribute to acceleration of rate. How does practice with this material (which, in the final analysis, does not actually resemble that used in the act of reading) promote more rapid reading? Is it possible that such training is, in effect, merely training in quicker visual discrimination? Does some transfer occur to the act of reading because the student is trained in more rapid and more accurate recognition of word gestalts, or in the reduction of cues needed for word recognition?

WHAT SHOULD MECHANICAL TRAINING EMPHASIZE?

We should like to suggest that mechanical training is successful in accelerating rate because the student is, in effect, being taught to read with fewer cues, to guess more readily what he sees peripherally, to overcome the caution exhibited in slow or word-by-word reading, and to be more confident in dealing with vague or indistinct portions of words, not because of any actual increase in perceptual span or other changes in eye movements.

It is now generally accepted that reading beyond the most primitive levels is achieved by the recognition of word wholes or a group of characters. Gray's (19) research in reading in a variety of languages proves that, regardless of the nature of the language or the type of early training, adult or good readers read by recognition of groups of symbols. In our language, reading is accomplished by recognition of word shapes or gestalts, identified by the gross shape, the initial letters, letters that protrude above the line, the context, and combinations of these and other minimal cues.

Recently, training in visual discrimination has been emphasized in reading readiness and beginning reading programs. This training has been offered to facilitate quicker and more accurate recognition, first, of geometric forms and figures and, later, of words (50). In work with retarded readers, some reading clinics emphasize similar training in visual discrimination, in recognition of words by configurations, and in other visual cues. Many other studies, such as that of Krise (21), have stressed the significance of accurate visual perception in successful reading. Collectively, this evidence seems to indicate the values of training in more rapid and more accurate visual discrimination. There is sound basis for stressing such training as a direct contribution to quick recognition of words and groups of words.

Certain cautions must be observed in selecting students for the perceptual training. We do not share the opinion that practically all persons can be taught to read more rapidly. We recommend permitting only the following types of readers to enter this program:

1. Those scoring low in rate, but distinctly higher in comprehension of the same material, that is, the slow, cautious, retentive reader.
2. Those scoring higher in an untimed power test of comprehension than in a timed test or in comprehension of timed material.
3. Those scoring distinctly higher in the untimed administration of a general vocabulary test than in timed administration.
4. Those clinically identified as habitually slow readers, lacking in flexibility, who tend to use the same rate in most materials but who show acceptable comprehension.

We recommend excluding from this program any students whose reading performances do not meet the first three criteria and those showing any coordination or fusional difficulties or tendencies to suppression. The Binocular Reading Test can detect these visual difficulties.

Perry and Whitlock (31) offer several other criteria for a mechanical training program that are relevant at this point. They suggest that the device should first produce striking evidence of the student's improvement in whatever skills are demanded. Secondly, improvement must be readily associated in the student's mind with the regular reading process. They imply that the training must resemble as closely as possible the subjective experiences of regular reading. These similarities should be present, they suggest, in the use of continuous material, permitting normal return sweep; with readability controlled to discourage regression; with rate controlled; with material constant in difficulty so that students may observe improvement in rate; with length and duration of fixation controlled; and with gradients of acuity in peripheral vision. Finally, to insure transfer, they suggest that the skills demanded should objectively resemble those that it is desired to train. Although these criteria were evolved to aid in the development of an improved version of the Harvard Reading Films, they are applicable also to our suggestions here.

OTHER PROBLEMS INHERENT IN CONTROLLED READING

Other questions that arise from the machine approach are the possibility of visual strain or visual fatigue, and the fact that a great deal of machine training is performed at far-point. Many of those who direct rate training programs with tachistoscopes or various controllers seem unaware of some of the inherent dangers to vision. When a darkened room is used, there is often too great a contrast between the lighted area on the screen and the rest of the room. This contrast is even greater with some types of devices in which the lighted area of the screen flashes on and off. In time these conditions may produce a type of visual strain known as retinal shock, as well as fatigue in other parts of the visual mechanism. Newer types of screens of greater reflective value could eliminate the need for a darkened room, but these screens are not yet widely used.

Users of controlling devices tend to ignore the implications of constant practice at far-point. Reading at this distance is—as we have pointed out several times—ordinarily quite appropriate for young children who are, for the most part, normally farsighted at this age. Accurate focus for sustained periods of reading is visually easier at far-point for such pupils, or for other individuals who are farsighted. But the same conditions do not hold for myopic children or most adults or those of limited acuity. For these, constant practice at far-point may be fatiguing or somewhat of a strain. Myopia, or nearsightedness, increases markedly during the school years until it affects perhaps 30–40 percent of the population at high school age. Thus it is apparent that machine training in reading at far-point may be relatively undesirable for a relatively large part of the population exposed to it. This problem could be solved by a careful visual screening test of all individuals who are to be subjected to this type of training. Those who are likely to experience difficulty in achieving a sharp focus at distance should be excused from the program, or they should be trained by the use of near-point tachistoscopes or by the use of pacing devices at near-point.

Another visual phenomenon ignored by those who use the controller type of machine is the significance of the after-image in aiding recall. Many controllers expose their material for a fraction of a second. An after-image of the digits or words persists before the eyes of the reader after the actual exposure of the material has closed. This after-image enables the reader to recall more than he was really able to read during the exposure. Thus a false impression is created of the amount or span of material read during the exposure time. This after-image is not present during the normal act of continuous reading, for different words are presented to the eye in each successive fixation with such short intervals of time intervening between fixations as to prevent a lingering after-image. The lack of an after-image may be a partial explanation of the reader's inability to transfer the span of recognition presumed to be present in reading tachistoscopically to ordinary reading.

One controlled reading device, the Tach-X of the Educational Developmental Laboratories, attempts to control the misleading effect of the after-image. Its projection simulates the action of the eye by bringing the training material into a sharp focus, as it would be seen in a fixation, and then causing it to recede to a blurred image. Thus, since the screen is not completely blank between successive exposures, the formation of an after-image is hindered. Other controlled rate training devices that use films or filmstrips avoid this after-image problem by projecting an entire page of material in which successive phrases are lighted up momentarily. Thus the act of normal reading of groups of words in too rapid succession for the formation of after-images is simulated. These devices that imitate natural reading are probably preferable to others, since they do not delude the reader or his teacher into false conclusions about improvement in rate or span of recognition.

Any device that exposes reading material in a constant fixed span introduces an element of artificiality, in our opinion. Ordinarily, reading does not progress in fixation spans of a constant size, but rather the spans vary from

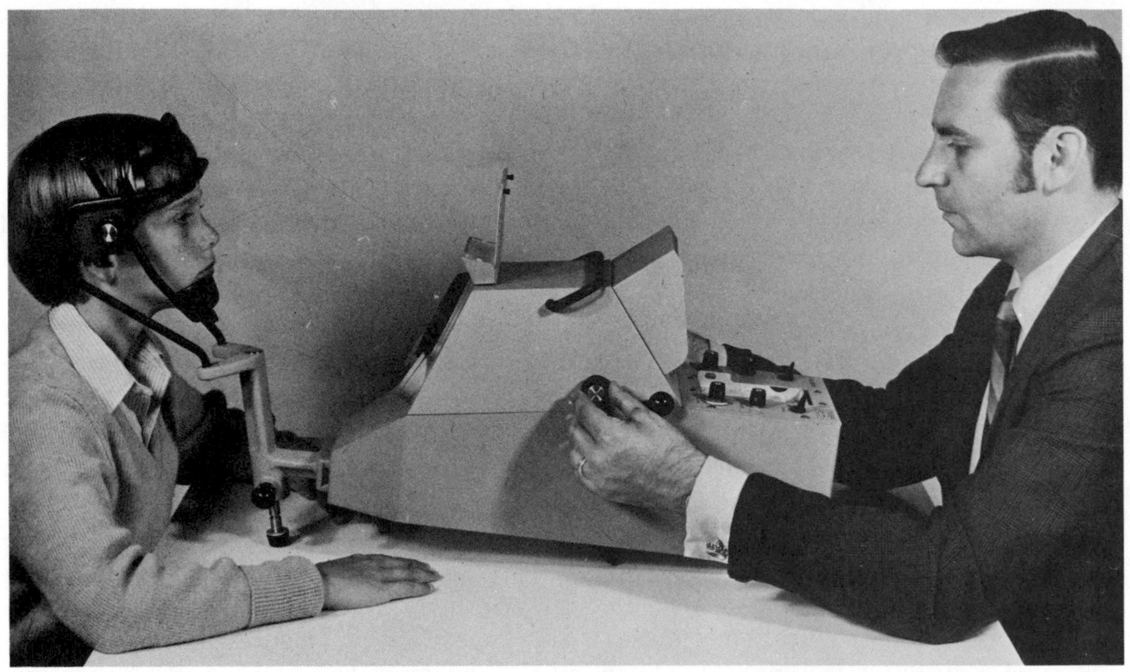

The Reading Eye Camera II
(Reprinted with permission from *Eye-Movement Analysis with the Reading Eye II* by Helen Frackenpohl Morris. New York: McGraw-Hill, Inc. 1973.)

one fixation to another. Difficulties of word recognition, word meaning, and comprehension usually affect eye movements by increasing the number of fixations at any point of difficulty, thus reducing the span of recognition. Many training materials used in controlled reading devices ignore this fact in presenting artificially constant spans of material. For the poor reader in the group, this type of training may be extremely frustrating, or may tend to disorganize his reading rate and comprehension. One solution to the inflexibility of this type of training lies either in using training materials that are simple enough for the poorest reader in the group or in homogeneous grouping from which students with below-average vocabulary or comprehension skills are eliminated. By these steps, the limitations of the device using fixed spans may be more closely fitted to the capacities of the students. Of course, an even easier solution is the selection for the training program of those devices that permit reasonable variations in fixation spans or have maximum flexibility in the rate of presentation of the reading materials.

In our experience, any device that presents material in some sort of an artificially fixed span becomes extremely difficult to follow when the rate of reading reaches approximately 300 words per minute. Poor readers who have gradually been trained to read at this speed with the aid of the machine may become used to the flickering. But good readers who read easily at this and greater rates are prone to react very negatively. For practice at these higher rates of speed, pacing devices or controllers that permit the reader to formulate his own fixation spans are preferable to those employing fixed spans.

There is one other element in machine training at far-point that seems to be ignored by most followers of this approach. This is the difference in the angle of vision or span of vision at near-point (14 inches) and at far-point (20 feet). The greater area visible at far-point makes possible the reading of a wide span of materials (four to five words of twenty to twenty-five letters) in a single fixation. At near-point, this span is reduced by the marked convergence of the eyes to approximately one word of about five letters per fixation, according to the norms for high school and college students on The Reading Eye eye-movement camera. It is true that at reading distance more than one word or five letters is actually visible, but peripheral images are so unclear that the normal reader is not aided by them but refixates approximately word by word. This simple comparison of the breadth of usable visual span at near-point with that at far-point should help clarify why it is relatively impossible to transfer the reading spans observed in far-point machine training to the act of book reading, even though the habits acquired during such training may promote faster book reading.

LEARNING PROJECT

Collect the advertising material and the manuals for several of the training devices now in the market. Ask also for reprints of any field work or research studies that the distributor can supply. Then compare these devices in terms of the following considerations:

1. Their claims regarding change in eye movement behavior that will be produced.

2. The actual outcomes of classroom and/or clinic use with poor or good readers.

3. The relationship of the claims found in (1) above with the measured outcomes of (2).

4. The degree to which the device simulates or permits the normal act of continuous reading of a book.

5. The provisions planned in the program to insure transfer of rate with the machine to reading without its assistance.

6. Their respective advantages and limitations, as you see them.

REFERENCES

1. Allen, M. R., "Adult Reading Improvement at an Army Service School," *School and Society,* 74 (1951), 72–76.
2. Anderson, Irving H., "Studies in the Eye-Movements of Good and Poor Readers," *Psychological Monographs,* 48 (1937), 1–35.
3. Anderson, J. A., "Seventh-grade Reading Program Lufkin Junior High School, Lufkin, Texas," *Educational Developmental Laboratory Newsletter,* 1, No. 1 (October 1956).
4. Barbe, Walter B., "The Effectiveness of Work in Remedial Reading at the College Level," *Journal of Educational Psychology,* 43 (1952), 229–37.
5. Barry, Robert E., and Smith, Paul E., "An Experiment in Ninth-grade Reading Improvement," *Journal of Educational Psychology,* 45 (1954), 407–14.
6. Bayle, Evalyn, "The Nature and Causes of Regressive Eye-Movements in Reading," *Journal of Experimental Education,* 11 (1942), 16–36.
7. Bellows, Carol S., and Rush, Carl H., "Reading Abilities of Business Executives," *Journal of Applied Psychology,* 36 (1952), 1–4.
8. Bryant, Norman Dale, "Follow-up Testing on Illinois Bell Reading Training Group," Perceptual Development Laboratories, St. Louis, 1957. Mimeographed.
9. Buswell, Guy Thomas, *Fundamental Reading Habits: A Study of Their Development.* Supplementary Educational Monographs, No. 21. Chicago: University of Chicago Press, 1922.
10. Causey, Oscar S., "A Developmental Reading Program for College Students," in *1st Yearbook,* Southwest Reading Conference, 1952, 27–29.
11. Colvin, Charles P., "A Study of Differing Treatments in a College Reading Program," *Reading World,* 11 (March 1972), 227–31.
12. Cosper, Russell, and Kephart, N. C., "Retention of Reading Skills," *Journal of Educational Research,* 49 (1955), 211–16.
13. Davis, Louise Farwell, et al., "First Grade Recognition Program," *Monograph on Language Arts,* No. 47. Evanston: Row, Peterson, 1946.
14. Fairbanks, G., "The Relations between Eye-Movements and Voice in the Oral Reading of Good and Poor Silent Readers," *Psychological Monographs,* 48 (1937), 78–107.
15. Fiehler, Rudolph, "The Reading Improvement Program at Southern State College," in *1st Yearbook,* Southwest Reading Conference, 1952, 19–20.
16. Freeburne, Cecil Max, "The Influence of Training in Perceptual Span and Perceptual Speed upon Reading Ability," *Journal of Educational Psychology,* 40 (October 1949), 321–52.
17. Gilbert, Luther C., "Functional Motor Efficiency of the Eyes and Its Relation to Reading," *University of California Publications in Education,* 11 (1953), 159–232.
18. Glock, Marvin D., "The Effect upon Eye-Movement and Reading Rate at College

Level of Three Methods of Training," *Journal of Educational Psychology,* 40 (February 1949), 93–105.

19. Gray, William S., *The Teaching of Reading and Writing.* UNESCO Monographs on Fundamental Education. Chicago: Scott, Foresman, 1956.
20. Jones, Nellie F., "Motorized Reading Project," *English Journal,* 40 (1951), 313–39.
21. Krise, E. Morley, "Reversals in Reading: A Problem in Space Perception?" *Elementary School Journal,* 49 (March 1949), 278–84.
22. Ledbetter, Frances Graham, "Reading Reactions for Varied Types of Subject-Matter: An Analytical Study of the Eye-Movements of Eleventh Grade Pupils," *Journal of Educational Research,* 41 (1947), 102–15.
23. Lewis, Norman, "An Investigation into Comparable Results Obtained from Two Methods of Increasing Reading Speed Among Adults," *College English,* 11 (1949), 152–56.
24. Luckiesh, Mathew, and Moss, Frank K., *Reading as a Visual Task.* New York: Van Nostrand, 1942.
25. Manolakes, George, "The Effects of Tachistoscopic Training in an Adult Reading Program," *Journal of Applied Psychology,* 36 (1952), 410–12.
26. Morse, William C., Ballantine, Francis A., and Dixon, W. Robert, "Studies in the Psychology of Reading," *University of Michigan Monographs in Education,* No. 4, April 1951.
27. Mullins, Cecil J., and Mowry, H. W., "How Long Does Reading Improvement Last?" *Personnel Journal,* 32 (1954), 416–17.
28. Needham, George, "Research Studies," as cited by Perry and Whitlock (32).
29. Olsen, Roger, and Amble, Bruce, "The Modification of Perceptual Span: An Experimental Study," *Journal of Reading Behavior,* 3 (Winter 1970–71), 42–50.
30. *The Perceptoscope.* St. Louis: Perceptual Development Laboratories, 1955.
31. Perry, William G., and Whitlock, Charles P., "A Clinical Rationale for a Reading Film," *Harvard Educational Review,* 24 (1954), 6–27.
32. Perry, William G., and Whitlock, Charles P., *Harvard University Reading Films, Series Two.* Cambridge: Harvard University Press, 1948.
33. Pilant, Richard, "Reading Improvement Programs," *English Journal,* 31 (1942), 235–37.
34. "Preliminary Evidence on the Permanency of Rate Increases Following Intensive Training in a Reading Laboratory." Air Command and Staff School, U.S. Air Force. Mimeographed.
35. Reach, D. D., and Dotson, F. D., "Developmental Reading for High School and College Students," *American School Board Journal,* 130, 36–38.
36. Renshaw, Samuel, "The Influence of Tachistoscopic Training at Far Point on the Scholastic Achievement of First Grade Children," *Psychological Optics,* 1945.
37. Robinson, Francis P., "The Tachistoscope as a Measure of Reading Perception," *American Journal of Psychology,* 46 (1934), 132–35.
38. Siebert, Earl W., "Reading Reactions for Varied Types of Subject Matter," *Journal of Experimental Education,* 12 (September 1943), 37–44.
39. Sisson, E. D., "Habits of Eye-Movement in Reading," *Journal of Educational Psychology,* 28 (1937), 437–50.
40. Sommerfield, Roy E., "An Evaluation of the Tachistoscope in Reading Improvement Programs," in *What Colleges are Doing in Reading Improvement Programs,* Oscar S. Causey, editor, 3rd Yearbook Southwest Reading Conference, 1954, 7–25.

41. Smith, Henry P., and Tate, Theodore R., "Improvement in Reading Rate and Comprehension of Subjects Trained with the Tachistoscope," *Journal of Educational Psychology,* 44 (1953), 176–84.
42. Staton, T. F., and Maize, R. C., "Voluntary Reading Improvement Program for Air Force Officers," *School and Society,* 76 (1952), 42–44.
43. Sutherland, Jean, "The Relationship between Perceptual Span and Rate of Reading," *Journal of Educational Psychology,* 37 (1946), 373–80.
44. Tinker, Miles A., "The Study of Eye Movements in Reading," *Psychological Bulletin,* 43 (March 1946), 93–120.
45. Thompson, Warren Craig, "A Book-Centered Course Versus a Machine-Centered Course in Adult Reading Improvement," *Journal of Educational Research,* 49 (1956), 437–45.
46. Traxler, Arthur E., "Value of Controlled Reading: A Summary of Opinion and Research," *Journal of Experimental Education,* 11 (June 1943), 280–92.
47. Walker, R. Y., "A Qualitative Study of the Eye Movements of Good Readers," *American Journal of Psychology,* 51 (1938), 472–81.
48. Weber, C. O., "The Acquisition and Retention of Reading Skills by College Freshmen," *Journal of Educational Psychology,* 30 (1939), 453–60.
49. Wedeen, Shirley U., "Mechanical vs. Non-Mechanical Reading Techniques for College Freshmen," *School and Society,* 79 (1954), 121–23.
50. Westover, Frederick L., *Controlled Eye-Movements versus Practice Exercises in Reading.* Contributions to Education, No. 917. New York: Teachers College, Columbia University, 1946.
51. Wilking, S. Vincent, "The Improvement of Reading Ability in College," *Journal of American Association of College Registrars,* 17 (1942), 183–84.
52. Williams, Gertrude H., "What Does Research Tell Us About Readiness for Beginning Reading?" *Reading Teacher,* 6 (May 1953), 34–40.
53. Wilson, Grace E., and Leavell, Ullin W., "An Experiment with Accelerated Training," *Peabody Journal of Education,* 34 (July 1956), 9–18.
54. Witty, Paul, and Fitzwater, J. P., "An Experiment with Films, Film Readers, and the Magnetic Sound Track Projector," *Elementary English,* 30 (April 1953), 232–41.
55. Witty, Paul, Stolarz, Theodore, and Cooper, William, "Some Results of a Remedial Reading Program for College Students," *School and Society,* 76 (1952), 376–80.
56. Wooster, George F., "An Experimental Study of the Reading Rate Controller," *Journal of Educational Psychology,* 45 (1954), 421–26.

12 Evaluating the Outcomes of Remediation

It may seem paradoxical for the author of these texts on reading disabilities to question seriously the basic values of remedial work. On the surface, there appears little justification for such an inquiry, for almost all reports of treatment programs are optimistic and apparently successful. Moreover, every worker in the field of remediation can recount happy personal experiences engendered by the great appreciation shown by their former students.

But, as we shall see, both these statistical records and the positive feelings of reading teachers are often based on very weak bases. The criteria of gains from treatment are crude and often give false impressions; the size of the gains considered significant is given exaggerated emphasis in many instances. To our knowledge, no one has yet answered the question of what is "normal" gain for a retarded reader under treatment for a given period of time. As a result, almost any degree of gain in a post training reading test is considered to indicate a successful treatment program. Our review of a sizeable number of reports of gains from treatment supports these criticisms.

Certainly the long-range effects of remediation are even more significant than the gains registered immediately after treatment. And like the short-term reports, these effects have generally been assumed to be quite positive. But comparison of the outcomes of twenty-five follow-up studies of disabled readers raises some grave questions regarding the ultimate values of remediation.

In reading this evaluation of remedial work, keep in mind such questions as:

1. Why are the reports of so many treatment programs almost meaningless?
2. What are some of the factors which tend to determine the effectiveness of remediation?
3. What long-term effects, if any, does remedial treatment during elementary or secondary ages seem to have?

MOST OF US who have been active in remediation of reading disabilities for any sizeable period of time are quite certain that such work is fundamentally successful. We see dramatic gains in reading test scores for most of the students that we have treated. They are appreciative of our efforts and even years later laud the help they received (43). They appear to have more positive attitudes toward reading and to have improved in their self-concepts as readers and students. Moreover, these convictions of the efficacy of remediation are constantly being reinforced by the reports of short-term treatments in our literature.

Our purpose in this examination of the outcomes of remediation is to raise the obvious questions that remedial teachers ought to be asking themselves. Such self-probing should query whether there is really evidence of long-term or permanent gain for our students, even for those who perform well in posttraining tests. As remedial teachers, we should also be questioning our methods of self-evaluation of our treatments and of predicting the probable outcomes of remedial training under varying conditions. We should be examining our data to discover what influences or factors in remediation are significantly related to the results that we obtain. In fact, it is difficult to see how any teacher or center can intelligently select pupils for remediation without the information about these modifying factors, if they really want to be efficient and to use their resources wisely. To aid in answering these questions, we have attempted to collate the facts that we could find about the outcomes of remediation.

BASIC PROBLEMS IN EVALUATION

Criteria for Gains

Critics of the reports of what appear to be successful remedial programs point out a number of flaws in the evaluation design as well as in the construction of most of these studies. For example, they see reports of gains for remedial work based on several posttraining reading tests that may give contradictory as well as different results. Typical of these is Bliesmer's (5) comparison of various ways of evaluating remedial gains. According to the Metropolitan Reading Test, gain for a seven-month treatment was a little more than eight months (.83), while the Gates indicated an average gain of over twelve months

(1.28), or about 50 percent more than that obtained in the Metropolitan. If we assume, as most teachers do, that the reading test indicates the level of reading materials that the children can comprehend adequately, what levels do we now use for these pupils—those only six–eight months more difficult than where they started or those a full year harder? About the only conclusion we could derive from data like these is that, if we want to impress our supervisors in the future, we had better use the Gates test. As we have stressed, reading tests are not really comparable and dual testing yields incompatible data.

Bliesmer suggests several other ways of judging remedial results such as the average yearly gain between two successive yearly tests compared with that from the remedial program; and the decrease in the gap between the child's potential (mental age) as a result of remediation. But again there are several questionable assumptions in these procedures. Do we know whether the average pupil grows a full year in test scores in a school year? Or whether his progress from year to year is characterized by continuous growth? First of all, even in a series of correlated reading tests for successive grades, the skills measured may vary dramatically. For example, most primary reading tests do not measure much more than word recognition or sight vocabulary, while intermediate-level and later tests emphasize the reasoning processes of silent comprehension. Comparisons from one of these levels to the next are relatively meaningless, for different aspects of the reading process are being sampled.

Even if we assume that all of Bliesmer's pupils were of intermediate-grade level, and that two forms of the same test were being employed for the measurement of gains, we do not know what is normal yearly increase. Rather we know that there are periods of rapid gains in reading skill and plateaus of growth during the school year as well as over all the years in school. Only in the extrapolated norms for reading tests do pupils seem to grow at a steady rate. Hopkins and Bracht (21) showed that pupil scores were only moderately stable in word recognition in the primary grades, and better in vocabulary than comprehension in the intermediate–junior high levels. For example, most of the gains each school year, as shown by repeated testing, occur in the first six months or so, relatively little test gain occurring thereafter; and, in fact, there may be losses for some children. Testing at the end of six–seven months of treatment would really sample the best performances of the year but not really indicate the actual gains by the end of the year or, in other words, not tell us how much gain was normal for these children in a year. Our point is that unless we give the test to children at the same time of the year, we are comparing gains in the most profitable early six–seven months of the treatment program, with what may be less gain for an entire year. Even averaging several years' growth to obtain an estimate of "normal" yearly growth, to compare with that from remediation, is questionable, for those years sampled may be periods of accelerated growth or plateaus of little growth, or of instability in growth (21).

The third way of judging gains from remedial treatment—by the decrease in the gap between achievement level and mental age level—is also faulty. Intelligence and reading achievement are related, to be sure, but not in parallel growth lines. High I.Q. children tend to fall below their mental age, while lower I.Q. pupils tend to exceed that standard. In only a very small proportion of children do reading and intelligence apparently grow at about the same rate. See chapter 4 on the intellectual factor for additional arguments against this practice.

In a continuous comparison of gains in reading over 276 training sessions, Jensen et al. (23) illustrated the irregularity of growth quite dramatically. Tests were given before and after each instructional series, probably of one semester each. Some methods produced gains in rate in each training period; others caused a decrease in rate during each period that was regained in the next series (pacer versus prereading questions). In this experiment, if Jensen had wanted to prove that the pacer was the best way of increasing rate (and decreasing comprehension), he would have ceased instruction after the first series and made the simple comparison of pretests and posttests.

What we are trying to point out is that evaluation of short-term remedial reading programs cannot be done accurately by comparison of pretests and posttests, by comparing gains with "normal" growth, or by noting the decrease in the gap in achievement and mental age. There is no good single criterion with which the pretest to posttest gain may be compared. There are, however, alternative methods that we have discussed in the related chapter on group testing in *Investigating the Issues of Reading Disabilities.* Among these are the use of a formula to find "true" gain by allowing for the initial status in the pretest and the reliability of the test. (This residual gain formula by Rankin and Tracy (34) is described in detail in our book mentioned above.) Other such formulas have been proposed by Cronbach and Furby (12) and several others. Use of these formulas in the dissertations of Dahlke (13) and Tillman (44) has shown that they produce very different interpretations of our remedial results and of the effects of factors influencing such results, as we shall point out later in discussing these factors.

Rankin and Dale (33) have proposed another alternative to the naive comparison of pre–post reading test scores to evaluate remediation. They recommend using a pre–post cloze reading test as a more accurate and sensitive measure of gains in reading comprehension. Applying their residual gain formula to the results, a gain yields residual cloze gains as contrasted to crude cloze gains from pretest to posttest, and in residual cloze gains the negative influence of initial status is reduced to nil. For those who are unwilling to take the time to construct appropriate cloze tests, or to apply the residual gain formula to pre–post gains from their cloze or standardized reading tests, Frederick B. Davis (14) has offered a number of alternative procedures. However, these involve using multiple pretests and posttests and other techniques that are equally time-consuming.

Other criticisms of the use of standardized reading tests to evaluate remedial outcomes emphasize the narrowness of reading test use as a significant criterion. We know and expect that remediation will reduce school dropouts (35), improve grades (not immediately but over time (46)), and perhaps reduce emotional problems (7). Other legitimate goals of the reading correction program are motivation, improvement of attention, and the breaking of old habits of inflexibility and dislike of reading—not to mention the positive effects upon self-concept. But how many of these goals, which in some instances are more significant than the actual gain in reading skills, does the average clinical report mention? If we believe that remedial reading has permanent values for the student's future, why do we not more often try to prove that it accomplishes these?

Gain Expectations

In most reports of remedial programs, it appears to be sufficient to convince the editor of the publication, the writer, and some of the readers by finding a statistically significant difference in the pre–post test gains. If such gains are present, it is supposed to show the validity of the procedures used, as well as the overall effectiveness of the program and teacher. Yet we really have very little idea of what degree or amount of gains that remedial work, in contrast with ordinary classroom instruction, should produce in a given time. Is every program that produces almost any gain greater than "normal" maximally effective? Or should we expect remediation to produce twice or three or *x* times the normal growth?

Because the reported programs vary greatly in length, it may be that the size of the gains would be affected. But this is probably not true, as we shall point out later in six of the seven studies reporting on this facet. In our tabulation of reports, we shall contrast these various factors that might have characterized the amount of gains. By using the ratio of gains for any period of time, we can hold the effect of the duration of remedial work constant.

GAINS FROM REMEDIAL PROGRAMS

AUTHOR	DURATION	AVERAGE CRUDE GAINS	GRADE OR AGES	RATIO
Aaron (1)	7 weeks	3.3 months	Mixed	1.8
Balow (2)	45 months	25 months	Sixth grade	0.55
	55 months	29 months	Seventh grades	0.52
	42 months	23 months	Fifth grades	0.54
Bliesmer (5)	7 months	8 months Metro.	Mixed	1.1
		13 months Gates		1.8
Bond and Fay (6)	5 weeks	5 months	One to six	4.0
Friedman (15)	First month	1.1 months	Retarded mentally	1.1
	Second month	1.0 months		1.0
Fry (16)	7-15 weeks	1 year	Mixed	3.5 to 7.4
Gwaltney (18)	7 weeks	0	H.S. Upward Bound	0
Heckerl and Sandsbury (20)	3 years	3.2 oral	"Primary" retardation	1.2
		1.9 silent		0.63
Lovell et al. (26)	1 year	2 years	Mixed	2.0
Pearlman and Pearlman (31)	4 to 19 months	15.1 to 46.4 months	Grades one to six	3.8 I
				2.4VI
Newman (30)	13 months	6.3 to 12.9 months	High school	0.5 to 0.9
Shearer (40)	10 months	2.44 years	9½-year-olds	2.9
Steirnagle (42)	1 year	2.3 years Botel	Grades four to twelve	2.3

The median ratio of remedial gain per period of instruction is 1.2 in these twenty-one reports. If we add five more studies from whom some additional data is available (5, 8, 24, 29, 45) for a total of twenty-eight ratios, the median becomes 1.8. The range is large, from 0. to 7.4, but the middle half of the reports cluster between .95 and 2.4. In other words, gains from remedial work are most commonly just about double the amount that might be normally expected in any period of time. Short-term gains for programs of five to fifteen weeks and those under six months yield a median of 1.8; longer programs, 2.0. Crude as it may be, and oblivious of long-range goals, we now have a criterion for judging the success of remedial programs in terms of the ratio of raw score gains to the length of the training, for those who insist on reporting in this fashion.

Computing the ratio of gain to duration of the treatment program would probably be more defensible if true gains rather than crude gains were employed. The ratios we cited above were, with two exceptions, those present in silent reading. The ratios for oral reading or word recognition or for auditory comprehension probably vary from the median that we found, and would also vary with the emphasis upon these areas in the program. For example, the ratios in word recognition were 4.0; in oral, 4.6; in silent reading, 6.6; and in auditory comprehension, 4.6 in Tillman's report (44), using true gains. Similarly, Dahlke found an average ratio of 6.6 in silent reading in terms of true gains (13). The markedly greater ratios in these two studies were not due to any unusual qualities of the program, for the tutoring was done by in-service teachers under supervision as part of a graduate course in diagnosis and remediation during a college summer session. Rather, the differences in these ratios reflect the correction of crude gains for the effects of initial status, a factor that most reporting ignores.

FACTORS AFFECTING OUTCOMES OF REMEDIATION

We think it correct to assume that most remedial services, whether by a solitary teacher or a staffed center, have more applicants than they can readily process. If this is true, it is essential to devise selection procedures that will use the professional time available at its maximum efficiency. We discuss this point to some degree in chapter 13, "Organizing for Remedial Work." Here we shall summarize data to help pinpoint certain factors that should be included in pretreatment selection procedures and should influence the evaluation of our results.

Duration of Remediation

Is there a maximally effective period of time for successful remediation, or should it be continued indefinitely in the hopes of promoting the greatest possible gain for the student? We skimmed the literature and, for thirty-three studies reporting the duration of remediation, found a median of twelve months, and a range from five weeks to fifty-five months. Five- and seven-week summer sessions, as in a college clinic, twelve months in school settings, and thirty-six months in private clinics are common arrangements. With the expected gains averaging twice the duration of each of these treatments, it seems difficult to justify the five- and seven-week programs. If the children are really retarded as much as a year or two below grade level, these brief treatments apparently do little to help them adjust to school demands.

The problem of determining the appropriate duration of remediation is complicated by a number of elements, as the limits of the school semester or year, the individuality of the pupils' responses to treatment, the cost to the parents, the availability of teaching staff, and other organizational problems. Other complicating factors are that six of the seven studies relating duration of remediation to gains find little or no interaction (43, 26, 44, 13, 2, 25 versus 10); and Collins (11) has reported from a large-scale Scottish study that the child's progress during treatment is not significantly related to the ultimate progress in reading. Lytton (28) also observes that good progress during treatment tends to result in higher posttreatment testing, but the reverse is also frequently true. Progress during treatment is not a good indicator of spontaneous growth after the treatment has ceased, Lytton also observes in reporting a large-scale British study of children treated in a child guidance clinic. Even the gains present in immediate posttreatment tests are not a positive indicator of future growth, for in some populations, such as school dropouts, the reverse is true (30). Several observers have pointed out that, for the best long-term results, contact with the pupil (and parents) should probably be continued, perhaps on a once-a-week basis, for some time after the formal treatment program has terminated (2, 11).

The decision regarding the optimum length for a remedial program becomes more difficult as we collate more relevant facts. It is probably true that the greatest gains are registered by the students in the first month or two of treatment because of the Hawthorne effect, if nothing else. Since the amount of gains is about double usual progress resulting from classroom instruction, this implies that it should continue, however, until the student reaches a level commensurate at least with his grade level so that he may be returned to classroom work with a reasonable chance of success. In other words, duration of remediation should be related to the extent of retardation below grade level (not necessarily below mental age). Since the progress during remediation, or even the posttreatment test result, does not indicate future growth rate, Balow's (2) and Collins's (11) recommendations for continued contact with the pupil, after treatment has ceased, seem very appropriate. This relationship would permit repeated reevaluation of the pupil's development and the resumption of treatment, if this is indicated. Despite the impressions we are given by some of the advertising matter and some of the program reports, there does not appear to be any magic in the length of any particular program.

Organizational Patterns

Much remediation is organized on a one-to-one or small-group basis. Although the problem of adequate staff is being helped by the use of tutors and aides, it would be profitable to ascertain the relative merits of individualized vs. small-group treatment. There were no observable differences from individualized or small-group therapy in Lovell's et al. report (27). Cashdan,

Pumfrey, and Lunzer (10) report that groups of four to six performed similarly, but that groups larger than seven gave poorer results (9). Steirnagle (42) found poorer results in one-to-one or one-to-two tutoring than in groups of five. As we might expect, treatments once or twice a week yielded similar results, according to Cashdan, Pumfrey, and Lunzer (10) in a large-scale British study. Most American centers and remedial teachers seem to prefer more frequent sessions per week with their pupils than this, but we find no real evidence regarding the values of this pattern. Since gains are related to amount of remedial time, and progress is more readily stimulated by frequent sessions, it may well be that the American pattern is preferable. In summary, it appears that small-group therapy with five or six pupils, occurring perhaps three or four times a week, may be the most economical and even profitable instructional arrangement, at least in terms of posttreatment test scores.

Initial Status

As we have pointed out in discussing factors indicating potential for reading development, initial status in reading when beginning treatment is positively related to gains from remediation. In a population of pupils, those with the higher initial test results tend to make the highest posttraining scores. Their gains may not be the largest among the pupils, for the regression to the mean of very low scores may create the impression that the worst of the poor readers make the greatest gains (10). But these trends are not contradictory, for both observations are usually based on crude gains from pretreatment to posttreatment tests. When initial status and reliability of the test are controlled (as they must be to make valid comparisons), only initial status, not degree of disability, is a reasonable indicator of probable posttreatment status (13, 34, 44). In other words, if our goal is to enable our pupils to return to the classroom with reasonable facility after a term of treatment, we should select pupils who, although below grade level, test higher in the remedial group of applicants—not the pupils who appear in greatest need of our services. This selection procedure could, of course, be modified if there is sufficient time and staff to include pupils of both types.

Age and Grade Level

As Balow (2) has shown, gains from remedial work with primary pupils can be very high, relatively speaking. Moreover, for some this is a crucial period during which long-term attitudes toward reading and a pattern of success or failure may be established. On the other hand, in the total retarded population, older pupils and secondary pupils respond more readily to treatment and show greater long-term profit (13, 43, 44). These relationships are affected, of course, by the nature of the disability and the relative ease with which it may be overcome. If, as is often the case, the secondary pupils exhibit largely problems of inflexibility of rate, rather than severe retardation in comprehension, training can be simple and direct and will yield good returns over time in both rate and comprehension (43). The generalization about secondary or older elementary pupils' greater response to treatment will not apply, of course, in cases showing very severe general retardation in reading or mental ability or in the case of those for whom the retardation persisted since elementary levels. The decision really amounts to choosing whether to accept primary children, probably for relatively short-term treatment, or to select older pupils because they may show greater response and long-term profit if the inception of their retardation is relatively recent. The question of the permanence of gains for primary pupils is relevant here, too.

Intelligence

The evidence regarding the significance of mental age or I.Q. in predicting gains from remediation appears conflicting. Mouly and Grant (29), for example, are so impressed with the relationship that they offer a regression equation for predicting remedial gain from I.Q. The use of such an equation would, of course, be impossible in other populations unless the same I.Q. and reading tests were employed and the remedial program was very similar to Mouly's (which, incidentally, was probably diversified). Gwaltney (18) quotes a correlation between intelligence and reading achievement of .83; and .86 for listening comprehension and reading. This relationship was much greater than others quoted, such as .12 to .38 by Lovell (27), and those around .50 to .60 in many samples of older pupils. Lovell (27) also points out that the correlation between I.Q. and progress during remediation was .19 to .34. It may well be that pupils with 70–84 I.Q.'s gain least (10) and that high I.Q. pupils gain the most and maintain their gains better (28). But these are only observable trends, not a one-to-one relationship, as we have repeatedly pointed out. And in large-scale studies, as that of 1227 pupils by Cashdan, Pumfrey, and Lunzer (10), the trends may be very weak above the 85 I.Q. level. The correlation between reading and mental age or I.Q. does increase with age of the pupil, for both tests are measuring reasoning processes, and often in the act of reading in both instruments. The probable error in both tests, the only moderate correlation, and the strong tendency for high I.Q.'s to underachieve and low I.Q.'s to overachieve for their respective mental ages do not support use of intelligence measures to predict remedial gains with any great degree of accuracy.

Nor—as we have pointed out in reviewing such predictive measures—are formulas juggling mental age, chronological age, and other factors, nor reading achievement quotients based on a comparison of reading and mental ages very useful in predicting gains from remediation. (These other fallible predictors are thoroughly reviewed in this text's chapter 4, "Diagnosis in the Intellectual Area," and in our *Investigating the Issues of Reading Disabilities.)*

Personality Adjustment and Socioeconomic Status

We proposed at length in chapter 5 that the personality adjustment of the retarded reader is a very significant element of his problem. We also pointed out that those who employ psychological or counseling strategies feel that treatment of this aspect of the child's problem is of paramount importance. As we view them, many of the reports of remedial treatments strongly support this view. As we might expect, Gwaltney (18) did not find a significant correlation between scores on a group personality test and gains. But his underachieving, black high school students showed literally no gains from a seven-week's reading improvement course. Similarly, Kassory's mental health clinic cases (25) were even further below age and grade level in a four–five year follow-up than at the end of their combined remedial and parental treatment program. Despite remediation, none had continued to progress in reading after treatment was terminated. The follow-up study by the Geneva Medico-Educational Service (17) indicated that only half had been effectively reeducated, and only 5 percent were in their proper grade placement for age. The Service considered emotional problems one of the primary factors determining eventual outcomes for these pupils.

We have noted the significance of the handicap of low socioeconomic status in reading progress elsewhere. The same obstacle seems to affect the outcomes of remedial work, for in one- and two-year follow-up studies of the British pupils treated in remedial centers, schools or in regular classes, lower-class children had made the least progress (11).

THE LONG TERM OUTCOMES

We have referred frequently to the findings of follow-up studies of the eventual outcomes of remedial treatments. Some remedial workers are quite certain of the positive nature of these results, while others wonder whether they have really affected the child's future. Part of these doubts may be attributed to the conclusions resulting from various ways of evaluating the long-term results. Some, simply ignoring the socioeconomic status of their subjects, claim success because such pupils persist in school or even go to college and may achieve white-collar employment status. They assume that such accomplishments imply quite adequate reading skills when, of course, they prove nothing about the present reading ability of their previous clients. Few studies try to establish the current reading status of pupils who have been treated a number of years earlier, depending rather upon questionnaires, correspondence, and telephone interviews. Other researchers try to ascertain the extent of dropouts and nonpromotions, grades, present school status, student reaction to the treatment program, and incidence of adjustment problems among their former pupils, often without comparing these with the statistics for the appropriate social-class segment of the population. We are inclined to believe that, with the exception of an actual reading test result, these supposed indications of successful treatment are often not very meaningful. Many very poor readers graduate from high school and college and find employment commensurate with those educational qualifications, by compensating for their poor reading and through the support engendered by their socioeconomic background, thus proving their motivation rather than their adequacy in reading. In any event, we shall try to summarize these follow-up studies to enable the reader to make his own judgments of their validity and meaningfulness.

The interpretation of these results is not simple and direct. Improvements attributed to the treatment in some studies are not present in others, or are shown to be just similar to the general population. This is true for the citations regarding high school graduation, college attendance, employment status, and even grades. When compared with the general population or the control groups who were not treated for their retardation, treated poor readers apparently do not differ greatly in these traits. When reading tests are administered as part of a long-range follow-up, twelve studies indicate no continued growth after treatment or at least less than normal development. Only two (19, 43) indicate that treated retarded readers are presently functioning at levels normal for age-grade status, on the average.

Considering only these two areas of progress for the moment, we might draw such conclusions as these:

Remedial treatment apparently does not affect school progress appreciably, over time. If sufficiently motivated—and provided socioeconomic support and educational opportunities—these pupils succeed about as well as

FOLLOW-UP STUDIES OF REMEDIAL TREATMENT

AUTHOR	FOLLOW-UP PERIOD	NUMBER OF CASES PRESENT AGES	RESULTS
Balow and Blomquist (3)	15 years	32—aged 20–26	Average rate 9.6; vocabulary 10.9; comprehension 10.2 for 9 cases. Of 32, 27 high school graduates; 19 some college; 6 still in college.
Birch (4)	2 years	332—aged 11–13	Percentage of retardation below M.A. had dropped from 40 to 16 percent in word recognition, for youngest pupils.
Buerger (7)	.3 to 5.6 years	72—grades four to twelve	No differences between remedial and controls in vocabulary or comprehension at grade nine; in English or social science grades seven and nine; but remedial group indicated fewer adjustment problems.
Cashdan and Pumfrey (9)	22 months	36 junior high	No differences in silent or oral reading from controls, or in attitudes.
Collins (11)	1 or 2 years	45 and 48 elementary	No significant differences; end results negligible.
Geneva (17)	5 years	90 elementary and secondary	62 percent in normal school, 38 percent still in remedial classes; 5 percent in proper grade placement. 85 percent satisfactory school grades.
Hardy (19)	Varied	40 secondary	Significant improvement in silent and oral reading since treatment.
Heckerl and Sansbury (20)	2 years	6—aged 11–14	Slight loss in oral, small gain in silent reading, after three-year tutoring treatment. But gain less than 1.0 ratio.
Jackson, Cleveland, and Merenda (22)	Varied	143—in grade four	No significant gains in twelve criteria including grades, personality tests, teacher judgments, or sociometric measures, after three-year treatment program.
Johnson and Platts (24)	2 years	284—aged 12	Rate of improvement diminished and were falling behind age group.
Kassory (25)	4–5 years	22—aged 10–18	All except one psychotic further below age and grade level; six actually lower than grade level during treatment.
Lovell, Byrne, and Richardson (26)	16 months and $3\frac{1}{2}$ years	240 mixed secondary	At 16 months, improvement continued but at slower rate; after $3\frac{1}{2}$ years, practically all in lower-level secondary school (non-college-preparatory) and no differences between treated and controls.
Lovell, Johnson and Platts (27)	12 months	259 elementary	I.Q. unrelated to reading age or to progress during treatment.
Lytton (28)	16 months	88 mixed elementary and secondary	Those now in secondary lost more and showed more loss over time. Most lost some of gains in reading.
Newman (30)	Varied	34 high school dropouts	Some had small gains. Those who apparently gained most from treatment as shown in posttest made least subsequent progress.

FOLLOW-UP STUDIES OF REMEDIAL TREATMENT (continued)

AUTHOR	FOLLOW-UP PERIOD	NUMBER OF CASES PRESENT AGES	RESULTS
Pearlman and Pearlman (31)	24 months	545—grades three to eight	Gains in follow-up ranged from 30 months for youngest (grade one) to 25 months for oldest (grade six) or ratios of 1.04 to 1.25.
Preston and Yarington (32)	8 years	50—aged 14 to 25	No differences from normal population in enrollment and graduation from high school; admission to college; white-collar employment; rate of unemployment. Repeated many grades; finished school later; none going into professional or graduate study.
Rasmussen and Dunne (35)	5 years	20 in grade nine	No difference from controls in gains after three years; reduced school dropouts, however.
Rawson (36)	20+ years	56 boys	No significant difference for "dyslexics" in years of college, graduation, vocational status.
Robinson and Smith (37)	10 years	44 mentally superior	Only three failed to complete high school; more than half graduated from college.
Schiffman (38)	1 year	240 mixed elementary and secondary	Elementary remedial made more gain than correctives or controls; secondary did not.
Shaw and McCuen (39)	Varied	53 underachievers in secondary	Significantly poorer mean grade point averages for grades three to ten for boys but not for girls.
Silver and Hagin (41)	10–12 years	35	Of twenty-four, fifteen now judged adequate readers because of perceptual maturation; inadequate still had perceptual deficits despite treatment.
Stone (43)	4–7 years	100 secondary and college	68 percent at average ability in comprehension for grade level or age. 58 percent now in college, 42 percent high school graduates. Those treated as secondary did better in reading follow-up test.
Wilson (46)	?	39 mixed	Today fifteen are good readers, twelve are fair, and twelve are still retarded. Most had improved in grades.

untreated poor readers or the general population. Some may improve their grades above the levels prior to the treatment, to a level sufficient for graduation eventually; but so do untreated poor readers, it would seem, if they are motivated for school success. The bulk of the follow-up studies indicate little or no further development of reading ability anything like the accelerated rate during treatment. After treatment, reading growth tends to revert to the less than normal ratio characteristic of most cases prior to their treatment. Eventual reading performances are poor for age-grade status in most studies.

The seven British reports give the same negative picture of posttreatment reading development as the American studies do. The former policy in Britain determining admission to college-preparatory secondary schools by school achievement tests tended to lessen the school opportunities of poor readers. Most were directed toward vocational training and deprived of further academic preparation for white-collar or professional work, with a rather dismal school progress picture thus created. Since this admission policy is no longer obligatory, British poor readers may well exhibit the average school progress of American secondary students in future reports.

Some of the positive side effects that may result from remedial treatment appear to be reduction of the degree of underachievement for mental capacities (assuming, of course, that pupils are supposed to function at capacity); fewer personal adjustment problems, at least from the pupils' own viewpoint, if not in personality tests or sociometric measures; reduction of school dropouts, at least sometimes at secondary and college levels; and perhaps some improvement in grade point average over time above previous levels.

Four studies included psychological techniques in the program, as parental counseling, teacher counseling, or psychotherapy in dealing with a normal sample of children referred to a mental health or child guidance clinic who may have exhibited other adjustment problems. No matter whether normal or possibly disturbed, the end results were also as negative as the studies employing ordinary remedial treatments. Even in the presumably normal sample reported on by Schiffman (38), these techniques plus remedial treatment seemed to produce reading gains only for elementary children, not for secondary. There may be the implications here that, when we talk in large-scale terms, treatment for the emotional problems of poor readers should be begun early in their school career; and that, even under those circumstances, combined treatments may not be the complete answer to the dual problem of reading and maladjustment, insofar as continued reading growth is the goal. Like other strategies, psychological approaches tend to produce temporary gains in posttreatment reading scores, not permanent gains. Whether this strategy achieves its avowed purpose of improving the life adjustment of the pupils is questionable. Only a few large-scale, long-term follow-up studies have attempted to sample the effects of remedial work through personality measures, as in the study by Jackson et al. (22) of fourth-grade underachievers; after a three-year treatment program, the results were negligible. We do not know whether psychological or counseling strategies were employed in this study, however. Other studies, like that of

Kathleen M. Holliday,* show more positive short-term results from combined therapies. Using eight groups of fifteen pupils each, she offered remedial treatment or combined remedial and psychological therapies (play therapy, bibliotherapy, art and music therapy, self-concept building, nondirective counseling). Five to ten months of a therapy program indicated that maladjusted children (identified by sociograms and a personality test) made more progress with psychological therapy than with remedial. Normally adjusted children made no greater gains with remedial than with combined treatments. Again results were measured in terms of reading gains rather than personality adjustment, and no long-term follow-up was made. Like other studies citing the short-term results of psychological strategies, these appear to indicate that they are effective in producing reading gains, with or without additional remedial reading instruction, for pupils who are maladjusted. But there is still little evidence of long-term effects either in reading or in personality changes.

Justifying Remedial Reading

If long-term results in either reading development or in life or school adjustment are not significant, can we justify remedial reading? In view of these results cited, perhaps the only generalization we can make is that remedial reading with or without counseling or other techniques is symptomatic treatment. It relieves temporarily the reading difficulty but produces, as far as we can discover, no long-range effects. In many respects, remediation of reading difficulties resembles the medical approach to treatment of the common cold. Since the exact cause of the cold is unknown, or at best can only be described as viral or nonviral, treatment is intended only to relieve the annoying symptoms and to prevent the progress of the infection (?) into more complicated ailments.

We remedial workers, too, often cannot establish why a reading disability appears in a student, although we know many factors that could have contributed. We are handicapped in treating the causes, such as intelligence, previous instruction, socioeconomic status, parental attitudes, and personality maladjustment of the pupil. Therefore, like the general medical practitioner we treat the symptom and give temporary relief to our client. His reading performances usually improve, and he resumes the struggle to compete in the classroom under somewhat more favorable circumstances. Like the medical

*Kathleen M. Holliday, "Values of Combined Remedial Reading Techniques and Certain Types of Psychotherapy for Emotionally Disturbed and Normal Pupils," Master's thesis, University of Florida, 1968.

treatment for colds, remedial reading is palliative, supportive and, perhaps, preventive, not curative. If our simile is accurate, there is as much justification for remedial reading as there is for treatment of the common cold.

If we make our services constantly available, like the physician, we may expect our pupils to return to us from time to time particularly during periods when their reading difficulties are disturbing, or at crucial transitional periods as in moving from elementary to junior high, to senior high, and to college. Like the medical profession, we should probably be promoting annual checkups to reassess our students' progress, to anticipate recurring reading difficulties, and to provide supportive treatment. We may never be able to change the pattern of reading problems for many cases, but we certainly can help make school life more tolerable for many by maintaining our helping relationship.

In summary, these conclusions may be pertinent to the organization of our remedial services and may act as guiding principles.

1. In estimating the probable duration of treatment, expect about twice normal growth for most cases. Progress may be less for those handicapped by socioeconomic status, language difference, emotional problems, or low intelligence.
2. If pupil evidences problems of personality maladjustment, consider the use of psychological or counseling techniques as preferable to skill instruction, at least during the early stages of the program.
3. Use small-group (four to six) instruction as most effective and economical of staff time.
4. If waiting list is excessive, consider selecting pupils with highest initial status, whether primary or secondary, to shorten treatment time, to produce the desired degree of improvement sooner, and, in the long run, thus to serve more pupils.
5. For primary pupils, plan relatively short-term treatments since degree of retardation is not so great as with older pupils. If ratio of improvement to duration of treatment is as great as expected, a favorable reading status may be obtained more quickly in these cases.
6. Maintain contact with former cases over the years to check progress, to offer resumption of treatment.
7. Terminate treatment when pupil demonstrates reasonable facility with ordinary classroom texts, as in open-book, silent reading tasks. Do not expect him to equal his mental age necessarily, or to perform precisely at grade level in a reading test. At primary grades, a few months' difference is insignificant; at intermediate grades allow about a year's variation, and two to three years at secondary levels in comparing posttreatment reading test with his grade placement. Remember that the middle 50 percent of the average class does not test exactly at grade placement but tend to vary these amounts from that hypothetical criterion.

8. Do not expect dramatic changes in grades or grade point averages. Such gains as do appear may not be obvious until at least six months to a year after treatment.

9. Unless parental and student aspirations for academic achievement are high or are increased by the treatment, do not expect remediation to prevent all dropouts.

10. If personality or school maladjustments are affecting the pupil's progress, do not expect ordinary remedial instruction to cure all these problems too. It may strengthen self-concept and alleviate some of the minor adjustment problems, but it is not a panacea for emotionally disturbed, poor readers.

11. If you emphasize skill development in remedial work, recognize it as a temporary, supportive effort to help the student deal with his current academic problems, not as a cure or even a preventative for future problems. The student's school career may well continue to be hindered by some of the factors that contributed to his present retardation; factors which, perhaps, you cannot alleviate but rather can help him to compensate for from time to time as he needs such assistance.

LEARNING PROJECT

Secure the report of a reading treatment program as published in the *Reading Teacher, Journal of Reading, Journal of Reading Behavior, Journal of Learning Disabilities, Elementary School Journal, Journal of Educational Research,* or other such sources. Try to answer these questions about the report.

1. How were the outcomes of the program in reading measured?

2. Were crude or true gains considered? Was initial status of pupils or reliability of the test controlled?

3. Were the median gains of the pupils considered significant? How large were the average gains?

4. What was the ratio of gains to the duration of the program? How does this compare with the gain expectations suggested by this text?

5. Were any other outcomes than reading test scores considered significant? How were these measured?

6. Was any attempt made to relate such factors as duration of remediation; pupil-teacher ratio; initial status, age, intelligence, or social class of the pupils to the outcomes for various pupils?

7. What is your evaluation of this report? What strengths and weaknesses do you recognize?

REFERENCES

1. Aaron, Ira E., "Contributions of Summer Reading Programs," in *Reading and Inquiry,* J. Allen Figurel, editor, Proceedings International Reading Association, 10, 1965, 413–15.
2. Balow, Bruce, "The Long-Term Effect of Remedial Reading Instruction," *Reading Teacher,* 18 (April 1965), 581–86.
3. Balow, Bruce, and Blomquist, Marlys, "Young Adults Ten to Fifteen Years After Severe Reading Disability," *Elementary School Journal,* 66 (1965), 44–48.
4. Birch, L.B., "The Improvement of Reading Ability," *British Journal of Educational Psychology,* 20 (June 1950), 73–76.
5. Bliesmer, Emery P., "Evaluating Progress in Remedial Reading Programs," *Reading Teacher,* 15 (March 1962), 344–50.
6. Bond, Guy L., and Fay, Leo C., "A Report of the University of Minnesota Reading Clinic," *Journal of Educational Research,* 43 (January 1950), 385–90.
7. Buerger, T.A., "A Follow-up of Remedial Reading Instruction," *Reading Teacher,* 21 (January 1968), 329–34.
8. Burt, Sir C., and Lewis, R.B., "Teaching Backward Readers," *British Journal of Educational Psychology,* 16 (1946), 116–32.
9. Cashdan, A., and Pumfrey, Peter D., "Some Effects of the Remedial Teaching of Reading," *Educational Research,* 11 (1969), 138–42.
10. Cashdan, A., Pumfrey, Peter D., and Lunzer, E.A., "Children Receiving Remedial Teaching in Reading," *Educational Research,* 13 (1971), 98–105.
11. Collins, J.E., *The Effects of Remedial Education.* Educational Monographs No. 4. Edinburgh: Oliver and Boyd, 1961.
12. Cronbach, L.J., and Furby, L., "How Should We Measure 'Change'—Or Should We?" *Psychological Bulletin,* 74 (1970), 68–80.
13. Dahlke, Anita B., "The Use of WISC Scores to Predict Reading Improvement after Remedial Tutoring," Doctoral dissertation, University of Florida, 1968.
14. Davis, Frederick B., *Educational Measurements and Their Interpretation.* Belmont, Calif.: Wadsworth, 1964.
15. Friedman, S., "A Report on Progress in an L.E.A. Remedial Reading Class," *British Journal of Educational Psychology,* 28 (1958), 258–61.
16. Fry, Edward, "A Reading Clinic Reports Its Results and Methods," *Journal of Educational Research,* 52 (1959), 311–13.
17. Geneva Medico-Educational Service, "Problems Posed by Dyslexia," *Journal of Learning Disabilities,* 1 (1968), 158–71.
18. Gwaltney, Wayne K., "An Evaluation of a Summer Reading Improvement Course for Disadvantaged High School Students," *Journal of Reading Behavior,* 3 (Fall 1970–71), 14–21.
19. Hardy, Madeline I., "Disabled Readers: What Happens to Them After Elementary School?" *Canadian Education and Research Digest,* 8 (December 1968), 338–45.
20. Heckerl, J.R., and Sansbury, R.J., "A Study of Severe Reading Retardation," *Reading Teacher,* 21 (May 1968), 724–29.
21. Hopkins, Kenneth D., and Bracht, Glenn H., "A Longitudinal Study of Constancy of

Reading Performance," in *Diagnostic Viewpoints in Reading,* Robert E. Leibert, editor. Newark, Del.: International Reading Association, 1971, 103–13.

22. Jackson, Robert M., Cleveland, John C., and Merenda, Peter F., "The Effects of Early Identification and Counseling of Underachievers," *Journal of School Psychology,* 7 (1968–69), 42–49.
23. Jensen, Philip, Mills, James W., and Hershkowitz, Martin, "An Evaluation of Four Methods of Reading Instruction as a Function of Time of Testing," *Journal of Reading Behavior,* 4 (Summer 1971–72), 32–37.
24. Johnson, L.R., and Platts, D., "A Summary of a Study of the Reading Ages of Children Who Had Been Given Remedial Teaching," *British Journal of Educational Psychology,* 32 (February 1962), 66–71.
25. Kassory, Esther, "A Follow-up Study of Children with Reading Disability," unpublished paper, Children's Mental Health Center, Columbus, Ohio.
26. Lovell, K., Byrne, C., and Richardson, B., "A Further Study of the Educational Progress of Children Who Had Received Remedial Instruction," *British Journal of Educational Psychology,* 33 (February 1963), 3–9.
27. Lovell, K., Johnson, E., and Platts, D., "A Summary of a Study of the Reading Ages of Children Who Had Been Given Remedial Teaching," *British Journal of Educational Psychology,* 32 (February 1962), 71–76.
28. Lytton, H., "Follow-up of an Experiment in Selection for Remedial Education," *British Journal of Educational Psychology,* 37 (February 1967), 1–9.
29. Mouly, G.J., and Grant, Virginia, "A Study of Growth to Be Expected of Retarded Readers," *Journal of Educational Research,* 49 (February 1956), 461–65.
30. Newman, Harold, "The Reading Habits, Attitudes and Achievements of High School Dropouts," in *Reading Disabilities: Selections on Identification and Treatment.* New York: Odyssey Press, 1969, 343–53.
31. Pearlman, E., and Pearlman, R., "The Effect of Remedial-reading Training in a Private Clinic," *Academic Therapy,* 5 (1970), 298–304.
32. Preston, Ralph C., and Yarington, D.J., "Status of Fifty Retarded Readers Eight Years After Reading Clinic Diagnosis," *Journal of Reading,* 11 (1967), 122–29.
33. Rankin, Earl F., and Dale, Lothar H., "Cloze Residual Gain—A Technique for Measuring Learning Through Reading," in *Psychology of Reading Behavior,* 18th Yearbook National Reading Conference, 1969, 17–26.
34. Rankin, Earl F., and Tracy, R.J., "Residual Gain as a Measure of Individual Differences in Reading Improvement," *Journal of Reading,* 8 (March 1965), 224–33.
35. Rasmussen, G.R., and Dunne, H.W., "A Longitudinal Evaluation of a Junior High School Corrective Reading Program," *Reading Teacher,* 15 (November 1962), 95–106.
36. Rawson, Margaret B., "After a Generation's Time: A Follow-up Study of 56 Boys: A Preliminary Report," *Bulletin of the Orton Society,* 16 (1966), 24–37.
37. Robinson, Helen M., and Smith, Helen K., "Reading Clinic Cases—Ten Years After," *Elementary School Journal,* 63 (October 1962), 22–27.
38. Schiffman, Gilbert, "Diagnosing Cases of Reading Disability with Suggested Neurological Impairment," in *Vistas in Reading,* J. Allen Figurel, editor, Proceedings International Reading Association, 11, 1966, 513–21.
39. Shaw, Menrille C., and McCuen, John T., "The Onset of Academic Underachievement in Bright Children," *Journal of Educational Psychology,* 51 (June 1960), 103–8.

40. Shearer, E., "The Long-Term Effects of Remedial Education," *Educational Research,* 9 (November 1966), 219–22.
41. Silver, Archie A., and Hagin, Rosa A., "Specific Reading Disability: Follow-up Studies," *American Journal of Orthopsychiatry,* 34 (January 1964), 95–102.
42. Steirnagle, Edward, "A Five-Year Summary of a Remedial Reading Program," *Reading Teacher,* 24 (March 1971), 537–43.
43. Stone, Evelyn W., "A Follow-up Study of Off-Campus Students Who Attended the University of Florida Reading Laboratory and Clinic," Doctoral dissertation, University of Florida, 1967.
44. Tillman, Chester Earl, "Crude Gain vs. True Gain: Correlates of Gain in Reading after Remedial Tutoring," Doctoral dissertation, University of Florida, 1969.
45. Valentine, Hugh B., "Some Results of Remedial Education in a Child Guidance Center," *British Journal of Educational Psychology,* 21 (1951), 145–49.
46. Wilson, Robert M., "The Scholastic Improvement of Successful Remedial Reading Students," Doctoral dissertation, University of Pittsburgh, 1960.

part five

ORGANIZATIONAL ASPECTS

13 Organizing for Remedial Work

Planning for the operation of a remedial service and then implementing those plans in actual services present a wide variety of problems. Among these are arrangements of the facilities, scheduling the cases, selection and in-service training of the staff, establishing selection procedures, and record-keeping. At the policy level, decisions must be made regarding the modus operandi of the treatment services, criteria for admission and discharge of the cases, and the goals of the center in the area of in-service training of teachers.

This chapter offers the combined experiences of the author and many others who have dealt with these organizational problems. As you read these suggestions, consider these questions.

1. If you have had the experience of establishing a remedial service, what alternative solutions to the problems discussed can you offer?

2. If you have not had the opportunity to plan such a service, are there problems that you anticipate that are not treated here?

THE MANNER IN WHICH REMEDIAL SERVICES for learning disabilities are established is often a rather unscientific and unplanned procedure. Someone in the administration becomes concerned about the number of failing pupils and decides to do "something" about it. He nominates a teacher or two to be the remedial staff, sometimes without even inquiring into their qualifications or willingness. In some instances, the teachers are logically selected because of their successes in the classroom. In others, they are being relieved of classroom duties because they have been incompetent with large groups. A sum of money is designated in the institutional budget, and within a short space of time the services are supposed to get under way for reducing the ratio of school failures. The questions of available permanent space, teacher training, integration with other school services, careful definition of objectives, and the nature and size of the remedial population to be served—all these are apt to be ignored in this administrative decision.

We have not described the worst possible conditions under which remedial services are initiated but merely those which are fairly common in public schools and colleges. The lack of guides for those thrust into this predicament has impelled us to offer this group of ideas about planning for remedial centers. We hope that they will be useful in the operation of services of all types, sizes, and levels. The aspects that we are stressing are not necessarily arranged in order of importance or primacy in decision making, as many of these facets are interdependent. Budget, space, size of staff, equipment, manner of case selection, and the like are closely interrelated. But each is a problem in planning the organization and operation of the services that must be faced in the early stages of the effort.

INTAKE PROBLEMS

Selection of Cases

One of the major decisions in initiating remedial services is that of determining who shall be eligible for the services of the center. Shall we serve students of all ages or only those drawn from a crucial stage in reading development, as at the beginning of the intermediate grades or the junior high school or the college freshman? What will the definition of retardation be—one, two, or more years below grade level, mental age, peer group, measured potential, or what? How long should retardation have persisted to be considered a real problem? Shall we accept only pupils who place above a certain I.Q. limit, as above 85? How large is the school population we are trying to serve, and approximately what proportion is really handicapped? Can we establish criteria of selection of cases and make them stand, or are we obligated to accept all referrals?

These would appear to be obvious questions that need to be faced even before the services begin. Their answers determine such crucial factors as amount of space, size of staff, case load and, of course, budget. Yet a visitor to many centers discovers that the objectives and the modus operandi have often never been explored in such detail. As a result, some centers are flooded with students referred by the administration and classroom teachers on other grounds than true retardation. They tend to refer pupils who show poor achievement because of behavior or personality disturbances, low intelligence, family problems, excessive school absence, and other causes that do not lend themselves to treatment by remedial efforts. Students on probation or those who appear likely to fail are often sent for remedial help, regardless of their actual reading performances. The number of these irrelevant referrals may well defeat the efforts of the center to serve those who truly present problems of reading or learning disabilities, if such referrals are accepted.

Once the age or grade levels to be served have been established, a general survey of that population is in order to determine the size of the needy population. In reading, a general survey test will usually suffice for this assessment, even though it does not discriminate well at its lowest levels.* The survey will usually reveal that about 60 percent are within a year above or below their grade placement. Under ordinary circumstances, those below grade level but within this range are receiving reasonably effective instruction in the classroom; they are not truly retarded. The client population will be drawn, in all probability, from the group retarded by two years or more on the general survey test. Since the probable error of the survey test is apt to be six months or more, we can ignore, temporarily at least, those who test between one and two years retarded since their true status could well be within the middle 60 percent.

In terms of pupil ability to deal with school demands, this two year

*A diagnostic test or one with reliable differentiation among several skills would actually be more serviceable both to the center and classroom teachers, but survey tests are more commonly familiar in school testing programs.

retardation criterion should be increased to three years in high school and college. There is evidence that at these levels a two-year retardation is not a great handicap to academic success requiring immediate remediation.

If taken at face value, the proportion of retardates as indicated by a survey test may range from 15 to 25 percent in middle-class populations to perhaps as much as 60 to 75 percent in inner-city groups. Since few remedial centers can conceivably service the total number identified as retarded, it becomes necessary to use some additional criteria to the two–three years below grade-level standard. Shall we retest the entire population in intelligence and then compare their achievement with their mental ages? Thus we might eliminate those who, while retarded, are performing at a level commensurate with their capacities. Many centers do employ such a criterion or, at least, establish a lower limit of I.Q. below which pupils are not accepted for remedial services. But, as we have pointed out elsewhere, this reasoning assumes a high correlation between academic performances and intelligence that just is not true. Rather the statistics show us that low-intelligence pupils tend to be overachievers in terms of mental age, while the reverse is true for those of superior intelligence. It may be useful to know a pupil's I.Q. to enable us to estimate his probable learning rate; but mental age versus achievement is not a suitable criterion for admission to the center or, as some use it, a criterion for discharge from the services.

An alternative approach is the criterion of the pupil's achievement in comparison with some other measure of potential than mental age, such as auditory comprehension. One school system with which we are familiar utilizes this approach in giving one form of a general reading test in the usual fashion and a parallel form by reading the entire test aloud to elementary pupils. When listening scores differ from reading by at least two stanines, pupils are considered to be underachievers in terms of capacity and are referred for remedial services. When used for a large school population, this is an expensive and time-consuming method of selection. It would be more practical to employ it as an additional criterion, after survey testing has tentatively identified the needy population, as Crowley and Ellis used it (3). Moreover, early studies show that most pupils score about two years higher in auditory comprehension than in reading at least until about the sixth grade. Beyond this point normal readers tend to test higher in reading than in listening. Thus this differential must be interpreted cautiously and in relation to other information (12).

There is evidence to support this use of auditory comprehension as a measure of potential to gain from remedial assistance. Several studies are cited in the Manual of the Spache Diagnostic Reading Scales indicating that testing in this fashion, which is an integral part of these Scales, is useful (9).

Measurement of the child's auditory comprehension—or potential level as it is termed in the Spache Scales—predicted gain in the instructional level as a result of remedial tutoring to a marked degree ($r = .66$), in a study by Anita B. Dahlke (4). A second study, by Chester Earl Tillman (11), revealed a correlation of .73 between potential level and gain in independent level (silent reading) and of .62 with gain in the word list tests, after remedial training. In both studies, gains calculated were true gain corrected for the reliability of the tests and for the expected regression to the mean.

However, as Crowley and Ellis's small study (3) demonstrated, this criterion of two stanines difference between reading and listening scores as prognostic of gain from remedial services is by no means perfect. Complications of emotional disturbance, bilingualism, visual or auditory deficits, and other factors may prevent the pupil from making the progress of which he is apparently capable. Thus, in actual practice when used in large-scale testing of potential candidates for remediation, the difference between reading and auditory comprehension must be reevaluated in terms of the constellation of problems by the individual case. Perhaps only when there are no major handicaps to the pupil's development or when these can be easily corrected (as in most visual defects) is this measure of potential for gain from remedial services very significant.

The criterion of two–three years below grade level is probably serviceable only in middle-class school populations. Certainly we cannot expect similar at-grade performances of many ethnic or racial minority groups, low socioeconomic or inner-city pupils or even rural pupils. When our school population includes sizeable proportions of these types of pupils, school grade averages should be substituted for the national norm standard. In other words, retardates are those who fall two–three or more years below their peer group (which may, as a group, test below grade level). Theoretically, it is true that many of the pupils who test below grade level in this population would benefit from remediation. But, pragmatically, few remedial centers can possibly service effectively anywhere near the total number of such cases in many school systems. The goal of the criteria of selection of cases is to find those truly retarded pupils who are most likely to benefit from the center's efforts. The obligation to other pupils who achieve below the national norms can be discharged in other ways, as we shall point out.

One other criterion is applied by many remedial centers in setting a lower limit of I.Q. below which pupils will not be accepted. In mixed racial and ethnic populations, as well as mixed socioeconomic groups, this criterion must be applied cautiously. Since I.Q.'s are dependent upon educational opportunities, language background, and the like, there are significant differences in the average performance of different groups. An I.Q. of 80 does not mean the same in low socioeconomic blacks and middle-class whites, for example. Hence, if a lower limit of I.Q. is set as a criterion of eligibility for remedial services, its application must vary with the known average performances of different groups on the intelligence test employed. For example, on a highly verbal test as the Stanford-Binet, an I.Q. of 80 is likely to indicate average mental ability for Southern blacks, not, as in middle-class white groups, a dull normal capacity. Again, this criterion must be evaluated in terms of peer group standards before it is perhaps significant in indicating capacity for learning.

Another caution regarding selection of cases is pertinent. Even though a pupil may meet the other criteria, the duration of his academic problem should be investigated before acceptance. Primary teachers, in particular, often refer pupils who are simply falling behind their peers for reasons not apparent to their instructors. While the center can and should lend help in dealing with such problems, as we shall discuss later, it should be careful not to permit itself to become overloaded with these cases. When available, records of repeated testing will help clarify this point. Pupils whose records show only a single instance of apparent retardation should be admitted only for diagnosis and/or observation, with a clear understanding that they are likely to be discharged in a short time. Perhaps only when retardation is shown in repeated testing or a constant downward trend has been present over several years should such pupils be seriously considered for remediation.

To summarize, criteria of selection for remedial services must be established and clarified to both administration and fellow teachers. This selection may be initiated by survey testing in the selected age groups to identify those pupils who fall two–three or more years below their peer group. The next identification is of those who give evidence on auditory comprehension and mental ability tests of adequate capacity to profit from remediation. The privilege of the remedial center to select or reject pupils, to refer them to other agencies as it seems desirable, or to reject referrals in terms of these criteria must be accepted by all concerned.

ORGANIZATIONAL PATTERNS

Modus Operandi

The manner in which the work of the center is to be conducted should be discussed early in this overview, for it determines many other aspects of the program. Centers vary greatly in their operations from one-to-one tutoring, to small-group, large-group and whole-class instruction. Some operate as though there is only one practical way to deal with the numbers that they serve, while others employ all types of arrangements with apparent ease. The staff of each center often seems quite assured that there is greatest efficiency in the particular organizational pattern that they employ. Are there any guidelines for the conduct of remedial work? Is individual, small group, or large group best? How often should the sessions occur? How long should they continue? When should pupils be discharged from the services? There are other questions, of course, that enter into the center's operational schemes, but we shall approach these later.

Let us first consider a comparison of individual versus small-group work. To our knowledge, there is no strong evidence in favor of either, at least in terms of reading gains (5). Individualized tutoring is a luxury that can be afforded only in special situations, as private centers with sizeable fees; in schools where a great deal of free or low-paid paraprofessional assistance is available; or in cases in which emotional disturbance or anxiety play a large part in the pupil's failure. Small-group instruction can produce as large gains as individualized work when the materials are carefully keyed to pupil needs; when sessions are well planned; and when pupils are reasonably similar in abilities, ages, and interests.

There is no magic number in small-group instruction, such as the total of five pupils often insisted upon in many places, for in other centers larger groups, as great as ten or so pupils, have produced as much gain. Beyond fifteen pupils, however, it is difficult to maintain the close working relationship between teacher and pupils upon which success heavily depends.

Many high school and college centers use large-group instruction under the mistaken assumption that they can thus serve the greatest number. But the attrition rate is usually high and gains in grade point average, which are really the primary goals at this level, are not generally great under these conditions.

An approach to solving the problem of numbers to be served is sometimes found in a laboratory arrangement. A portion of the center is equipped with many self-directing materials, which pupils are permitted to use before and after school hours, during any free periods of the day, and, of course, during their regularly scheduled periods. A staff member is usually available in the area for consultation and advice, as well as for interviews and planning. With mature pupils, this arrangement permits services to more students than even large-class instruction, a very important advantage in its favor. It also provides a greater opportunity for the pupil to become involved in his own progress, for, rather than being dependent upon the directions and efforts of a teacher, he is given the opportunity of assuming some responsibility for his improvement, of pacing his efforts, and evaluating himself.*

Scheduling

Many centers operate on a semester basis, particularly those above elementary grades. A schedule of a certain number of sessions per week is made, students being discharged automatically at the close of the term. This type of arrangement assumes that the same amount (and often type) of instruction suffices for all students, regardless of the nature or degree of their retardation. That this is a false assumption is shown by the failure of many of these students to persist in attendance (or effort), in the frequent lack of effect upon school grades, and sometimes even in the failure to show gain on a posttraining reading test. The degree of retardation present in some high school students, in many freshmen entering junior colleges with an open-door policy, and even in many who gain admission to state and private universities is often not overcome under this plan. In our opinion, one-semester programs are appropriate only for students weak in a specific skill, such as flexibility of rate, not for those whose general retardation has persisted for a number of prior years. We are implying, of course, that remedial centers, instead of simply imitating course arrangements, should maintain an open-door policy for all students in its client population. Ideally speaking, students who meet the criteria of selection should be permitted to seek assistance in the center at any time or times that they feel the need during their school career. We are referring here, of course, to students above elementary grades, for these latter do not always have sufficient self-insight to recognize their needs.

It is apparent that we are opposing in principle the practice of requiring students who test below a certain cut-off score on the survey test to attend the center. Many institutions operate in this fashion by requiring students who test poorly—or sometimes the entire freshman class—to enter the center. This may seem a desirable practice in some populations with poor academic achievement, but it ignores the reactions of the individual students. Someone has observed that there are all types of students in remedial centers: those who expect the training to help in their reading and grade point average, and it does; those who expect to improve in reading ability, but see little relevance to

*The laboratory approach assumes that, following the usual diagnostic procedures, the nature of the remedial work is planned jointly by the pupil and teacher and that self-evaluation techniques are present in the remedial program.

grades, and these expectations are realized; and those who do not expect to or see no need for improvement in reading or its relevance to grades, and they improve in neither respect after the training. We have often met a fourth type who is under the illusion that faster reading skill will solve all his academic problems and mistakenly expects these results from the center's training. What we are trying to say is that the student's expectations regarding the center's training tend to determine its actual effects. Forcing students who have negative attitudes or mistaken assumptions, or those whose personal goals are not academically oriented, to take remedial reading is a waste of professional time and money. Carl Rogers, the father of nondirective psychology, has long insisted that we cannot help an individual who does not have a felt need; we are strongly inclined to agree.

When the proportion of retarded readers in the client population is great and we are anxious to serve as many as possible, we can persuade many to seek assistance without forcing them by administrative fiat. A public relations program addressed to the student body, such as will be outlined later, is a sounder approach, in our opinion.

In terms of actual attendance at the center, the frequency and duration of sessions is related to the age or attention span of the pupil. Sessions are usually a half or a full hour, or whatever length of class period is common, repeated from several times a week up to daily sessions. There is little evidence regarding the effectiveness of remedial sessions in terms of their frequency, duration, or length of session. Among young pupils, sessions should probably be not much more than a half-hour and perhaps as frequent as every day. Among older pupils, fewer sessions per week of about an hour each seem reasonably effective. Some doubt that sessions once or twice a week will produce gains as great or as rapidly as three or four at any grade level. In our experience in a college laboratory, students permitted to attend daily made only superficial progress in transferring their learning to the study situation. While they learned the concepts and practices offered in terms of ability to repeat them verbally, they had not had sufficient time between sessions to apply, modify, or adopt these new practices. Hence, we limited sessions to three a week, distributed over the entire five days. The total number of sessions should, in our opinion, be related to the degree of retardation and the pupil's progress, as well as to his felt needs.

Should remedial sessions be scheduled in place of classroom lessons in reading? If possible with elementary pupils this is often a wise procedure, particularly if the classroom teacher persists in offering a program that is inappropriate. With older pupils, we prefer to let them set their own schedule, since that involves them in the planning of the program.

Diagnostic Cases

Earlier we implied that some referrals should be accepted only for diagnosis, such as those who have just begun to show signs of failure at primary or other levels. This discrimination between diagnostic and remedial functions of the center is an important one. Many pupils are only temporary failures because of emotional or family problems, inappropriate grade placement, school transfers, abrupt introduction to a new method, or personality clashes with an instructor. Many referrals that may have to be temporarily accepted for politic reasons do not present deep or long-standing problems. And, certainly, some pupils appear to fail because of classroom emphasis upon a sensory approach or a skill that they cannot deal with. In such cases, classroom observation, interviews with pupil or teacher or parents, and a minimum of diagnostic tests will often suffice to reveal the basic problem and to indicate appropriate corrective steps, without any need for extended remedial effort. Scheduling staff time for these diagnostic cases is an important aspect of public relations with the school staff and student body. Through them the center creates a favorable image of a service that is readily available and really helpful in a wide variety of problems related to academic achievement. Besides, the practice helps establish the facts that the center is not omnipotent, for many of these cases involve referral to other agencies; also, that the center does not necessarily take in all cases for extended periods of time. Since each diagnostic case is followed by an explanation of the pupil's needs and of the fact that he is not really a retarded reader according to the center's selection criteria, this type of service also helps clarify the center's true function and standards to those referring cases.

Some centers function only for diagnosis or for short-term therapy. After a week or two of observation, diagnosis, and initial treatment, the pupil returns to his school. Center staff members then visit the school regularly, offering individual or small-group remedial treatment to these pupils for as long as necessary. Pupils of several schools may thus be served by a center staff member.

Discharge

An important part of the center's modus operandi is its manner of final disposition of cases. When should a pupil be discharged from remediation? What criteria lead to this decision? What contacts with his teachers should be made at this time? Some centers simply use the comparison of the pupil's mental age and reading performance as the sole criterion for discharge. When the pupil tests in reading at a level commensurate with his mental age, it is assumed that his problems have all been solved and that he has been trained to the limits of his capacity. As we have suggested earlier, this assumption of equivalence between mental and reading ages is true for only a small proportion of the general population, probably only that group between 90 and 110 in I.Q. There just is not any good reason to expect each pupil to perform in reading at his mental age level, any more than we could expect it in arithmetic, handwriting, spelling, social science, or any other content area. Pupils do not develop evenly in these areas, but rather differ more and more in strengths and weaknesses as they mature. Probably only at the undifferentiated age of five to six is the pupil similarly advanced in many areas. A better criterion, perhaps, is that present in a comparison of his performances with the grade averages of his peers, for that is the real situation in which he must function in the future. A pupil is then ready for discharge when it appears both by test and in actual use of classroom materials that he can compete with his peer group on favorable terms.

Though it is useful in selecting cases, auditory comprehension, like mental age, is not very relevant to determining the proper time to discharge pupils. This measure of potential continues to excel the average elementary child's reading performance, and the difference may even be increased by remedial work that has produced general language development. Only at about the sixth grade do reading scores begin to equal and finally to surpass listening scores in the development of the normal reader. Retarded readers may continue to score higher in listening beyond this point, until remedial work creates the opposite trend. Hence a simple comparison of reading and auditory comprehension scores does not reveal the extent to which reading has developed toward its potential limit, or whether the pupil is ready to be discharged.

Another factor entering into the decision to discharge is the nature of the situation to which the pupil will return. Will the teacher accept and follow through on our suggestions for future assistance for the pupil? Is her program reasonably flexible, and does it show cognizance of individual differences? What are her attitudes toward this pupil and her expectations for him? What are her expectations about the center's help to the pupil; that is, does she think that all his problems are solved and that he will no longer need any special attention? If the answers to these questions are unfavorable, and they cannot be altered by better communication between the center and the teacher, it may be wise to delay discharge. We might decide to continue remedial work until his performances are as good or better than the average of his peer group in order to insure his success in a highly demanding situation. We might also consider alternative solutions such as placement with a different teacher, or a continued relationship with the center at gradually increasing intervals until he is completely capable of standing on his own. All the efforts of the center can be vitiated by returning the pupil to a classroom situation that initially contributed to his failure. Many improved pupils retrogress seriously in reading achievement within a year or two after having been returned to the classroom. While some centers do not have the absolute privilege of placing children in the most favorable setups, it is certainly only common sense to try to convince the administration of the need for some of these changes. The need to pay careful attention to the classroom conditions to which pupils discharged from the center are being returned is reinforced by the implications of many follow-up studies that demonstrate this regression tendency.

Grades

It is a moot question whether school grades can or should be given for attendance at the center. If so, how should these grades be determined: by the amount of gain on a posttraining test; by the degree of student effort at self-improvement; by the faithfulness of attendance; or in terms of the readiness of the pupil to resume normal classroom work? Gains on a posttraining test may or may not really mean anything, for they appear as a result of regression to the mean, the practice effect of repeated testing, and a result of increasing test-taking sophistication. A number of studies show that just a bit of knowledge about how to take the test can apparently produce as much gain as lengthy remedial training. Besides, how do we equate gains of similar amount by pupils who started with different degrees of retardation? For example, is one year's gain by a junior high school pupil who originally tested at third-grade level equal to the same gain by a similar pupil who began with seventh-grade ability? Or is a gain from the 5th to the 10th percentile equal to a gain from the 40th to 45th? Certainly not, for in both examples the pupil with the lower initial status has made much more gain in development than the other. Moreover, if we consider the I.Q. of the pupil as well as his initial status—since both tend to enter into his rate of gain—we are even more puzzled regarding the appropriate grades to be given.

There are, of course, many mathematical techniques for removing the influence of regression to the mean, the reliability of the test, the practice effect of repeated testing, and that of initial status. These are discussed in the preceding chapter and should be consulted if an objective method of comparing gains is to be used. For those unwilling to make this effort, we suggest that they consider ignoring the exact amount of gain as a primary basis for grades, subordinating this to emphasis upon pupil effort toward self-improvement as manifest in industry in the sessions and persistence in attendance. Much of the student's future success in dealing with reading tasks is dependent upon his belief in his own improvement and his involvement in the remedial process. His statements about the benefits he receives from the training are not closely related to his actual gains on a posttraining test. But the feelings they imply, his observable effort in the remedial sessions, and his attendance are the foundations of his self-concept as a reader. And many poor readers succeed in school and college, if they think they can, and apply their weak skills industriously.

STAFFING THE CENTER

Selection

For the sake of this discussion, let us assume that the staff of the center has not been preselected by administrative order but that there is the opportunity to select and develop a working group. Under these conditions, the director will seek persons who have a variety of professional skills. Some of the staff should certainly have had successful classroom teaching experience, preferably at the grade levels from which the majority of the clients will be drawn. Others should have had training in diagnosis of speech disorders; or in the administration of intelligence and personality tests; or in psychological methods of therapy such as counseling, play therapy, behavior modification, and the like. If some are drawn from the ranks of classroom teachers, they should be selected from those who have, or are attempting to acquire, the qualifications for reading specialists as outlined by the International Reading Association. We are quite aware that we are emphasizing ideal conditions, for, as some surveys show (2), a large proportion of remedial teachers do not meet these basic qualifications and *some have not even had a recent course in reading methods.* These facts reflect, of course, the offhand way in which many remedial services are established, a situation that we hope these guidelines will help correct.

We are also aware that centers in some public school systems cannot readily find staff members with these various types of qualifications. Often the staff must be drawn almost entirely from the body of classroom teachers, who lack training in these specialized areas that we think significant. In these cases, public school centers have alternative approaches to finding qualified specialists. One is to arrange with a nearby university to employ graduate students who have the desired training. In some majors, graduate students are required to obtain field experience or to serve an internship; their professors may be willing to have them fulfill this requirement in the remedial center. This practice of loaning qualified graduate students to school systems is much more common than many public schools seem to realize. A second source of varied professional personnel may be present within the school system. Parttime services may be obtained from school psychologists, speech correction teachers, counseling and guidance personnel, and others. In attempting to avail the center of such assistance, it is wise to approach the individuals concerned to ascertain their willingness to collaborate before making application to the school administration for formal approval of a working relationship. While useful, these part-time interdepartmental arrangements are often only temporary because of changes in school personnel and they may present real problems in scheduling. There is also the problem of pecking order, for these are, in a sense, consultants for the center; they are not subordinate to its demands or perhaps even concerned about its needs. But these arrangements are possible, at least until the center staff can increase.

When qualified specialists are lacking in the school system, centers may seek them among the professional workers of the community. Some of the time of clinical psychologists, for example, may be contracted for by the center. Centers that have adequate budget avail themselves of a wide variety of specialists, including optometrists, pediatricians, psychiatrists, social workers, and the like. In a few cases, some of these specialists may donate a small portion of their time to aid the center, or they will accept referrals at reduced rates when the center demonstrates the client's need and lack of funds. The possibilities of these various relationships with universities, other school personnel, and professional workers of the community should certainly be explored in any case. Remedial centers will inevitably handle cases arising from a wide variety of etiological causes with which they should have professional assistance of a high order.

Two other sources of staff for the center are present in the average community. One of these is paid or volunteer paraprofessionals drawn from the ranks of parents, retired teachers, and older pupils in school. There is a growing trend toward the use of these paraprofessionals and supporting evidence that their work is profitable for retarded pupils. Some centers make wide use of the nonprofessional workers, both in the center proper and in farming out pupils for tutoring in other settings. Training for these student or adult helpers is most desirable, and we shall discuss this later in detail. With this training and careful selection of the instructional materials by the center, small-group or one-to-one tutoring by paraprofessionals has been shown to be a practical approach to the problem of numbers faced by most centers (5, 6, 7, 8). There are hazards, of course, in this situation in terms of personality clashes, inadequate information regarding the process of learning to read, and lack of experience in methods of handling younger individuals. But careful selection of the cases to be handled by paraprofessionals and a continued in-service training program, plus constructive supervision by the center staff, will keep these to a minimum.

Particularly in the early stages of establishment of the center, university reading or learning disability specialists can be a good source of assistance. We suggest seeking those who have conducted remedial services rather than those professors whose work is solely in the preparation of undergraduate education majors. Also, from time to time after the center is in operation, these remedial specialists should be invited to visit the center as consultants to evaluate its progress and to bring a fresh viewpoint to its operations.

Responsibilities

The division of responsibilities of the staff may be approached in several ways. The director could devise a hierarchy of positions and titles with stipulated duties. In the beginning, these assignments would be based upon the particular skills and experience of the initial staff. For example, some members might be assigned solely to diagnosis in the area of reading skills, while others would concentrate on remediation or on psychometric testing. Some would be given responsibilities in the area of public relations because of their public-speaking skills, while others would be more effective in working with parents or children. Some will work with groups of teachers; others will be assigned to home visits with parents. Obviously, these responsibilities are to be assigned gradually, as the capabilities of the staff become apparent.

Each center eventually evolves its concept of a complete case study. Some centers prefer that all responsibilities or actions concerning each case be conducted by one staff member. This arrangement is believed to give greater coherence to the data and the reports. Other centers, as we have mentioned, employ each staff member in his area of competence, and then assign one person to collate the facts and prepare the case history. The various reports may be brought together and discussed in a staff meeting, or they may be simply gathered by the assigned worker and incorporated in a final statement. The choice of these methods of processing a case is determined in part by the number of cases being accepted, as well as the breadth of competencies of the staff. When the intake of cases is small, the staffing of each case by all members concerned is feasible. But when large numbers of cases are being admitted, use of each staff member largely in his area of training, with eventual collation of these observations, is more practical.

Ideally speaking, each staff member should broaden his professional experience by participating in almost every aspect of the center's activities. But when the staff is eventually composed of a number of specialists, they may not be particularly interested in becoming competent in many areas. Or the personal characteristics of the staff members may fit them only for certain types of work. Not all good remedial teachers are good at diagnosis; not all good diagnosticians are competent in small-group or individual tutoring. The eventual nature of the staff tends to determine its manner of operation and the division of responsibilities.

Training

In-service training of the staff of the center is essential for its professional competence and growth. It may be arranged in obvious ways, such as requiring members to take those courses needed for professional certification; inviting consultants to observe and discuss the center's operations; and asking specialists from other school departments to speak to the staff regarding their functions. Demonstrations by salesmen and publishers' representatives are another good source of professional information about instructional materials and devices. Less formal in-service training, which is probably even more realistic than those mentioned, is present in the staff's interrelations. In staffing cases, for example, members constantly learn more about other specialized areas and their relevance to their own spheres of interest. When regular staff meetings are held to discuss the policies of the center, each member gains a broader background in the whole operation—its successes and failures and problems—and also feels a sense of identification with the administration of the center.

When the staff is composed of remedial or classroom teachers or comprises a number of graduate students, a planned in-service training program in most of the details of the center's operation is necessary. For example, each staff member could be processed through the entire procedure (from initial interview to final disposition) as though he were a client of the center. He would be tested for sensory defects, intelligence, personality, reading skills, and so on, with instruments appropriate to his age. Each body of results would then be interpreted to him privately by the tester. Later he would practice the administration of tests of each area under supervision, until he was judged reasonably competent by his more experienced colleagues.

The results of this testing and training would be reported to the director, with the knowledge of the staff member. Then the director could suggest corrective steps that the staff member might take to improve his effectiveness. This same type of in-service training would, of course, be followed with new staff members, unless they were being engaged for one specific function.

It is most desirable that the staff training activities and the atmosphere of the center create the impression that participation in the center is a remarkable professional experience. Staff members should be led to feel that, whether they expect to continue in this type of work or to return to the classroom, they have had a wonderful opportunity to broaden their professional skills and information. The variety of in-service training activities to which they are exposed, and the frequency of professional and social relationships with the director, specialists, and other members of the staff, as in consultations and staff meetings, can foster this realization. It is probably true that the primary goal of any remedial center is service to its client population. But this is only the short-range goal. Few centers can serve more than a small proportion of the retarded pupils in their client population. Hence, a long-range goal should be the inspiration and training of more competent workers in the field. This inspirational and staff training aim cannot be lost sight of or completely subordinated to the daily remedial services to clients.

In the same vein, the center serves a greater function than just service to clients in the training efforts that extend beyond its own staff. If, as we argue, many cases of retardation are created by faulty classroom practices, then the staff has an obligation to work with teachers to correct these situations. This broader service can be offered by short courses or workshops within the center, by college courses under the sponsorship of a cooperating university, and by inviting groups of teachers to visit the center. The relationships between the center and the teachers of pupils referred to it are another opportunity to help teachers improve their practices. Some centers have a regular schedule of visitations for such classroom teachers to enable them to view and understand the center's approaches to remediation. In fact, some centers will not accept a pupil unless his teacher agrees to be interviewed and to visit the center a certain number of times. A few centers arrange with the local school administration for groups of teachers of a certain grade level to visit the center to observe. After the observation, staff members meet with the group to explain their remedial procedures, to display their instructional materials, and to answer questions.

One center with which we are familiar entered into in-service training for teachers by bringing both a teacher and her class into the center for a period of time. Other teachers of the same grade level were asked to observe this class as conducted by the remedial teacher and afterward to discuss the relevance of the procedures they observed to their own classrooms. Another ongoing relationship with teachers is present in the center's sharing of its diagnostic and remedial observations of each pupil. We shall discuss this sharing later in greater detail, mentioning it here simply as another example of the ways that the center can help improve classroom instruction. Finally, one large school system used its reading centers as a training base for new teachers entering the system. All new teachers were assigned to the center for a portion of their first year's service, attending one or several afternoons a week to function as aides in the center. Thus they could be introduced to the methods and materials they might be using in the classroom. This arrangement was initiated by a superintendent who had authored several of the materials that were used in his system. Naturally, he was anxious that his methods and materials be used appropriately. We have reservations about such a use of a center, preferring the idea of a thorough introduction to the latest techniques by this sort of plan. Teachers should be brought to the center, not to indoctrinate them in a certain approach, but rather to broaden their knowledge of methods and to combat some of their unsound ideas and practices.

Although some studies seem to have been successful without any training for pupil tutors or paraprofessionals, most teachers would be likely to feel that some introductory training is most desirable. Certainly the handling of the pupil-tutor relationship would be more effective if the tutors had some basic ideas about how to operate. Niedermeyer (7) has shown that even sixth graders trained to function as tutors learned such techniques as how to relate to the pupil by conversation prior to, during, or after sessions; how to confirm or correct pupil responses; how to give praise for each effort; and how to offer the correct response when the pupil errs, and have him repeat the correction before continuing. Allen, Della-Piana, and Stahmann (1) have concentrated on the training of parents who would act as tutors, as well as a type of training for parents of remedial subjects who are not functioning in a tutorial fashion. Several of these researchers have outlined the content of the training of tutors and included such areas as these:

1. Offering a structured or programmed body of materials for the tutor and pupil to follow. Directions to the tutor and expected responses of the pupil, as well as programmed reading materials, are present in this approach.
2. Some instruction in child development and language growth and the influence upon these of the tutor's active, responsive role.

We would add the following:

3. Concepts of the reading process and important reading skills at various stages.

4. How to support, encourage, praise, and reward pupil effort phsyically and verbally in a positive manner.

5. How to use workbooks, readers, trade books, and programmed materials effectively (whether such materials are selected by the tutor or the remedial teacher-supervisor).

6. How to use a variety of questions to evoke thought and interpretations as well as recall.

7. How to conduct questioning strategies by interspersing clarification and explanation of the question after an erroneous response; how to progress from recall and memory to interpretation and discussion questions, in preference to the reverse.

8. How to conduct questioning or discussion in a small group, that is, deemphasizing competition to be the first to answer; directing questions directly to pupils rather than vaguely to the entire group; insuring active participation of all members; adjusting the difficulty of the question to the probable abilities of the pupil addressed.

9. How to conduct an oral reading session without allowing it to degenerate into a word-pronouncing contest; to use oral reading for what are basically communication situations, in a variety of types of materials.

Size of Staff

The size of the center staff is, or should be, related to the size of the retarded population that it will serve, and to the modus operandi of the remediation as well as, of course, the budget. Some centers in a public elementary school will work almost daily with small groups of children, and thus yearly serve most of the retarded pupils with a staff of two or three (assuming the school has a total population under 1,000). In large high schools and some colleges, large-group instruction is a common approach, with each remedial teacher conducting sessions two or three times a week for each of perhaps as many as five to eight groups. In one junior college center we visited, this type of mass operation was arranged by dividing the freshmen into ten levels according to their percentiles on a survey test, selecting a workbook or two for each level, and then assigning each staff member to work with the students of a particular level in whole class arrangements. The problem of numbers may seem to be solved by these class approaches, but the only results that they are likely to achieve is some sort of gross improvement of general reading ability, as measured by the total score on a survey test. This type of results satisfies many and is reported frequently in our reading journals. As we have pointed out earlier in discussing the question of school grades for remediated pupils, gains on a reading test after instruction are no real evidence of the validity of the program. Most really poor readers respond to training in the expected fashion whether or not the program has really enabled them to function better in school.

Our prejudice against whole class instruction without intraclass grouping and related differential instruction is by now apparent. We do not believe it is any better than whole class instruction by competent classroom teachers, which, as we have seen, continuously produces candidates for remedial help. Nor is it necessarily a good solution when large numbers of students must be served. Our own experience in a remedial center has shown us that literally hundreds of students can be helped on an individual basis in an open laboratory. Following group and individual diagnostic testing, each student can follow a program of self-improvement that is directly related to his needs, at his own pace, with guidance available when necessary from a staff member. For example, in a thirty-five-hour week in which students attend three times a week, thirty to forty can be readily accommodated each hour for a total of over 400 students, with a total staff of three to four. We are not suggesting that this is an ideal arrangement, for it is difficult to promote close working relationships between staff and students (as the same teacher may not be present in the laboratory each time that a student attends). But regular visits with one staff member can be woven into the student's schedule, since the counseling sessions need not be very long in this type of self-directing plan.

The ideal case load of a staff member is a very difficult question. In one-to-one tutoring, the teacher can handle not much more than twenty-five cases in a week, and even this would leave little time for other staff responsibilities. In small-group arrangements meeting as often as three times a week, the case load might include eight groups or perhaps as many as seventy to eighty pupils. In whole class arrangements, a teacher may work with six to eight groups with as many as thirty in each. It must be recognized that, as the number of pupils handled by a staff member increases, the possibilities of continued diagnosis of needs and individualization of treatment tend to decrease. The pressure of numbers to be served also often leads to losing sight of the fact that a remedial worker has other important functions than just remedial instruction.

The work schedule of a remedial teacher should include a time provision, perhaps as great as the equivalent of one day per week, for basic functions. Among these are staff meetings, maintenance of records, planning for instruction and assembling materials, and liaison with the classroom teachers of her pupils, or with other faculty. Time must also be planned for visits to or with parents, the administration of individual or small-group diagnostic and progress tests, and contacts with the personnel of referral agencies or with consultants to the center. All too often, these essential activities that tend to determine the ultimate effectiveness of remedial treatment are not provided for in the worker's schedule. Her working time may be monopolized by instructional activities and these other basic functions left to be done in her free moments or in postcenter hours. We feel that definite blocks of time, each of three or four hours, should be designated in the schedule for these functions. This is preferable to considering scattered one-class periods, during which she is free of instructional duties, as sufficient or appropriate.

Secretarial staff is essential for any center of almost any size beyond one or two members and, even in this case, secretarial services should be available as needed. The time of professional workers should not be wasted in activities such as typing, filing, answering telephones, receiving guests and visitors, preparing reports in final form, and the like. Once routines and forms have been evolved, these can be executed more efficiently and economically by clerical workers than by the staff itself.

Records

Among the types of records that an efficient center must evolve are data collection forms to assemble the facts available from parents, school records, referral agencies, and community professionals. Each of these will differ according to the source to which it is addressed, but there will be overlap in the facts sought in order to improve accuracy and the depth of information. For example, the forms sent to the parent and the school might include the forms shown on pages 370-373.

These forms should be sent to the parent and school as soon as the initial contact with the center is made, and their return requested by a date prior to the first interviews. In many instances, the factual contradictions or contrasting viewpoints of the pupil's problem will be revealed and can be explored profitably in the initial interviews. These forms will be an integral part of the case record and filed with it, after corrections or comments have been added by the interviewer.

Some centers evolve a record sheet on which the results of all tests administered are entered after the diagnostic sessions. Others simply place the front page of each test record form on which the test results are inscribed in the file. The latter, a space-saving procedure, avoids duplicating test results

CASE HISTORY REPORT

* PARENT EDITION *

last name first name middle

residence address

city county state

school grade age

THE READING LABORATORY AND CLINIC
University College, Anderson Hall
UNIVERSITY OF FLORIDA
Gainesville, Florida

Page 2.

Child's Name ______ *Birth Date* ______ *Today's Date* ______
Address ______ *Telephone* ______
Present School ______ *Grade* ______ *Teacher* ______
Family Doctor ______ *Address* ______
Person Interviewed ______ *by* ______
Referred to Clinic by ______

I. Physical History

1. Any unusual birth conditions *(Full term—Injuries—Prolonged labor—Natural—Caesarean or Instrumental)* ______

2. Early illnesses, accidents, or operations. *(Age—Severity—Effects)* ______

3. Development; Age at walking ______ Talking ______
(Outstanding traits as a young child; slow or early development) ______

4. Child shows symptoms of undue fatigue, visual or hearing defect, or any oth problem contributing to difficulties? How? ______

5. General health. *(Colds, sore throat, nausea, underweight, etc.)* ______

NOTES: ______

Page 3.

II. School History

School attended	In grade	Progress and success *(Parent's comments on school.)*

Any long absences? Duration	When? In grade	Why?

Parent satisfied with school? Why not? ______
Child's relations with present teacher. ______
With previous teacher. ______
NOTES: ______

III. Reading Problems *(Parent's concept)*

When reading problem began? ______ How or why? ______
______ Present difficulties ______

Any previous remedial help? ______ By whom? ______ When? ______
For how long? ______ Of what nature? ______
With what results? ______
Is present school giving special help? ______ Of what nature? ______

Page 4.

Is parent helping? How?__________

About how many books does child own?______ Magazines?______ Comics?______

Spontaneous reading—How much? ______ Kinds?______

Child's attitude toward reading. ______

NOTES: ______

IV. Child's Attitudes and Interests

Playmates and friends—How many?______ What ages? ______

Relations with other children - Good? Why not? ______

Show aggressiveness? Leadership? How? ______

Hobbies ______

Child's attitude toward school ______

Any special abilities? ______

Out-of-school lessons ______

NOTES: ______

V. Parent-Child Relationships

By whom is child usually disciplined? ______ How? ______ Any difference of opinion between parents? ______

In what respects? ______

Father's relations with child ______

Mother's relations with child ______

NOTES: ______

Page 5.

VI. Family History

Any unusual events during early childhood? Any problems in home conditions *(Finances, relatives, religion, companions for child, relations with brothers and sisters, foreign language)* ______

Father—Name ______ Age ___ Occup. ___ Elem. ___ H.S. Educ. ___ Coll. ___

Mother—Name ______ Age ___ Occup. ___ Elem. ___ H.S. Educ. ___ Coll. ___

Brothers—Name ______ Age ___ Sisters—Name ______ Age ___

Other members of family in home *(relationship, ages)* ______

Marital status of parents ______

Occasionally, we find it desirable to record a testing session or permit observation by a graduate student. Do you have any objections to such observation of your child?

NOTES: ______

General Summary

NAME ________ last ________ first ________ middle ________ SCHOOL ________ GRADE ________ AGE ________

CASE HISTORY REPORT

* SCHOOL EDITION *

____
last name *first name* *middle*

____
residence address

____
city *county* *state*

____
school *grade* *age*

THE READING LABORATORY AND CLINIC
University College, Anderson Hall
UNIVERSITY OF FLORIDA
Gainesville, Florida

Page 2.

Child's Name ________ *Date* ________ *School* ________

I. Physical Status

Child shows visual or hearing troubles? How? ________

Any other physical defects or conditions that contribute to child's difficulties? ________

II. School Attendance and History

Age at entrance to first grade ________ Any long absences? When? Why? ________

Duration of absences	In grade	Reason

Comments on progress and success *(summarize reports or ask for teacher's comments)* ________

Grade ________ Comments ________

Grade ________ Comments ________

Grade ________ Comments ________

Testing Results—Intelligence

Name of Test	Date	MA or IQ results

Achievement *(Reading and Spelling)*

Name of Test	Date	Score	Name of Test	Date	Score

Page 3.

III. Reading Problems

Is child showing evidence of reading or language difficulty? Since when? How? ____________

Causes of difficulties ____________

Any other subject difficulties? ____________

What level reading materials are being used with him? ____________

Has he been given special help in this school? By whom? ____________

Since when? ____________ Of what nature? ____________

With what results? ____________

IV. Child's Attitudes and Interests

Playmates or class friends—How many? Who? Ages? ____________

Relations with other children—Good? Why not? ____________

Shows aggressiveness? Leadership? How? ____________

Spontaneous reading—How much? ____________ Kinds? ____________

Child's attitude toward reading ____________

Child's attitude toward school ____________

Any special abilities? ____________

Extracurricular activities ____________

Best school subjects ____________

Page 4.

V. Family Conditions

Any home problems that may contribute to child's difficulties *(finances, relatives, religion, child's companions, relations with brothers and sisters, forsign language).* ____________

Use this space, if you wish, to make any other comments regarding this child that will help the Reading Laboratory and Clinic to understand his reading difficulties. ____________

____
signature

____
title

in both the diagnostic report and on a separate sheet. Saving only the front page of the test record form—provided that raw and derived scores for all subtests are noted—will suffice for most circumstances, unless some research involving item analysis is planned in the future.

The format and content of the typical diagnostic report should be evolved by joint action of the staff. Among other areas that should be covered are a summary of the developmental, school, and health history; a summary of the interviews with the parent and/or the pupil's teacher; results of the screening for visual and auditory handicaps; interpretation of the strengths and weaknesses revealed in the intelligence testing; interpretation of the personality tests given the pupil, the interaction in the family constellation, and teacher-pupil relationships; the results of tests of perception, reading, spelling, and related academic areas, with interpretation; a tentative summary of all these diagnostic data; and recommendations for treatment, referral or other action. Some discretion in the fullness of the report in each area is necessary, as, for example, the early developmental history becomes less significant for older-aged cases. Information about the family and its problems may often be obtained from a social service exchange and should be added to the file.

There are a number of values to be derived from the staff's planning of the outline of a diagnostic report such as this. New staff members will have a clearer picture of the entire intake procedure to guide them. Older members will be guided away from following their own diagnostic tangents while neglecting to assemble the basic data. This does not prevent staff members from adding new or experimental instruments to the diagnostic process, for this should be encouraged, after the nature of the experimental test has been discussed and its use approved in staff meetings. Standardization of the format and content of the diagnostic report insures greater clarity, decreases the tendency to esoteric jargon, and makes reports more readable for those outside the center to whom frequent reports are sent.

Copies of the diagnostic report should be given to parents and teachers, with oral explanations, and sent to referral agencies, for every case. The exact wording of the report may need to be different in the copies for the parent and the teacher, for there may be confidential matter that is obtained from one of these sources that need not be revealed to the other. For example, when marital problems, parental conflict, or pupil-teacher conflict or the like assume a significant role in the pupil's difficulties, it may be sounder to omit this emphasis in the report either to the parent or the school, although it may have been discussed in the interview with one or the other. These facts would be included in supplementary notes in the center's copy, however. Some centers find it serviceable to use the same outline for the report to parents or schools as that agreed upon for the center's records, simply adapting it as necessary.

We believe it most advisable to send progress reports to both parents and classroom teachers from time to time during remedial treatment. Again, the content may vary according to its recipient, but it should include such information as the nature and grade level of the instructional and recreational materials being used; the reading skills being emphasized, or the nature of the therapy employed; some interpretation of the child's specific and general progress; and specific suggestions for reinforcement activities that could be used in the home or classroom. Including the center's telephone number and an invitation to call for interpretation of this progress report is advisable. The frequency and outline of these progress reports is also a staff decision, but for good public relations the intervals should probably not be any greater than two or three weeks. Progress reports can contribute to the interest and concern of both parents and teachers in the pupil's progress and, in the case of the teacher, lead her to a clearer understanding of the pupil's needs in classroom work. Keeping parents and teachers informed of the progress helps produce better comprehension of the final report and of the child's potentials for performance in the classroom, as well as a more realistic interpretation of the center's success in its remedial efforts.

In a sense, the final report issued when the pupil is discharged is a résumé of the diagnostic and progress letters. It should review the initial status, describe the measures taken, and evaluate the pupil's progress. It should also offer recommendations for the future to prevent regression in the pupil's gains, along with repeating the invitation to call the center or visit again if further help is desired.

In individual or small-group arrangements, a log of the teacher's observations or an anecdotal record, as it were, contributes to the personalization of the progress and final reports. As a cumulative record of the pupil's behavior, success in skill development, and responses to materials and methods, the log aids in planning or modifying the remedial program. Needless to say, copies of the progress, final reports, and the log become part of the permanent case record.

Cross-indexing of the case records for reference and research purposes is most desirable. We found a coding system punched into McBee Keysort Cards of great value. Holes were designated for each item of identification as age, date, sex, and grade level; for each diagnostic test administered; for the major etiological factors; and for the posttraining test results. Other areas that can be included on a single card are treatments used, skills emphasized, experimental tests employed, number of treatment sessions, and the like. The McBee Keysort Card will accommodate almost a hundred identifying items using single or multiple hole punches. Cards containing any certain item are readily sorted out by inserting an ice pick through the relevant hole, and shaking a stack of cards. Those punched at the item in question then fall to the desk. Once the coding system has been determined, each staff member simply indicates the holes to be punched as he turns the case record over to the secretary for filing. She adds the pupil's name to the card, punches the proper holes, and files the card in an appropriate-sized box in an alphabetical order.

As the number of case records increases, it may well exceed the storage space. Some centers meet this problem by reproducing the contents of each file on microfilm or microfiche, which require very little storage space. Sometimes this can be a relatively expensive operation if done by commercial firms. On the other hand, reproduction of dozens of pages can be made on a single microfiche for perhaps as little as ten–fifteen cents when the proper equipment is available.

Equipment and Space

It often seems to be the lot of a center to be assigned the last (and worst) space available. We have visited centers conducted in a cellar and worked in one situated in a remodeled attic. In one school, we did our work in an oversized closet in the corner of a fourth-grade classroom. (Fortunately, the closet had a window.) Some centers that we have visited recently have had much more luxurious quarters, with wall-to-wall carpeting, air-conditioning and the like, which is an encouraging trend.

If the director of a center is permitted to plan the layout of the operation, he will need to include space for such aspects as the reception area; the professional and the pupils' library; the storage area for supplies and records; a secretarial area; and small rooms for testing, interviewing, and other individual staff work. If necessary, some of these areas can, of course, serve a dual function as secretarial-reception, library-individual tutoring, secretarial-storage, library-staff meeting room. The site of the center should not be near administrative offices, or its functions may be confused with the regulatory and punitive functions of these school officers.

Space for instructional purposes will be determined by the size of the clientele and the modus operandi. Open laboratories require a large or double-sized classroom, close to or adjoining the center proper. Small groups can be accommodated in a half-classroom, or one divided into two segments by a folding partition. Individual tutoring can be conducted in almost any small area, free from traffic or interruptions. Whole-class arrangements may be conducted in the lab or any ordinary classroom in which instructional materials can be shelved permanently. We believe that instructional areas should be as close to the center proper as possible and should be permanently designated as such. The staff can be frustrated and ineffectual when compelled to run from room to room carrying the necessary materials for a session (and frequently forgetting something essential). This transporting of materials cannot be avoided when the staff works at nearby schools, but even here some permanent storage and instructional areas are most desirable. If groups are to be accommodated for demonstrations and the like, one-way vision mirrors should be installed between instructional areas and adjoining spaces.

The equipment and furnishings can be categorized under four rubrics: testing, training, library, and office supplies. Testing supplies should include an ample supply of those commonly used for individual and group diagnostic, posttraining, and survey purposes; a sample file of practically all other parallel tests available; and a supply of any used in testing programs of adjacent school systems. Testing instruments would include a vision screening device, as the Bausch-Lomb Ortho-Rater or Titmus Sight Screener; an audiometer; the Spache Binocular Reading Test; the fly Stereo test; or similar devices; as well as an audiometer for individual testing. Training materials, which should be relevant to the age groups served, include workbooks, programmed and regular; ditto masters; teacher-constructed exercise folders and seatwork; perceptual training devices, such as the Getman School Skill Board, pegboards, puzzles, Lummi sticks, walking beam, balance disc, and the like.* Reading improvement manuals, content field reading skill texts, study skills workbooks, and similar commercial materials will also be needed.† A broad selection of filmstrips, slides, and movies; a bulletin board; chalkboards; chart paper or newsprint for language experience material and various displays; and the necessary projection machines will be needed. Kits of parallel strips, records or tapes, and trade books are now widely available, for those to whom a multisensory approach appeals. A tape recorder and record player will be very useful.

Many centers seem to believe that, particularly at secondary and college levels, reading machines are a necessity. Some centers that we have visited

*See George D. Spache, *Good Reading for Poor Readers* (Champaign, Ill.: Garrard Publishing, 1974), for comprehensive list of training materials.
†Ibid.

devoted most of their initial budget to these training devices, now scheduling much of the instructional time in their use. There is little doubt that those students who present problems of inflexibility of rate—and no major difficulties with vocabulary or comprehension—can be helped by some of these devices. But this approach is preferable only when large groups are being trained, for then the machines are economical of instructor time. In individual or small-group work or in an open laboratory, other approaches to rate improvement are equally as effective, requiring only a minimum of machines. Among those suitable for individual and small-group work that do not stress the fallacious increase in span as a means of improving rate are the Tach-X, the Controlled Reader, and the hand Flash-X. Some films and the Perceptoscope also are sound and will be serviceable for the group deficient in this single skill. Other possibilities are the SRA Reading Accelerator, the Shadowscope, or similar instruments not emphasizing span increase.

There are a great many devices currently being offered that claim to contribute to the correction of learning disabilities. Some are based on theories of handedness and eyedness that are indefensible on physiological grounds; others offer a wide variety of kits of games, seatwork, and so on, purported to improve visual perception. We have reviewed the research on perceptual training elsewhere and indicated that many of these package deals were of dubious value, despite their present popularity and the hard sell being given them.

Office equipment will include such essentials as dictating machines, typewriters, copying machines, an adding machine or calculator, a microfilm or microfiche reader, and some centers include a Polaroid camera for adding a picture of each client to his record folder. Record folders are often ordinary manila folders or microfiche reproductions of the records. We found that printing facsimiles of the record form for each test given, on and in the manila folder, eliminated saving separate test records and provided a permanent, accessible record requiring less storage space. As each test was given, the results were immediately transcribed onto the manila folder in detail. Case records containing diagnostic, progress reports, and final reports—as well as correspondence, the log, and staff notes—became easier to handle by this elimination of tests and their record forms. These printed folders also provided a convenient place for identifying data and interview notes and similar matter; they and their contents could be filmed on microfiche if desired. A supply of stationery, typing paper, and so forth, is, of course, necessary for the secretarial work.

We believe that a library of recreational books spanning the reading levels of the clients is an essential part of the center's equipment. Since favorable attitude and interest in reading are a primary goal of the remedial program, we should make suitable books an integral part of our relationships and have them immediately accessible. Frustrated readers, particularly of elementary ages, cannot be expected to seek books at the local or school library. They should be available to be handled, sampled, perhaps read, and discussed with the teacher. To facilitate appropriate selection, these books should be graded, perhaps by the Spache or Dale-Chall formulas, coded by colored stickers, and then organized by interest areas. A variety of dictionaries and other basic reference books, plus children's and teen-age newspapers and magazines suited to the clientele, should be included.

The selection of books for the pupil library should certainly reflect the nature of the clientele population. For example, for a middle-class white population, one might well choose standard classics, series books, adapted classics, and a cross-section of contemporary fiction and nonfiction representing various areas of interest. For inner-city pupils or those of mixed racial or ethnic origins, a large part of the selection, we believe, should be drawn from materials reflecting those origins. Development of self-concept and racial identification are promoted by this highly relevant literature.* The pressure that these pupils feel to read the classic materials often required in their classrooms can be met by providing some of the adapted or simplified versions readily available, if desired.

A professional library of recent texts, handbooks, sample remedial materials, and professional magazines is essential for professional growth of the staff. A file of research studies on microfiche from ERIC/CRIER would be most worthwhile to help the staff in their individual and group research efforts. Binders for assembling back issues of the journals help prevent their loss, and a check-out system for borrowing from the library is desirable for both staff and students.

Games for reinforcement of sight vocabulary, meaning vocabulary, phonic and structural analysis, and other skills are in wide supply. We strongly prefer those that stress the associative learning of meanings of words, as classifying, categorizing, defining, synonyms, antonyms. We doubt the values of those that demand visual matching or rote memory, and those that make no distinction between function words (prepositions, adverbs, adjectives) and meaningful words (nouns, verbs). If the fun element is exploited, some of these learning games may make a positive contribution to the pupils' development. Those constructed by teacher and pupil can be even more relevant to the immediate needs than general commercial items.†

*See George D. Spache *Good Reading for the Disadvantaged* (Champaign, Ill.: Garrard Publishing, 1975).
†See Evelyn B. Spache, *Reading Activities for Child Involvement* (Boston: Allyn and Bacon, 1976).

The reader will probably note that we have not included standard school materials as basal readers and their workbooks in our proposed pupil library. We might place sample copies of those used by adjacent school systems in the professional library for occasional use with pupils as, for example, near the time of discharge to determine readiness for the usual classroom reading. But we strongly object to their frequent use in remedial work as in tutoring pupils in the basal. If the pupil has had classroom instruction of any good quality before, this approach has probably been tried and has apparently failed. Remediation is not just an adjunct or supplement to good classroom instruction, but also an attempt to discover and correct the factors that interfered with the pupil's progress under such instruction. Basal readers may be used from time to time to reinforce the pupil's belief in his ability to deal with required materials, not as a basic tool in remediation ignoring the previous failure in these under similar instruction.

Let us share one other experience related to this assembling of equipment and instructional materials. To supply the variety of materials needed to help high school and college students and to enable them to work independently in the lab, we assembled open files of exercises in reading and study skills. Each exercise was selected from a text or workbook, cut out, and mounted in a manila folder with explanatory and self-evaluation matter we devised. After mounting, the contents of each folder, which might be simply an exercise or an entire chapter, was sprayed by an aerosol devised for library use. The spray saturated the paper and strengthened it, covering the printed matter with an invisible, inkproof coating. Folders providing for continuity among a group of exercises or work-sample applications of the skill, or those replacing the commercial materials found inadequate were typewritten in multiple carbon copies and similarly sprayed. We found that carbons did not smudge and that the life of the workbook pages in the folders was lengthened appreciably. Except for doodling, which was easily erased, no writing was done in each folder, answers being placed on a standardized mimeographed answer sheet.

Among the advantages that we found in this approach were economy, complete flexibility, individualization in skill development, self-pacing, and involvement of the student in his self-evaluations and attempts at application. After discussion of the diagnostic tests with the student, areas to be studied were agreed upon by student and counselor, and he was given outlines of the practice materials in a certain area or two with appropriate numbered folders indicated. We found that this approach had similar positive effect upon gains in measured reading skills but greater impact upon student habits and attitudes in study situations than did group or machine instruction presenting the same concepts and practices (10).

Public Relations

We have already referred to many of the center's activities that involve public relations. Among these were frequent reports to parents, teachers, and referral agenices; conducting demonstrations for groups of teachers; individual staff public relations with interested groups through talks to PTA, school staffs, and student groups; personal visits with parents and teachers in the center, the home, or classroom to discuss pupil needs and the like. A great deal of the center's success as a service organization, as well as with the individuals it treats, depends upon positive public relations efforts of these types. The center must acquire a reputation for pragmatic helpfulness, particularly among students, if it is to serve its basic purposes.

Since the center is often dependent upon administrative approval for its existence, a distinct effort should be made to improve communications in the upward direction. Reports on the number of students served; lists of those in attendance; simple summaries of the measured progress of the students, perhaps accompanied by charts or graphs; notation of any services to other school departments, PTA, and other groups, brief descriptions of collaborative efforts with counselors, deans, and so on, are some of the informational materials that should be distributed to any and all administrative officers, deans, principals, and the like who relate to the center. The center must discover what types and how much information it should send regularly to these personnel, rather than flooding them with unwanted matter. These decisions will gradually evolve from the professional interrelationships with these school or university personnel.

Public relations with students will include posters, bulletin board displays, talks to the student body about the results of survey testing, and the available center services for those who feel the need. Small-group illustrated talks to dormitory groups, in study halls, to fraternities or sororities, or to any interested student group or club will help carry the message of the center's functions.

Relations with community agencies and individual professionals are promoted by regular reports on students referred to the center; exchanges of visits to and from the center; invitations to open house and social occasions arranged at the center; and demonstration of sincere effort to avail oneself of the agency's professional services in helping one's own clients. The center staff should early recognize its limitations in diagnosis of possible physical factors; of its need for information assembled by social service agencies; of the possibilities of professional help with family or marital problems of all types that may be contributing to the pupil's learning difficulties. Assistance in the treatment of emotionally disturbed pupils can often be found in psychiatric social service agencies, and other therapies are available from local psychiatrists, optometrists, psychologists, and other specialists. There is little doubt that pupil difficulties in these areas are among the causes of failure in learning and few centers have the breadth of personnel to explore and treat those problems, without outside help. The center staff must be alert to recognize symptoms of these problems and to seek the appropriate resources. Much remedial work is wasted, as many reports show, when early correction of underlying physical and psychological factors is not attempted.

The center's public relations also have certain negative aspects. There is real need for adequate insurance against theft or malpractice suits and to cover accidents by personal liability policies, in addition to the usual protection against damage by fire, water, malicious mischief, and the like.

Research Activities

The possibilities for research by the center and its staff are very diverse. Whether the research can be published (forming the basis of a thesis or a dissertation of one of the staff) or it is simply an exploration to find information of internal significance for the operation of the center is not very significant. The value lies in the stimulation of the staff to professional interest and self-improvement. Some centers ask their staff to devote a definite portion of their working schedule to research; perhaps as much as 10 percent. Projects are proposed and evaluated in staff meetings; after criticism for adequacy of design, plans are made to aid the staff member complete the project. Not all staff members are necessarily research-minded; for some, curiosity must be aroused to lead them to try to face the unanswered questions inherent in their own practices. Informal research based on careful personal observation, on simple comparisons of methods or materials, or on evaluation of the apparent values of an experimental test or procedure may be all that some staff can or wish to attempt. But these experiences should be encouraged for professional alertness, if for no other reason.

A few centers make it a practice to share their professional reading in staff meetings, or even to pool their notes on what they have read in some codified form. Here again (as in expecting staff to engage in formal or informal research), there should be a distinction between demands imposed by the director and the exploration of questions on professional practices evolving out of staff discussions.

Budget

It would be pointless for us to attempt to stipulate a budget plan for any center, for each differs in size of staff, salary schedules, manner of operation, types of equipment, sources of income, and other financial details. Some centers are given almost complete freedom to plan their expenditures, while others must plan entirely within the strictures of a stipulated amount. Some are underwritten completely by the sponsoring institution, while others must depend in part or wholly upon a fee basis. And a few, believe it or not, must pay rent for the space and furnishings that they borrow from their institutions. All we can really offer in this area are the earlier descriptions of center activities that may help in planning the operation of another such center.

One source of information on the costs of operating a center is in a brochure published by the International Reading Association.* Costs vary from $206 per pupil for 200 pupils to $540 per pupil for 235 pupils, according to the sources quoted in this brochure. Other figures are gross amounts for the operations of school clinics, mobile trailers, and centers for service and teacher training, which are relatively meaningless without some indication of the number of clients served. It is obvious that the cost of a center is determined by the nature and size of its program and, of course, its modus operandi. The costs cited were for 1969 and have probably increased considerably since that time.

LEARNING PROJECT

Draw a floor plan for a remedial center with a staff of five. Assume that the case load would be several hundred per year. Label each room and indicate the approximate dimensions; the entrances and exits; the furniture; any booths or carrels or other construction, such as shelving, built-in or movable screens, and the like. Show any one-way vision mirrors or other such arrangements. If any rooms are to be multipurpose, list their functions in the legend below your drawing. Review the chapter, if you need to, for detailed suggestions regarding essential areas.

You may want to preface your attempt to complete this learning project by visits to the nearby centers where you may find helpful ideas regarding such facilities.

REFERENCES

1. Allen, J. E., Della-Piana, Gabriel, and Stahmann, R. F., "The Effect of a Parent Training Program upon Reading Achievements of Children," in *Forging Ahead in*

---

*Carl B. Smith, *Establishing Central Reading Clinics: The Administrator's Role* (Newark, Del.: International Reading Association, 1969).

Reading, J. Allen Figurel, editor, Proceedings International Reading Association, 12 (1968), 523–32.

2. Bowren, Fay F., "The Status of Reading Services in New Mexico Secondary Schools," *Journal of Reading,* 13 (April 1970), 513–18.
3. Crowley, H. L., and Ellis, Bessie, "Cross Validation of a Method for Selecting Children Requiring Special Services in Reading," *Reading Teacher,* 24 (January 1971), 312–19.
4. Dahlke, Anita B. "The Use of WISC Scores to Predict Reading Improvement after Remedial Tutoring," Doctoral dissertation, University of Florida, 1968.
5. Klosterman, Sister Rita, "The Effectiveness of a Diagnostically Structured Reading Program," *Reading Teacher,* 24 (November 1970), 159–62.
6. McWhorter, Kathleen, and Levy, Jean, "The Influence of a Tutorial Program upon Tutors," *Journal of Reading,* 14 (January 1971), 221–24.
7. Niedermeyer, F. C., "Effects of Training on the Instructional Behaviors of Student Tutors," *Journal of Educational Research,* 64 (1970), 119–23.
8. Rist, R. C., "Black Studies and Paraprofessionals: A Prescription for Ailing Reading Programs in Urban Black Schools," *Journal of Reading,* 14 (May 1971), 525–30, 583.
9. Spache, George D., *Examiner's Manual, Diagnostic Reading Scales.* Monterey: California Test Bureau, 1972.
10. Spache, George D., Standlee, Lloyd, and Neville, Donald, "Results of Three College Level Remedial Reading Procedures," *Journal of Developmental Reading,* 4 (Autumn 1960), 12–16.
11. Tillman, Chester Earl, "Crude Gain vs. True Gain: Correlates of Gain in Reading after Remedial Tutoring," Doctoral dissertation, University of Florida, 1969.
12. Young, W. E., "Relation of Reading Comprehension and Retention to Hearing Comprehension and Retention," *Journal of Experimental Education,* 5 (September 1936), 30–39.

APPENDIX I

Resources and References

For those instructors and students interested in reading in depth or perhaps in finding studies related to their own interests or research, we offer this list of resources and references.

U. S. Department of Health, Education and Welfare, *ERIC Research in Education.* Washington, D.C.: Government Printing Office. A monthly summary of reports, articles, and projects collected by the Educational Research Information Centers.

As the eighteen ERIC centers cover practically all aspects of education, this is probably the best single source of educational research. Almost every item listed in the monthly summary can be obtained in microfiche or hard copy from ERIC Document Reproduction Service, P.O. Drawer 0, Bethesda, Maryland 20014. Although the first issue of *Research in Education* appeared in November 1968, many items antedate the publication, for the massive personal library of William S. Gray, which covered most of the preceding half-century, was made available to the center specializing in reading. Thus many or most of the materials mentioned in the remainder of this list are available from ERIC.

Traxler, Arthur E., et al., *Ten Years of Research in Reading.* Greenwich, Conn.: Educational Records Bureau, 1941.

Traxler, Arthur E., and Townsend, Agatha, *Another Five Years of Research in Reading.* Greenwich, Conn.: Educational Records Bureau, 1946.

Traxler, Arthur E., and Townsend, Agatha, *Eight More Years of Research in Reading.* Greenwich, Conn.: Educational Records Bureau, 1955.

Traxler, Arthur E., and Jungeblut, Ann, *Research in Reading During Another Four Years.* Greenwich, Conn.: Educational Records Bureau, 1960.

Each of these summaries includes about 400–750 articles and research reports, beginning with those published in 1930 and extending through 1959.

Gray, William S., et al., "Summary of Reading Investigations," *Journal of Educational Research,* usually in the February issue.

Beginning about 1930, William S. Gray and later Helen M. Robinson summarized each year's research studies and articles in the field of reading. Although Dr. Robinson transferred her annual review to the *Reading Research*

Quarterly in 1965, an annual review has continued in this magazine under other reviewers.

Robinson, Helen M.; Weintraub, Samuel; and Smith, Helen K., "Summary of Investigations Relating to Reading," *Reading Research Quarterly,* Winter issue.

Since 1965 each Winter issue of this quarterly has been devoted to a yearly summary of research and articles in the field of reading.

Most of the major reading conferences held each year in this country and Britain present the papers read at each meeting in a yearbook or other such organ. Recently many of these papers have been selected for reproduction by the ERIC center for reading and are being listed in *Research in Education.* If a particular article or research report is not abstracted in that source, we suggest writing to the director of the reading conference at the relevant institution. *A Guide to Information Sources for Reading,* by Bonnie M. Davis (Newark, Del.: International Reading Association, 1972) will help in finding the sources of these elusive materials.

If a reader has special problems in finding research articles relevant to his interests, he may write for assistance to ERIC Clearing House on Reading and Communication Skills, National Council of Teachers of English, 1111 Kenyon Road, Urbana, Illinois 61801.

APPENDIX II

An Incomplete Sentence Test for Elementary Children

For Primary—This is a game called "Say the First Thing." I will say a word or a few words and then pause. When I stop, you tell me the very first thing that came to you. I will write down just what you say. Are you ready?

For Older Pupils—Finish each sentence with the first idea that comes to your mind. Let's try the first one together.

1. Reading is fun with ______________________
2. My teacher reads ______________________
3. Reading is ______________________
4. I cannot read when ______________________
5. Reading is not fun with ______________________
6. I find reading ______________________
7. Reading about ______________________
8. My classmates read ______________________
9. Reading is most fun when ______________________
10. My reading group ______________________
11. Reading in school is ______________________
12. The best reading group is ______________________
13. Reading with ______________________
14. I read ______________________
15. Reading games ______________________
16. When I read all by myself ______________________
17. Reading is best ______________________
18. When reading, new words ______________________
19. Reading before the class ______________________
20. I like reading when ______________________

21. Reading out loud ______
22. The best reader in my class is ______
23. I read best ______
24. Last year's reading teacher ______
25. Reading in the group ______
26. I don't like reading when ______
27. I always want to read about ______
28. I read better ______
29. I learn reading best when ______
30. I don't want to read about ______
31. I cry when I read about ______
32. I don't read when ______
33. The best thing about reading ______
34. I began reading ______
35. I laugh when I read about ______
36. When reading I feel ______
37. My class thinks I read ______
38. When I read at home ______
39. At home I read ______
40. At home my mother reads ______
41. My teacher thinks I read ______
42. My teacher makes me mad when ______
43. I like reading when my teacher ______
44. I like it when my teacher ______
45. My reading teacher ______
46. My teacher makes me happy when ______
47. I like my teacher best when ______

48. I don't like my teacher best when ______________________
49. If I were the teacher______________________
50. My teacher smiles ______________________
51. The teacher thinks the reading class ______________________
52. Last year my teacher did ______________________
53. The teacher talks loud when ______________________
54. This year my teacher does ______________________
55. The teacher thinks I ______________________
56. The teacher is angry when ______________________
57. The teacher is happy when ______________________
58. Next year I want my teacher to ______________________
59. The teacher thinks the class______________________
60. The best book I know about ______________________
61. Books with pictures ______________________
62. My books______________________
63. Books with no pictures______________________
64. The book I like______________________
65. The school's books ______________________

Summary Sheet

Write the student's response to each item listed in each problem area, if the response seems related to that area. If a response obviously reflects another problem area, or several, enter it there. Summarize your evaluation of the tone and specific indications in each problem area.

Teachers—2, 24, and 41 to 59.

Reading Lessons—5, 8, 10, 11, 12, 13, 19, 21, 25, 26, 29, 43

Peer Relations—1, 4, 5, 8, 10, 12, 15, 16, 22, 25, 37

The Act of Reading—3, 4, 6, 7, 9, 17, 18, 19, 21, 26, 28, 32, 36

Reading Interests—3, 7, 9, 14, 16, 17, 20, 23, 27, 30, 31, 33, 35, 38, 60, 61, 62, 63, 64, 65

Other Areas—34, 38, 39, 40